Labor in the USA: A History

DATE			

Labor in the USA:
A History

Ronald L. Filippelli

The Pennsylvania State University

Alfred A. Knopf

New York

Library of Congress Cataloging in Publication Data

Filippelli, Ronald L.
  Labor in the USA.

  Includes indexes.
  1. Labor and laboring classes—United States—History.
2. Industry and state—United States—History.   3. Trade-
unions—United States—History.   4. Industrial relations—
United States—History.   5. Technological innovations—
United States—History.   I. Title.   II. Title: Labor in
the U.S.A.
HD8066.F54   1984   331'.0973   83-23458
ISBN 0-394-34149-X

Printed in the United States of America

10 9 8 7 6 5 4 3

For My Parents

PREFACE

Attempting to write the history of a subject so varied and rich as labor history is a humbling experience because, in its broadest sense, the history of labor encompasses much of the story of human activity. But this book has more modest goals. This book is intended for undergraduate labor history classes, and as supplementary reading for courses in American social and economic history. It is an overview of the impact of the triumph of industrial capitalism on American workers. As such, it is concerned with workers' attempts to cope with the profound changes they experienced from technological change, the hierarchical organization of production, and the power of business enterprise. The conflict between workers and bosses engendered by these changes came to be called the "labor question." It took many forms and dominated Western society for most of the nineteenth and twentieth centuries, providing the axis around which the major social divisions of industrial society rotated.

Unions, as the primary working class institutions in American history, were in the vanguard of this conflict and they receive the most attention in this book. This focus is balanced with traditional institutional history and social and intellectual history. Fortunately, in recent years labor and social historians have provided a wealth of studies of what we can call the cultural history of industrialization. These scholars have gone beyond the narrow economic framework of the institutional historians and have studied the impact of the Industrial Revolution on the social structure, values, and traditions of working class people over periods of social change. The inclusion of some of their findings in this book recognizes that unions did not exist in a vacuum, nor did they ever enroll more than a minority of workers. In order to understand why workers, both in and out of unions, made certain choices in confronting the challenges they faced, the book stresses the impact of change on the lives of workers both on and off the job that is an essential part of the story.

Any book that seriously tries to portray the history of American workers must attempt to correct the omissions of a past rooted in a different social and cultural reality. Thus, material on women and minorities has been stressed. In each section of the book the roles of these groups as workers have been included, with particular emphasis on their often-problematic relationships with the labor movement. One deliberate omission is that slavery is treated only in a most superficial fashion. This is not done to denigrate its tremendous importance as a labor system, nor its inhumanity, but only because the decision was made to deal only with free labor.

While it is a risky enterprise to make historical judgments on recent events, they too have been included to bring the story up to date. This is especially important because the events of the past twenty years cast doubt on standard interpretations of the long-term viability of the dominant form of American trade union structure and function. Knowledge of organized labor's current dilemma will help the reader evaluate labor's past decisions.

One of the perils of writing survey history is the difficulty of incorporating the kind of anecdotal and biographical information that brings history alive. This is overcome through the inclusion of biographical sketches. The people chosen represent the activists who took part in the struggles for workers' rights. I hope that these biographies will give the reader an idea of the variety of the labor movement, both in terms of personality and ideology. The individuals written about represent radicals and conservatives, well-known union leaders and forgotten organizers, men, women, and minorities.

Incorporating so much new material requires the sharpening of the selection process. In order to keep the book to a reasonable length, the choice has often been made to add new material at the expense of more familiar information, and to emphasize ideas instead of the usual litany of names, dates, and statistics. Special emphasis has been placed on acquainting the reader with the varied ideas, often conflicting, which guided workers and contended for their loyalties as they struggled to come to grips with the realities of industrial capitalism.

The book is organized into eight major sections, a prologue, and an epilogue. Every section contains three parts, each of which is structured topically within a chronological framework. In most sections, Part I provides a general overview of the societal factors that most directly affected workers. This is usually followed in Part II by a discussion of the ideological and organizational response of workers to these changing conditions. Finally, most sections conclude with a detailed look, in the nature of a case study, at selected events and issues that illustrate major themes of the period under study.

The goal is to provide a series of overlays going from the general to the specific. But history has a way of disrupting even the most ambitious organizational schemes, and it soon becomes apparent that symmetry is not an absolute virtue. Thus, of the three sections covering the period from the Civil War to World War I, only Section Two includes a broad, introductory overview covering the entire period. This is because the powerful social and economic forces that led to the triumph of industrial capitalism in this period do not lend themselves to easy division. Because of the importance of these forces, labor's responses to them were also much more complex than in the earlier, preindustrial era. Consequently, Sections Three and Four concentrate on these responses and on the ideological conflict in the labor movement that was so crucial in shaping the course of workers' organizations in the United States.

Each section, except the prologue and epilogue, is followed by a list of discussion questions to encourage critical thought and debate. A list of key words and phrases has been included after each section to help guide the reader, and there is also a chronology covering the years from 1648 to 1981.

In addition, there are bibliographies at the end of each section that have a dual purpose. First, they credit the historians whose work was most heavily drawn on in the writing of the book. Second, they provide a guide to suggested readings for students who wish to pursue the subject beyond the limitations of an introductory survey. It is for this reason that only the most recent labor historiography is included.

No book is a solitary effort. I thank the many historians whose research provided the raw material from which this book was fashioned. I also thank Gerald Eggert, Richard Hindle, Alice Hoffman, and Helmut Golatz of Penn State University; Charles Craypo of Cornell University; Simeon Larson of Rutgers; William Pratt of the University of Nebraska at Omaha; John Bennett of the Empire State College Center for Labor Studies (SUNY); Jacqueline Brophy of the George Meany Center for Labor Studies; and David Montgomery of Yale. All read the manuscript and made invaluable suggestions and corrections. Patricia Hindle, Irene Kirk, and Arlene Smith skillfully typed the manuscript, and Sandy Stelts helped much more than she realizes. Errors and omissions, of course, remain solely the responsibility of the author.

University Park, PA   **Ronald L. Filippelli**
August 1, 1983

CONTENTS

PROLOGUE

Workers in the Garden

On July 23, 1778 thousands of artisans of New York City marched to celebrate the ratification of the Constitution. Their colorful banners and floats announced confidence in a prosperous and harmonious future in which all classes—journeymen and masters, merchants and farmers— would share. It demonstrated the pride of the artisans in their ancient trades, in the role they had played in the struggle for independence, and in their place in the community.

The artisans had good reason for optimism. A vast continent endowed with splendid rivers, rich soil, endless forests, and undreamed-of wealth lay before them. Heir to all of this were less than five million people, free and slave. They clung to a narrow strip of land stretching south from the forests of New England to the savannahs of Georgia and inland to the Appalachian barrier. Most of them were farmers and barely one in twenty lived in towns with a population of a few thousand or more. Most grew food for their own tables, made their own clothing, and built their own dwellings.

Only a few of them were artisans, or mechanics as they were more commonly known. This free laboring class developed in the seaport towns and cities and slowly migrated to the small towns that served as commercial centers for the agricultural hinterlands. Shipbuilding, brewing, flour milling, cooperage or barrel making, tanning, saddlery, and iron manufacturing provided the bulk of the opportunities for skilled workers. Shipbuilding was most important in the major cities of Philadelphia, Boston, and New York, and in smaller port towns such as Newport and Charleston. The industry created a demand for carpenters, smiths, joiners, shipwrights, caulkers, ropemakers, sailmakers, and a host of others, both skilled and unskilled. As early as 1687 a French visitor to Boston noted that "there are here craftsmen of every kind, and particularly carpenters for the building of ships." Only a quarter of a century later there were 3500 sailors in the port of Boston alone.

In the colonial period few artisans and craftsworkers worked for wages. In the larger towns they produced "bespoke" or custom-ordered goods in small shops that often were part of their homes. Other craftsworkers, itinerants, traveled from farm to farm carrying their own goods to produce goods from raw materials provided by the farmers. For these traveling masons, smiths, shoemakers, and carpenters payment usually came in kind—corn or wheat or goods—and the employment arrangement also provided for food, rum, and lodging while the work was being performed.

As shipbuilding and oceangoing commerce spurred economic development, the cities grew and wealth increased. A growing class of wealthy merchants and planters provided a market for luxury goods, and craftsworkers in the luxury trades proliferated. In 1720, the small village of New York had thirteen silversmiths, four watchmakers, two goldsmiths, and one jeweler.

Like their brethren on the farms, most artisans worked according to traditions rooted in premodern practices. They knew little of the tyranny of the clock and the discipline of the factory. They worked at their own pace and output was controlled more by the demands of quality than by the promise of profit. The employer's, or master's, authority rested not so much on the control of capital as on his skill in the mysteries of the craft. The master worked beside the journeymen, shared their value system and was, for the most part, their social equal. In all probability master and journeyman cooperated not only at work but also in their civic duties and recreational activities. Theirs was a world characterized by stability, by a kind of unity, in which life was a piece and its rhythm knew few distinctions between work and leisure.

It would be wrong to view this era as some kind of idyllic epoch. The societies from which so many colonists had come were also in large measure preindustrial. In England this had meant rigid class stratification, recurring famines, and political powerlessness. Colonial America too was a stratified society from the beginning and became increasingly so as the colonial period progressed, but because it was a pioneer society in need of labor, a higher value was placed on what one could contribute than on an inherited place in society. Especially in the seventeenth and early eighteenth centuries, class differences were less in evidence than in Europe.

ENGLISH LAW AND CUSTOM

Colonial workers were English subjects and the conditions under which they worked owed as much to the economic needs of that country as they did to the circumstances of life in the colonies. The colonies existed to serve the mother country in three basic ways. First, they were to supply raw materials and foodstuffs to fuel England's Industrial Revolution. Second, the colonists provided a captive market for English manufactured goods. Third, they served as an outlet for surplus labor.

As early as the sixteenth century Englishmen believed their island to be overpopulated. In his influential *Discourse of Western Planting*, which appeared in 1584, Richard Hakluyt pointed to the New World as the answer to England's unemployment problem and as a means to empty her prisons.

The rise of unemployment in England was directly related to the rise of industrial capitalism. The woolen industry in particular changed the nature of English agriculture when sheepherding replaced grain farming and displaced large numbers of agricultural workers. With industrialization came urbanization and unemployment. Poverty and crime increased. Landowners and industrialists used the legal machinery of the state to regulate wages while the price of food soared.

The dramatic changes that industrialization brought to the preindustrial English working class led to severe social tensions. Riots and violence became commonplace as class divisions hardened. It is not surprising that the English ruling class viewed the colonies as a safety valve for the pressure building up at home. In 1611 the Spanish ambassador in London wrote that the ". . . principal reason for colonizing . . . is to give an outlet to so many idle, wretched people as they have in England, and thus prevent the dangers that might be feared of them."

While the ambassador might have overstated the case, there is no doubt that in many ways English workers were more slave than free. Their wages were regulated, their right to collective action nonexistent before the law, and they faced imprisonment if they left their jobs without the employer's permission. Early attempts at collective action were smashed by the courts as illegal conspiracies while combinations of employers to set prices, monopolize markets, and control the labor supply went largely unmolested.

The needs of English industry for a guaranteed labor supply at subsistence wages were provided for in a body of laws called the Tudor Industrial Code. While in theory the code also provided for the protection of workers against exploitation, in practice it operated to their disadvantage. It provided for compulsory labor for all able-bodied persons. Youths, usually orphans or the children of the poor, could be subjected to forced labor. Workers who refused to work at the rates set by local authorities were considered petty criminals who were subject to whippings and forced labor in houses of correction.

Little wonder then that Britons willing to undergo the rigors of an ocean voyage to an unknown world were plentiful. John McBeath, a Scottish farmer and shoemaker who came as late as 1774, no doubt spoke for many of his fellow colonists who had preceded him when he said he was leaving because his crops had failed, he had lost his cattle, his rent had increased, and he could find no work to support his family. He had heard from friends in America that there a man could find work at high wages and support his family in comfort.

The world of work that John McBeath found on arrival in the colonies was not as different from the one he had left as he might have expected. In an attempt to hold down inflation, the colonies experimented with wages and price regulation. With the wishes of employers uppermost, wage regulation took precedence over price regulation. Many of the colonies attempted to put a ceiling on wages and a floor on hours in the seventeenth century with some success. But the practice generally fell into disuse in the eighteenth century, so that by the eve of the American Revolution only the monopolistic trades—those that operated under license, such as ministers, schoolteachers, chimney sweeps, and porters—remained under regulation.

Strictures against higher wages, the natural result of a tight labor market, went beyond public regulations. Ministers and businessmen pointed to high wages as a temptation to violence and vice. Low wages were advocated by some as a way of keeping laborers in their place. Too much money, they claimed, tended to encourage "the insolence of servants," and there was frequent emphasis on the necessity for working people to dress and act in keeping with their station in life. One colonial official expressed "utter detestation and dislike that men and women of mean conditions should take upon themselves the garb of gentlemen."

Many of the restrictive provisions of the English system of labor regulation also applied in the colonies. Idleness was not tolerated. Pennsylvania law stipulated that all children reaching the age of twelve were to be taught some useful skill. Vagrancy, or idleness, could be punished by whipping and by the eighteenth century workhouses where vagrants, the unemployed, or orphans served labor sentences for minor offenses were common.

Compulsory labor was not confined to the unemployed. Most men were required to donate some time to public works projects, such as road building and repair; but in order to attract skilled workers local authorities often exempted them from these duties.

While English law and customs established the framework in which people worked in early America, Englishmen by no means made up the entire labor force. Increasingly workers came as well from Ireland, Scotland, Africa, and Germany and in smaller numbers from a score of other countries. Only a minority came as free workers. The majority arrived in some form of bondage, either as indentured servants or chattel slaves.

BOUND LABOR

The combination of the colonies' need for labor and England's interest in exporting her excess population led to the establishment of a system of indentured servitude. A means had to be found to ensure a steady flow of emigrants and at the same time cover the cost of their passage. Emigrants bound themselves to service for a period of years, usually not more than seven, in exchange for the cost of transportation. These written contracts, called indentures, were usually held by the ship's master who sold them to planters or farmers on arrival in America. The system was a adaptation of the old institution of apprenticeship.

After a horrible trip packed in the fetid holds of small ships, during which many people died, parents were often forced to sell their children, and husbands and wives were sometimes separated. Frequently buyers, called "soul drivers," purchased large numbers of indentures and drove the servants inland like cattle, offering them for sale at farms and villages along the way.

Most, but not all, came of their own free will; but kidnapping was a thriving industry in the cities of London and Bristol in England where criminals called "spirits" abducted all manner of people, especially children, and indentured them to ship captains. Convicts also made up a considerable part of the human cargo that flowed into American harbors. England used the indenture system to empty her crowded jails of petty criminals of all kinds. A sense of the makeup of this diverse trade in human beings can be gathered from the comments of the Mayor of Bristol who described the unfortunates who flocked to his city to sell themselves for passage.

> Among those who repair to Bristol from all parts to be transported for servants to his majesty's plantations beyond the seas, some are husbands that have forsaken wives, others wives who have forsaken their husbands. Some are children and apprentices run away from their parents and masters. Often times unwary and credulous persons have been tempted on board by men stealers, and many that have been pursued by hue and cry for robberies, burglaries, or breaking prison, do thereby excape the prosecution of law and justice.

While the vast majority of bound servants were propertyless casual laborers who worked off their indentures on the plantations of the South or the prosperous farms of the middle colonies, a significant number were skilled artisans. The notice of the arrival of a vessel bearing ". . . a parcel of young likely men-servants, consisting of weavers, joyners, shoemakers, smiths, brickmakers, bricklayers, sawyers, tailors, staymakers, butchers, chairmakers and several other trades . . ." was not uncommon.

By the early eighteenth century England began to have second thoughts about the tremendous outflow of her population. Having become the workshop of the world, the old worries about overpopulation were replaced with a renewed hunger for labor, especially skilled labor. Soon mostly convicts made up the passenger manifests of the English fleet. Workers from Scotland, Ireland, and Germany took up the slack. Many came as "redemptioners" or "free willers." They signed no contract beforehand but were given transportation with the understanding that on arrival they had a few days to indenture themselves to pay their passage. If not successful, their indentures reverted to the ship captain who could sell them as he pleased.

Aspects of indentured servitude were also found in the apprentice system. Although public officials frequently bound out, or apprenticed, orphans and other wards of the state to less desirable trades or to an "apprenticeship in husbandry" (a euphemism for child labor on the farm), the apprenticeship of children to a trade was most often voluntary. Parents saw apprenticeship as a means to provide skills and opportunities for their sons. Not all trades were equally desirable. A hierarchy existed—from silversmith, through printer or ship carpenter to shoemaker at the bottom. Binding a son out to the more desirable trades was often a privilege reserved to parents who could afford to pay a handsome fee to the master craftsman. Benjamin Franklin's father could not afford to apprentice young Benjamin, the youngest of eight sons, to the cutlery trade because of the payment demanded.

The apprentice was bound to a master craftsman who provided training in the mysteries of the trade in exchange for service. Often the employer took the child into his own home. Conditions of the contract were carefully set down as follows.

Jonathan Hurst, Jr., by consent of his mother Anne Hutchins, indents himself apprentice to James Gottier, of Philadelphia, cooper, for eight years from this date to have six months schooling and six months evening schooling to learn to read, write, and cipher, to be taught the trade of cooper, and at the end of his time to have two suits of apparel, one of which is to be new.

The law required employers to care for their apprentices and retain them in hard times as well as good. The usual term was seven years, normally beginning at around fourteen years of age, and often new journeymen remained in their master's employ after the apprenticeship ended. Though for the most part the apprenticeship system was more humane than indentured servitude, it was often restrictive and notices of runaways appeared frequently in colonial newspapers.

Six Cents Reward

Ran away from the subscriber on Saturday evening, the 29th ult. an indentured apprentice to the cabinetmaking business, named John Rimbey, between nineteen and twenty years of age. He had on when he went away a new black fur hat, blue coat and corded pantaloons and striped vest. The public is hereby cautioned against employing or harboring said apprentice, as the law shall be enforced against any person doing so.

It is difficult to overemphasize the importance of indentured labor to the development of the new nation. Without it the middle and southern colonies could hardly have been established. One-sixth of the white population of Virginia in 1683 was under conditions of servitude and nearly two-thirds of the immigrants to Pennsylvania during the eighteenth century came as servants. In Pennsylvania, Maryland, and Virginia at the time of the Revolution some three out of four persons were or had been indentured servants.

Conditions for bound servants were harsh, sometimes even worse than those for black slaves. The slave represented a lifetime investment and there was some natural interest in protecting one's investment. But indentured servants belonged to the employer for a limited number of years and his interest was in extracting the maximum amount of work during that period. Servants did have the right to complain against harsh treatment, but failure to prove their cases in courts dominated by employers often resulted in a lengthening of their required service.

Oppressive conditions led to frequent desertions and occasional strikes. But by far the most serious reaction occurred in Virginia, a colony in which masters frequently treated bound servants with brutality. In 1676 resentment over this treatment led to an armed insurrection by indentured servants, small farmers, and slaves led by Nathanial Bacon. Aimed primarily at royal rule, those rebelling believed, according to Bacon, that "the proverty of the country is such that all the power and sway is got into the hands of the rich, who by extortious advantages, having the common people in their debt, have always curbed and oppressed them in all manner of ways."

Harsh as the system was, indentured servants did have rights. They could sue or be sued and testify in court. At the end of their period of servitude the law entitled them to "freedom dues" such as clothing, perhaps a gun, and in some cases a grant of land. Because the system was so widespread and so many had passed through it, there was little or no stigma attached to having once been in a condition of servitude. Two signers of the Declaration of Independence, George Taylor and Matthew Thornton, had been white, bound servants. Yet even though some made their way out of indentured servitude to fortune and fame, most remained poor. For a great many, according to historian Richard Hofstadter, the hardship of the journey across the Atlantic "proved in the end to have been only a epitome of their journey through life."

Most important, however, was the fact that the bondage was temporary and the servant could look forward with some hope to the future. It was this hope of ultimate freedom that most differentiated the system of indentured servitude from chattel slavery. Africans had no rights and no hope. Their lives and the lives of their children were to be spent in forced service to white masters.

The first Africans came to America as indentured servants. Not until the middle of the seventeenth century did the passage of slave codes in most colonies transform them to slaves. After 1690 the expansion of the tobacco economy increased the demand for slave labor, leading to the massive importation of Africans. By 1775 a half-million black slaves lived in the colonies. The vast majority worked on the tobacco plantations of Virginia, North Carolina, and Maryland and on the rice and indigo plantations of

South Carolina and Georgia. Only after the invention of the cotton gin in 1793 did the majority of slaves devote their time to cotton cultivation.

Although Africans were overwhelmingly engaged in agriculture, as were all Americans, they were also in demand in other occupations because of the scarcity of labor. Slaves represented a fixed investment and it made economic sense to use them in place of free labor wherever possible. The need for agricultural labor was seasonal and by contracting out his slaves, the slaveowner could recoup a portion of his investment. This was particularly remunerative if the slave had skills, as many did because of the need for a wide variety of craftsmen on the complex business enterprise that was the southern plantation.

Slaves predominated as workers in the small manufacturing enterprises of the South. They labored in the lumber mills, shipyards, cooperages, furniture shops, and countless other enterprises. The *South Carolina Gazette* between 1732 and 1776 gives notice of slaves practicing at least twenty-eight crafts, including the entire range of the building trades. These occupational opportunities increased the personal freedom of skilled slaves because they frequently worked away from the plantation, and skilled blacks constituted the largest class of runaways.

Naturally the presence of slave artisans had a disruptive effect on the free labor market. White artisans understandably found the situation less than attractive and their migration patterns reflected this attitude. Relatively few chose the South to practice their trades. In 1744 a white South Carolina shipwright complained that slaves worked in Charleston and other places at his trade and as a result white tradesmen could find no work, were reduced to poverty, and would have to leave if not given relief. This conflict between white and black worker, rooted in the exploitation of Africans, was to become a regular feature of American history.

OPPORTUNITY AND INSECURITY

The size and importance of the two systems of bound labor emphasized the favored position of free labor, and those who practiced skilled trades as free citizens constituted an elite of the labor force. Relatively high wages and the opportunity to become independent businessmen or farmers attracted a steady stream of skilled immigrants from Europe. The lure of available land drained off many artisans, who, like most people from the land-scarce old world, viewed land as the only real guarantee of status and security. Where agriculture was not the goal, it was not unheard of for a skilled tradesman to become an employer, purchase land, and construct a substantial house.

An anonymous craftsman, in a letter home, wrote that "It is a great deal better living here than in England for working people. Poor working people doth live as well here as landed men doth live with you thats worth twenty pounds a year. I live a simple life and hath builded a shop, and doth follow weaving of linen cloth, but I have bought 450 acres of land in the wood." Occasionally ship carpenters purchased shares in a vessel and became capitalists. Given this relative opportunity, when colonial agents scoured Europe touting the advantages of emigrating to America, they met with considerable success. In 1767 the *New York Journal* announced that "Thirteen of the best Hammer men and Forge men in the Iron Manufactory have been engaged to come from Sheffield to America for which a handsome premium is given them, and great wages for two years certain, and six shillings a week to each of their wives and families as stay behind for that time. They have also given one-hundred guineas for each of the best saw-makers, and the same money for their wives that stay." Terms such as these must surely have interested the workmen of the English Midlands.

But not even the inducements of high wages and the salesmanship of Colonial agents could slake the thirst for labor in the growing country. Both women and children were pressed into service. Indeed the labor shortage was one incentive for the high birth rate of the colonial period. Single women found themselves courted both as potential wives and workers. One disgruntled contemporary wrote that "even the meanest single women marry well and being above want are above work." In addition to household industries, particularly the spinning and weaving of cloth, women were found in a variety of occupational roles. They mainly worked as domestic servants although working conditions were often less than ideal. Maids in New York joined together in order to give notice that they would not take work where they would be subjected to beatings by their mistresses' husbands, "they being too strong and perhaps may do tender women mischief." Although most tailors, furriers, and staymakers were men, women filled jobs as milliners, menders, dyers, and wool scourers and most of those engaged in the laying out and dressing of the dead were women.

The premium placed on skill also conferred on the artisan class a higher status and greater independence than in Europe. But artisans did not constitute the whole of the urban working class. There were also teamsters and porters, watermen and seamen, dustmen and dockers, and workers in a number of other categories of common labor. By the end of the seventeenth century each colonial city had a large population of unskilled laborers whose economic fortunes fluctuated according to the ups and downs of the economy, but which rarely rose much above subsistence level. In 1684 14 percent of the adult male population of Boston had no property and were not dependents, grown sons living at home, apprentices, or indentured servants. These men were propertyless by virtue of owning no real estate, nor any investments or merchandise from which to derive income. Many were journeymen, laborers, or seamen, and they were transient. Only 35 percent remained in Boston eight years later.

In the eighteenth century the proportion of this class in the urban centers rose dramatically and so did the incidence of poverty. All of the major cities reacted to this situation by building almshouses in the 1730s in order to bring as many of the growing number of poor people under one roof as possible. Aimed at reducing relief costs, the system no longer cared only for the aged, widowed, crippled, or incurably ill, but increasingly for the seasonally employed, new immigrants, and migrants from the agricultural hinterlands as well.

Statistics on poor relief in Philadelphia, Boston, and New York leave little doubt that the problem worsened as the century wore on. From midcentury on the colonies underwent several severe economic and social dislocations. In New York City the incidence of poverty rose fourfold between 1750 and 1775. In the decade before the Revolution, Philadelphia admitted more than 900 persons a year to the city's almshouse, workhouse, and hospital for the sick poor. Without question, by the end of the colonial period, a large number of urban dwellers were without property, without opportunity, and except for public aid, frequently without the means of obtaining the necessities of life.

Periodic depressions, prices that outstripped wage increases, and war taxes that fell with unusual severity on the working class also hit hard at the lower middle classes. The economic well-being of master artisans, skilled journeymen, and shopkeepers began to decline in the middle of the eighteenth century and continued its downward trajectory for the remainder of the colonial period. The pattern was illustrated by the declining number of taxpayers in the urban centers. Boston's "taxables" dropped from 3600 in 1735 to 2600 by 1771, while the population of the city remained almost static. This meant that almost one-third of the city's taxpayers had to be dropped from the rolls because of economic misfortune. In Philadelphia, the number of taxpayers removed from the list jumped significantly after 1740 and reached one in ten taxpayers in the fifteen years before the Revolution.

Probate records paint a similar picture of the growing insecurity of the middle groups in the cities. In Boston, among the middle classes, median wealth at death dropped considerably between 1685 and 1735 and then made a small, but uneven recovery as the Revolution approached. Historian Gary Nash has shown that the average carpenter, baker, shopkeeper, shipwright, or tavern keeper dying in Boston between 1735 and 1765 had less to show for a lifetime's work than his counterpart of a half century before. In Philadelphia as well assets of those in the middle ranges of the middle class also declined steadily for most of the eighteenth century. Although it is true that some city dwellers, such as Benjamin Franklin, had risen from the bottom to the upper reaches of colonial society; for most skilled workers, as well as for their less skilled brothers and sisters, the dominating fact of late colonial life was economic frustration and insecurity.

If economic development and population growth did not bestow significant benefits on the majority of the population, it did further enrich those at the top of colonial society. Indeed, the most striking alteration in the social structure of the eighteenth-century cities was the narrowing of the distribution of wealth. Eighteenth-century tax lists for Boston, Philadelphia, and New York demonstrate this long-range trend toward a less even distribution of wealth. By the early 1770s, the top 5 percent of Boston's taxpayers controlled 49 percent of the taxable assets of the community, up from 30 percent in 1687. The top 12 percent owned 78 percent, fifteen times that held by the lower half of the adult male population.

Colonial probate records tell a similar story. There were few estates of 5000 pounds sterling in northern cities before 1730, but by midcentury estates of 20,000 pounds sterling, exclusive of real estate, were becoming common, and those in the 50,000 range—equivalent in purchasing power to about $2.5 million today—were not unheard of.

PROTEST

The maldistribution of wealth and the shift of political power to the rich that accompanied it led to frequent conflicts between rich and poor, and workers and merchants in the eighteenth century. As the century wore on, the growing resentment of wealth and of political control by the rich gained momentum.

"A poor man," lamented a resident of Philadelphia, "has rarely the honor of speaking to a gentlemen on any terms and never with any familiarity but for a few weeks before the election. . . ." Such social division prompted another observer to warn that "that community cannot be pronounced happy in which from the lowness and insufficiency of wages, the laboring class . . . are reduced to beggary, whenever employment fails them, or age and sickness oblige them to give up work."

Protest against such conditions broke out in Boston during the depression of 1713 when angry townspeople attacked the grain warehouses of a wealthy merchant who chose to export grain to the West Indies at a high profit rather than sell it at lower prices to hungry Bostonians. During the same depression a spokesman for the poor and unemployed of Boston protested against those who grew rich "by grinding the poor," and by studying "how to oppress, cheat and overreach their neighbors."

In Philadelphia, such resentment led to the formation of working class and lower middle class political clubs that greatly affected political control of the city for most of the 1720s.

When a recession caused a rise in unemployment, a spate of small business failures, and an increase in suits for debt in New York City in the 1730s, workers expressed their resentment in the political arena. A 1734 election tract reminded New Yorkers that the best interests of the city lay with the fortunes of "Shuttle," the weaver; "Plane," the joiner; "Drive," the carter; "Mortar," the mason; "Tar," the mariner; "Snip," the tailor; "Smallrent," the fairminded landlord,; and "John Poor," the tenant. Working against the city's interests were "Gripe," the merchant; "Squeeze," the shopkeeper; and "Quible," the lawyer.

The long movement of protest that gained momentum as the Revolution approached was not informed by a radical working class ideology in any modern sense. Instead it was the reaction of those laborers, artisans, and small shopkeepers, who, along with farmers, counted themselves the "producers" of society, and who believed that the rewards they received for their work were not equitable, and that economic security and social status were slipping away from them.

WORKERS IN THE REVOLUTION

The demands of these producing classes made up an important part of the revolutionary spirit. Hand in hand with the issue of "home rule" for the colonies went the issue of "who would rule at home." Much of the agitation centered around the issue of male suffrage. The vast majority of workers, because they did not own property, did not enjoy full political rights. As the movement against British rule grew in the late eighteenth century, so too did the frequency of protest at home against the control exercised by the propertied classes. Those wealthy colonists who supported the move to end the economic and political control of Great Britain also understood the dangers inherent in their alliance of convenience with the more radical workers. "The heads of the mobility grow dangerous to the gentry," wrote the wealthy Gouverneur Morris, "and how to keep them down is the question."

Indeed, mechanics, artisans, and small tradespeople voiced the more radical demands in support of colonial liberties and kept up the agitation when the merchants and planters were willing to compromise. Mechanics benevolent and protective associations usually supported the revolutionary movement. The Sons of Liberty who played a strategic role in organizing and rallying the colonists against British rule consisted largely of workers from the docks, shipyards, and ropewalks. The same working class character marked the Daughters of Liberty and the various committees of correspondence. The "Loyal Nine," which instigated the mob action that led to the Boston Massacre and the Boston Tea Party, included two distillers, two braziers, a printer, a jeweler, a painter, and a ship captain.

In fact, the Boston Massacre grew directly out of a dispute that had arisen between colonial workers and British troops over a labor issue. A Boston employer precipitated the incident when he fired a ropemaker for objecting to the hiring of an off-duty British soldier instead of a colonial worker. When British troops fired into the angry mob that had gathered as a result of the dispute, they killed five workers—two seamen (one black and one white), a ropewalk worker, an artisan, and a joiner's apprentice. While it is certainly an exaggeration to say that the American Revolution was primarily the result of radical agitation against two ruling classes, one British and one American, there is considerable truth in Samuel Adams's opinion that it was the "firm patriotism" of the town workers and small farmers, those "two venerable classes of men stiled mechanics and husbandmen, that must finally save this country."

ECONOMIC ORGANIZATION

Because colonial America was a preindustrial society with relatively few permanent wage workers, economic organizations representing the interests of urban workers did not develop to any degree during the colonial period. Those that did were of two types, benevolent societies and guilds. Little remains to document their activity, but it appears that the benevolent societies—composed of masters, journeymen, and sometimes apprentices—paid sick and death benefits, provided funds for indigent members, and occasionally made small loans. The societies represented the community of interest that existed among all practitioners of the trade. The guilds on the other hand, were more like trade associations of master craftsmen, or employers, which attempted to regulate everything from entry into the trade to the quality of workmanship. The most notable of these was the Carpenters' Company of Philadelphia, which built and owned Carpenters' Hall where the first session of the Continental Congress convened. Chartered in 1724 for the purpose of "obtaining instruction in the science of architecture and assisting such of their members as should be in need of support," the Carpenters' Company soon broadened its interest in the economic well-being of its members. Its activities included regulating prices for all carpentry, including architectural or building work. A "book of prices" containing rates was directed at both employers and employees in order to assure fair wages and fair value. The Company arbitrated disputes between masters and journeymen and regulated apprenticeship. As a mutual aid society it provided benefits for widows and orphans and furnished carriages for the funerals of members.

Most of what appear to be strikes during the colonial period were really protests by craftsmen against prices set by local authorities in the regulated trades. In 1684 truckmen employed by the city of New York refused to work until the price per load was increased, and in 1741 the bakers of the same city struck to protest the regulated price of bread. Protection from unlicensed or cheaper labor also caused job action occasionally. As early as 1675 Boston ship carpenters drove an interloper out of town because he had worked in the yard without having served his full apprenticeship.

The descendants of these workers would toil in a world in many ways unrecognizable to their parents and grandparents. Even as the parades celebrating the victory over Britain were in progress, the industrial age was dawning in America.

Signs of change were everywhere. In the small artisan's workshop, the master, usually without the capital to undertake large-scale production, increasingly found himself acting as a contractor supplied with raw materials by a wealthy merchant who set the price of the finished commodities in advance. In such an arrangement the journeymen no longer performed "bespoke" work at agreed-on prices, but was instead transformed into a wage worker.

Soon after the Revolution there were signs of the beginnings of the factory system. The enterprise established in 1775 by the United Company of Philadelphia for Promoting American Manufacturing turned out cotton goods and employed 400 women under one roof. It was a harbinger of things to come.

As their relations at work began to change, some skilled workers in the seaboard cities began to turn to trade unions as the best form of organization to protect their interests as wage earners, and strikes of journeymen against their employers began to occur. In 1785 New York shoemakers struck for three weeks and one year later Philadelphia printers walked out to protest a reduction in wages. Shoemakers in the city of brotherly love struck for higher wages at least three times before the end of the century.

The extent of the growth of the labor movement in Philadelphia can be measured by the fact that when the union of cabinet and chairmakers fought an attempt by employers to blacklist union members in 1790, they were able to call for support from unions of hatters, shoemakers, house carpenters, tailors, goldsmiths, saddlers, coopers, painters, printers, and others.

Clearly the old harmonious patterns of work that had characterized the preindustrial period were disintegrating as a result of changes in the organization of production. Rather than harmony, the next century would be marked by mounting conflicts as workers searched for ways to protect themselves against the onslaught of industrial capitalism.

KEY WORDS AND PHRASES

Mechanics	Chattel Slavery
Bespoke Goods	Almshouses
Tudor Industrial Code	Revolutionary Workers
Indentured Servants	Benevolent Societies
Apprenticeship	Guilds

BIBLIOGRAPHY

The material for the prologue was drawn largely from:

Bailyn, Bernard. *The Ideological Origins of the American Revolution.* Cambridge: Harvard University Press, 1967.

Bridenbaugh, Carl. *Cities in Revolt: Urban Life in America, 1743–1776.* New York: Alfred A. Knopf, 1955.

———. *The Colonial Craftsman.* New York: New York University Press, 1950.

Hansen, Marcus Lee. *The Atlantic Migration, 1607–1860.* New York: Harper and Row, 1961.

Henretta, James. "Economic Development and Social Structure in Colonial Boston," *William and Mary Quarterly,* vol. 22 (January 1965): 75–92.

Hofstadter, Richard. *America at 1750: A Social Portrait.* New York: Alfred A. Knopf, 1971.

Herrick, Chessman A. *White Servitude in Pennsylvania: Indentured and Redemption Labor in Colony and Commonwealth.* Philadelphia: McVey, 1926.

Jernegan, Marcus W. *Laboring and Dependent Classes in Colonial America, 1607–1783.* New York: Frederick Ungar, 1931.

Kurtz, Stephen G. and James H. Hutson, eds. *Essays on the American Revolution.* Chapel Hill: University of North Carolina Press, 1973.

Maier, Pauline. *From Resistance to Revolution: Colonial Radicals and the Development of American Opposition to Britain, 1765–1776.* New York: Alfred A. Knopf, 1972.

Morris, Richard B. *Government and Labor in Early America.* New York: Columbia University Press, 1946.

Nash, Gary. "Social Change and the Growth of Prerevolutionary Urban Radicalism," in Alfred Young, ed., *The American Revolution: Explorations in the History of American Radicalism.* Dekalb: Northern Illinois University Press, 1976.

SECTION
ONE

A World Turning Upside Down

The years between 1800 and 1865 were years of transition and transformation in the United States. Three wars scarred the period, including the Civil War. Racial, religious, and sectional conflicts raged as the nation extended its borders to the shores of the Pacific.

Underlying these conflicts and changes lay the dynamic effects of the Industrial Revolution. The founding fathers' dream of an agrarian republic of independent, self-reliant farmers and artisans slowly slipped away. A fever for internal improvements—roads, canals, and railroads—spurred a communications revolution that bound the nation together in a continental market.

As the master craftsman's opportunities expanded along with the potential market, so did his capital requirements. Faced with the need to expand his workforce, increase his stock of raw materials, and extend credit to his far-flung customers, he spent less and less time at the trade and more on the functions of management. The social and economic distance between him and his journeymen increased.

For the most part, however, master craftsmen were unable to seize the opportunities presented by the expanded markets. Their access to capital was too limited. Into this void stepped the merchant capitalist. His commercial experience provided him with funds and the marketing expertise to put them to good use. He knew little or nothing of the trade. His access to capital allowed him to purchase raw materials in large quantities, have them prepared for finishing, and then contract the finishing out to a master and his journeymen. Marketing of the finished product remained entirely in the hands of the merchant who developed the markets and delivered the product.

The impact of this change on handicraft manufacture was severe. Thrust into a highly competitive world and beholden to the merchant capitalist for contract work, the master craftsman came under constant pressure to reduce costs. His earnings depended on it. He sought to hold down wages, lengthen the working day, and where possible, employ cheap labor. The bulwark of the trade was the apprentice system. Any subdivision of the work to reduce its complexity so as to enable the use of less skilled labor ran head on into the apprenticeship system. Frequently technology, in the form of new machinery, aided the employer in this process and as the trades slowly changed women and children began to appear in the workshops. The merchant capitalist was a transitional figure. It is true that he gradually replaced the master artisan as dominant figure in workshop enterprise. But, more importantly, he ushered in the factory system.

The reorganization of workshop enterprise lacked two things to transform it into the factory system. An external source of power came first. This America had in abundance in its magnificent system of rivers and streams. But in order for the factory system to develop, water power had to be combined with machinery. The solution to the problem appeared as early as 1791 when Samuel Slater, an English immigrant, developed a cotton-spinning machine driven by water power. Out of this came the first American factory in Pawtucket, Rhode Island. To be sure, it was a crude beginning, but soon machinery was developed that permitted the carding, spinning, and weaving of cloth under one roof. By 1850, America's first great industry—cotton textile manufacturing—was wholly mechanized. Similar changes took place in other trades like boot and shoemaking. In the shoe center of Lynn, Massachusetts, the introduction of the sewing machine first had a catastrophic effect on the employment of female binders. By 1862 the machine had been adapted to the work done by journeymen shoemakers and permitted a semiskilled operator to stitch eighty pairs in the same time that a journeyman used to sew the seams on one. With this kind of mechanization the factory system came to the industry. As one Lynn newspaper noted in 1863, "The hum of machinery is heard on every hand, old things are passing away, and all things are becoming new."

The transformation did not take place overnight. Even in 1865 it was an indication of things to come rather than a reality for most Americans. Artisans working in traditional ways still produced most manufactured goods. The rural village rather than the industrial town or the commercial metropolis still characterized America on the eve of the Civil War. Old patterns and traditions rather than the factory bell and the clock still governed the lives of the vast majority of workers. Yet while most workers did not operate power-driven machinery, the majority had become wage earners rather than independent artisans and they saw the impact of the machines and realized their implications. In 1844 a writer in the *Working Man's Advocate* lamented that the following was happening.

Machinery has taken almost entire possession of the manufacture of cloth; it is making steady—we might say rapid—advance upon all branches of iron manufacture; the newly invented machine saws, working in curves as well as straight lines, the planing and grooving machines, and the tenon and mortise machine, clearly admonish us that its empire is destined to extend itself over all our manufactures of wood; while some of our handicrafts are already extinct, there is not one of them but has foretasted the overwhelming competition of this occult power.

If workers were apprehensive and a bit bewildered by the "occult power" of new technology, many Americans embraced the future enthusiastically. While much of the early technology had been imported from England, Americans soon rushed headlong into developing their own. The chronic shortage of labor encouraged a spirit of inventiveness. For many, progress became increasingly identified with technological advances. Machines became more than utilitarian instruments. They had symbolic meaning for the nation's future. Americans lionized inventors such as Fulton, Morse, Franklin, and Whitney. The patent office issued 5942 new patents in the 1840s and almost five times that many in the next decade. Fascination with technology so pervaded the culture that visiting Swedish novelist Fredrika Bremen discovered schoolboys using a period of undirected drawing to sketch "smoking steam engines or steam boats, all in movement." Not surprisingly American inventions began to amaze the world.

In the course of several decades the nation seized the leadership of the Industrial Revolution through the creation of what came to be called the American system of manufactures. The system developed, as did the encouragement of technological innovation, because of the need to produce for a rapidly expanding market with a rapidly growing, but largely unskilled, labor force. The doubling of the population between 1820 and 1840 increased both the supply of unskilled labor and the market for manufactured goods. Even greater waves of Irish and German immigrants came in the next twenty years. In addition, canals and railroads tied the agricultural west to the heavily populated east, thus releasing thousands of young men and women from eastern farms for factory work. An American working class was developing.

In order to capitalize on these opportunities manufacturers increasingly turned to a system of mass production that divided the production of goods into a series of sequential machine operations. The system relied on machinery especially designed for the work and requiring little from the workers but endurance and discipline. The system also profoundly changed the lives of the artisans away from work. Instead of a social and political system based on rough equality that had reflected an economic order characterized by numerous small producers, society slowly came to reflect the widening gulf between capitalists—both merchant and industrial—and wage earners. As control of the trade slipped away from the artisans, so too did control of their communities.

THE BOSSES

If the tireless and efficient machine created industrial wealth, the men who directed it created a social and economic revolution against formidable opposition. Workers resisted in a variety of ways, and they were not alone. Others also questioned the wisdom of straying so far from the republican dream. Thomas Jefferson warned that the introduction of large-scale manufacturing would undermine the economic base of agriculture by competing for scarce labor. Jefferson and others also feared that factory work would degrade American workers and result in the creation of an urban proletariat, a development fraught with danger for an egalitarian society. They feared the division of society into the rich and the poor and the inevitable class conflict that would follow. Agriculture, they argued, was the foundation on which the hope for a society based on equality existed. Undermine it and the Republic would be undermined as well.

But the rising manufacturers were not without resources in the struggle. They argued that industry did not necessarily mean the weakening of the nation's agrarian base. They pointed out that through the use of labor saving machinery and the employment of immigrants and women, manufacturing could coexist with agriculture and lead to the enrichment of all. In other words, there was a place for the machine in the garden.

The struggle for power between agrarians and industrialists, like other great conflicts in pre-Civil War America, was carried on in the state legislatures, the halls of Congress, and the courts over issues such as governmental support for internal improvements, the creation of a national banking system, the protective tariff, and the creation of a national market. The sectional and economic alliances that did battle over these issues were fluid and complex. Issues such as slavery and sectionalism intertwined with the struggle for economic dominance.

Slowly the champions of industrialization prevailed. By 1828 they had secured the protection they wanted from foreign competition. A series of Supreme Court cases guaranteed both an open national market and the inviolability of corporate charters. By 1830 manufacturers had taken their place beside the agricultural and commercial interests as arbiters of the nation's destiny. With the defeat of the agrarian South in the Civil War, their triumph, both political and economic, was complete. Through it all they grew more confident of their right to command.

THE WORKERS

Historian Edward Pressen tells us that a variety of factors determined a worker's place in society in the early nineteenth century. These included skill, income, type of workplace, degree of freedom, living conditions, property ownership, and opportunities for advancement.

In the years between the turn of the century and the Civil War a significant number of workers received payment in kind, rather than cash. Food, living quarters, and goods and services of various kinds were frequently exchanged for services. Nor was this only a rural phenomenon. Skilled weavers in the New England textile mills typically received three-quarters of their pay in yarn or goods.

In the cities, unskilled laborers, teamsters, dock workers, seamstresses, and domestic workers made up nearly half of the urban work force and, along with railroaders and canal workers, were always among the lowest-paid categories of workers and were usually propertyless. An observer of the time claimed that the average worker lived "on the brink of starvation, has nothing left for his old age, if he lives to attain it, becomes a vagrant supported by charity, and is finally buried at the expense of the parish."

Skilled artisans constituted the elite of the laboring classes. Paid nearly double that received by the unskilled workers, artisans sometimes owned property and their own tools and these factors gave them a sense of independence and influence in the social, economic, and political life of their communities. But although craftsmen fared a good deal better than the unskilled, they too frequently lived with little margin of security. The head of the Journeymen House Carpenters of Philadelphia estimated that the cost for a decent house with a bathroom, cellar, furniture, bedding, clothing, and amusements left his fellow workers without money to feed their families properly.

These skilled workers produced the bulk of the nation's manufactured goods in the first half of the nineteenth century. Most of this production came out of the artisan's shop or the home as part of the putting-out system. In 1810 the secretary of the Treasury reported that two-thirds of the clothing worn by the 90 percent of Americans who did not live in the cities resulted from home manufacture.

Many small communities were nearly self-sufficient. Inhabitants frequently made almost everything they needed, including carpets, candles, and linens. Butchers, tanners, tailors, weavers, and shoemakers visited the residents, offered their services, and frequently performed them on the buyer's premises. Artisans working in their own shops making furniture, hats, wagons, and barrels, for example, bartered them in part for the raw materials required in their trades.

In the cities most products, including carriages, cabinets, residences, and bricks, to name just a few, were still made by artisans in response to special orders, but not all artisans enjoyed the relative independence of those engaged in the custom order trade. The manufacture of cloth and munitions had already moved into the factory setting. Shoemaking illustrated an industry that combined both factory and artisan techniques. Historian Alan Dawley has described the Massachusetts boot and shoe industry in the 1830s as one in which wealthy merchants had brought skilled cutters from the small artisan workshops, or "ten footers," into central shops to cut the leather. They then hired thousands of semiskilled farmers and fishermen to complete the work in their homes as part of the largest "putting-out" system in the history of American manufacturing.

In Philadelphia, instead of sending work to rural farms and villages, merchants who owned the raw materials produced cheap, wholesale boots and shoes by contracting with "garret bosses" who hired semiskilled shoe-makers to bind, last and bottom the shoes in sweatshops. Both the putting out and the sweatshop systems under cut the independence of the artisans and, as methods of organizing mass production of ready-made goods, they presaged the coming of the factory system to the industry.

The entrepreneurs who organized these systems were the midwives to the birth of the Industrial Revolution and they, along with their allies in government, transformed an entire society. They built the new factory towns that spread out along the rivers and streams of the New England and Middle Atlantic States that lacked accommodations for workers, as did the growing industrial cities. Eager to start production, employers brought workers to dismal communities lacking sewers, streets, or schools. Rents soared as factory workers were packed eight to ten to a room in dwellings built for one family. As this landless population gathered in the new towns and old cities, lack of proper sanitation led to periodic epidemics. Social tensions exacerbated existing racial, ethnic, and religious antagonisms. White workers resented blacks, native Americans blamed their condition on immigrants, and Protestants took out their frustrations on Catholics. Crime, poverty, and violence increasingly disfigured the urban scene.

If the price of the rapid industrialization of America was to be paid by the workers, they soon learned that they were to share only marginally in its bounty. In Holyoke, Massachusetts, in 1856 the Board of Health discovered whole families huddled into "low, damp and filthy cellars." Others existed in attics without ventilation. "It is only a wonder," remarked the Board, "that life can dwell in such apartments."

THE CHANGING WORKPLACE

If the environment in which factory workers lived was hardly conducive to well-being, the factory where they spent twelve to sixteen hours a day, six days a week, was no improvement. Two distinct types of factory labor systems emerged in the New England and Middle Atlantic States. One, the less common, relied on female labor recruited from surrounding farms, the most famous of which was at Lowell, Massachusetts. These firms were usually located in rural areas and were the centerpieces of company towns where the operatives were quartered in boarding houses supervised by matrons and controlled by the employers. Most American factory settlements, however, retained the English system of hiring whole families, usually including school-age children. In the South, slave labor made up as much as half of the industrial labor force. One white foreman in a southern textile mill attributed this to the fact that slaves did just as much work as whites and were more careful workers. He failed to mention that their condition rendered them a good deal cheaper and less contentious.

Whatever the system in use, industrial workers spent their days in large, rectangular structures with poor ventilation and no safety provisions, cold in the winter and hot in the summer. The factory bell summoned the workers to the mills and regulated their lives. In each room an overseer closely monitored their behavior and "dishonorable discharge" could result not only from improper work, but also for profanity, improper conduct, or insubordination. Leaving employment under these conditions frequently resulted in blacklisting.

"A cotton mill in motion," wrote historian Anthony Wallace, "was a shuddering, creaking, hissing mass of shafting turned by the great water wheel outside . . . belts whirred and hummed; gears clicked; cams and cranks clanked. The ,whole mill must have seemed to come alive with vibration when the power train was connected at the wheel in the morning." Noise was not the only hazard. A Pittsburgh physician described several Pennsylvania cotton mills as follows.

> . . . *ill ventilated. Their atmosphere . . . constantly impregnated, and highly surcharged with the most offensive effluvia—arising from the persons of the inmates, and the rancid oils applied to the machinery. The temperature of their atmosphere is generally high, approaching a medium of from sixty to seventy degrees in winter, and rising to eighty and even ninety degrees in summer. Their atmosphere is constantly filled with floating particles of cotton; the finer the yarns to be spun, the higher the temperature must be. . . . The cotton wool, when impregnated with the oil used to diminish friction in the machinery, and in the usual temperature of the rooms, emits a most offensive fetor. This fetor, acted on by the ozate and hydrogen abounding in the rooms, gives an atmosphere which none but those accustomed to it can respire without nausea. In the rooms where the cotton wool undergoes the first process of carding and breaking, the atmosphere is one floating mass of cotton particles, which none but those accustomed to it can breathe, for an hour together, without being nearly suffocated.*

Workers toiled from sunup to sundown under these conditions. Most Americans saw nothing wrong with this. It was no more time than the farmer gave to his fields or the artisan to his trade. Most factory workers had known long hours before on farms or in the shops, but they were not prepared for the unpleasant environment of factory work. In the mills the machines, not they, set the pace of work. On the farms and in the handicraft trades the nature of the work and the dictates of the seasons had contributed to an irregular work process, alternating between intensive periods of work and leisure activities. The discipline of the factory reached beyond the factory's walls into other areas of work. Efficiency became the test. Even building tradesmen who previously had worked from sunrise to sunset in all seasons found that those financing new construction now crowded work into the late spring, summer, and early fall when the days were long. This meant greater exertion for part of the year and little or no work during the winter.

HABITS OF INDUSTRY

To many people, the early fears that industrialization would degrade the workers seemed to be coming true. This bothered the masters of industry little because they did not consider their workers, particularly the immigrants, free and equal citizens of the Republic, but rather an undisciplined mass of inferiors. To break them to industrial discipline, far from a threat to democracy and stability, would be a public service. A Fall River foreman told a visitor in 1855 that he regarded his workers—for the most part immigrant Irishmen—just as he regarded his machinery. "When my machines get old and useless," he explained, "I reject them and get new, and these people are part of my machinery."

If bringing order to an unruly workforce could be defended as a noble social mission by manufacturers, then long hours could just as easily be defended as a means to this end. Shorter hours, argued the defenders of the system, led to idleness, mischief, drunkenness, gambling, and violence. Thus the factory served as an institution of social control. One company's regulations admonished employees to devote themselves to their duties during working hours and "on all occasions, both in their words and in their actions, show they are penetrated by a laudable love of temperance and virtue, and animated by a sense of their moral and social obligations."

This solicitous concern for the moral and social well-being of workers also extended to children. For them, too, idleness was seen as a threat to the values of hard work, sobriety, subservience, and self-discipline that the factory owners saw as necessary for a productive workforce. Early in the nineteenth century, child labor became a regular feature of the factory system. In the 1820s and 1830s children under sixteen comprised one-third to one-half of the industrial labor force in New England and about one-fifth in Pennsylvania. Usually hired as part of the family system, they worked the same hours as their parents. Whatever the supposed moral benefits, the immediate effects were plain to see. Disfigurement from industrial accidents, fatigue, mental dullness, and a host of other afflictions were everyday reminders of the price of child labor.

The process of implanting a value system in accord with the needs of the factory system proved difficult. Preindustrial values, customs, and traditions frustrated employers. Workers used to the irregular quality of traditional work habits carried those habits into the factories. There they conflicted with the regimentation required by the factory. The workplace became a place apart, separate and distinct from the rest of their lives. Socializing at work, characteristic of the handicraft trades, was not tolerated.

The struggle for control of the workplace is characteristic of all societies undergoing industrialization. Machines require workers to adapt older work habits to new routines. The struggle is always intense and frequently violent, but in most homogeneous societies, where ethnic, religious, and cultural differences are minimal, a new value system can be achieved in a finite period. As a new consensus forms, it can be reinforced through stable institutions whose legitimacy is recognized by most of the population. But in the United States, because of the successive waves of preindustrial immigrants and the large migrations of rural people within the country, the process never stopped. The American working class was in a constant state of alteration because of these movements of peasants, farmers, and artisans, all carrying with them customs and values incompatible with the demands of industrial discipline.

Such customs meshed with the irregular work routines of the handicraft shops but played havoc with the efficiency of the factory. Work rules of the period indicate the degree to which the problem vexed employers. A New Hampshire cotton factory that hired mostly women and children forbade drinking, smoking, and other kinds of amusements in and around the factory and threatened the disgraceful dismissal of workers found gambling, drinking, or committing "any other debaucheries." The Parkmount Woolen Mills near Philadelphia prohibited "Fighting, swearing, obscene language, undue familiarity between the sexes . . . tobacco smoking or possession of alcoholic beverages within the mill."

In the working class neighborhood pubs played an important part in the lives of the workers. Pubs served as meeting places and centers for political discussions as well as social centers. After employers began to prohibit drinking on the job the pubs grew in importance.

Workers regularly took part in a variety of other leisure activities as well. Traveling circuses and road shows, hunting and shooting matches, harvest festivities, wedding parties, and election and independence day celebrations were popular. Membership in militia units and volunteer fire companies was common and annual musters became occasions for celebrations frequently lasting several days. Leisure pursuits begun on Sundays, the only regular holiday from work, often carried over into Monday. As early as the 1750s Benjamin Franklin had lamented the absence of regular work habits. "Saint Monday," he said, "is as duly kept by our working people as Sunday; the only difference is that instead of employing their time cheaply at church, they are wasting it cheaply at the ale house." These habits carried over to the early factories, and plagued employers with inefficiency and absenteeism. In 1836 a New Jersey manufacturer stated with relief that he was no longer plagued with a workforce infected with "the brutal leprosy of blue Monday habits. . . ." No wonder then that a Connecticut textile manufacturer justified the twelve-hour day and the six-day week because they kept workers from "vicious amusements."

To prepare the mass of American workers for the new economic order required more than long hours. Employers agreed with John Adams when he said that "manufacturers cannot live, much less thrive, without honor, fidelity, punctuality, and private faith, a sacred respect for property and the moral obligation of promises and contracts." What was needed was no less than a new industrial morality emphasizing order, self-discipline, propriety, and the work ethic, not only at the workplace but in all aspects of life.

In pursuit of this goal manufacturers established churches, moral reform societies, schools, and temperance organizations to impart the values and ideology of industrial capitalism to workers. In their effort manufacturers enlisted the aid of the professional classes, in particular the Protestant clergy. In a sense, the manufacturers and the ministers were the carriers of a new culture—one that sharply distinguished between work and leisure and regarded preindustrial culture as wasteful and sinful. Many clergymen became moral police for the manufacturers, providing them with a disciplined labor force, imbued with "habits of industry," respectful of property and orderly in its behavior.

According to a prominent Philadelphia Presbyterian the task would not be easy. He warned that "the lower stratum of society . . . that dense and dark mass, the population of alleys and cellars, and garrets—the ignorant, the degraded, the grossly sensual, the idle, the worthless—the refuse of society . . . are not in a condition where revival of religion can be expected . . ."

Apparently the crusade for industrial morality made only slight inroads into the working class in the 1820s and 1830s. But during the terrible depression following the Panic of 1837, it began to make considerable progress among factory workers and artisans. The reformers urged the closing of the taverns, teaching the poor the virtues of self-denial, and placing the children in schools. Thus the assault on the moral laxity of preindustrial customs and traditions was to have two major thrusts: temperance and public education.

No problem so troubled industrialists as the effect of preindustrial drinking habits on efficiency. Indeed, one early New York temperance advocate claimed that the effect of liquor on labor efficiency constituted the strongest argument for temperance. Religious leaders and industrialists warned against the harmful effects of drinking, and employers urged workers and their children to substitute time in church for time in the ale houses. Poverty and economic ruin were attributed to drink. In spite of the intensity of the crusade workers did not succumb easily to the urgings of their employers and the clergy. But the dismal conditions of the depression of 1837 seemed to some a sign of God's wrath and the temperance movement began to make considerable progress in working class districts. Even labor leaders, who previously had seen the sense in moderation, but rejected total abstinence, began to attack the use of liquor. In their eyes liquor degraded workers, kept them permanently in debt, and made them untrustworthy comrades in any attempt to confront the rising power of their employers through collective action.

But rather than foster solidarity, there is evidence that the success of the temperance movement contributed to conflict among the working class. The movement succeeded in bringing large numbers of workers into active membership in the evangelical Protestant churches. This created conflict with the Irish Catholic immigrants flooding into the country. To be sure some of this conflict can be attributed to the threat that the new immigrants posed to the jobs and wages of those already employed. But perhaps equally important was the perception that Irish immigrants did not share the new moral code of sobriety, respectability, and self-control. In other words the anger of Protestant workers was turned not against employers, but against Roman Catholics as in Kensington, a manufacturing suburb of Philadelphia, where Catholic and Protestant workers battled for four bloody days in 1844. Religious differences also divided workers in the political arena. Anti-Catholic political parties triumphed at the polls in 1844 in New York, Philadelphia, and Boston with significant support from Protestant workers.

Moral reformers came to see public education as the best means to ensure that the working class absorbed the new industrial morality. It would be a gross misrepresentation to claim that only individuals interested in social and industrial discipline supported educational reform. People of all classes and political persuasions took part in the movement for free public education. But while humanitarians viewed public education as the road to social justice and equality, industrialists and moral reformers emphasized that it would increase production, lower the crime rate, and counteract radical doctrines among the working class. For labor leaders public schools had other purposes. They would put an end to the "hereditary bondage" into which ignorance had cast workers and also put an end to the monopoly of talent that the private schools had assured to the elite. An educated working class would "remove the veil of ignorance by which the poor who suffer are prevented from penetrating into the mysteries of that legislation of the rich by which their sufferings are produced," and have its eyes opened to the "monstrous frauds perpetrated upon it."

The broad base of support for free public education, whatever the motives, assured its success. But the values the public schools taught were largely those desired by the emerging business elite and the religious reformers. Textbooks, such as the famous and influential *McGuffey Reader*, were handbooks of common morality that extolled the habits of industry. Stressing sobriety, hard work, and obedience to superiors, these books testified to a value system well on its way to triumph.

THE DISSENTERS

The economic changes of the Industrial Revolution intensified competition among wage earners, cheapened their skills, undercut their security, attacked their standard of living, and lowered their social status. Increasingly labor leaders emerged who saw an inherent conflict of interests between workers and employers. They argued that the manufacturer whose control over production rested exclusively on ownership of capital was a parasite. Labor leaders blamed manufacturers for creating unemployment, for reducing wages, and for forcing workers to spend their days in dangerous and debilitating conditions. They identified wealth, the system of producing it, distributing it, and transmitting it across the generations as the source of power within society.

Against this accumulation of power based on the unrestricted use of private property, the leaders had their own ideas of how society should be organized and how its economic benefits should be distributed. Almost universally accepted by labor was the belief that labor created all wealth. Labor, as its leaders interpreted it, and as the artisan journalist, George Henry Evans, described it, meant the following.

Those who do the work and fight the battles; who produce the necessaries and comforts of life; who till the earth for its treasures; who build the houses and the ships; who make the clothes, the books, the machinery, the clocks and watches, the musical instruments, and the thousands of things which are necessary to enable men to live and be happy.

For Evans and his contemporaries, this included not only artisans and laborers, but farmers, shopkeepers, master craftsmen, and small manufacturers. Indeed, the inclusion of small businessmen and manufacturers was important because many artisans aspired to that status and saw the growth of large scale enterprise as a threat to their opportunity to reach that goal.

A strong sense of social and economic decline motivated the labor leaders. They believed strongly in the ideals of the American Revolution. They saw equality as the true goal of the labor movement—an equality that they defined as the dignity of labor, freedom for the worker, and the social equality of all producers. They viewed industrial capitalism as a fundamental threat to that goal. The labor leaders knew that because of it, in the words of one leader of the Lynn shoemakers, "Labor had become a commodity, wealth lay in capital, and the natural order of things entirely reversed."

Labor's leaders by no means universally accepted that large-scale manufacturing should be regarded as exclusively the province of private capital. Industrial capitalism had not yet swept all before it. Some argued that there were alternate ways to use the new technology. It is true that some few rejected industrialization and longed to return to an earlier, simpler time. But the majority saw promise in the machines. One reformer, Robert Dale Owens, spoke for this viewpoint when he argued that it was not labor saving machinery itself that caused the problems, but rather "labor saving machinery, as at present directed and controlled." To these emerging labor leaders, according to historian Norman Ware, "The American worker was not actively opposed to machinery. He was opposed to the method of its introduction, for exploitive purposes, as he conceived it, in the hands of a group alien to the producer."

These early labor leaders faced formidable opposition. But their accomplishments in the face of overwhelming odds were impressive. They took the lead in organizing unions, reform associations, consumer and producers' cooperatives, and worker's political parties. They were artisans for the most part and they looked forward to a more egalitarian society in which the benefits of the machine age would flow to all of the people. Their ideas dominated the labor movement for most of the nineteenth century.

WILLIAM ENGLISH

English described himself as a "mechanic, born to toil from early childhood (who) never . . . entered a school by the light of day." In fact, in spite of his concern to be identified by his trade of shoemaking, English spent relatively little time as a cordwainer. Like a handful of his contemporaries, he dedicated his life to the labor movement, and through his commitment and his skills as a public speaker he became one of the leaders of the attempts to organize unions and labor parties in Philadelphia and beyond.

By the late 1820s he was actively involved in the Philadelphia Mechanics Union of Trade Associations, a short-lived citywide federation formed as a result of a house carpenters strike in 1827. He became a vice-president of the Mechanics' Library Company of Philadelphia, which published the first labor newspaper, the *Mechanics Free Press,* and emerged as one of the key leaders of the Philadelphia Workingmen's Party between 1829 and 1831. English considered the political system a hoax with the purpose of the major parties to make the rich richer and the poor poorer. In advocating a labor party he argued as follows.

> . . . *once a year they call us* men; *once a year we receive the proud appellation of freemen; once a year we are the* intelligent, virtuous orderly working men. *But then they want our* votes, *and they flatter us; they want our interest, and they fawn upon us; and it grinds them to the very soul, to have their delicate fingers clenched in the friendly gripe (sic) of an honest hand, but they dare not avow it then. There is contamination in the very touch of a man who labours for his bread; but it will not do to say so on the election ground, for that would lose them our votes. They know our strength; although it would seem we do not; and hence they resort to every stratagem to distract and divide us; to cut us up into parties and fragments of parties; to set each man against his neighbor; to turn, almost, our very brains with political excitement; and all for what? To elevate themselves!!!*

English eventually became recording secretary of the National Trades Union in 1835 and president of the Philadelphia Trades Union in 1836. This union—consisting of mechanics, factory workers, and day laborers—carried out a successful strike for the ten-hour day in 1835.

PART II
The Response of Free People

Workers in William English's trade of shoemaking formed the first "permanent" trade union in 1792. There had been strikes before and even rudimentary attempts at collective bargaining, but in these cases workers in a particular trade joined together for the duration of the struggle and then disbanded. The attempt by the shoemakers was different. Though they lasted only one year, they reconstituted themselves in 1794 and remained in existence until 1806. Others soon followed. By 1820 shoemakers had organized in a number of eastern cities as had carpenters, cabinetmakers, coopers, masons, and tailors.

These were local craft unions with membership limited to one trade. They concerned themselves primarily with the protection of the trades through the establishment of apprenticeship systems and minimum wages. Both, they believed, would protect them from cheaper, less skilled workers who were increasingly appearing in the shops as the reorganization of production divided the skills. They also attempted to establish the closed shop by compelling employers to hire only union workers. In the absence of this protection they resorted to "shunning," or refusing to associate in any way with nonunion practitioners of the craft.

The rise of the early unions and their limited successes led to a reaction on the part of employers who turned to the courts for support in what was to become a time-honored tactic. The courts responded with a series of decisions that retarded the growth of the labor movement for four decades.

Called the Cordwainer Conspiracy Cases, they took place between 1806 and 1815 and involved shoemakers in Philadelphia, Pittsburgh, and New York. The issue was the demand for a minimum wage. The courts ruled that although the right of workers to form unions was in some doubt, almost any actions that unions could take to increase wages or endorse the closed shop were illegal. In effect the courts applied English common law to American industrial relations and found that combinations of workers to compel employers to take actions against their will constituted illegal conspiracies. The conspiracy doctrine grew out of the English Tudor industrial code that had sought to ensure a profit to the agricultural or industrial proprietor by guaranteeing him an adequate low-wage labor supply, and at the same time to safeguard the worker against undue and unrestrained exploitation, but it had never before been applied to trade unionism in the free market conditions that existed in the United States.

The combination of the conspiracy doctrine and the depression that followed the War of 1812 had a chilling effect on the growth of the labor movement. As infant American industries collapsed in the face of renewed British competition, unemployment soared and the tiny, struggling labor movement disappeared. But as prosperity returned so too did the labor movement. In a pattern that was to repeat itself with regularity through the boom and bust economic cycles of the nineteenth century, labor declined in hard times and regrouped in periods of inflation and prosperity. The unions that reappeared were no different from those that had preceded them and conflicts with employers continued to center around wages. But as the 1820s developed it became clear that unions were to make up only a small portion of the labor movement. Only a tiny fraction of workers were in unions and the class interests of the vast majority of workers went well beyond questions of wages. The issues that united the mass of workers into something resembling a movement were numerous, but the one that provided the most solidarity proved to be the ten-hour day.

In 1825 Boston house carpenters struck for the ten-hour day and lost. New York building tradesmen and others cooperated with considerable success on the same issue soon after. In Philadelphia the ten-hour movement led to the formation of a citywide federation of local craft unions called the Philadelphia Mechanics Union of Trade Associations, often called the beginning of the modern labor movement.

EQUAL RIGHTS

The fact that almost immediately after its formation the Mechanics Union of Trade Associations converted itself into a political party says a great deal about the pre-Civil War labor movement. To the leaders of labor all of the specific issues around which workers rallied were merely facets of the larger, more fundamental issue, equality: economic, political, and social. Such a wide-ranging struggle could not be fought only at the workplace. It had to be carried into all of the institutions of society, and particularly into the political arena. Indeed it was in the political arena in which the battle seemed most equal. Although universal white manhood suffrage did not come in some states until the 1830s, white American male workers had the right to vote in the early nineteenth century in numbers unheard of for workers in any other part of the world. Workers also believed widely in the potential of the ballot for social change and in the guarantees of the Constitution. Not surprisingly they looked often to political action as a weapon in their struggle for equality.

Out of their sense that they were losing that equality grew a group of issues around which working people rallied in the political arena. First among them was the demand for the ten-hour day. Although skilled tradesmen had made some progress in a few cities, workers for whom unions were only a distant hope—and especially for factory operatives—any change in the sunrise-to-sunset system would have to come through action in the state legislatures.

Logically then, the second most important issue became the call for universal, white male suffrage. As long as property qualifications kept a significant part of the working class without the right to vote, labor's interests could more easily be ignored.

Free public education also gained almost universal support. Only with equal access to education could the children of the working classes use their intelligence in the political system to ensure a more equitable society.

There were other issues as well and all, in one way or another, dealt with equality. Labor's political leaders called for the end of imprisonment for debt, a system that fell most heavily on the small debtor. They also wanted an end to the militia system that required attendance at periodic drills under pain of fine or imprisonment—a fine that the well-to-do paid with ease, but which represented as much as ten days' wages to the worker. Political leaders also urged passage of mechanics' lien laws in the various states to ensure that workers would have first call on the assets of bankrupt firms in order to collect wages owed them. Finally the leaders joined in the general reaction to the rising power of capital by opposing chartered monopolies.

The fight against monopoly went to the heart of the issue of equality. When state legislatures granted monopoly charters to banks, transportation, or manufacturing enterprises, it stifled competition and relegated the master and worker to depend on the capitalist for contracts and wages. Banks were seen as the worst offenders of all because they financed the merchant capitalists and manufacturers at rates well below those available to tradespeople. Banks also issued paper money in which workers were paid—paper money that often turned out to be worth a good deal less than face value when exchanged for goods and services. In other words, concentrations of economic power reduced the independence and opportunity of Americans and struck a blow at the republican dream of an egalitarian society.

Around these issues, as well as the continued hostility of the courts to unions, and the effects of the depression of 1828 and 1829, the first labor parties in the world developed in the United States. These worker's parties, derisively called "workies" or "dirty shirt parties" by their enemies, appeared in a number of cities and towns in the late 1820s. The first, as we have seen, grew out of the Philadelphia Mechanics Union of Trade Associations that had unsuccessfully fought for the ten-hour day. New York workers followed suit one year later in 1829.

The leaders of this political movement were by and large the same men who led the early labor unions—men like William Heighton, a Philadelphia shoemaker, and Thomas Skidmore, a New York machinist. But they were not alone. Intellectuals, reformers, and propagandists who knew or thought they knew how to cure the ills of society also joined in. That their main concern was for the welfare of workers rather than their class standing qualified them as allies of working people. It should also be remembered that these early labor parties were broad based in the belief that all who lived from their own labor, rather than that of others, were workers. Considering this,it is not surprising that the parties included farmers, entrepreneurs, and even small manufacturers. One of the main arguments for the creation of the workers parties was the increased domination of the major parties by the rich.

THOMAS SKIDMORE

Skidmore exemplified the versatility and wide ranging interests of the early leaders of the labor movement. Born at the turn of the century and self-educated, he began teaching at the age of thirteen, left a few years later to become an inventor, and finally moved to New York City in 1819 to work as a machinist.

In 1829 Skidmore emerged as one of the leaders of the Workingmen's Party of New York, which resulted from an employers' attempt to lengthen the working day. Skidmore led the "mechanics" present at the founding of the party to resolve to defend the ten-hour day and to criticize the unequal division of property.

After an internal split in the party, Skidmore withdrew and spent the few years until his death in 1832 writing and speaking on behalf of the theories on land distribution that made him famous. In 1829 he published *The Rights of Man to Property! Being a proposition to make it equal among the adults of the present generation; and to provide for its equal transmission to every individual of each succeeding generation, on arriving at the age of maturity.* Skidmore advocated that every man over twenty one and every single woman receive 160 acres of land to be held as long as he or she tilled it. The land could not be disposed of by sale or rental. Those currently owning more than 160 acres would not be disturbed, except after death when inheritance laws would expropriate all but 160 acres. Skidmore argued that because great wealth is an instrument that is used to extort property from others, it ought to be taken away from the rich on the same principle "that a sword or pistol may be arrested from a robber. . . ." Although Skidmore also urged the poor to expropriate cotton factories, iron foundries and other industrial property as well as land, he emphasized the distribution of land. His philosophy came to be called agrarianism.

Whether the workers parties were true labor parties in the modern sense of the word is irrelevant. It is difficult to argue with the fact that the parties were formed by workers and allies devoted to the interests of workers, and that their programs championed the causes of working-class people. That these programs, built around the "workingmen's platform," were wide ranging was in keeping with the times. This was a political movement, not a trade union movement, and its goals extended far beyond the problems of the workplace.

The downfall of the New York party illustrates the problems the organizers faced in holding such a diverse membership together. The party declined because of a split between agrarian reformers who supported Skidmore's call for equal property to all adults and educational reformers (such as Robert Dale Owen and Fanny Wright) who proposed a radical system of state-supported boarding schools. But all of these programs, no matter how utopian they might seem to us now, were taken seriously in their day and were part of the ferment of the so-called "Age of the Common Man." It was a period marked by an impulse toward democracy aimed at restoring a semblance of equality to a society that was rapidly changing in ways which common people perceived to be harmful to their interests.

ROBERT DALE OWEN AND FRANCES WRIGHT

Robert Dale Owen, son of Robert Owen, the famous British utopian socialist reformer of the nineteenth century, came to the United States in 1825 to help his father found the pioneer utopian community at New Harmony, Indiana. At New Harmony young Owen edited the *Gazette*, in which he expounded his views against organized religion and in support of liberal divorce laws, industrial education, and the distribution of wealth.

After the failure of the New Harmony experiment, Owen and Frances "Fanny" Wright, whom Owen had met at New Harmony, established an experimental community in Nashoba, Tennessee, aimed at ending slavery. The plan called for white benefactors to purchase slaves from their owners and send them to Nashoba. There the slaves were to pay off the purchase price from profits they hoped to earn through work on the cooperative plantation. While working off the purchase price, the slaves were to be educated for future self support.

When the project failed amid rumors of sexual license among the participants, Owen and Wright moved to New York City and became active in labor and reform politics. Both joined the Workingmen's Party, which the press labeled the "Fanny Wright" party. The two reformers attacked Thomas Skidmore's plan for equal distribution of land as "crude communism" and put forward their own panacea for the problems of wealth and poverty in the form of a system of state guardianship education in which all children would be taken from their homes and placed in national schools where they would receive equal education at public expense, thus ending inequality and regenerating society.

The plan caused a split in the Workingmen's Party when the majority of artisans holding more traditional social and cultural values rejected it as a menace to family and religion. Disillusioned, Owen ended his labor activities and embarked on more than half a century of agitation for reform causes. Wright became well known for her advocacy of free love, abortion, and the abolition of slavery, and "Fanny Wrightism" came to be a standard term of derision for reform ideas.

The phenomenon of the workers parties lasted only a few years. But in that short time the movement spread to a number of communities, large and small, in the New England and Middle Atlantic States. They had few successes. For the most part they melted away into whichever of the major parties championed their goals in a given locality. But the attempt had not been futile. Many of the principles for which the workers parties stood became part of major party programs in a number of areas. As popular support for the democratic goals of the "workies" spread, many of the reforms became reality. By the end of the 1830s imprisonment for debt had been abolished. The free public education movement made impressive gains in the New England and middle states. Mechanics' lien laws appeared and compulsory militia duty disappeared. Ironically, only labor's primary goal—the ten-hour day—remained for the majority of workers only a distant dream.

The workers political movement failed to develop into a permanent labor party for several complex reasons. Probably most significant was that as small parties with real influence in only a handful of cities, the movement was most effective when acting as a pressure group within the Democratic Party. Where the workies could demonstrate their clout, the two major parties simply adopted their programs and absorbed them. In other areas, such as New York, internal bickering contributed to their disappearance. But whatever the causes, the flirtation with independent political action had been short lived. In the mid-1830s workers, although remaining active in the major parties, turned most of their attention to rebuilding their trade associations and continuing the fight for the ten-hour day.

TEN HOURS

The ten-hour movement, which accompanied the revival of the labor movement in the 1830s, took place in a period in which capitalists brought heavy pressure on many of the traditional trades. The key to this process was the development of the central shop system in which preparation of the material for finishing took place under the watchful eyes of the merchant capitalist. This divided the skill and struck a blow at the apprenticeship system, the main method with which to protect the integrity of the trade. Necessary skills could now be learned in a few months and half-trained boys, women, and children began to replace the skilled journeymen. By 1837 women could be found in one hundred different trades.

Threatened by these unskilled workers the skilled tradesmen reformed their unions and developed citywide federations in most major cities. These federations became the cornerstones of the antebellum labor movement. They consisted largely of local associations of journeymen artisans. Typical of the movement was the Philadelphia Trades Union in which William English had been prominent. The city centrals spawned a lively labor press that served not only as a forum for problems in the trades but also as organs for a variety of political, social, and economic reforms that labor's leaders championed. First among these was the ten-hour day.

In 1835, a general strike by seventeen Philadelphia craft unions, acting in concert under the coordination of the city federation, and with the support of the city's unskilled workers, succeeded in winning the ten-hour day for some of the trades. Encouraged by the Philadelphia example, skilled workers throughout the Middle Atlantic States struck for ten hours with considerable success. In New England it was a different story. There an organization uniquely representative of the period formed around the issue of the ten-hour day. The New England Association of Farmers, Mechanics and Other Workingmen attempted to draw together skilled and unskilled workers with farmers and small businessmen—the producing classes.

The impulse toward cooperation also reached New York. There unionists took the lead in forming the National Trades Union. Although it was little more than a series of meetings of representatives of local trade assemblies at which political and economic issues were discussed, the organization did support the broad reform issues of the Workingmen's parties. Though it never achieved real stability and fell victim to the Panic of 1837, it did help to convince President Andrew Jackson to establish the ten-hour day in the Philadelphia Navy Yard.

Once again depression destroyed the struggling labor movement. By the beginning of 1838, one-third of the nation's workers were unemployed and the wages of those working dropped dramatically. But with recovery, the movement returned. In 1844 two hundred delegates formed the New England Workingmen's Association to carry on the struggle for the ten-hour day.

FREEDOM'S FERMENT

The severity of the long depression had brought other, more radical solutions to the attention of workers. Inside the New England Association and elsewhere in the labor movement, reformers put forth utopian plans calling for nothing less than the reorganization of society along cooperative lines. The ten-hour day and more mundane concerns generally received less emphasis than calls for sweeping societal reforms. The 1840s were years of reform ferment. Issues such as land reform, utopianism, abolition of slavery, and feminism captured the attention of the nation.

Although in retrospect it is difficult to understand the deep impression that the utopian movement made on American society in the 1840s, it should be remembered that it took place in a nation undergoing rapid change, a change that threatened the very consensus on which the Republic had been founded. To be sure the movement to create a cooperative society did have its odd aspects, ranging from food faddism to free love. But for the most part it was a serious movement that attracted a number of the most influential people in the country to its ranks. Horace Greeley, the famous editor of the *New York Tribune*, became one of the most vigorous supporters of associationism, the mainstream of utopian thought during the period.

It is no easy task to summarize the main tenets of a movement with so many varied, and often exotic, strains. But common to all of them was an impulse toward equality of effort and reward within a cooperative system.

The utopian movement was clearly an attempt to create a society based on pure democracy in a setting of small, harmoniously balanced agricultural and industrial communities. In a sense they were not unlike the company towns, such as Lowell, Massachusetts, that envisioned a carefully planned integration of technology, social structure, and education. The difference was in who was to control the machine and its benefits. In the capitalist company town, no matter how idealistic the original concept, the profits flowed to the owners and the lower the wages the higher the profits. Utopian reformers envisioned a model society, free of crime and poverty, where all would share equally the fruits of their labor.

No matter how unrealistic the hundreds of experiments that took place proved to be, labor leaders of the time gave them a respectful hearing. For the most part they had no real philosophical differences with the ideas of the utopian reformers. But to agree in principle was one thing. To convince working people to leave their homes and jobs to move to experimental communities proved all but impossible. That, and the hostility of the churches to the radical social ideas of the reformers, spelled their doom.

Nevertheless, to dismiss the experiments as only an aberration and distraction for workers is not accurate. The associationist movement alone attracted some 8000 members to forty communities during the 1840s. Labor leaders such as William Heighton (the Philadelphia shoemaker who founded the Mechanics Union of Trade Associations, a mechanics library, and the *Mechanics Free Press*) was a strong supporter of one strain of utopian socialism. Labor papers of the 1840s gave ample space to arguments for utopian experiments, publicized appearances by various reformers, and urged their members to join the new communities.

The extent to which labor leaders accepted the basic tenets of utopian reform can be seen in their fascination with the idea of producers' cooperatives. After all, shorn of their elaborate social justification, the utopian experiments were basically producers' cooperatives. It is not surprising that the movement for the establishment of producers' cooperatives as a solution for labor's problems also began in the 1840s. Labor newspapers paid a great deal of attention to experiments of this kind in Europe. Horace Greeley urged their formation in the pages of his *New York Tribune*. The Iron Molders of Cincinnati pioneered in their formation in 1847 in order to sustain themselves during a strike. By 1850 several dozen were in operation. Most failed because of inadequate funding, poor management, and cutthroat competition from capitalist firms. But the idea of cooperatives made a lasting impression on labor leaders who came to maturity before the Civil War. More than the other reform issues that dominated the labor movement before the Civil War, producers' cooperatives maintained their allure well into the postwar period.

Land reform also captured the interest of workers during the 1840s. As a means to relieve pressure on themselves, the workers advocated the distribution of the public domain to actual settlers, rather than selling it to speculators. The idea of free public land as one cure for society's ills had been around for a long time, and in a particularly radical form had been partially responsible for the split of the Workingmen's Party of New York in the early 1830s. But the agrarianism of the 1840s and 1850s was more moderate and of broader appeal to workers. Its main proponent, George Henry Evans, an Englishman by birth and a printer by trade, had long been involved in the whole range of labor reform issues. He argued that the people had a natural right to the public land and that it should be equally distributed to anyone who would farm it in lots of 160 acres. Land reform, Evans argued, would free workers from complete dependence on the masters of capital. It would also drain workers from the east, create excess housing and lower rents, and raise wages. Land reform, like free public education, had many supporters outside the ranks of labor. Nevertheless, Evans' National Reform Association, to which a number of labor leaders were attracted, played a major role in winning passage of the Homestead Act during the Civil War.

IN UNION THERE IS STRENGTH

Despite the attention given to general reform issues in the two decades following the Panic of 1837, workers never lost sight of the goal of the ten-hour day. Organizations such as the Female Labor Reform Association of Lowell carried on the fight by petitioning New England state legislatures. At the end of the 1840s several states responded with legislation fixing the legal working day at ten hours. But the laws contained a fatal flaw. All of them contained a provision whereby workers could contract to work longer hours if they chose. In the hands of the employers this quickly became a blanket requirement for all workers. Any resistance to signing such contracts was quickly broken by the use of blacklists and the presence of large numbers of immigrant workers desperate to work under any conditions.

In the Middle Atlantic States, a revived labor movement consisting largely of city federations of skilled workers agitated for ten-hour legislation. Although most skilled tradesmen in the cities had already won the shorter day through their economic power, these artisans pressed the state legislatures of New York, New Jersey, and Pennsylvania on behalf of their brothers and sisters in the factories. Legislation similar to that passed in New England followed with the result that by 1860, of 350 manufacturing enterprises reporting to the Bureau of the Census, workers in some 67 percent of them worked eight to eleven hours per day. Although these are meager statistics, they do reflect considerable success for a movement waged almost entirely through the use of political pressure. The lesson was clear. For the growing army of industrial workers, effective trade unions were a long way in the future and reform could only come when working people could bring sufficient pressure to bear on the political process. It was to take almost a century more for that to become a reality.

The city federations that took an active part in the ten-hour movement were but one sign of a revival of the labor movement. Beginning early in the 1850s, trade unionism spread in the building and service trades among skilled artisans, led by carpenters, bricklayers, printers, painters, tailors, and bakers. That the return of prosperity gave them some leverage can be seen in the fact that they carried on more than 400 strikes between 1853 and 1854, many of them successful.

But although these unions resembled earlier attempts at stable unionism, there were also significant differences. Conscious of the reasons for earlier failures, the unions developed strict apprenticeship codes, raised initiation fees and dues, and created strike funds. To protect their members against nonunion labor, the locals pooled information concerning job opportunities and scabs with other locals in the trade. Members in good standing carried traveling cards when seeking employment in other cities. Usually organized on a citywide basis, these locals continued the old practice of publicly posting their demands for all the employers to see, and threatening to strike if they were not met.

An even more significant development in the 1850s was the spread of trade unionism to the more skilled workers in the factories. British immigrant workers in the Fall River, Massachusetts, textile mills organized the Mule Spinners Association, while their countrymen in Lynn and Natick organized unions of skilled shoemakers. British miners agitated for unions in the Pennsylvania anthracite coal fields, and in 1861, Daniel Weaver organized bituminous miners into the American Miners Association, perhaps the first American industrial union encompassing everyone working at the trade. Around the same time, skilled puddlers, heaters, rollers, and molders in the growing iron industry also formed unions.

Out of this movement grew the first attempts to form national trade unions. The printers from five states met in convention in New York City in 1850 and out of that meeting, in 1852, came the National Typographical Union. Plumbers, hatters, cigar makers, mule spinners, cordwainers, and others followed until by 1860 there were ten important national unions. All of them continued the trend toward common apprenticeship standards, centrally controlled strike funds, and common welfare funds.

Except for the Typographical Union, the Hat Finishers, and the Stonecutters, most of the nationals proved too fragile to survive the depression of 1857. But as the economy revived in 1860, so did the labor movement. Once more, workers in the Massachusetts shoe towns were in the forefront. But where earlier shoemaker unions had been composed of highly skilled craftsmen who worked in artisan shops, the 1860 revival of unionism involved factory hands, both male and female, who ran machines.

Begun in Lynn, Massachusetts, the movement spread to other New England shoe centers and resulted in one of the largest and longest strikes in the pre-Civil War era. From February to April of 1860, 20,000 novice factory hands and craftsmen transformed into machine operators by the introduction of the sewing machine struck against a wage cut. The militancy of the workers and the support of other townspeople for the strikers led many employers to rescind the wage cut, but recognition of the union did not follow. Still, the great strike of New England shoe workers was a harbinger of the industrial conflicts between capital and labor that were to characterize the United States after the Civil War.

PART III
Lowell

No single industrial experiment illustrated the conflict between the desire for industrialization and the fear of its impact on a republican society as did the textile city of Lowell. The businessmen who developed Lowell were aware of the disgust that so many American travelers felt when they visited the textile centers of England and saw the misery and poverty of the industrial workers. The businessmen heard the chorus of influential voices raised against the introduction of a similar system here.

The concern of those who feared such a development did not rest solely, or even mainly, on sympathy for the workers. Most important was their fear that industrialization on the English model would lead to the creation of a debased proletariat that would threaten the existence of the traditional republican community—a community based on the ideal of a society of rough equality in which all citizens were bound together by mutual responsibilities.

Most of the skeptics believed that the idea of equality depended on the existence of a largely agrarian society where men and women worked and lived in independent and direct contact with nature. Had not Thomas Jefferson, the main exponent of the virtues of an agrarian society, warned that industrialization could lead to class conflict in America?

The contrast between the agrarian ideal and the popular image of the effects of industrialization was clearly stated by one appalled visitor to Manchester, England.

Heaven forbid that America should ever be cursed with such a manufacturing system as that which is now the curse of England. May the day never come, when any great proportion of the labouring classes of America shall be taken from the broad fields and rich soil, where the muscles grow strong and the frame sturdy in the open air; where the wages of a few months will purchase . . . enough of the earth's surface to be dignified by the name of home, and which will produce the grand necessaries of life for the working man's family.

The founders of the textile mills of Lowell were not immune to such sentiments; indeed, they shared them in part. Nevertheless, they argued that manufacturing need not necessarily follow the English pattern. Simplistically, they reasoned that many of the evils of the English system resulted from the location of the factories in the large cities where a permanent proletariat perpetuated itself. Their answer was to locate the mills in the countryside, import the workers, and provide a system of strict moral supervision that would guarantee their health and virtue. With the machine placed in the garden, rather than in the city, factories could coexist harmoniously with agriculture.

For their experiment the textile manufacturers chose a sight at a falls on the Merrimac River where barely 200 families lived in 1820. By 1826 the tiny hamlet held six textile mills and a workforce of over 1000. The phenomenal growth continued and, by the Civil War, Lowell had become the leading textile center of the nation.

Lowell's uniqueness as an industrial center flowed from two basic decisions. The first was to establish a community with a rotating, rather than permanent, population, and the second was to hire women for the most part. Previous factory settlements had depended on the labor, of whole families. This required a permanent workforce and raised the specter of class conflict. This conflict could be avoided if young women could be recruited from surrounding farms to work for only a few years. There was also another reason for using women. Men could not be spared from the farms and any aggressive attempt to lure them from agriculture could confirm the fears of agrarians that industry would undermine agriculture. By employing young farm women who would send their earnings home, the enterprise could actually contribute to the stability of the family farm. This made eminently good sense at a time when a combination of cheap European imports and the beginnings of the factory system had resulted in declining opportunities for household manufactures, an activity through which farm women had traditionally contributed to the financial security of the family. But while it made sense economically, it was no easy matter to convince the parents of rural New England girls to allow their daughters to leave home to work in the mills far from parental supervision. In order to calm their fears and also because no housing existed in Lynn, the boarding-house system evolved.

In the Lowell system, the female operatives (the vast majority of whom were under thirty) were to be under total supervision both in the mills and in the boardinghouses. They were to be watched over by upright matrons and provided cultural advantages and compulsory religious services. Factory work, too, would contribute to their moral well-being. In the mills the women would learn "habits or order, regularity and industry, which [would] lay a broad and deep foundation of public and private future usefulness." In the propaganda of its founders, Lowell was to be a combination of private enterprise, finishing school, and moral reform society.

Of course, the motives of the manufacturers proved to be not entirely altruistic: they expected women to be a docile, more easily managed workforce. The fact that women would not be permanent workers would retard the development of deep-seated resentments. In the words of one employer, "Women are much more ready to follow good regulations . . . and do not clan as the men do against the overseers."

Company agents working on commission traveled the New England countryside to recruit workers for the mills. They extolled the virtues of a harmonious community where virtuous young women would learn the habits of industry, be exposed to cultural advantages, and receive moral and religious instruction. In truth, many young women looked forward to leaving the restrictions of family life. Besides, they viewed mill work as temporary. They could always return home if they wished, but work at Lowell offered them an unprecedented independence from home and family while at the same time providing them with the opportunity to assist their families or earn a dowry for a future marriage. And even though pay at Lowell was never good, the women earned more in the mills than they could have earned in any other occupation open to women at the time.

There was more than a little truth in the propaganda about the benefits of the Lowell system. In the early years it did provide a working and living environment far superior to those that existed in the mill towns based on the family system. But the renown of Lowell probably had as much to do with the intellectual level of the workers as it did with the good intentions of the manufacturers. Many women from the farms were intelligent and literate and they attended lectures, concerts, and literary discussions. They even produced their own literary journal, *The Lowell Offering*, which printed their poems and stories and served to reinforce the image of Lowell as a cultural center and the factory woman as a virtuous and intelligent collaborator in the harmonious industrial experiment.

The fame that Lowell attracted as an economic and cultural attraction rested primarily on its heralded social achievements. It appeared to many people that the Lowell system might be the key to resolving the conflict between the desire for industrial progress and the fear of its social consequences. Countless visitors from the United States and abroad came to see the great experiment. They took away with them the image of a model industrial community, a paternalistic technological order that shone in comparison with the dismal conditions of the Lancashire textile mills. Davy Crockett saw the workers "enjoying all the blessings of freedom, with prospect before them of future comfort and respectability." *The Lowell Offering* so impressed Charles Dickens that he gave it credit for challenging the European opinion of the abilities of the working class. Another European visitor, Harriet Martineau, was even more enthusiastic. To her, the minds of the workers were "kept fresh and strong, and free by knowledge and power of thought; and this is the reason they are not worn or depressed by their labors." Credit for all this went, of course, to the employers who had it in their power "to do more for the morals of society . . . than the clergy themselves."

Not everyone saw Lowell as paradise, not the least the women themselves, but the naysayers were in the minority and one wonders how many listened when Charles Douglas, a New England labor leader, described Lowell in 1834 as a horrible example of the possible future of the nation. Rather than cultured, virtuous maidens happily operating the looms and spindles, he saw women in the wretched condition of industrial slavery. Douglas warned that Lowell was an attempt to establish a new aristocracy. To Douglas, Lowell represented an attack on freedom, indeed, on the very system of republican equality it claimed to reinforce.

Considering the course of later events at Lowell, a majority of the workers apparently agreed with Douglas. It might be true that conditions at Lowell in the early years approximated the claims of its founders and its numerous visitors, few of whom ever saw the inside of a mill. But Lowell was a capitalist enterprise and whatever its other trappings, profit was its reason for existence. As competition increased, the enterprise responded with tighter control over the workers and less attention to the moral and social dimensions of Lowell. Employers tightened work rules, fired women for minor offenses, required a year's employment for an "honorable discharge," and blacklisted uncooperative workers.

Boardinghouse life also declined rapidly. During the inflationary spiral of the 1830s, matrons could no longer provide a comfortable environment on the $1.25 a week they received from the workers' wages for room and board. Crowding resulted, sometimes as bad as six or eight women to a room and three to a bed. Under these strained conditions workers began to see the matrons as agents of the company whose primary function was to report their activities, particularly any sign of discontent, to the overseers.

Perhaps more than any other factor, the boardinghouse environment led to the development of community among the workers, and community led to collective action against the company. The Lowell women lived in an almost totally controlled environment. Three-quarters of them lived in boardinghouses and considering that they worked an average of seventy-three hours a week, they related to practically no one but their fellow workers.

What social life the women had they carried on in the boardinghouses. There they ate, read, sewed, wrote letters, and talked among themselves. A sisterhood developed out of this intense common experience. In many ways the sisterhood provided a surrogate family in which peer pressure was very strong. The boardinghouses also provided a climate in which new workers could be integrated into the system. Women frequently came because a sister, cousin, or friend already worked at Lowell. Often, women from the same family or the same town lived together.

The structure of work also reinforced the sense of community. The newcomer was assigned to an experienced operative as a helper for several months until she learned the job. This eased the transition for rural girls for whom the factory seemed an alien world. *The Lowell Offering* described one such experience.

> *The next morning she went into the mill; and at first the sight of so many bands, and wheels, and springs in constant motion, was very frightful. She felt afraid to touch the loom, and she was almost sure she could never learn to weave . . . the shuttle flew out, and made a new bump on her head; and the first time she tried to spring the lathe, she broke out a quarter of the threads.*

Textile mills were dangerous places, all the more so for newcomers. The novices quite naturally became dependent on experienced workers. But the mutual dependence existed among experienced workers as well. Informal sharing of work frequently occurred. Other workers covered up for workers who were too ill or too weak to keep up with the pace. Out of this solidarity based on the structure of the work and the boardinghouse system, a new consciousness developed among the women and resulted in a series of protests against the company.

The mill women of Lowell were not the first American female industrial workers to strike. That honor goes to the women of Pawtucket, Rhode Island, who joined the men in a walkout in 1824. Four years later women struck the Dover, New Hampshire, textile mills on their own. But Lowell was a symbol and industrial conflict there received a good deal more attention. The conditions that led to collective action in Lowell affected the entire industry. Increased competition led to overproduction and declining prices. As profits declined so did working conditions and wages. In the face of these pressures the Lowell workers struck in 1834 and 1836.

Solidarity was reinforced by the peer pressure of the workplace and the boardinghouses. The strikes signified more than simple opposition to wage cuts. The women made clear that they did not measure their liberty by dollars and cents alone. The "haughty, overbearing disposition" and "purse-proud insolence" of the employers also rankled them. The protests indicated the importance of values and attitudes that were formed in an earlier period. An 1834 poem linked the strike to a republican and revolutionary heritage:

"Let oppression shrug her shoulders
  and a haughty tyrant frown,
And little upstart ignorance
  in mockery look down.
Yet I value not the feeble threats
  of Tories in disguise,
While the flag of independence
O'er a noble nation flies."

The failure of the 1834 strike led to the organization of the Factory Girls Association, which carried out the 1836 strike. The immediate issue was an increase in board charges that amounted to a 12.5 percent pay cut. But once again the larger issue concerned their rights and status as free-born citizens. As the women marched through Lowell they sang the following.

"Oh! Isn't it a pity that such a pretty girl as I
   Should be sent to a factory to pine away and die?
Oh! I cannot be a slave,
   I will not be a slave,
For I'm so fond of liberty
   That I cannot be a slave."

And they pointedly announced to the employers: "as our fathers resisted unto blood the lordly avarice of the British ministry, so we, their daughters, never will wear the yoke which has been prepared for us."

The Lowell women lost their strikes and returned to work, but through their actions they had laid to rest the myth of Lowell. They were the daughters of free men, as well as industrial workers, and they understood that the control of capital had turned their labor into a commodity and them into dependent wage workers.

In Lowell, as elsewhere, the depression of 1837 destroyed any real hope for labor organization. Wages dropped and the speed-up continued as employers drove the workers with little fear of turnover or strikes. Any job was precious and a growing army of unemployed workers stood ready to work under any conditions.

Following the defeats of the 1830s the women turned their attention to politics and took an active part in the campaign for the ten-hour day. Under the leadership of Sarah Bagley and her Female Labor Reform Association, Lowell became a center of the movement to petition state legislatures for ten-hour legislation. In 1843, 1600 people signed petitions and two years later the number climbed to 5000. With it all, however, the campaign failed.

Disheartened by their failures and driven ever harder in the mills, the women began to leave the mills in ever-increasing numbers. Some returned to the farms but many others found work in newly mechanized industries such as shoemaking and clothing manufacturing. Their places were taken by Irish immigrants fleeing the terrible famine in their homeland. Soon Lowell discarded the boardinghouse system and any pretense at social experimentation. The family system that dominated the industry everywhere else came also to Lowell. No attention needed to be paid to the cultural and moral well-being of the Irish. They were seen as an alien and inferior people, fit only for the discipline of the factory. England's "dark satanic mills" had indeed come to America, and with them a restive and volatile working class.

SARAH BAGLEY

Sarah Bagley came to Lowell around 1836 to work in the mills. A strong believer in education and trade unions, Bagley conducted evening classes for the mill girls and initiated a lecture series on industrial problems. She also contributed articles to *The Lowell Offering*, but when those critical of the companies were rejected, she began publishing the *Voice of Industry* to create a forum for dissent.

In early 1845 she and a small group of co-workers formed the Female Labor Reform Association to work for the ten-hour day. Bagley knew the troubles of the mill women from firsthand experience. When she became active in trying to correct those conditions and affiliated her association with the New England Workingmen's Association, the press attacked her for "unladylike" behavior. At the group's first joint convention, the fiery Bagley declared that "For the last half a century, it has been deemed a violation of woman's sphere to appear before the public as a speaker; but when our rights are trampled upon and we appeal in vain to legislators, what shall we do but appeal to the people?"

Bagley's spirit is clear in the constitution she drafted for the Lowell Female Labor Reform Association. Swearing all members to "Labor actively for reform in the present system of labor," the constitution charged the mill workers "to assert and maintain that independence which our brave ancestors bequeathed us and sealed with their blood."

After many of her reform attempts failed because of the hostility of male legislators in Massachusetts, Bagley withdrew from her leadership role. But before she disappeared from history she became the first woman telegraph operator in the United States when the new telegraph station opened in Lowell in 1846.

DISCUSSION QUESTIONS

1. How did improved transportation, rising population, and the need for increased capital to engage in manufacturing change the traditional relationship between master craftsmen and journeymen in handicraft enterprise?
2. Why did the need to produce for rapidly expanding markets with a growing, but largely unskilled, labor force lead to an emphasis on technological innovation in early American industry?
3. Why did manufacturers argue that harsh workplace discipline and long hours contributed to public order and social progress as well as economic growth?
4. What roles did institutions such as the schools and churches play in

providing workers with the "habits of industry" necessary for productive work in the factory system?
5. Why did labor leaders and reformers view the growing power of the merchant capitalists and industrialists as a threat to democracy? What were their ideas about reforming American society?

KEY WORDS AND PHRASES

American System of Manufactures
Putting-out System
Garret Bosses
Child Labor
New Industrial Morality
Labor Theory of Value
Cordwainer Conspiracy Cases
Workingmen's Parties

Ten-Hour Movement
City Centrals
Utopian Movement
Producers Cooperatives
Agrarianism
Trade Unionism
Lowell Mill Girls

BIBLIOGRAPHY

The material for this section was drawn largely from:

Cochrane, Thomas C. and William Miller. *The Age of Enterprise: A Social History of Industrial America*. New York: Harper & Row, 1961.

Dawley, Allan. *Class and Community: The Industrial Revolution in Lynn*. Cambridge: Harvard University Press, 1976.

Dublin, Thomas. "Women, Work and Protest in the early Lowell Mills," *Labor History*, vol. 16, no. 1 (Winter 1975): 99–116.

Gutman, Herbert. *Work, Culture and Society in Industrializing America*. New York: Alfred A. Knopf, 1976.

Kasson, John F. *Civilizing the Machine: Technology and Republican Values in America*. New York: Penguin Books, 1977.

Montgomery, David. "The Shuttle and the Cross: Weavers and Artisans in the Kensington Riots of 1844," *Journal of Social History*, vol. 5, no. 4 (Summer 1972): 411–446.

———. "The Working Classes of the Pre-Industrial American City, 1780–1830," *Labor History*, vol. 9, no. 1 (Winter 1968): 3–22.

Pessen, Edward. *Most Uncommon Jacksonians: The Radical Leaders of the Early Labor Movement*. Albany: State University of New York Press, 1967.

Smith, Timothy. *Revivalism and Social Reform in Mid-Nineteenth Century America*. New York: Abingdon Press, 1957.

Vogel, Lise. "Hearts to Feel and Tongues to Speak: New England Mill Women in the Early Nineteenth Century," in Milton Cantor and Bruce Laurie, eds., *Class, Sex, and the Woman Worker*. Westport, Conn.: Greenwood Press, 1977.

Wallace, Anthony. *Rockdale: The Growth of an American Village in the Early Industrial Revolution.* New York: Alfred A. Knopf, 1978.

Ware, Norman J. *The Industrial Worker, 1840–1860.* Boston: Houghton Mifflin, 1924.

Wertheimer, Barbara M. *We Were There: The Story of Working Women in America.* New York: Pantheon, 1977.

For additional reading see:

Faler, Paul. "Cultural Aspects of the Industrial Revolution: Lynn, Massachusetts Shoemakers and Industrial Morality, 1826–1860," *Labor History,* vol. 15, no. 3 (Summer 1974): 367–394.

Feldberg, Michael. "The Crowd in Philadelphia History," *Labor History,* vol. 15, no. 3 (Summer 1974): 323–336.

Gordon, David M., Richard Edwards, and Michael Reich. *Segmented Work, Divided Workers: The Historical Transformation of Labor in the United States.* Cambridge: Cambridge University Press, 1982.

Kulik, Gary, "Patterns of Resistance to Industrial Capitalism, Pawtucket Village and the Strike of 1824," in Milton Cantor, ed., *American Working-class Culture.* Westport, Conn.: Greenwood Press, 1979.

Laurie, Bruce. "Nothing on Compulsion: Life Styles of Philadelphia Artisans, 1820–1850," *Labor History,* vol. 15, no. 3 (Summer 1974): 337–366.

Parrington, Vernon L. *American Dreams, A Study of American Utopias.* Providence: Brown University Press, 1947.

Starobin, Robert S. *Industrial Slavery in the Old South.* New York: Oxford University Press, 1970.

Sullivan, William A. *The Industrial Worker in Pennsylvania, 1800–1840.* Harrisburg: Pennsylvania Historical and Museum Commission, 1955.

SECTION
TWO

PART I
From Civil War to World War

Never has an era been so appropriately named: Mark Twain called the years between the Civil War and the turn of the century the "Gilded Age," and historians ever since have adopted this title for this period of superficial brilliance underlain by poverty, corruption, violence, and wrenching change.

Population tripled between 1850 and 1900. From 1859 to 1919 manufactured goods increased almost fivefold in value. Industries like steel and petroleum, which had barely existed in 1860, grew to world leadership four decades later. In 1860 the nation had some 30,000 miles of railroads; by 1900 it boasted of almost nine times that many. By 1915 automobiles, hardly known before the turn of the century, were being manufactured at the rate of nearly a million a year.

Nothing so dramatized the growth of American industry in the period between the Civil War and World War I as the change in the size of manufacturing enterprise. The industrial labor force grew from 2¾ million in 1880 to over 8 million in 1910. By 1900, 240,000 machinists built and maintained the mechanical devices that increasingly set the pace of American life.

During the last third of the nineteenth century the average plant in eleven of sixteen major industries more than doubled in size. Before 1870 textiles was practically the only industry of large-scale factory enterprise. Labor forces of more than 400 were rare. By 1900 there were 1063 factories with 500 to 1000 workers and 443 with more than 1000 employees. Of those, 14, mostly in the steel industry, employed over 6000 and by 1920 plants with 15,000 workers were common.

The increased size of industrial enterprise fundamentally changed the worklives of industrial workers. Jobs in huge, impersonal structures with increasingly high-speed technology led to monotony and danger. Repetitive motions dulled concentration and boredom, and exhaustion often led to accidents. In 1913 alone some 25,000 died and nearly 100,000 sustained injuries in American factories.

The dynamic growth of American industry also gave rise to a change in the leadership of American business. Whereas employers had once assembled small working forces for shops and mills, they now had to call on financial resources and organizational skills unheard of before. Huge industrial workforces had to be recruited, organized, and disciplined. Great financial resources had to be gathered. The leaders who undertook these tasks became the symbols of the age. They rode their leadership of American business to dominance in the social, economic, and political life of the nation.

Fortified with a belief in their own natural superiority, the captains of industry set the standards for a growing middle class of clerks, accountants, technicians, and professionals who mimicked their values and aspired to their position and wealth. And that wealth was astonishing. In the 1830s, a man worth $5000 was considered well-to-do, and assets of $50,000 put him in a category almost unimaginable to most people. But, by the turn of the century, millionaires were common and Andrew Carnegie, the steel baron, had an income of $40,000 per day. Men such as Leland Stanford, Cornelius Vanderbilt, Jay Gould, J.P. Morgan, and others matched Carnegie both in income and conspicuous consumption.

The life-styles of the millionaires captured the attention of the nation and set the tone for the Gilded Age. A growing number of popular newspapers and magazines exposed millions to the social activities of the great industrialists, and more importantly, to their value system—a system based on the idea that in America, the land of opportunity, a man could rise as far and fast as his own hard work and enterprise could take him. Those who made it to the top congratulated themselves for triumphing in an economic system in which the law of the jungle prevailed. Survival of the fittest became the justification for the enormous power and prestige possessed by the business elite. The wealthy had established their right to command without interference from government or unions, and little of importance escaped their domination.

The economic arena in which the industrialists and financiers transformed American society was not without risks. Business failure was commonplace in the intense competition of a period when the general price index fell from a high of 129 in 1864 to a low of 71 in 1894. The rhythm of production proceeded unevenly and when overproduction led to intense competition, business failures mounted and the nation slipped regularly into recession or depression. Two of these economic declines—in 1873 and 1893—rank among the worst in American history. In all, depression scarred fourteen of the twenty-five years between 1873 and 1897.

But as businessmen learned the hazards of competition, they moved, under the guide of financiers like J.P. Morgan, away from the jungle toward the safer, more comfortable terrain of combination and cooperation. Even as businessmen preached the gospel of competition, they bent their efforts to limit competition in the marketplace. Mergers and corporate takeovers resulted in the creation of giant "trusts," huge industrial combinations, which controlled 40 percent of the nation's manufacturing capital by 1894.

THE WORKERS

For the growing army of American industrial workers the land of opportunity offered long days of debilitating work and crowded, disease-ridden urban slums. It is true that competition and technological innovation provided a general rise in the standard of living between 1865 and 1898, but even in these circumstances workers bore the brunt of depression, periodic unemployment, inadequate housing, hazardous working conditions, and increasingly harsh industrial discipline. Clearly not everyone benefitted from the bounty of industrial expansion. By the end of the 1880s an income of roughly $500 per year was necessary for a family of five to enjoy more than a subsistence standard of living. Approximately 40 percent of working-class families earned considerably less than that. Robert Hunter, in his book, *Poverty*, estimated that in 1904 there might have been as many as 15 or 20 million people out of a population of approximately 76 million living in poverty.

To the anxieties over conditions of work and unemployment were added the difficulties of existence in the working-class quarters of the industrial towns and cities. Uncontrolled industrial growth created slum overcrowding of a scandalous magnitude. In one notorious district in New York, 30,000 people crammed into a five- or six-block area. Other major cities and industrial towns were almost as bad. In one block in Holyoke, Massachusetts, 105 people existed in seventeen rooms. Naturally, overcrowding led to sanitation problems that spawned disease. Memphis, Tennessee, lost almost 10 percent of its population in 1873 in an epidemic, and the fear of typhoid and influenza contagion was a constant companion of urban slum dwellers. The slums took their heaviest toll on the children. In 1870 the infant mortality rate in New York amounted to 65 percent more than in 1810.

A remarkable increase in the nation's population accompanied the growth of American industry after 1865. Population increased from 23 million in 1850 to 76 million in 1900. Much of this could be attributed to a sizable increase in the native population, but a dramatic increase in immigration provided the bulk of the industrial workforce. Twelve million immigrants came to America between 1865 and 1900. Approximately half came from Germany and Ireland, while nearly a million came from Great Britain. Many immigrants came with trade union experience in their homelands and were to provide the bulk of the leadership of the labor and radical movements in the United States until well into the twentieth century. After 1890 the character of the immigration changed, and of the 12 million immigrants who came between 1900 and 1914, the majority were Italians, Jews, Slavs, and Greeks with little union tradition.

By 1909, nearly two-thirds of all workers in twenty-one important branches of industry were immigrants. As more and more factory jobs went to the newcomers, indifference toward the plight of industrial workers was combined with prejudice. The middle class, conditioned to seeing immigrants as inferiors, assumed that the monotony of the factory matched the abilities of these seemingly strange people. But coupled with indifference and hostility was a fear of the social consequences of harboring such a mass of alien, disaffected workers. The fear that the "dangerous classes" would undermine American society could be found in much of the social thought of the era. While reformers attempted by a variety of means to "Americanize" the immigrants, others placed their faith in police forces, a professional army, and the order and discipline of the factory.

Americanizing or disciplining such a varied workforce proved to be no easy matter. The Immigrants resisted adjustments to the factory regimen. Old work habits persisted and each new wave of immigrants required the same attention. In no area was this resistance to industrial life so striking as in turnover. Certainly some of the drastic turnover rates of the period can be attributed to the chronic instability of the economy. Boom and bust cycles caught workers in repeated patterns of overtime and unemployment. Many industries such as clothing, glassmaking, and foundry work followed seasonal work schedules, as did the construction industry. Irregular demand characterized the coal and steel industries. Even in 1892—a good year—most of Pennsylvania's major industries closed for a month or more. Still, the labor turnover of the period was so massive that it cannot be wholly attributed to the fluctuations of the business cycle. Even the highly disciplined New England textile mills in the 1870s had difficulty running efficiently because of the frequent absence of workers. In the anthracite coalfields, "blue Monday" plagued employers. Where immigrants predominated, and that was almost everywhere, old country traditions, religious holidays, and an endless number of celebrations competed with the factory for the attention of workers.

Men and women simply walked off the job in startling numbers. In good times the turnover rate increased. It rose in spring and declined in winter. Although statistics are difficult to come by, we do know that even at the supposedly model plant of the Pullman Palace Car Company in 1894, one-fifth of the men employed had less than one year's tenure. Statistics for the first two decades of the twentieth century show that workers changed jobs at a rate of about once in every three years. The Armour meat-packing plant in Chicago in 1914 hired 8000 workers in the course of the year in order to maintain its full complement of 8000 employees. Between 1907 and 1910, turnover in the woolen industry ranged between 113 and 163 percent per year. Turnover reached 232 percent among New York City cloak, suit, and skirt shops in 1912. Surveys of other industries tell the same story. An intensive study by the United States Bureau of Labor Statistics in 1913–1914, discovered a normal turnover rate in the factories of some 115 percent. Obviously there were many reasons for such a phenomenon, but dissatisfaction must certainly have been one. The country possessed a highly mobile workforce, resistant to industrial discipline.

Although turnover plagued employers, it did nothing to challenge management's control over the workplace. Workers' control of the process of work posed a much greater threat. In most industries before 1880, management techniques, particularly those involving relations with workers, had not changed a great deal from the days of workshop enterprise. This was partly because the relatively small size of the pre-1880 factory precluded the development of supervision and personnel relations as distinct administrative functions. In this setting, the employer, preoccupied with financial matters, relegated control of the production process to the foremen and skilled workers. In industries where technological innovation had not led to something resembling continuous process operations, the factories resembled collections of craftsmen's shops in which certain groups of skilled workers exercised considerable control over their own work.

In such industries workers established their own work rules that frequently undercut formal rules and frustrated managers. Building tradesmen, operating in a fragmented industry, regularly determined their own output. But in the factories as well, glassblowers, iron molders, and other workers maintained either openly acknowledged or clandestine limitations on their day's work. This occurred in both union and nonunion shops. Where formal arrangements proved impossible, the old practice of "shunning" was used against workers who worked harder than the commonly accepted group norm. According to a Bureau of Labor Report, "The common sentiment of the workmen is strong and severe against those whose output is materially above the average."

Knowledge of the trade and the production process gave skilled workers considerable control. Above the level of foreman, management's knowledge of the work being done was markedly inferior to that of the workers. Bill Haywood, a radical leader of the Industrial Workers of the World, put it most succinctly: "The manager's brains are under the workmen's cap." This superior knowledge often made workers almost self-directing in their tasks. In addition, skilled workers exercised a variety of management functions in the shops, including the supervision of helpers and apprentices. Historian David Montgomery discovered this functional autonomy among iron molders, glassblowers, coopers, paper machine tenders, locomotive engineers, mule skinners, pipe fitters, iron rollers and others.

The iron rollers of the Columbus Iron Works in Ohio are a case in point. Three twelve-man rolling teams constituted the union. They negotiated a single tonnage rate with the company for each specific rolling job. The workers then decided how to divide the rate among themselves, how the work would be done, at what speed, and what special arrangements should prevail for the extremely hot work of the hookers during the summer. In short, according to Montgomery, the skilled rollers controlled all of the elements of production. The buying of equipment and raw materials and the marketing of the product were left to management.

In the absence of new technology, employers could counter the system only by turning the skilled rollers into individual subcontractors who then could be expected to "sweat" their helpers in order to maximize their own profits. Workers responded to this tactic by collectively codifying the autonomy of the shops. This signified a shift from spontaneous to deliberate collective action, from an informal group code to formal rules and sanctions. Rules generally specified a fixed term of apprenticeship, established a standard wage, prohibited helpers or handymen from performing journeymen's work, and forbade any member from running more than one machine at a time or accepting any form of piecemeal payment. The key to the work rules was the control of the rate of production. In 1884 a Knights of Labor assembly of window glass workers in Pittsburgh carried out a successful strike to maintain the union's limit of forty-eight boxes of glass a week, a rule that the union considered the key to the preservation of the dignity and welfare of the trade. By 1899 the same assembly had sixty-six "rules for working" in their by-laws.

Building trades workers also faced the threat of subcontracting. The Bricklayers Union forbade its members to work for any contractor who could not raise enough capital to buy his own bricks. Every building trade union instructed its members not to allow contractors to work at the trade on the job.

When employers attacked work rules established by one trade, other trades frequently went out on sympathetic strikes. In 1891, 11.5 percent of all strikes fell into this category. Seventy percent of the sympathy strikes in New York between 1890 and 1892 took place in the construction industry. New York cabinet makers struck to preserve their union in 1892 and carpenters, gilders, marble cutters, painters, plasterers, porters, blue stone cutters, tile layers, upholsterers, varnishers, and wood carvers closed more than 100 firms in support.

A BROAD OFFENSIVE

In the face of this challenge employers began to cooperate in the early 1980s to resist sympathy strikes and break down union work rules. Lockouts to deny striking workers other employment opportunities became common as did legal prosecutions charging unions with conspiracy in restraint of trade. The increased size and complexity of factories also created opportunities for management. Technological and organizational innovation led to increased specialization of function and the bottlenecks which permitted workers to use their skills as leverage disappeared. Employers gradually substituted managerial direction and control for the informal, ad hoc methods of the past that had relied on the judgment of the workers.

The decline of the functional autonomy of skilled workers in the late nineteenth century went hand in hand with the decline in apprenticeship. For skilled workers, particularly, control over the supply of new entrants to the trade was essential in the face of the subdivision of labor created by new technology. Despite their efforts, control over apprenticeship slipped away from them. The weakness and decentralized nature of unions had always made uniform regulations difficult to enforce. Workers themselves often ignored the regulations by bringing in children or relatives in violation of union-established quotas. When rules were strictly enforced, employers complained that an insufficient number of journeymen were available when business was good. Workers countered by arguing that a constant number of skilled journeymen would ensure steady employment and quality production. Employer demands to relax apprenticeship rules frequently led to strikes, such as one as early as 1864 by St. Louis iron molders who argued that to increase the number of apprentices in boom times would lead in slack time to the laying off of journeymen "and only the boys kept at work."

Whatever the attacks on apprenticeship, none would have carried the day without the aid of the division of work and the machine. Mechanization drove a wedge between skilled and nonskilled workers and the breakdown of apprenticeship created conflict. In the carpenters trade, machine-made doors and sashes replaced those fashioned at the construction site, and allowed the trade to be invaded by less skilled workers, their wages declining relative to the other building trades. Plumbers faced the same kind of pressure from the cutting of pipes with machines and the building of tubs and sinks with couplings, as painters faced with the introduction of ready-mixed paints.

Although unions still maintained that workers' control of apprenticeship assured the quality of the work performed, the rapid introduction of job-changing technology pushed the argument into the background. Control of the labor supply became the main justification. The question had become, according to a Chicago judge in 1887, "whether a craft will teach a boy a trade to its own destruction." Union leaders argued that if labor had become a commodity, then workers, like industrialists, should be able to combine to regulate the supply of their commodity in order to sell it for the highest price. At the plumbers union convention in 1897 one delegate stated the case in clear terms. "A labor organization is a monopoly from start to finish," he said, "and we are entitled to have it just as much as the coal and sugar trust is entitled to monopoly."

If workers had a property right in their skill equal to any other property right in society, unions argued that closing the trade to competitors was a legitimate exercise in self-interest. In the absence of any protection from government, they were justified in joining together to protect the value of their property. By the late nineteenth century, apprenticeship rules enforced through union regulation had become the principal means to protect the property rights that skilled workers claimed in their jobs.

For the growing army of unskilled and semiskilled industrial workers, the struggle over the survival of apprenticeship had little meaning. But employers understood that some sort of preparation for industrial life was required, even in the new industrial setting. New and more sophisticated technology required workers with basic mathematical and literacy skills, as well as some manual dexterity. For this service, employers turned increasingly to the public schools. What they wanted was industrial education.

Businessmen rapidly took control of the industrial education movement from reformers like Jane Addams, who had a broader vision of its goals. Employers stressed the need for the schools to produce efficient workers. What they wanted was job training matched to the needs of industry. Or, as J.B. Taylor summed it up in the *Educational Review* in 1900: "The whole drift of present educational thinking is to produce the efficient man, the man related by forceful needs to the world without."

By World War I the industrial education movement had succeeded in placing trade and commercial components in a growing number of high schools. Increasingly the children of the working class experienced an education that stressed "vocationalism."

In addition to industrial education, employers instituted a variety of measures in the late nineteenth century to motivate workers and tie them to employers in a community of interest that left no room for trade unions. The deadening effect of industrial work had become apparent to nearly everyone. Employers gauged its negative effects by shoddy workmanship, malingering, or, as they called it, "soldiering," and the formal and informal arrangements workers developed to resist management control. Day wages, they reasoned, provided no incentives to workers and allowed no room for individual initiative. If a worker's rewards could be tied directly to his or her effort, productivity would increase and the interests of workers and employers would converge. To this end they instituted compensation systems based on piecework and profit sharing.

Many reformers also shared in the enthusiasm for these experiments because they believed they had the potential to return a semblance of individualism to workers in the impersonal world of the factory. In theory each worker would be an entrepreneur. Employers were more interested in higher profits and less collective resistance on the part of workers.

Employers began to install piecework systems in a number of industries. Railroad repair shops converted in the 1880s and companies such as Singer Sewing Machine and Bethlehem Steel followed. However, piecework was incredibly complex to install in large operations and no one had yet determined how to set the rates. Unions rejected it as an obvious attempt to weaken their control over the work. They had good reasons for their suspicions. It soon became clear that business could not resist taking the lion's share of the profits created by increased productivity. When output and thus wages rose significantly above the norm, management frequently lowered the piece rate. This, of course, neatly undercut the incentive as well as the justification for the system in the first place.

Profit sharing proved to be the anemic descendant of the old labor dream of producers' cooperatives. What was missing was cooperative ownership and management. What was left was a share of the firm's profits for the workers. Not surprisingly the idea gained prominence in the 1880's, a period filled with strikes, boycotts and industrial violence. Profit sharing originated as an incentive device, not far removed from piecework. But its appeal to naive reformers lay in its cooperative essence. Industry could become an industrial partnership between workers and employers, both sharing the same goals and rewards. In truth, of course, management envisioned no partnership. Nicholas P. Gilman, a leading advocate of profit sharing, assured businessmen that the employer was to remain "just as much of an autocrat as before."

Workers asked why, if the company could distribute profits, could it not pay higher wages? Participation in profit sharing, or its close relative, stock option plans, provided no protection against layoffs. Moreover, voluntary resignation denied workers any benefits they had built up, thus diminishing their freedom to move and tying them more closely to the company. And finally, as with piecework, companies could not resist cutting wages if large profits were being distributed.

Attempts to forge a productive and cooperative workforce out of the diverse and often unruly mass of industrial workers culminated in the industrial efficiency or scientific management movement of the early twentieth century. Although the goal of the movement was to bring order and system to industrial enterprise at every level, its heart lay in the extreme division of work, and its starting point was piecework.

Frederick Taylor, the father of the movement, reasoned that the fatal flaw in piecework lay in the inability of management to set accurate standards for each job. As long as this could not be done, workers could manipulate their jobs and connive to set output levels far below their actual capacity. This lack of knowledge on management's part led them to reduce the piece rates when workers consistently performed above the norm. To Taylor, these two problems, worker "soldiering" and management's lack of information, constituted the two major defects of the incentive system.

To correct this situation, one had only to determine on a "scientific" basis how long a normally efficient worker should take to do each job in the shop. Taylor's method for accomplishing this was time study, the heart of his proposed system. It would provide a method to determine a fair day's work and a fair piece rate. By timing each operation in minute detail, Taylor and his followers went well beyond rate setting: they instituted breaking down jobs into a series of repetitive operations. Decision making, no matter how minute, was to be taken from the workers. In the well-run factory, according to Taylor, it was essential that every man "become one of a train of gear wheels."

Taylor's justification for his system did not differ appreciably from the earlier proponents of piecework. He realized that he was creating boring and meaningless jobs, but the compensation would be in the incentive to exceed the scientifically determined standards. Taylor believed that nothing could be done to make factory work interesting. One could only strive to make it more efficient. If every task could be separately monitored and precisely measured, then so could each worker, and the best workers could be identified and rewarded. In essence, while claiming to recreate a setting in which individual initiative could thrive, the industrial engineers removed whatever freedom workers had left.

Companies embraced time study with great enthusiasm. They rationalized assembly lines, introduced piecework payment wherever possible, and offered special incentives for speed. Some, like United States Steel, spurred their workers with contests between various plants. Where workers still had some leverage, they resisted. Molders and machinists at the Federal Arsenal in Watertown, Connecticut, feared that the stopwatch would lead to the ruin of their trades. They attacked the process as degrading and "un-American." The idea that a man should account for his time by seconds conflicted with the craft traditions of the Watertown workers.

Organized labor fought Taylorism from the beginning. Samuel Gompers, president of the American Federation of Labor, damned it as reducing men to "mere machines." Labor leaders saw it as a death blow to the skilled trades. They had seen it all before and they knew that whatever the grand social justification for the experiments, employers always benefitted and workers always suffered.

Labor's sense that scientific management included a great deal more than time study and piecework was correct. At issue was control of the work process. Time and motion studies, while they were concerned with the systematic organization of production, redesigned jobs in ways determined not by workers using their experience and knowledge but by engineers using "scientific" methods. Taylor and his disciples had faith that standardized selection, training, job classification, and work flow, when coupled with incentive pay, would create an efficient workplace peopled by loyal workers under the firm control of management. Employers were also beginning to recognize the cost to efficiency of job-related accidents and illness, not to mention that during the first decade of the twentieth century, the growing recognition of the plight of industrial workers had led to agitation for state labor legislation in the areas of child labor, female labor, and industrial safety. In this climate companies implemented safety programs and improved the work environment. Social activities were encouraged and employee clubs, newsletters and other activities became common. Of 431 establishments studied by the U.S. Bureau of Labor Survey in 1916–1917, 223 provided lunchrooms for their employees, 141 employed welfare secretaries to organize social activities, and most had some form of safety program.

By the 1920s the campaign for industrial betterment had given rise to specialized personnel departments. Their primary goal was to fit the worker to the job in order to reduce the possibility of frustration, shoddy work, and turnover. Personality and aptitude testing for new employees spread throughout industry. Personnel management grew into a specialized field and these new human relations experts strove to recreate the old handicraft shop contact between management and the worker. Workers could now air their individual grievances and problems to the personnel specialists. The message was that the company cared. The myth that the worker could deal with the company on an individual basis was reinforced. But for all the talk of teamwork and cooperation, the new welfare capitalism left the unequal power relationship between workers and management intact. The system made no provision for independent unions and without them any semblance of equality between workers and management was impossible.

PART II
Reform or Rebellion

The American Civil War created demands for industrial production and organization unprecedented in American history. As such, it served as an added impetus for the tremendous growth of industrial activity already underway. The Civil War also stimulated trade union growth as workers took advantage of the tight labor market to revive unions that had collapsed in the great depression of 1857. By 1864 union membership reached 200,000. Much of this activity resulted in the rapid increase in national unions. Wartime organizing activity led to the formation of twelve national unions, and by 1870 there were thirty-two. By and large they resulted from the activities of skilled workers, most of whom worked in factories but retained leverage because of their skills.

Typical of such unions was the Knights of St. Crispin in the shoe industry, the largest trade union of the Civil War era. Although led by skilled workers, many of whom had learned their trade in the artisan shops of the prefactory era, the Knights sought to organize all workers in the shoe industry regardless of skill or sex. The goal was control of the work, not of the enterprise. The Crispins had made their accommodation with the new factory methods of shoe production, provided that union members operated the machines following union rules and at union wage rates.

The Crispins and the other national unions that formed during and immediately after the Civil War remained deeply involved in radical and reform politics. But it is true that interest in sweeping societal reforms was increasingly linked to concern for the more immediate problems faced by workers on the job.

THE NATIONAL LABOR UNION

The first significant attempt to continue the labor and reform alliance of the pre-Civil War era took place in Baltimore in 1866 with the founding of the National Labor Union (NLU). From its beginning, the National Labor

Union reflected the growing disparity of interests between the skilled workers in the young trade unions and the advocates of political and cooperative solutions to labor's problems. The National Labor Union's ideological debt to its reform predecessors could be seen clearly in its diverse membership. Once again reformers and trade unionists rubbed shoulders in the same organization. In language reminiscent of an earlier time, the National Labor Union called for a grand coalition of the producing classes.

In calling for a coalition of all producers, the National Labor Union sought to remake American society. This remaking was only one manifestation of the impulse toward community in the period. At the same time, reform clubs, fraternal organizations, and political parties developed for much the same reasons. Industrialization was fragmenting society and workers formed organizations not only to fight the trend, but also to provide themselves with the status and sense of community they saw slipping away.

"Labor," said William Sylvis of the Iron Molders Union, the driving force behind the National Labor Union, "is the foundation of the entire political, social and commercial structure. . . . It is the base upon which the proudest structure of art rests—the leverage which enables man to carry out God's wise purposes—the source from which science draws the elements of its power and greatness, . . . the attribute of all that is noble and good in civilization."

With this grandiose attitude, the organization proceeded. In this spirit the National Labor Union advocated an economic system based on producers' and consumers' cooperatives. For Sylvis, the issue was still who should control the means of production. Even though the emphasis was to be on cooperatives, the immediate problems of workers were never entirely neglected. Indeed, the issue that attracted the trade unions in the first place was the eight-hour day, but the attitude of the organization on this key issue illustrated the curious blend of pragmatism and idealism that was the National Labor Union.

WILLIAM SYLVIS

Born into an Armagh, Pennsylvania, wagonmaker's family in 1828, Sylvis and his eleven brothers and sisters spent their young lives in poverty. At the age of eighteen, Sylvis apprenticed himself to an iron molder. He soon learned the perils of the trade when the Iron Works failed. Like many skilled journeymen of the period, Sylvis's goal was to go into business for himself, but when an attempt at self-employment failed in 1849, he took his growing family to Philadelphia where he took a job as a molder, became active in a strike, and joined the local molders union. The year was 1855, and Sylvis made the union his life from that point on. His dream of a national union of molders came true in 1860—in large measure because of his efforts. In 1863 he became president of the National Union of Iron Molders.

To build the struggling union, Sylvis went on the road. In all, he traveled over 10,000 miles and helped create some eighty local unions. Sickness and poverty were frequent companions. For his work, he received no pay, only small donations collected from members of locals along the way.

Although a dedicated trade unionist, Sylvis believed that unions were only the first step in the emancipation of workers—"mere preparatory institutions, without power to do other than defensive battle and frequently unequal to the task." For Sylvis, cooperatives offered "the only true remedy for low wages, strikes, lockouts, and a thousand other impositions and annoyances to which workingmen are subjected."

Sylvis's death on July 27, 1869 was a severe blow to organized labor. Shortly after his death the great depression of 1873 wiped out many of the gains that Sylvis had helped unions secure.

EIGHT HOURS

The eight-hour movement began in 1865 with the formation of the Great Eight-Hour League in Massachusetts. By 1868 similar organizations appeared in most northern states. By this time the trade unions were beginning to see the eight-hour day in basic terms, as a job-creating measure in the face of the increasing displacement of labor by technology. But many people also accepted the arguments of Ira Steward, a Boston machinist.

Steward argued that the basic standard of living of the nation at any particular time—not the labor supply, availability of capital, or the activities of trade unions—determined wages. He meant that the habits, customs, and expectations of workers determined their wants and these wants were what employers responded to. Steward reasoned that these wants were too low to enable workers to absorb the production of American industry, a fact that led to overproduction and unemployment. Shorter hours would allow workers the time and energy to cultivate their tastes and desires and thus raise their level of wants. Wages would rise accordingly. Central to Steward's argument was that wages must not be reduced along with hours.

Steward placed great faith in the productive capacity of technology. Machinery was the key to expanding production in order to meet increased demand. In his belief in the machine, Steward parted company with the skilled members of the trade unions. He realized the impact of the machine on skilled workers, but he believed that what was lost in status and control of work would be replaced by the increased ability to consume, which would accompany shorter hours.

But what of the workers displaced by the machines? Steward recognized the problem but he contended that displacement would only be temporary. As long as hours and not wages were reduced, the increased consumer demands of workers would lead to the creation of new industries and provide jobs for more workers. Beyond its immediate benefits, Steward's theory was a basic attack on the wage system and a step toward a cooperative society. He reasoned that if hours but not wages were reduced, the portion of the value of the workers' production that went to the employer in the form of profits would be reduced. With more leisure time, workers would formulate even stronger demands in the form of even shorter hours and higher wages. This would eventually eliminate profits altogether, giving workers the time and resources to turn their attention to establishing cooperatives, thus bringing an end to the wage system.

Whatever their motives, the National Labor Union, the Eight-Hour Leagues and the trade unions succeeded in lobbying through Congress an eight-hour law for federal employees. But like the earlier ten-hour legislation, the eight-hour law contained so many loopholes as to be nearly worthless. Trade unions turned to industrial action and demanded the passage of eight-hour laws in a general strike in Chicago in 1867 and a three-month walkout of thirty trade unions in New York City in 1872. The rationale behind these strikes was a long way from Ira Steward's program. The New York tradesmen believed that unless employers reduced hours, mechanization would result in either seasonal unemployment or a permanent oversupply of labor. To the tradesmen, shorter hours meant more workers producing the same volume of goods, less unemployment, and the elimination of the pressure of the unemployed on their wages.

COOPERATIVE DREAMS AND CHEAP MONEY

Cooperation had a less divisive impact on the NLU. Though no more successful than the eight-hour movement, the idea of producers' cooperatives had a powerful hold on labor leaders of the period. They realized that the deeply ingrained idea that a person could rise from worker to entrepreneur was being severely undercut by industrialization. Fewer and fewer workers could hope to accumulate enough capital to become masters of small shops. The cooperative idea offered a collective means by which workers could conform to the primary American value of independence. On this limited basis it appealed to many. For others, like William Sylvis, it offered a means to restructure society. For both groups it offered the possibility of independence from industrial and finance capital. If most single workers could no longer achieve independence, perhaps workers could collectively pool their resources and share in the management and rewards of a cooperative enterprise. To these workers, industrial capitalism was still new enough for them to have faith in the possibility of other forms of economic organization.

The National Labor Union's emphasis on cooperatives conditioned its attitude toward strikes. Sylvis, from his experience as president of the molders, viewed strikes as defensive actions that did nothing to remove workers from their dependency on wages. He believed that strikes were no more than holding actions that could do nothing about the implementation of new machines and the absolute control over industry by the masters of capital. Only the elimination of the wage system through the cooperative control of the means of production offered a lasting solution.

Sylvis took heart from the operation of a successful cooperative foundry by his iron molders in Troy, New York. By 1868 he had organized eleven more. "Divide the profits among those who produce them," he counseled workers, "and drive the nonproducers to honorable toil or starvation." A variety of skilled workers answered his call, but, in the end, cooperatives could not compete for the same reasons that small businesses of every kind were falling by the wayside. Cooperatives had difficulty in raising capital from banks hostile to the whole idea, and they lacked sophisticated management and marketing skills increasingly necessary in highly competitive markets. Sylvis died in 1869 before he knew the fate of many of his cherished cooperatives. But those who remained did not give up the faith. They attributed their lack of success to the inability to raise sufficient capital, which they blamed on the private control of the banking system by big business. Understandably they turned their attention to currency reform.

The National Labor Union's interest in currency reform was part of a broader movement, largely agrarian in nature, to combat declining prices through an inflationary money policy. Based on the ideas of Edward Kellog, a New York merchant, "Greenbackism," as it came to be known, argued that the nation's monetary laws permitted banks to create and loan money, and in so doing, allowed them to withhold capital, thus creating a scarcity and driving up interest rates. In place of this system, currency reformers proposed that the federal government issue paper money carrying 1 percent interest and backed not by gold, but by the physical wealth of the country. This action would remove the deflationary shackles created by the gold standard, take control of the supply of money out of the hands of bankers, and allow farmers and workers to secure loans at rates they could afford.

Labor's interest in "Greenbackism" was in keeping with the broad reform orientation of the NLU. Greenbacks loaned by the government directly to workers at 1 percent interest would enable cooperatives to obtain start-up and operating capital. These loans would also allow small businessmen to enlarge their enterprises and hire more workers. Nothing illustrates the ambivalence of the reform labor leaders of the period toward trade unionism better than the greenback movement. At bottom, it offered a means to eliminate the wage system and replace it with a cooperative society—to turn workers into entrepreneurs. To Sylvis, this meant a society in which "there will no longer exist any necessity for trade unions."

FUNDAMENTAL CONFLICTS

Currency reform required political, not trade union, action. This did not bother the leaders of the NLU, because from the beginning they had envisioned the organization as the basis for a political party.

Encouraged by labor political action in Massachusetts and Pennsylvania in 1869 and 1870, led by the Knights of St. Crispin and the anthracite miners, the National Labor Union moved toward an emphasis on political action at its 1870 congress. These unions that had joined the NLU primarily to facilitate cooperation among workers in the hope of spreading trade unionism left because they no longer saw any benefit to belonging. Many objected to the emphasis on political action over the more immediate concerns of workers. But the main objection rested on the fact that the NLU, dominated by workers at its founding, had become, by 1870, "a strange mixture of mechanics, workingmen, ministers, lawyers, editors, lobbyists and others of no particular occupation, some intent upon organizing a political labor party, others using their efforts to defeat that measure and benefit existing parties," according to William Jessup of the New York State Workingmen's Assembly. The complaint that the organization had lost its working-class character also led the socialists—surely not hostile to political action—to refuse to send a delegate to the 1871 meeting of an organization they believed was dominated by bourgeois reformers.

Although political action and the make up of the NLU provided points of conflict, there were other important areas of disagreement within the organization. Most important were controversies over the admission of black and female workers. The abolition of slavery had resulted in the addition of several million black workers to the nation's free labor supply. During the late 1860s, black workers, refused admission by most white unions, began to create their own organizations and, in 1869, under the leadership of Isaac Myers, a Baltimore caulker, delegates from nine black unions asked for admission to the National Labor Union. After lengthy debate the delegates were seated and the convention called for the organization of "colored" unions. Myers accepted the challenge and created the National Colored Labor Union, which hoped to affiliate with the NLU at its 1870 meetings. Affiliation never took place because of the NLU's turn to independent political action. Black workers remained politically loyal to the Republicans, the party of Lincoln; emancipation; and radical reconstruction in the South.

Although the ostensible split between blacks and the NLU came about over the issue of independent political action, conflict between the races had deeper roots. Sylvis favored the organization of blacks on the prag-matic grounds that if not incorporated into the labor movement, blacks would pose a constant threat to wages and job standards. But even more significantly, he realized that the new black voters had the potential to be a significant political factor that would either be used for or against labor. Sylvis envisioned the potential of black and white workers in independent labor political action.

Most trade unionists, however, held the prevailing racist stereotypes of the times and refused to believe that the blacks would uphold union stan-dards. No pleas from reformers and black unionists convinced them other-wise. Thus racial prejudice and misguided self-interest combined to keep blacks out of all but a few of the white unions.

Women caused a similar problem in the NLU. They made up at least one-fourth of the workforce from the end of the Civil War on, and most were single, young and childless, or widowed. Women rarely found work in the skilled trades, save for scattered cases in the printing and telegraph industries where they sometimes found opportunities through male rela-tives in those trades. By far the largest female occupational category was domestic service, in which nearly a million women worked in 1870.

Working women found no relief from household duties. Child rearing, marketing, baking, cooking, and mending remained women's work. In-deed, the strong conviction among male workers that women's work was household work underlay their standard approach to the issue. Labor lead-ers argued that the way to save the family from the unhealthy conse-quences of women working was to raise men's wages so as to make it unnecessary for women to work. Frank Foster of the Typographical Union argued that "There is greater necessity than all others that our industrial system shall be so regulated that the head of a family shall be able to preserve his family intact."

The trade unions reacted against the threat of women being used to cheapen the labor of men. Women recognized this fear and countered with the same rational argument that Isaac Myers had made on behalf of blacks. An article in 1868 in *The Revolution,* a women's suffrage journal, reasoned that "it is yet to be seen whether workingmen are wise enough to see, that so long as woman is disenfranchised her labor is degraded, and capitalists will use her cheap labor to cheapen that of the man by her side."

William Sylvis agreed that the "defenseless condition" of women was a threat to male labor. From the beginning he and most of the NLU leader-ship supported the admission of women and urged them to join existing unions or form their own. More than altruism could be found in the NLU's position. Equal pay for women would reduce the threat to male labor, many thought, because if women had to be paid as much as men, employ-ers would see no benefit in hiring them. That the NLU was not prepared to go beyond the question of self-interest can be seen from the fact that although it urged women to join unions, it never endorsed the vote for women. Even this narrow acceptance of the rights of women workers proved too much for most of the trade unions, few of whom accepted women as members.

The history of the National Labor Union held mixed lessons. The sentiments of those who believed that the organization had fallen under the control of nonworkers who had little interest in trade unionism were reflected in an editorial in the Chicago *Workingmen's Advocate*. "Labor's educators must come from labor's ranks," the paper counseled. "Theorists, experimentalists and demagogues who have gained what notoriety they possess by prating about laborers' wrongs, must now take back seats." Those in the reform tradition concluded that a labor movement based primarily on economic organizations of skilled workers could never hope to solve the problems of the majority of American working people. For these individuals the demise of the NLU did not mean the end of a radical labor movement, but only one phase in a long process aimed at the fundamental restructuring of society.

PART III
Depression and Disorder

The terrible depression of 1873 hit an industrial society with a ferocity that the earlier, more agrarian society, had never experienced. Angry crowds of homeless and jobless people demonstrated in the cities for bread and work. Fearful public authorities reacted with little restraint. A police assault on an unemployed rally in New York's Tompkins Square Park in 1874 resulted in scores of injured.

In such conditions the trade unions collapsed. Of the thirty national unions in existence in1873, only nine remained by 1877. Those that survived, like the Typographers, lost more than one-half of their members. Strong and proud unions like the Knights of St. Crispin were destroyed by the combination of hard times and hostile employers. Industrial violence captured the attention of an apprehensive public, especially the events in the anthracite coal fields of Pennsylvania.

By 1870 tens of thousands of miners dug anthracite coal in the rich beds of northeastern Pennsylvania. Largely Irish, and 25 percent of them under the age of sixteen, the miners worked in conditions of semislavery. Huddled in the bleak company towns, under the harsh control of the companies' coal and iron police, they subsisted on low wages and worked under conditions so dangerous that in one seven-year period, 566 miners were killed and 1655 injured in Schuylkill County alone. The hazards of coal mining were horribly illustrated in September 1869, when 175 men and boys died as a result of a mine fire in Avondale, Pennsylvania.

Out of the discontent in the coal fields, John Siney, an Irish immigrant who had learned trade unionism in England, had forged the Workingmen's Benevolent Association in 1868. The new union had startling success and 1869 forced the coal operators to grant a minimum wage and a sliding scale of wages tied to the price of coal.

The operators chafed under the agreement and in the depression year of 1874, under the leadership of Franklin B. Gowen (head of the Philadelphia and Reading Railroad, a company with vast anthracite holdings) refused to renew the agreement. The miners struck for six months in what became known as the "long strike." But in the end, the bitter miners, reduced to near starvation, returned to the dark and dangerous tunnels with a 20 percent wage cut and without a union.

Before, during, and after the long strike, the conflict inherent in the autocratic social and economic atmosphere of the coal fields broke out in sporadic acts of violence. A kind of guerrilla war scarred the coal fields in what came to be known as the "Molly Maguire" riots. Although there is still no conclusive proof that a terrorist organization named the Molly Maguires ever existed, there is no doubt that a series of assaults and murders were committed against company officials and strikebreakers. Determined to stamp out the last vestige of resistance to his dictatorial control of the mine fields, Gowen hired the Allan Pinkerton detective agency to crush the miners' resistance. Pinkerton had gained some fame as a Northern spy during the Civil War, and, following Appomattox, he offered his skills to industry in the more lucrative undertaking of destroying unions. In the late nineteenth century, "Pinkertons" became a fixture on the volatile labor relations scene.

By planting an undercover agent, one James McParland, in the Ancient Order of Hibernians, an Irish fraternal organization, Pinkerton collected dubious evidence that led to the conviction of nineteen men. Twelve Irish miners were eventually executed. There is no doubt that in the violent atmosphere of the coal fields crimes had been committed. But there is considerable doubt whether the men convicted were responsible for those crimes. There is also little doubt that the trials were a travesty of justice. Gowen himself acted as state prosecutor in some of the trials and McParland presented the only evidence against the accused. Corroboration of his testimony came from accused men who won freedom in return. In the end Gowen had gotten what he wanted. Unionism in the anthracite coal fields was tarred with the brush of terrorism and destroyed.

Soon after the Molly Maguire trials disappeared from the newspapers, a new and frightening example of the frustrations building up among industrial workers exploded. The great railroad strikes in 1877 dwarfed any industrial dispute the nation had ever seen. They went beyond any one trade and any one geographical area and seemed to engulf the entire nation.

No one industry so typified the changing nature of America as did the railroads. Fattened on government land grants and monopoly routes, railroads tracked across the continent at a pace that astounded even their ardent boosters. Whole regions lay in their economic grasp. Communities flourished or disappeared at the whim of their leaders. In the process railroads alienated workers, farmers, and small businessmen alike. It is no wonder then that when the first great spasm of industrial discontent struck the new order, it happened on the railroads.

The desperate economic conditions of the depression brought these accumulated grievances to the surface. The railroads had systematically cut wages until by 1877, on some roads, workers had undergone a 35 percent cut in wages. In addition, management had seized the opportunity to crush the young brotherhoods of locomotive engineers, firemen, and conductors. When the Baltimore and Ohio reduced wages again in the summer of 1877, the workers at Martinsburg, West Virginia, refused to allow freight trains to move until the company restored the wage cut. Local militia, called up by the governor at the company's request, sided with the strikers and only the use of federal troops cleared the tracks at Martinsburg. By then the strike had spread to other railroad centers and by August, when it ended, it had affected railroads as far west as California. Hundreds of thousands of workers took part. In Pittsburgh, the Allegheny County militia, like its counterpart in Martinsburg, refused to take action against their friends and relatives. An ill-advised attempt to use a Philadelphia militia company led to rioting that resulted in enormous damage to railroad property. Violence flared in other cities, such as Reading, Pennsylvania, where outside militia killed ten citizens. By the end the cost approached $10 million, an extraordinary sum at the time, and hundreds of lives.

Historian Joseph Rayback described the significance of the strike to America's working class. The Railroad Strike of 1877, he wrote, "was not only a strike of railway workers. In every community it was aided by other elements. Miners from the surrounding coal fields supported the strike actively in Martinsburg and Pittsburgh; they ran the strike in Scranton; they turned out in sympathy in St. Clair and Madison Counties in Illinois. Millhands and unemployed workers assisted in the strike in Pittsburgh; unemployed helped . . . in Cincinnati; 20,000 workmen joined the strikers in Chicago. Negro sewermen in Louisville and Negro stevedores in Cairo, Illinois, held sympathetic strikes. Farmers in West Virginia and along the route of the Erie Railroad in New York joined the movement. Small businessmen aided in Martinsburg and Pittsburgh."

The support of the strike by so many elements of society showed that the resentment of the growing control of society by big business was not restricted to workers. In the small towns and cities of the nation, the huge corporations and their absentee management were aliens and interlopers who were destroying the traditional bonds of community. In 1877, industrial and finance capitalism had not yet succeeded in isolating workers from other elements of that community.

The remarkable events of 1877 and the nation's recovery from the depression spurred a revival of labor activity in both political action and union organization. The year 1877 had demonstrated to labor leaders the overwhelming coalition of political and economic power arrayed against them. Some reasoned that only through political action could the power relationship be fundamentally altered. In the wake of the great strike, new political parties appeared in most major cities. The movement developed into a coalition of labor parties and greenback parties, most notably in Pennsylvania and Ohio. Limited success in those states led to the formation of the Greenback-Labor Party in 1878. In addition to currency reform, the party called for legislation reducing hours, an end to convict labor, creation of national and state bureaus of labor statistics, and the end of the importation of "servile labor." The last was aimed at Chinese immigration, but also mirrored the growing resentment of workers to unrestricted immigration. In its resemblance to the goals of the National Labor Union, the platform of the Greenback-Labor Party demonstrated the continuity of the labor reform tradition in the nineteenth century. The Greenback-Labor Party did have some success in the 1878 election, but the internal contradictions of the movement led to its decline soon after.

DISCUSSION QUESTIONS

1. As businessmen achieved economic, social, and political dominance in the second half of the nineteenth century, how did they justify their absolute right to command? Did this dominance imply the triumph of property rights over human rights?
2. How did the preindustrial work habits of workers, particularly the immigrants, clash with the requirements of industry for a dependable and disciplined workforce?
3. What methods did management use to challenge the control of work by skilled workers in the factories? How did some skilled workers use unions to respond to the challenge?
4. Why were labor leaders so interested in cooperatives in the nineteenth century? Why were cooperatives, rather than unions, frequently seen as the solution to workers' problems?
5. The issue of the eight-hour day captured the attention of workers in this period. Some viewed the shorter work day as a means to reform society, while others saw it in more limited terms, as a way to create jobs. Discuss how this division illustrated the growing split between reform and pure-and-simple unionism.

KEY WORDS AND PHRASES

Gilded Age	National Labor Union
Turnover	Eight-Hour Movement
Shunning	Ira Steward
Work Rules	William Sylvis
Apprenticeship	Greenbackism
Industrial Education	Women's Suffrage
Piecework	Franklin P. Gowen
Profit Sharing	Molly Maguires
Scientific Management	Allan Pinkerton
Frederick Taylor	Railroad Strike of 1877
Knights of St. Crispin	

BIBLIOGRAPHY

The material for this section was drawn largely from:

Clawson, Dan. *Bureaucracy and the Labor Process: The Transformation of U.S. Industry, 1860–1900.* New York: Monthly Review Press, 1980.

Cochrane, Thomas C. and William Miller. *The Age of Enterprise: A Social History of Industrial America.* New York: Harper & Row, 1961.

Filippelli, Ronald L. "The Railroad Strike of 1877 in Reading," *Historical Review of Berks County,* vol. 38, no. 2 (Spring 1972): 48–51, 62–71.

Foner, Philip S. *Organized Labor and the Black Worker.* New York: Praeger, 1974.

Gersuny, Carl. *Work Hazards and Industrial Conflict.* Hanover, New Hampshire: University Press of New England, 1981.

Grob, Gerald N. *Workers and Utopia.* Evanston, Ill.: Northwestern University Press, 1961.

Kasson, John F. *Civilizing the Machine.* New York: Penguin Books, 1977.

Kirkland, Edward Chase. *Dream and Thought in the Business Community, 1860–1900.* Chicago: Quadrangle Books, 1964.

Montgomery, David. *Workers' Control in America.* New York: Cambridge University Press, 1979.

Nelson, Daniel. *Managers and Workers: Origins of the New Factory System in the United States, 1880–1920.* Madison: University of Wisconsin Press, 1975.

Rogers, Daniel T. *The Work Ethic in Industrial America, 1850–1920.* Chicago: The University of Chicago Press, 1978.

Spero, Sterling and Abram L. Harris. *The Black Worker.* New York: Atheneum, 1972.

Ware, Norman. *The Labor Movement in the United States, 1860–1895.* New York: Appleton, 1929.

Wertheimer, Barbara M. *We Were There: The Story of Working Women in America.* New York: Pantheon, 1977.

Yellowitz, Irwin. *Industrialization and the American Labor Movement, 1850–1900.* Port Washington, N.Y.: Kennikat Press, 1977.

For additional reading see:

Broehl, Wayne G. *The Molly Maguires.* Cambridge: Harvard University Press, 1964.

Hays, Samuel P. *The Response to Industrialism: 1885–1914.* Chicago: University of Chicago Press, 1957.

Josephson, Matthew. *The Robber Barons.* New York: Harcourt, Brace and World, 1962.

Montgomery, David. *Beyond Equality: Labor and the Radical Republicans, 1862–1872.* New York: Alfred A. Knopf, 1967.

Walkowitz, Daniel J. *Worker City, Company Town.* Urbana: University of Illinois Press, 1978.

SECTION
THREE

PART I
An End and a Beginning

During the dark years of the depression of 1873, with the labor movement in disarray and industrial violence seemingly everywhere, the next great attempt at reform unionism developed. The Noble Order of the Knights of Labor represented the flowering of the ideas of labor reformers who rejected the wage system and strove to bend the productive capacity of the Industrial Revolution to the benefit of all who worked. At the heart of the Knights's ideology lay the old dream of equality in a cooperative society. Its high-sounding name, elaborate rituals, and colorful paraphernalia appealed to workers attempting to recover their status through brotherhood in an age of increased depersonalization and social fragmentation.

The Knights grew out of the search of a small group of Philadelphia garment workers for a viable form of union organization. Their own small union succumbed to hostile employers and the effects of recession in the late 1860s. Their leader was Uriah Stephens, half reformer and half religious mystic, who believed strongly in a universal vision of the brotherhood of man. Although Stephens drifted away from the Knights into greenback politics before the organization's greatest success, his vision of an organization that would include all workers, regardless of craft, race, skill, sex, or nationality made the Knights unique in an era of fragmentation, racial and ethnic hostility, and rising craft consciousness on the part of skilled workers. The all-inclusive nature of the Knights owed its inspiration to Stephens and they were the first great attempt at industrial unionism.

Local Assembly No. 1 of the Noble Order of the Knights of Labor, as the Philadelphia garment workers called their new local union, began in December 1869. Fearful of being blacklisted, the workers devised an elaborate ritual based on secrecy. The members of Local Assembly No. 1 proved to be effective missionaries for their cause. By 1874, there were some eight more assemblies in and around Philadelphia, and one in New York. Most were craft assemblies, built on individual trades like ship carpentry and masonry.

The fact that most of the early assemblies of the Knights were, in effect, trade unions reflected the fact that craft workers, their national unions devastated by the effects of the depression, were ready to seize any opportunity to reconstitute their unions. But the founding principles of the Order pointed to inclusive, not exclusive, unionism. The mixed assembly, including skilled and unskilled workers, not the craft assembly, was to become the building block of the organization, and eventually the divergent interests of the two organizations created an internal contradiction in the Knights, which contributed to its decline and fall.

But decline was well in the future in 1878 in Reading, Pennsylvania, when the first general assembly of the Knights met and formed a national organization. One year later, Stephens stepped down and Terence Powderly, the man who was to guide the Knights through most of their effective years, assumed the post of Grand Master Workman.

Born in Carbondale, Pennsylvania, the son of Irish immigrants, Powderly, a machinist by trade, was a personification of the reform labor leader in an age of dramatic change. At one time or another before and during his tenure as head of the Knights, he served as Greenback-Labor mayor of Scranton, served as a county health officer, owned and managed a grocery store, and became vice-president of the Irish Land League. Small wonder, then, that Powderly threw his energies behind an organization like the Knights, which welcomed everyone except professional gamblers, stockbrokers, lawyers, bankers, and liquor dealers.

This busy man, who never devoted more than part of his time to his labor activities, became America's most famous labor leader in the 1880s. He presided over an organization that grew to a membership of almost three quarters of a million at its peak, and he doggedly propagated his view that the Knights were to be more than a trade union—they were to serve as the embryo of a cooperative society based on the brotherhood of man. Well into the 1890s, after the decline of the Knights and the effective end of reform unionism, Powderly continued to advocate cooperatives as the crucial step toward the end of "that curse of modern civilization—wage slavery."

Said Powderly,

"The Knights of Labor is higher and grander than party." "There is a nobler future before it than that which clings to its existence amidst partisan rancor and strife. . . . We seek and intend to enlist the services of men of every society, of every party, every religion, and every nation in the crusade which we have inaugurated against these twin monsters, tyranny and monopoly; and in that crusade we have burned the bridges behind us; we have stricken from our vocabulary the word fail; we aim at establishing the complete rights of man throughout the world. . . ."

ONE BIG UNION

Powderly's all-inclusive vision was demonstrated by the Knights' willingness to welcome black and women workers into the fold. "Why," the leadership asked, "should workingmen keep out of our organization anyone who might be used as a tool to aid the employer in grinding wages?" No labor organization before, or for some time after, rivaled the Order in its willingness to accept blacks. At its peak in 1886, some 60,000 black workers belonged in either all-black or racially mixed assemblies. In 1885, the General Assembly approved the appointment of a black organizer for each of the southern states.

To be sure, the Knights' concept of industrial brotherhood did not completely break down the color line in the organization. Nevertheless, even the craft element in the organization lowered the racial barriers to some extent. Bricklayers and carpenters admitted blacks in several craft assemblies or helped them create their own.

The appeal of the Knights to black workers lay in the nondiscriminatory principles of the Order. Even during the years of decline in the late 1880s blacks remained loyal, even as white workers—particularly those in the craft assemblies—left in droves. The eventual collapse of the organization dealt a serious blow to the hopes of black workers for equality in the labor movement.

Nondiscrimination applied to sex as well as race. There was a good deal of self-interest, as well as principle, in the Knights' appeal to women. Uriah Stephens pointed out that machinery seeks cheap labor and finds women and children. He believed that equal pay for equal work would cut the attractiveness of female labor. Much of this self-interest became cloaked in humanitarian justifications. Society was the loser when the exploitation of women and children led to the "degradation" of the race. Equal pay would, in effect, remove women from the factories and protect the "motherhood of the next generation" from being turned into "machine slaves."

Any organization interested in organizing all workers could not ignore women, a fact that was evident in the statistics. Women constituted at least one-fourth of all nonagricultural workers after 1870. Outside of domestic service, most worked in the sewing trades, in teaching, and in the cotton and woolen mills. Along with child labor, according to the Massachusetts Bureau of Labor Statistics in 1875, women supplied one-quarter to one-third of a typical working-class family's income in that state. The 1880 census discovered 2.6 million females over ten years old gainfully employed, 25 percent more than in 1870.

The Knights responded to the reality of women workers by extending membership to them in 1881. By 1886, 192 women's assemblies existed, and a significant number of women also belonged to previously all-male assemblies. At the organization's peak, 50,000 women held Knights of

Labor cards. As part of its commitment, the Order also created a women's department and appointed its director a general officer of the organization. The militance of the women members so impressed Powderly that he gave them the dubious honor of calling them "the best men in the Order."

LEONORA MARIE BARRY

Born in Kearney, County Cork, Ireland, Barry emigrated to the United States with her family in 1852 at the age of three. After a short career as a teacher and the death of her husband, she took a job as a millhand in Amsterdam, New York, in 1881. Angered by the poor wages and working conditions, Barry joined the Knights of Labor in 1884. She quickly made her mark on the Knights, rising swiftly through the ranks to become the order's first general investigator of the department of women's work. Her investigations of industrial conditions affecting women and child labor resulted in the first systematic inquiry into the abuse of women and children at work. The documentation she provided led to the passage of the Pennsylvania Factory Inspection Act of 1899.

Like many of her male colleagues in the leadership of the Knights, Barry saw the wage system as the major cause of the deplorable plight of industrial workers. She established two cooperative shirt factories, one in Baltimore and the other in New York. Barry's reform interests also extended to the fight for the vote for women, and, like many of her sisters in that crusade, she also preached against the evils of liquor as part of the temperance movement. Through public speeches and tireless private work she promoted increased education and industrial training for women, improved safety legislation, and an end to child labor.

In 1887 she became a general officer of the Knights with the title of General Instructor and Director of Women's Work. Throughout her career she suffered from the criticism of the Roman Catholic Church, of which she was a member. She defended her right as "an Irishwoman, a Catholic, and an honest woman" to help women workers. Barry retired from the Knights after remarrying in 1890 but continued her reform activities until her death in 1930.

The Knights believed that all existing workers had to be included in the organization for it to succeed. But they also realized the ruinous effect of unrestricted immigration on the ability of existing workers to create effective organizations. In calling for restrictions on immigration, the Order placed itself in the mainstream of organized labor's attitude toward unrestricted immigration since the Civil War. Initially, labor had opposed only the importation of contract workers from abroad, *that is, workers who were recruited to perform specific tasks by private enterprise or government agencies.* As early as the 1860s, labor leaders began to interpret contract labor as a threat to unions and labor standards. The importation of workers with specific skills, such as molders and miners, at times when Americans with the same trades were unemployed particularly incensed them.

The argument against contract labor was clearly motivated by understandable self-interest. But when self-interest combined with racism, the labor movement, including the Knights, demonstrated the ugly side of antiimmigrant sentiment. Ethnic and racial hostility was a basic feature of American society in the nineteenth century. This hostility had resulted in the attacks on the Irish in the 1850s and would be demonstrated in the resentment for the southern and eastern Europeans who flooded into the country between 1880 and 1914. But American labor, with the exception of attempts to limit contract workers, never turned these private prejudices into a full-scale campaign for exclusion except against the Chinese, who began to arrive in large numbers after the Civil War.

Hatred of the Chinese centered in California, where they could be found in the greatest numbers and where white workers saw them as the greatest threat. Until 1870, when employers imported Chinese strikebreakers into a Massachusetts shoe factory, eastern labor had not bothered much with the issue. But under the goading of the Knights of St. Crispin, the National Labor Union went on record opposing Chinese immigration.

The combination of the depression and the presence of large numbers of Chinese led to a virulent outbreak of anti-Chinese violence in California in the midst of the volatile climate created by the Railroad Strikes of 1877. Tension in that state led to a racist working-class political movement that had considerable, in brief, success. The issue assumed national proportions in 1880 when Congress ratified a treaty with China that appeared to ensure the continued flow of Chinese immigrants. Some labor papers characterized the Chinese as immoral, bestial, and filthy and stressed that the Chinese were different from other workers. These papers attacked the Chinese for clannishness, for their reluctance to become citizens, and for their penchant for sending part of their wages home to relatives, a practice common to all immigrant groups.

The Knights took an active part in the Chinese exclusion campaign. They refused membership to Chinese and lobbied in Washington for restriction. In 1882, Congress gave in to the pressure and passed the first Chinese Exclusion Act. This pleased Powderly, who considered Chinese competition with white labor "one of the greatest evils with which any country can be afflicted." Proof that the rank and file shared these sentiments was demonstrated by Knights in Wyoming when they massacred twenty-eight Chinese workers in 1885. Powderly had second thoughts about the implications of his organization's position on the issue when he learned the grisly details.

By the time Congress had abolished contract labor in 1884, the Knights and much of the rest of the labor movement had broadened their objections to include all unrestricted immigration. The threat of competition from newcomers had become an obsession in the labor movement and remained so until after World War I.

TO STRIKE OR NOT TO STRIKE

While the status of blacks, women, and immigrants provided lively debate in the councils of the Order, the struggle between the trade unionists and the reformers became the fundamental issue that plagued the organization. Powderly and the majority of the leadership consistently reaffirmed the reform goal of producers' cooperatives. The trade unionists in the craft assemblies just as ardently tried to direct the Order toward collective bargaining. The issue became most clearly defined over the use of the strike.

Powderly, in the tradition of William Sylvis, viewed the strike as a defensive weapon that did nothing to alter the basic evil—the wage system. He directed the treasury of the Order toward the establishment of cooperatives. His efforts resulted in the creation of some 135 producer and consumer cooperatives, all of which ultimately failed, because of underfunding and cutthroat competition.

This attention to cooperatives rankled the trade unionists, who argued that the money could be put to better use in a strike fund. When strike activity accelerated in the nation in the 1880s events began to overtake Powderly. Trade assemblies of the Knights took an active part in these strikes and several of the most notable—against the Union Pacific and the Southern Railway System—resulted in victories.

The rush of skilled and unskilled workers to the Knights as a result of these victories proved that workers, whatever their skills, were looking for an organization that could be effective in maintaining labor standards and wages in the face of hostile employers and economic distress. Events in 1885 reinforced this trend. Craft assemblies on the Wabash, a railroad controlled by Jay Gould, one of the titans of American finance, struck in response to an attempt to break their unions. Powderly reluctantly supported the strike because he realized its implications for the survival of the Order. When Gould surrendered, a deluge of workers clamored for membership in the Knights. By 1886, membership had ballooned to approximately 750,000. The tide overwhelmed the general officers. At almost one stroke the Knights had become the hope of a frustrated and combative working class.

JOSEPH BUCHANAN

Buchanan, a journalist and a typesetter, moved from his native Hannibal, Missouri, in 1878 to Colorado, where he tried his hand at editing a newspaper, operating his own print shop, and prospecting for gold. He began nearly a half a century of labor and radical activities when he joined the Denver affiliate of the International Typographical Union in 1878. In 1882 he joined the Knights of Labor and began publishing a weekly newspaper, *The Labor Enquirer.*

Buchanan became the Knights' most legendary organizer. In 1884, he led the successful strike of the railroad shopmen against the Union Pacific and one year later won himself and the Knights a national reputation by winning a strike against a number of railroads on notorious financier Jay Gould's Southwest System. The strikes had an electrifying effect on workers who had seen attempt after attempt at unionization fail because of economic collapse or employer resistance.

A believer in labor unity, Buchanan tried to mediate the growing split between the Knights of Labor and the independent craft unions between 1884 and 1886. His sympathy for the demands of the craft unions brought him into conflict with Terence Powderly, who expelled Buchanan from the Knights' General Executive Board in 1886. The dispute between the two men also sprang from Buchanan's resentment of Powderly's failure to support the strikers when Jay Gould counterattacked in 1886 and drove the Knights from the Southwestern System.

After an unsuccessful attempt to lead a secessionist movement from the Knights, Buchanan became active in the campaign to gain amnesty for the anarchists who were convicted as a result of the Haymarket bombing. He then moved east to New Jersey where he ran unsuccessfully for Congress and served as labor editor of the *New York Evening Journal.* He took part in the organization of the People's Party in 1892 and was a socialist for most of his adult life.

Overnight Powderly became known as America's "Labor Czar," arbiter of the destiny of millions, seemingly possessed of a power unmatched in the nation. Nothing could have been farther from the truth. The Knights' small administrative staff could barely cope with the new registrants, let alone direct them in any coherent fashion. Nor had Powderly changed. He remained the part-time leader who believed in cooperation rather than conflict and disdained the idea of the existence of a permanent working class. But he and the majority of the general executive board who supported him could do little to control his combative members. Heady with their recent successes, assemblies struck again and again, ignoring the Knights' strict procedures for sanctioning strikes, yet expecting the financial support of the Order. The small strike fund that the craft assemblies had succeeded in establishing over Powderly's objections proved pitifully inadequate to support the numerous strikes. Practically leaderless and with little or no discipline, the Noble Order reeled toward collapse at the very moment when it appeared invincible.

Employers, concerned with the apparent success of the Knights, gathered forces to crush strike after strike. The most telling defeat took place in

1886, ironically on the scene of the Knights' greatest victory over Jay Gould's Southwest System. This time, Gould used strikebreakers, troops, and Pinkertons to smash the union. Opposed to what they considered an unauthorized strike, and helpless in the face of events, the Knights' executive board abandoned the strikers and other defeats followed.

A MODEST CHALLENGE

Into these chaotic circumstances a small, struggling organization of craft unions, searching for a means to attract support, interjected the issue of the eight-hour day—the issue that would finally topple the Knights over the precipice into oblivion. The Federation of Organized Trades and Labor Unions (FOOTALU) grew out of the revival of the national trade unions after the depression of the 1870s. While the remarkable growth of the Knights held center stage, the craft nationals also made steady if less spectacular progress. By 1883, the nationals boasted 100,000 members, and a similar number could be found in unaffiliated locals. The revived nationals paid little attention to transforming society and concentrated on collective bargaining, strikes, and boycotts. One of the strongest, the Amalgamated Association of Iron and Steel Workers, which grew out of the old puddlers union, the Sons of Vulcan, had enough resources to lead a strike of 35,000 iron workers in six states.

The nature of the movement is best illustrated by the success of the cigar makers. Under the leadership of Adolph Strasser, the union increased its membership to 13,000 by 1883. Strasser had been a socialist who gradually became convinced that socialism offered no immediate solution to the problems of skilled workers in the United States. Instead, he turned to the British "new model" unionism for an example. He created a strong, central authority in the union, raised dues to ensure the financial stability of the organization, and placed financial control at the national level so that funds could be used where they were most needed. Strasser also introduced a system of death and accident benefits. The benefit system tied workers to the union in order to enjoy the benefits and helped ensure discipline because loss of membership meant loss of benefits. Most significantly, Strasser directed the union toward immediate job-related goals and away from reform. His associate in this undertaking was a British immigrant of Dutch-Jewish heritage, Samuel Gompers, who had risen to the presidency of the cigar makers' most important New York City local.

As this movement grew and was reflected in other crafts, the old impulse toward national federation surfaced again. Interest also came from the increasingly restless craft assemblies of the Knights. In 1881, delegates from a variety of nationals, unaffiliated locals, and a number of Knights craft assemblies formed the Federation of Organized Trades and Labor

Unions. The meeting established the dominance of the national craft unions. Reform organizations were pointedly not included.

Although the young organization structured its first program around legislative demands, its pure and simple nature was clear from the nature of these demands themselves—uniform apprenticeship regulations, removal of unions from state conspiracy laws, prohibition of contract labor, Chinese exclusion, safety legislation, and an end to child labor.

While the Federation struggled for survival, the attention of the labor world turned to the outbreak of a rash of strikes. In addition to strikes carried on by the Knights on the railroads, workers everywhere struck to protect wages against cuts during the business slump. The ferocity and longevity of many of these strikes testified both to the improved stability of the national unions and the increased militance of unorganized industrial workers. For example, stove molders in Troy, New York, held out for five months, and Cincinnati cigar makers endured a thirteen-month lockout. In Fall River, Massachusetts, 5000 spinners walked out, as did 4000 coal miners in Ohio. Labor also turned to the boycott in this period with some success. From 1884 on it became a regular weapon for both the national trade unions and the Knights of Labor assemblies. In fact, the tension between them on some issues notwithstanding, cooperation between the Knights assemblies and trade union locals during boycotts was common in many communities.

The Knights continued to grow throughout the turmoil. Their legislative gains reflected their organizational success. In 1885, Congress prohibited the importation of contract labor. A Federal Bureau of Labor was created in 1884, and soon most of the industrial states had established state bureaus of their own.

EIGHT HOURS AGAIN

As the Knights grew, FOOTALU languished. Many unions were leery of joining any national federation, seeing little direct benefit in affiliation. The issue that was to break down this reserve was the eight-hour day. Searching for an issue with which to attract membership, FOOTALU championed a national movement for eight hours. It is significant that the drive was to rely on the economic—not political—action of the workers. The Federation set May 1, 1886 as the day after which "eight hours shall constitute a legal day's labor." Unions were left free to determine the best means to the end.

For most workers the shorter work day had been the "question of questions" since the Civil War. It was not chosen as a means to attract interest to FOOTALU. As Samuel Gompers later reflected, no matter how much workers differed on other matters, they could unite in support of the shorter workday. To unorganized industrial workers, the issue had an almost mystical attraction while at the same time the proud carpenters could refer to it as the most important goal of their union. Talk of eight hours dominated the labor scene. Workers bought "eight-hour shoes," smoked "eight-hour tobacco," and sang "eight-hour songs."

The issue also gave the struggling federation a tactical advantage over the Knights. The leadership of the Noble Order had largely been silent on the issue for the same reason that it abhorred strikes. It viewed the shorter workday as little more than a palliative, a temporary adjustment that left the wage system intact.

Ironically the eight-hour movement contributed to the great influx of workers into the Knights between 1884 and 1886. Workers caught up in the idea naturally looked to the most powerful labor organization for support. Inside the Knights, the trade assemblies enthusiastically supported the campaign, further widening their split with Powderly and the reform leadership. Beset with a membership out of control and fearful of being identified with a call for a general strike, Powderly issued a secret circular advising the assemblies to shun the movement. The members paid little attention and it became clear that, like it or not, the fortunes of the Knights were to be closely linked with those of the eight-hour movement.

Into this complex situation a new, more volatile element, was introduced. But first it is necessary to review the development of another major current in the labor world of the late nineteenth century: Marxian socialism.

RUMBLE ON THE LEFT

German radicals fleeing the repression following the unsuccessful revolution of 1848 in their homeland first brought the teachings of Karl Marx to America. For the next quarter century the doctrine remained largely confined to German immigrant communities in the large cities, where it took root in the trade unions of skilled German workers. Except for the adherence of Section 12 of the Marxist International Workingmen's Association to the National Labor Union, the scattered and divided socialist movement went largely unnoticed until the 1870s. During that tumultuous decade socialists began to move out of their ethnic isolation. They played a minor role in the "long strike" of the anthracite miners, organized the Tompkins Square unemployment demonstrations in New York in 1874, and led the Railroad Strikes of 1877 in Chicago and St. Louis.

Socialists came together in 1876 in the Workingmen's Party of North America, their first attempt at a national political organization. One year later, the party changed its name to the Socialist Labor Party. Outside of the Germany immigrant community, socialism made little impact on the American working class, but it did attract a number of influential labor leaders, like Adolph Strasser of the Cigar Makers and Peter J. McGuire of the Carpenters, to its standard.

TENNESSEE CLAFLIN AND VICTORIA WOODHULL

The history of Section 12 of the International Working Men's Association—the First International—illustrates some of the problems Marxism had in America because of its attraction to reformers of the most unconventional kind. Key figures in Section 12 were two sisters, Victoria Woodhull and Tennessee Claflin. Children of a mother who earned a living as a clairvoyant and a father who deserted the family while fleeing the police under suspicion of arson, the sisters spent their childhood telling fortunes as part of a traveling wagon show. After a brief career as spiritualists in Cincinnati, the women moved to New York in 1868 to seek their fortunes.

As luck had it, Tennessee soon met and became the mistress of the railroad baron, Commodore Vanderbilt. Vanderbilt set the sisters up as the first female stockbrokers and supplied them with enough inside tips on the market to ensure their success. In the course of the business Victoria met Stephen Pearl Andrews, a wealthy gentleman scholar who, among other interests, was involved in radical causes. With Andrews's help, the sisters published a newspaper called the *Woodhull and Claflin Weekly*, which they filled with articles on free love, abortion, and an occasional exposé of a prominent citizen. One such exposé of the illicit love affair between the prominent minister, Henry Ward Beecher, and the wife of a journalist, brought the paper great fame.

The *Woodhull and Claflin Weekly* also had the distinction of being the first journal to publish Marx's Communist Manifesto in English. At Andrews' suggestion the women joined Section 12 where they quickly alienated the upright, family-oriented German workers who lost little time in expelling them. Victoria then called a convention of all "male and female beings of America" to form the Equal Rights Party, on whose ticket she ran for president with the famous black reformer, Frederick Douglass, as her vice-presidential candidate.

Both sisters eventually moved to London. Claflin married a wealthy businessman and lived in luxury until her death in 1924. Woodhull married a wealthy banker and continued her reform activities by publishing *The Humanitarian*, a journal devoted to redressing the evils caused by "unequal distribution of wealth." She died in 1927.

Internal disagreements among socialists, many of which mirrored the sectarian conflicts of the more developed European socialist world, led to a bewildering number of splits in the movement. These disagreements are too complex to treat in detail here. Some were purely personal, but the tactical issues that preoccupied the socialists centered on where to place the emphasis of their activities. Should socialists concentrate on the organization of revolutionary trade unions? If so, should these efforts take place within existing organizations such as the Knights and the nationals? Or should the emphasis be placed on the creation of independent Marxist unions? Perhaps trade unionism, while always important, should be relegated to secondary importance in a nation where universal manhood suffrage provided the theoretical basis for effective political action.

Chicago—by then the center of American socialism—became the focus of the debate. Chicago socialists had great influence in the city's labor movement. Already the city had gained a reputation for bitter antiunion repression. To many of the hardened and bitter workers of Chicago, the majority of whom were immigrants, revolutionary trade unionism rather than timid political action seemed to offer the quickest means to redress their grievances. Out of this sentiment developed the Revolutionary Socialist Party, which put its faith in militant unions following "communistic principles."

The spark that ignited this tinderbox of discontent was another import from the European radical world. Anarchism, a bitter rival of Marxism, arrived in the United States in 1882, carried by a battle-scarred veteran of European revolutionary politics—Johann Most. Most preached a message of conspiracy and violence. Where Marx had placed his faith in a mass movement of the working class, the anarchists advocated terror against the ruling class carried out by small, secret groups of dedicated revolutionaries. Where Marx believed in the replacement of the bourgeois state with a state controlled by the working class, the anarchists opposed all states as inherently oppressive.

Johann Most made few converts among American socialists, although he did generate enough interest to lead to the formation in Pittsburgh in 1883 of the International Working People's Association, or as it was more commonly known, the Black International. He also made a significant impression on several leaders of the Chicago labor movement. One such leader was Albert Parsons, a leader of the Revolutionary Socialist Party and a power in the Chicago Labor Council.

The arrival of Johann Most's brand of anarchism in Chicago corresponded with FOOTALU's call for a general strike for the eight-hour day. In its Chicago version, the conspiratorial aspects of anarchism merged with the emphasis on revolutionary trade unionism. This undoubtedly occurred because Chicago was one of the few cities where radicals possessed any real organizational power in the labor movement. Ironically the eight-hour issue could hardly have been expected to appeal to anarchists. Their views on the issue, although arrived at from very different perspectives, did not differ a great deal from those of Terence Powderly. To anarchists, support of eight hours was to recognize the legitimacy of trade union struggle— that is, to recognize the value of reform rather than revolution.

But eight-hour fever had spread to Chicago's workers as it had to workers everywhere, and, sensing the potential of the issue to radicalize the workers, Albert Parsons and his anarchist supporters seized control of the movement in the city, mixing calls for the eight-hour day with inflammatory rhetoric.

Chicago workers had other things on their minds in the spring of 1886. A lockout had already been in progress for three months at the McCormick Harvester plant. Four days after the eight-hour strike in Chicago began, violence erupted when police attempted to escort strikebreakers into the plant. In the riot that followed, several strikers were killed. The following night at a mass meeting held in Haymarket Square to protest the killings, an unknown assailant threw a bomb into a contingent of Chicago policemen on their way to break up the rally. The explosion and resulting gunfire from the panicked police left seven dead and sixty-seven wounded.

The incident filled the general citizenry of Chicago with fear and rage. The city's newspapers tarred the entire labor movement with the brushes of anarchism and radicalism. While a fascinated nation followed the events in the press, Chicago's police disregarded all constitutional guarantees as they arrested workers indiscriminately, smashed printing presses, and invaded workers' homes and union halls at will.

At the trial, eight men were convicted of murder. Only one had been present when the bomb incident occurred. They were, in fact, convicted for being radical agitators. No direct evidence linked these men to the actual crime. Anarchism was really on trial in Chicago and the convicted were meant to be examples to their followers. Four of the convicted men, Albert Parsons among them, died on the gallows on November 11, 1887.

ALBERT PARSONS

Parsons's journey from youth in rural Texas to execution in Chicago as a revolutionary anarchist spanned the period in which the United States passed from being a largely agrarian, preindustrial society to become the greatest industrial power in the world. Born in Montgomery, Alabama, in 1848, Parsons was raised by his brother in Texas until the age of thirteen when he joined the Confederate Army and served for four years. He returned to Texas after the war to take up the printing trade, but decided to move north to Chicago in 1871 in search of greater opportunity. Soon after his arrival the great depression of 1873 struck and the effects of that economic calamity on ordinary people began to turn Parsons into a radical. He joined the International Typographical Union during the depression and helped to organize a branch of the Knights of Labor.

At about the same time, Parsons joined the Socialist Labor Party and he gained prominence as a socialist orator during the railroad strikes of 1877. But Parsons' labor activism was taking him increasingly to the left. He became part of the revolutionary wing of American socialism, joined the anarchist, or "black" international in 1881 and became editor of the anarchist paper, *Alarm*, in 1884. Caught up in the sweep of anarchist rhetoric, the personally nonviolent Parsons published a number of inflammatory articles in the *Alarm*, including one advocating the placing of dynamite near "rich loafers who live by the sweat of other people's brows."

Although clearly not involved in the throwing of the bomb at the Haymarket rally in Chicago in 1886, Parsons and others were convicted of the crime and he, along with three others, was hanged on November 11, 1887. When the Governor of Illinois intimated that he would grant clemency to Parsons if he would petition for it, Parsons refused because it would injure the chances of his comrades. After his death, his wife, Lucy, herself a labor activist, sought for years to clear his name. She became one of the founders of the Industrial Workers of the World in 1905.

Overshadowed by Haymarket, the general strike for the eight-hour day proved to be a disappointment. Only some 200,000 workers participated and only a quarter of those achieved their goal. Most of those gains were lost in the antiunion offensive that followed the events in Chicago. Although they had disassociated themselves from the Haymarket defendants and withheld their support from the eight-hour campaign, the Knights, as the leading labor organization, became the chief victim of the antilabor feeling which swept the nation.

After Haymarket, employers, alarmed by the growing labor discontent, had a new and more popular justification for their actions: protection of the nation from anarchists and radicals. Industrial unrest became increasingly attributed to "outside agitators"—carriers of foreign ideas—rather than to the real conditions of labor in industrial America. The use of lockouts, blacklists, yellow-dog contracts, and the like by employers could now be justified in defense of the "American way of life." Courts and state legislatures contributed to the reactionary atmosphere by regularly convicting workers of conspiracy, incitement to riot, and a variety of other charges, and by passing laws designed to further restrict the abilities of workers to unionize.

DAVID AND GOLIATH

It would be an oversimplification to view the conflict between the Knights and the craft unions as a clear-cut struggle between business and reform unionism, one side based on skilled workers with limited economic aims and the other on inclusive membership and fundamental societal reform. The rhetoric of the national leaders obscured a much more complex situation at the local level where many of the same people belonged both to independent craft unions and the Knights. The amount of cooperation depended on the local situation. Loyalty to one or another organization was often based on personal loyalties or local politics rather than commitment to a particular ideological position. Nor were the socialists excluded; in certain cities, such as Detroit, socialists formed the backbone of the Knights. On the national level, before Haymarket, members of the Socialist Labor Party exercised an influence in both the Knights and the craft unions far out of proportion to their numbers. This was not surprising. All organizations interested in the labor question drew on the same constituencies, and activists at the local level tended to move rather easily among them.

In 1885, jurisdictional conflict broke out between the Knights and the trade unions. One such incident involved the Cigar Makers Union, of which Gompers was president. Gompers responded by calling a trade union conference just two weeks after Haymarket. The conference demanded that the Knights recognize the exclusive jurisdiction of the trade unions and that they transfer their craft assemblies to the appropriate unions. The Knights' rejection of the terms led to the calling of a trade union-FOOTALU convention in December 1886 in Columbus, Ohio. There the representatives of twelve nationals, six dissident Knights of Labor craft assemblies, and seven independent locals dissolved FOOTALU and created the American Federation of Labor (AFL), with Samuel Gompers as its first president.

Reeling under the employer offensive, the defection of the trade assemblies, and the disillusionment of the unskilled, the Knights declined almost as fast as they had risen. In 1893, Terence Powderly was removed as president. The core of the once great Noble Order of the Knights of Labor had been captured by agrarian elements. For the next few years these elements concerned themselves with agrarian reform politics and then quietly disappeared.

The Knights's dismal end does not overshadow its very real accomplishments. Through its vision of a unified working class it had created a model for the industrial union movement of the twentieth century. It brought dignity, hope, and a brief sense of power to workers for whom unions had been only a distant dream. As the major working-class organization of its time, the Knights contributed to the coalition of progressives and humanitarians who mounted a widespread campaign of political action after Haymarket. The conviction of five workers for leading a boycott by a Knights assembly of musicians against a New York music hall led to the formation of the Independent Labor Party of New York in 1889, in which all elements of the labor movement participated. The party lost in New York by a close margin, but a similar coalition won the mayoralty of Milwaukee. Less remarkable, but still substantial, gains came in Chicago. Across the land the Knights of Labor helped dozens of prolabor candidates to win local office.

Intense lobbying by the Knights and progressive allies led to the enactment of legislation, most of which ultimately proved ineffective, aimed at correcting some of the more obvious evils of the industrial system. Between 1886 and 1900, twenty-two states passed voluntary arbitration laws. Such legislation had been a long-time goal of the Knights. The Order also led the fight for child-labor laws that resulted in minimum age and maximum hour legislation for children in a number of states. Agitation by the Knights spearheaded the partially successful drive for the passage of safety legislation. The Knights also played a major role in other areas, such as industrial accident responsibility and maximum hours legislation for men and women. As the major working-class organization of the second half of the twentieth century, the Knights provided both the numerical strength and the spirit of unity that underlay the united labor-reform front of the period.

PART II
The Little House of Labor

The organization that replaced the Knights as the heart of the American labor movement—the American Federation of Labor—took its basic principles from the short-lived Federation of Organized Trades and Labor Unions. Like that transitional organization, it claimed to represent all workers, skilled and unskilled alike. Indeed, the preamble to the American Federation of Labor's (AFL) constitution spoke in ringing terms of the class struggle. But the structure of the new organization belied its rhetoric. Voting procedures assured the dominance of the affiliated unions over the administrative units, such as city centrals, of the Federation. The guiding principle was strict recognition of the autonomy of each trade. The Federation itself, guided by an executive council dominated by the strongest unions, exercised little real power. It spoke for the organization on national affairs but had no control over the affiliates. Charged with solving jurisdictional disputes, the Federation's decisions usually reflected the relative strength of the contending unions. Membership in the Federation was voluntary, and the affiliated unions could leave at will. The organization's survival depended on their support and per capita tax they paid.

The autonomous craft unions were reluctant to adhere to any organization that limited their independence. Nor did the craft unions want their fortunes linked to those of unskilled and semiskilled industrial workers whom they viewed more as threats to their own security than brothers and sisters in a common struggle. The craft unions believed that only by concentrating on what workers had in common—their conditions of occupational life—could a labor organization hold together in the face of the power of business enterprise. Therefore, emphasis had to be placed on economic matters—hours of work, apprenticeship regulations, wages and working conditions. Collective bargaining, boycotts, and strikes were means to those ends.

An organization built on such limited objectives had a much more restricted view of the uses of political action. In part this was because of the lack of success such attempts had experienced in the past. But there was also a fundamental philosophical reason. Most of the reform political action of the past had been built on two concepts. First, that universal suffrage provided the means to fundamentally alter and reform the economic system, and second, that it was in the interest of all who lived from their own labor, whatever their class, to use their votes to do so. Gompers, in rejecting the concept of the producing classes so important to the reform labor movement of the nineteenth century, also rejected the idea that the theoretical power of the ballot was a match for the real power of American business enterprise: its economic power. What good was the right to vote if capital controlled both political parties? Capitalists had the only real freedom because they had the only real power. Gompers reasoned that without power there was no freedom, no matter how many theoretical political rights one possessed. "Rights?" he said in 1908, "Yes, there is no hesitancy on the part of our country to grant us certain rights—for instance, the rights to be maimed or killed without any responsibility to the employer; the right to be discharged for belonging to a union of labor; the right to work as long hours for as low wages as the employer can impose upon working men and women. These rights—these academic rights which we do not want—are frequently conceded, but there is a denial to us of the rights that are essential to our welfare."

Individual rights meant little in an unequal contest. Most of the shorter-hours legislation of the past supported his argument. This legislation had almost universally included "right to contract" clauses that theoretically protected the workers' right to choose to work longer hours. But these rights had no meaning because the lone worker was weak and the company strong. The real choice lay between working longer hours or not working at all. To Gompers, this imbalance of power could not be changed primarily through the ballot; it could only be changed by giving the worker some equality of strength with the employer. The answer, of course, was for the workers to band together to replace individual weakness with collective strength. Gompers saw that individual freedoms were meaningless in a society consisting of powerful interest groups. Labor, he reasoned, must combine and create its own monopoly—a monopoly of labor power with which to confront monopoly capital. Only then could equality prevail; and only then could there be true freedom. To Gompers, individual freedom had no meaning unless protected by collective power.

This justification was not surprising in an age when employers, church leaders, and educators attacked unions an infringements on the individual freedoms of workers. This was particularly true of the closed shop, which opponents labeled as a limitation on the worker's right to work wherever he or she pleased, without the interference of a union. The attacks were based on the prevailing social philosophy of the period, which argued that society should be allowed to function unfettered by organizational restraints, either governmental or private. Only then could an individual rise to full potential. Gompers was a product of his age, and in theory he accepted this argument based on the survival of the fittest. But Gompers also believed that free and unregulated competition would take place between organized groups—not individuals—because the organization of large-scale business enterprise was already an established fact.

In a sense, what Gompers and the AFL did was institutionalize the philosophy of survival of the fittest, or Social Darwinism, as it was called, by creating a labor federation well suited to the needs of the strongest workers, the most skilled. What this meant was that pure and simple unionization, which, while Gompers theoretically advocated it for all workers, in reality applied only to skilled workers whose scarce skills gave them some leverage with their employers. This meant a labor movement representative of a shrinking minority of American workers. There were exceptions. The United Mine Workers, an AFL affiliate, included all who labored in and around the mines, regardless of skill. But the few unions organized industrially were not to be found in the mass production industries. They succeeded only in highly competitive, decentralized industries, such as bituminous coal mining and brewing, in which the union was more powerful than any one employer.

The AFL's exclusive nature was reflected in its attitude toward political action. Samuel Gompers believed that the American working class was too diverse to be led to support one or the other of the national political parties. But he never suggested that unions should not take part in political action. He developed the position that labor should reward its friends and punish its enemies, regardless of party affiliation. This approach also made organizational sense. Any attempt to impose a uniform political line would have violated the autonomy of the affiliates. They were a diverse group with diverse interests and wanted to be left free to support candidates and form political alliances at the local and state levels that best served their interests.

The Federation's national political action did not aim so much at securing favorable legislation for labor, as much as it tried to keep government out of the industrial relations arena. Gompers realized that government, in the form of injunctions and police power, had long been an active participant in labor relations, always on the side of management. In light of his belief in a free economy of contending interest groups, he wanted the removal of governmental interference of any kind so that free collective bargaining could take place.

A related reason for Gompers's lack of interest in reform political action was his belief that if government did not interfere in labor relations, the AFL unions could obtain more in the way of shorter hours and higher wages through collective bargaining. With this rationale, the Federation began to oppose eight-hour legislation. By 1914, most of the AFL's craft affiliates had already achieved that goal on their own. Gompers feared that if legislation enshrined eight hours as the standard workday, the AFL unions would find it difficult to use their bargaining power to go below that. It was a classic argument for the economic freedom of the affiliates. But lack of legislation meant quite a different thing to the industrial workers unprotected by unions. These workers needed government intervention on their behalf.

Gompers recognized the plight of the industrial workers and he took every opportunity to speak out on their behalf, but he also realized the immense power of the corporations and their allies in government. Although he was well-versed in socialism, his experiences in the Cigar Makers Union had led him to reject the possibility of revolutionary change in the United States. He accepted the permanence of industrial capitalism and believed that labor must forge organizations that give it the power to wrench as much from the system as possible. In order to do this, he advocated the creation of an economic power base for workers that could survive. For Gompers, this could only be done by concentrating in areas where workers had strength: the crafts. He believed that this strength became diluted once one moved it from the workplace. Thus he advocated "pure and simple" unionism. Pure, because it excluded nonworkers, and simple, because it concentrated on immediate material goals rather than sweeping reform.

THE LOGIC OF EXCLUSION

Gompers shared the prevailing social and economic values of turn-of-the-century America. This basic harmony with society contributed a great deal to the Federation's ability to survive and eventually thrive. But it also conditioned the Federation's attitudes toward, blacks, women, and immigrants. AFL concentration on the economic protection of skilled workers led it to confront nonskilled workers in terms of its own self-interest. Given the histories of the national craft unions, such a position was hardly surprising. Most craft unionists had always resisted the admittance of women and blacks and their actions had caused friction within the NLU and the Knights. With their autonomy assured in the Federation, the craft unions could be as exclusive as they pleased. Most excluded women outright or did so indirectly by restricting admittance to apprenticeship to men. Some unions, which had no formal policy on women, left the decision to the locals, usually assuring exclusion. Some nationals did accept women, usually in all-female locals. Where they were accepted into mixed locals, they frequently found dues so high that they could not afford them. When dues were reduced to more closely reflect the lower wages of women, it meant reduced benefits and practically no voice in union affairs. By 1895, women made up only 5 percent of all union members and the number shrank to 3 percent by 1910.

Although few in number, women gave nothing away to the men in militance. Iowa cigar makers reported in 1899 that women strikers stood fast even as the men abandoned the fight. According to the male president of the Boot and Shoe Workers, women compromised less willingly. "They are more likely to hold out to the bitter end . . . ," he lamented. During the "Great Uprising" of 1909, 20,000 women walked out of New York's garment shops against the wishes of the male leadership, worrying Jewish men who were afraid "for the security of their jobs."

AFL attitudes cannot be entirely blamed for the low organizational rate for women. Their position in the workforce also retarded unionism. At the turn of the century, most women workers were unmarried and nearly half were under twenty-five. For the most part, they still worked in manufacturing jobs that proved difficult to organize. Between 1890 and 1900 the number of women working increased by 33 percent to 5.319 million. Much of the increase came in office and sales work, also extremely different groups to organize.

This heavy presence of women in the workforce, and the often terrible conditions under which they worked, alarmed labor leaders who thus supported legislation to limit the hours and improve conditions of work for women. Along with humanitarian reformers, the leaders stressed the negative effects of industrial work on the health and morals of women. They argued that female labor injured the motherhood and family life of the nation. "In our time, and at least in our country," Gompers stated in 1905, "there is no necessity for the wife contributing to the support of the family by working . . . the wife as wage earner is a disadvantage economically considered, and socially is unnecessary." The more important reason for the AFL's position, however, came through in an 1896 editorial in the *American Federationist*. "Every woman employed," claimed the paper, "displaces a man and adds one more to the idle contingent that are fixing wages at the lowest limit."

Reaction to black workers was a bit more complex. The AFL had embraced an antidiscrimination policy and even refused affiliation to unions of boilermakers and machinists on the grounds that their constitutions included "white only" clauses. Throughout the 1880s and 1890s Samuel Gompers frequently urged AFL representatives to organize black workers in integrated locals, if possible, and in all-black locals, if necessary. But by 1893, with the nation in the midst of yet another depression—and at a time when legal segregation began to harden in America—Gompers and the Federation began to change. Pressure from the craft unions for the exclusion of blacks increased. Some of the immediate hostility came from the use of blacks as strikebreakers during the depression. This practice had been a thorn in labor's side since before the Civil War, and as industrial conflict grew, exploited black workers became a regular weapon in the arsenal of industrial capitalism. Although immigrants had been employed as strikebreakers to a much greater degree, racial prejudice singled black workers out for the most severe hostility. Part of the reason for this lay in the fact that most black leadership, frustrated in their attempts to have blacks admitted to unions, believed that employers were to be preferred to unions as allies.

Faced with a choice between principle and the stability of the Federation, Gompers gave in to the craft unions. Any attempt to enforce the nondiscriminatory policy under the circumstances would have resulted in either the disaffiliation or expulsion of many of the strongest affiliates. Beginning in 1895 with the International Association of Machinists, unions evaded the antidiscrimination policy by removing white-only clauses from their constitutions and either putting them in the ritual, as the Machinists did, or leaving it to local option. By the turn of the century, not even these small deceptions were necessary. By 1910, eight national craft unions denied membership to blacks either by ritual or constitutional provision. The fact that the remaining fifty or so member unions had no such clauses did not mean that they admitted blacks. In 1902, W. E. B. Dubois, a black leader, discovered that forty-three national unions, including the independent railroad brotherhoods, had no black members. Twenty-seven others had very few because they barred black apprentices. Of the AFL unions, the only one with significant black membership was the United Mine Workers.

Gompers denied prejudice as a factor before the U.S. Industrial Commission. He told the Commission that the reason for exclusion was because blacks "so conducted themselves as to be a continuous convenient whip placed in the hands of the employers to cow the white man and to compel them to accept abject conditions of labor." He also argued that blacks did not possess the skill required to become members of the craft unions. It is certainly true that the craft orientation of the AFL severely limited the necessity for the organization to deal with the problems of black workers, the majority of whom were unskilled. But it is also true that racial prejudice played the most significant role. Blacks were not seen mainly as rivals for jobs, but as racial and social inferiors. When a union refused to admit blacks, the main result was to preserve the status of its members and the reputation of the union in the white community.

RICHARD DAVIS

In the early years of the AFL no union had a better record of organizing black workers than the United Mine Workers. By 1900, there were approximately 20,000 black miners in the UMW, one quarter of the union's members. Much of the credit for this success belonged to a dedicated band of black organizers, few of whom have left a record. One who did was Richard Davis. Born in Roanoke, Virginia, in 1864, Davis went to work in a tobacco factory at the age of eight and remained there for nine years. Disgusted with the "very low wage rate and other unfavorable conditions," he left to work in the West Virginia coal mines. He moved to Ohio in 1882 and became a union activist. Davis worked tirelessly to organize black miners. His union work brought him election to the National Executive Board of the United Mine Workers in 1896 and 1897; it also brought him frequent firings from his employers and finally, in 1898, blacklisting. Unable to find work in the mines or with the union, he wrote this letter on May 16, 1898.

I have as yet never boasted of what I have done in the interest of organized labor, but will venture to say that I have done all I could and am proud that I am alive today, for I think I have had the unpleasant privilege of going into the most dangerous places in this country to organize, or in other words, to do the almost impossible. I have been threatened; I have been sandbagged; I have been stoned, and last of all, deprived of the right to earn a livelihood for myself and my family.

I do not care so much for myself, but it is my innocent children that I care for most, and heaven knows that it makes me almost crazy to think of it. I have spent time and money in the labor movement during the past sixteen years, and to-day I am worse off than ever, for I have no money, nor no work. I will not beg, and I am not inclined to steal, nor will I unless compelled through dire necessity, which I hope the good God of the universe will spare me. . . . I can not think of my present circumstances and write (more), for I fear I might say too much. Wishing success to the miners of this country, I remain, as ever, a lover of labor's cause.

Davis died in 1900 at the age of thirty-six, without work and in despair.

The reaction of organized labor to women and black workers can be understood in the context of the threat that union members felt during a period of massive industrialization that was accompanied by a tremendous influx of immigrant workers between 1880 and 1914. Some 12,000,000 came between 1890 and 1910 alone. The response of labor to these new competitors did not require elaborate justifications based on protection of the family or the race, although there was some of that. Labor stood four-square on economic survival. Immigrants had always provided a strikingly high percentage of the leadership of the labor movement. British and Irish immigrants had taken the lead in almost every industry. But the new immigrants of the late nineteenth century came at a time when industrialization was in full swing and when an increasingly urban and industrial America was especially vulnerable to the hardships caused by periodic economic downturns.

Arrival of the immigrants brought a dramatic change of personnel in American industries. Before 1890, most miners in the Pennsylvania bituminous coalfields had been American born, English, Scotch, Welsh, Irish, or German. After 1890, Magyars, Slovaks, Poles, or Italians replaced them. Italians, Portuguese, Greeks, Syrians, and Poles took the places primarily held by British, Irish, and French-Canadian workers in the New England textile and shoe factories. In the garment trades of Philadelphia, New

York, and Chicago, Russian Jews and Italians replaced Germans, Bohemians, and Irish.

By the early twentieth century foreign-born workers constituted the majority of wage earners wherever manufacturing and mining thrived. A 1910 federal study determined that foreign-born workers, most from southern and eastern Europe, constituted 57.9 percent of the workforce in the twenty-one industries studied. In textiles, the garment industry, coal mining, and meat packing, the figure was considerably higher.

Private labor agencies funneled these masses into jobs, often as strikebreakers. Skilled workers feared that any gains they had made in the fight for shorter hours would be overwhelmed by the crush of new immigrants. Unlike earlier arrivals from northern and western Europe, these newcomers had little familiarity with unions. Cultural and religious differences, which employers played on to keep the immigrants divided, made them seem impossible to organize. The multitude of languages created the "tower of Babel" effect in which workers in the shops often could not talk to each other.

Of course the main reason that most immigrants remained unorganized lay in the fact that they were industrial workers in whom most AFL unions had little interest. When such unions as the United Mine Workers carried on vigorous organizing campaigns, the newcomers flocked to join. In the clothing industry, Jewish and Italian workers formed their own industrial unions.

Throughout the second half of the nineteenth century, labor organizations had consistently objected to certain forms of immigration. But with the exception of Chinese workers, labor had made a distinction between contract labor and free immigration. In the 1880s the AFL moved toward a policy of broader restriction. As one Teamster put it in 1885, "I am not opposed to a man because he is a foreigner, but I think there are too many here for the work there is to do." In 1897 the AFL went on record in support of a literacy test and a means test. From that point on, the AFL consistently supported restrictive immigration legislation, which finally became a reality following World War I.

The future of the AFL looked far from secure as the 1890s began. Membership had grown slowly since the organization's founding only five years earlier. In addition, depression cast its shadow over much of the decade. As always, employers increased antiunion activity during hard times and the viciousness of their tactics increased as well. Still, the young organization continued to grow. Struggling new unions came into the fold. What was later to become the International Brotherhood of Electrical Workers grew out of a meeting of a small group of electricians gathered in St. Louis in 1890. They had come from around the country to wire the buildings and exhibits for the St. Louis Exposition of that year. For every strong affiliate there were many weak ones to be nurtured.

What strength the Federation had rested on its few strong member unions, like the Carpenters and Miners. Without them the Federation could not have survived. The unions provided the funds and the leadership. In a sense the unions were the parents and the AFL the child.

Much of the credit for the growth and survival of the AFL must go to Samuel Gompers. He devoted all of his energy to the union cause and became, from an obscure immigrant cigar maker, the central spokesman and leader of the American labor movement for the remainder of his life.

PART III
Frick's Fort and Pullman's Paradise

A 1969 U.S. government commission studying violence in the United States concluded that this country had the bloodiest and most violent labor history of any industrial nation in the world. Historian Richard Hofstadter found the level of industrial violence in America to be unusual considering the lack of militant class-conflict idealogies in the mainstream of the labor movement. The explanation to the paradox of a maximum of industrial violence and a nonrevolutionary labor movement, according to Hofstadter, lay more in the ethos of American capitalists than in that of the workers. Events in Homestead, Pennsylvania, and Pullman, Illinois, in the 1890s proved just how willing American capitalists were to use violence to retain total control over business enterprise.

In February 1892, Henry Clay Frick, director of Andrew Carnegie's Homestead works, near Pittsburgh, and representatives of the Amalgamated Association of Iron, Steel and Tin Workers began negotiations for a new contract. The Amalgamated represented the skilled workmen and was one of the strongest affiliates of the AFL. In 1888 a company attempt to lock out the Amalgamated members had floundered when community support prevented strikebreakers from working. This time things were to be different. After three months of negotiations, during which time Frick had fortified the mill, the company delivered an ultimatum. Accept the company offer or lose union recognition. When the Amalgamated refused, Frick locked the men out.

Events that transpired during the Homestead lockout captured the attention of the nation. The union, supported by the overwhelming majority of all of the workers, strung pickets around the mill and the company began making arrangements with labor agencies to recruit strikebreakers. When the company tried to outflank the pickets by bringing armed Pinkerton guards into the mill by barge on the Monongahela River, the workers countered with armed resistance of their own. In the ensuing fight, nine Pinkertons and seven workers died. Forced to surrender, the Pinkertons were led through Homestead to the railroad station while the crowd, enraged by the bloodshed, stoned and assaulted the invaders.

Six days later, although the town had remained calm since the violence, 8000 state militia converged on Homestead at the request of Henry Clay Frick. Under the protection of the troops the company imported a sufficient number of "scabs" and resumed operations. Leaders of the union were indicted on charges of rioting and murder.

In the midst of this tension a young anarchist, Alexander Berkman, attempted to assassinate Frick. Although he had no association with the union, Berkman's deed shifted public opinion against the workers. The lockout dragged on for another month but legal costs involved in the defense of their leaders drained the Amalgamated's treasury and the men slowly gave up the struggle.

The defeat of the Amalgamated at Homestead was the beginning of the destruction of unionism in the steel industry. The union never regained its strength and by 1910, after several other defeats, the industry had become the bastion of the open shop.

While the struggle at Homestead held center stage in 1892, labor suffered other defeats as well. Frequently, federal and state troops were involved. Silver miners were defeated in Idaho, railroaders in Buffalo, and coal miners in Tennessee. Gompers gave what moral support he could to the strikers, praising the men of Homestead for refusing to bow before the autocrats, but moral support, unfortunately, was all that the weak federation could offer.

Although public opinion generally turned against the strikers as a result of biased newspaper coverage, there was some support for the workers. An Illinois senator told his colleagues that there seemed to be two regular armies abroad in the country, the United States Army and the Pinkerton army, whose commander-in-chief, "like the barons of the Middle Ages, has a force to be increased at pleasure for the service of those who would pay him."

Hard on the heels of Homestead, and in the midst of depression, the Pullman strike of 1894 broke out. In many ways the Pullman strike differed from Homestead. As an attack on paternalistic capitalism, the Pullman strike resembled the earlier protests of the mill women of Lowell. George M. Pullman, president of the Pullman Palace Car Company, had established a "model" community for his workers, immodestly called Pullman, Illinois. It was, in the words of Pullman's press agent, "a town, in a word, where all that is ugly and discordant and demoralizing is eliminated and all that which inspires self-respect is generously provided."

For the workers, however, Pullman presented a different reality. Those workers who lived in the town paid exorbitant rates for rent, utilities, and services., It is true that Pullman's streets were wide and its houses pleasantly arranged. But Pullman earned substantial profits for the company by recycling the bulk of the workers' wages back to the enterprise. Behind the pleasant facade, workers lived in crowded company houses where high rents forced them to take in lodgers. Mark Hanna, himself an industrial baron, summed up the reality of Pullman very well. "Oh, Hell!" he commented, "Model—Go and live in Pullman and find out how much Pullman gets sellin' city water and gas ten percent higher to those poor fools!"

Pullman also supervised the morals of the inhabitants of his company town. Liquor was forbidden, church attendance was encouraged, and while libraries were provided, one could not read about unions because among other things, unions were forbidden at Pullman.

During the depression of 1893, the Pullman Company laid off over one-half of its workers and reduced the wages of those still working by 25 to 40 percent. Rents stayed the same, however, and the company continued to pay dividends. When, in May 1894, a committee of workers asked for relief, the company refused and discharged three of the delegation. During the preceding year a number of Pullman workers had secretly organized several locals of the new American Railway Union.

Railway unionism had first developed among the skilled workers in the 1860s with the aim of protecting workers against the hazards of the trade. The six railroad brotherhoods, consisting of the engineers, conductors, firemen, trainmen, switchmen, and yardmasters, concentrated their energies on the establishment of widows, orphans, and disabled members' funds, as well as a death benefit system. The brotherhoods were, in reality, not unions, but mutual aid societies.

Attempts to turn the brotherhoods toward trade union action foundered because of internal squabbles and conflict with the Knights of Labor. In 1888 an attempt at cooperation in a strike against the Burlington Railroad failed, but not before alerting railroad management to the growing discontent among the workers. In an attempt to split the skilled from the unskilled workers, the employers granted the brotherhoods wages and working conditions that turned them into something of a privileged elite.

Under these conditions, unionism among the unskilled and semiskilled railroaders languished until 1892 and the emergence of Eugene V. Debs as the apostle of industrial unionism. Debs had long been an active member and national officer of the Brotherhood of Locomotive Firemen. But the events of the 1880s and 1890s had a profound effect on him. When the Buffalo switchmen were defeated in 1892 because of a lack of support from the other brotherhoods, he began to organize all railway workers, regardless of craft or skill, into the new American Railway Union (ARU).

Debs's call for an industrial union of railroad workers hit a responsive chord. Workers rushed to the standard of the ARU as they had to the Knights after the brief victories on the Wabash. A remarkable victory in a strike against the Great Northern Railroad, a corporation with 9000 employees, further stimulated growth and by 1894 the union boasted of 150,000 members.

Among those who had joined in the euphoria following the defeat of the

Great Northern, were the workers of the Pullman Palace Car Company. They qualified for membership because of the existence of a small, company railroad on Pullman's property. Their decision to seek help from the ARU was a fateful one. It was to bring Debs's fledgling union its greatest glory and led to its ultimate destruction.

Following the discharge of their representatives, the Pullman workers struck and appealed to the ARU for support. After a futile attempt to convince the Pullman management to settle the dispute through negotiation, Debs ordered ARU members everywhere in the country to refuse to handle Pullman cars. The boycott quickly spread to most of the eastern and western lines.

The General Managers Association, an organization of twenty-four railroads centered in Chicago, decided to come to Pullman's aid. Member railroads ordered the discharge of any worker refusing to handle Pullman cars, but the workers countered by closing down every line where this occurred. From a dispute between one company and its workers, the boycott became in Debs's words, "A contest between the producing classes and the money power of the country." Debs realized the power of the forces arrayed against his union and he cautioned the members to stand fast and operate in a peaceful and lawful manner.

The General Managers Association wanted just the opposite. In addition to the time-honored tactic of importing strikebreakers, the Association ordered its lines to attach mail cars to the rear of Pullman cars so that the strikers could be charged with interfering with the U.S. mails. Using this as a pretext, the railroads appealed for help to the U.S. Attorney General Richard C. Olney, a railroad lawyer by profession and a board member of several railroads.

Olney quickly appointed another railroad attorney, Edwin Walker, as special counsel to the federal district attorney in Chicago, with instructions to employ "all legal remedies" to break the strike. Walker proceeded to deputize private company police as federal marshals. Their primary mission was to move the trains. As conflict between the marshals and the strikers escalated, the newspapers began to describe the strike as the "Debs Revolution."

On July 2, 1894, at Olney and Walker's urging, the Federal District Court issued a sweeping injunction prohibiting the strikers from "interfering with or stopping any of the business of any of the railroads in Chicago," on the grounds of interference with the mails and as an unlawful conspiracy in restraint of commerce. The court based its decision on the Sherman Antitrust Act, which had been passed by Congress under pressure from farmers and small businessmen to control business monopolies in restraint of trade. Unions had never been considered as falling under the provisions of the law.

Olney then convinced President Grover Cleveland to dispatch federal troops to protect the mails and enforce the injunction. Governor John Peter

Altgeld of Illinois protested the sending of troops, but the army poured into his state and some twenty others. The appearance of the troops on behalf of the companies enraged the strikers and more violence followed. The growing magnitude of the strike drew the entire labor movement into the crisis. The Knights of Labor offered what little support they could, and 100 Chicago unions voted to call a general strike. Gompers, too, felt the pressure to act, but he resisted agitation from within the AFL for a general strike. Instead, the Federation sent money to the strikers and pleaded with President Cleveland to use his good offices to bring the dispute to a just end.

In the interval, a federal grand jury indicted Debs and other leaders of the ARU for conspiracy to obstruct the mails, and the judge who had issued the injunction cited Debs for contempt of court in refusing to honor it. In all, some 700 strikers were arrested on a variety of charges. Under indictment for conspiracy and contempt of court, his union in shambles, Debs called off the strike on August 2, 1894. The cause of industrial unionism had been crushed and the injunction became a regular feature of industrial disputes.

The use of injunctions in labor disputes was not new. But between 1890 and 1894, state and federal courts began to expand their use. According to historian Joseph Rayback, these new injunctions had a different basis. They were issued to prevent violations of the Sherman Antitrust Act or the Interstate Commerce Act, or to protect private property. It is quite clear that neither act was designed to include labor. Injunctions to protect private property were a different matter. In order to enjoin workers, it had to be proved that irreparable injury to property had occurred. When strikes had already resulted in the destruction of property, there was no problem. But the injunction in the Pullman strike had been issued to prevent strikes, picketing, and boycotts. These actions, in themselves, were not illegal activities, and courts could not enjoin workers from exercising their legal rights. Nor were these actions, in themselves, a threat to physical property. In order to satisfy the requirement that real property be threatened, the courts began to rule that strikes and boycotts threatened the future expectations and goodwill that companies had built up with their customers, and that these were property rights with a monetary value. Even so, there could be no recovery of damages resulting from the legal acts of others. Therefore strikes, picketing, and boycotts had to be made illegal. In order to do this, the courts resurrected the old conspiracy doctrine, but in new form. Where the old doctrine—as developed in the cordwainer conspiracy cases—held that strikes were a criminal offense because they damaged the public, the new interpretation held that they were civil offenses because they threatened the employer's future expectations.

In sum, union actions that adversely affected relations between a business and its customers were illegal conspiracies in restraint of trade and in violation of the Sherman Antitrust Act. This dubious body of law had been developing in the state courts since 1890. But before the Pullman strike, the federal courts had not been involved. Debs's conviction for contempt of court reached the U.S. Supreme Court where the conviction was upheld. Thus, for the first time, the Supreme Court sanctioned the widest possible use of injunctions in labor disputes. One year later, in 1897, the Supreme Court expanded this tremendous antilabor weapon when it ruled that anyone who knew of the issuance of an injunction, not just those directly named, were obligated to obey it.

The defeat of the Pullman strike by the combined power of the railroad corporations and the government profoundly changed Eugene Debs. He entered prison a trade unionist and a Democrat. When he emerged six months later as a populist, he began an ideological journey that would bring him to the leadership of American socialism. Throughout all the tribulations that followed, he never abandoned the cause of industrial unionism.

DISCUSSION QUESTIONS

1. How did the Knights of Labor's form of organization reflect its program for social reform?
2. Discuss the reasons why the Knights of Labor, at least officially, placed little faith in the strike as an effective weapon for workers to use.
3. Why did Adolph Strasser's "New Model" unionism have more relevance to skilled workers than to unskilled and semiskilled workers?
4. What were the differences between Samuel Gompers and the socialists on the primary functions of unions? Pay particular attention to their different attitudes toward political action.
5. It can be argued that Gompers's emphasis on pure and simple economic unionism was in harmony with the prevailing value system, which stressed competition and survival of the fittest. Discuss why.

KEY WORDS AND PHRASES

Knights of Labor	Samuel Gompers
Terence Powderly	Social Darwinism
Chinese Exclusion	Pure and Simple Unionism
Contract Labor	New Immigration
FOOTALU	Pullman Boycott
Eight-hour Movement	American Railway Union
Anarchism	Eugene V. Debs
Haymarket Riot	Injunction Law
American Federation of Labor	Homestead Lockout

BIBLIOGRAPHY

The material for this section was drawn largely from these works:

Fink, Leon. *Workingmen's Democracy: The Knights of Labor and American Politics.* Urbana: University of Illinois Press, 1982.

Foner, Philip. *Organized Labor and the Black Worker, 1619–1973.* New York: Praeger, 1974.

Ginger, Ray. *The Bending Cross: A biography of Eugene V. Debs.* New Brunswick: Rutgers University Press, 1949.

Grob, Gerald. *Workers and Utopia.* Evanston: Northwestern University Press, 1961.

Kaufman, Stuart. *Samuel Gompers and the Origins of the American Federation of Labor, 1848–1896.* Westport, Conn.: Greenwood Press, 1973.

Lens, Sidney. *Radicalism in America.* New York: Thomas Crowell, 1969.

Rodgers, Daniel. *The Work Ethic in Industrial America, 1850–1920.* Chicago: University of Chicago Press, 1978.

Rogin, Michael, "Voluntarism: The Political Functions of an Anti-Political Doctrine," *The Industrial and Labor Relations Review,* vol. 15 (July 1962): 521–535.

Spero, Sterling and Abram Harris. *The Black Worker.* New York: Atheneum, 1972.

Taft, Philip. *The A.F. of L. in the Time of Gompers.* New York: Harper and Row, 1957.

Ware, Norman. *The Labor Movement in the United States, 1860–1895.* New York: Appleton, 1929.

Wertheimer, Barbara. *We Were There: The Story of Working Women in America.* New York: Pantheon, 1977.

For additional reading see:

David, Henry. *The History of the Haymarket Affair.* New York: Farrar & Rinehart, 1936.

Eggert, Gerald. *Richard Olney: Evolution of a Statesman.* University Park: Pennsylvania State University Press, 1974.

Gordon, David M., Richard Edwards and Michael Reich. *Segmented Work, Divided Workers: The Historical Transformation of Labor in the United States.* Cambridge: Cambridge University Press, 1982.

Kogan, Bernard, ed. *The Chicago Haymarket Riot: Anarchy on Trial.* Boston: D. C. Heath, 1959.

Lindsey, Almont. *The Pullman Strike.* Chicago: University of Chicago Press, 1942.

Livesay, Harold. *Samuel Gompers and Organized Labor in America.* Boston: Little Brown, 1978.

Mandel, Bernard. *Samuel Gompers: A Biography.* Yellow Springs, Ohio: Antioch Press, 1963.

McLaurin, Melton A. *The Knights of Labor in the South*. Westport, Conn.: Greenwood Press, 1978.

Salvatore, Nick. *Eugene V. Debs: Citizen and Socialist*. Urbana: University of Illinois Press, 1982.

Saxton, Alexander. *The Indispensable Enemy: Labor and the Anti-Chinese Movement in California*. Berkeley: University of California Press, 1971.

Wolff, Leon. *Lockout, The Story of the Homestead Strike of 1892*. New York: Harper and Row, 1965.

SECTION
FOUR

PART I
The Radical Alternative

As the utopian radicalism of the nineteenth century declined with the demise of the Knights of Labor, the mainstream of the labor reform tradition fell to the growing American socialist movement.

Permanent organization of American socialism began with the formation of the Socialist Labor Party (SLP) in 1877. Involvement in the 1886 mayoral campaign of Henry George, the candidate of the United Labor Party in New York City, brought the SLP in contact with the man who was to become the dominant figure in American socialism until the close of the century.

A native of Curaçao, an island off the Venezuelan coast, Daniel DeLeon had become professor of international law at Columbia University. He moved through several reform movements; when he found little enthusiasm in them for the organization of labor, he joined the SLP and quickly rose to leadership. DeLeon based his concept of revolutionary political action on what he called the new trade unionism—a trade unionism that did not concentrate on immediate gains but struggled to create the "cooperative commonwealth and freedom." Pure and simple unionism was anathema to DeLeon who, as a Marxist, rejected the legitimacy of private ownership of the means of production.

DeLeon first attempted to capture the Knights of Labor but succeeded only in helping to drive Terence Powderly from office and hand the Noble Order over to a group of western agrarians. He then set about creating his own labor federation, the Socialist Trades and Labor Alliance, with which he hoped to do battle with the AFL in the cause of revolutionary industrial unionism. This was to be a militant movement under the tight control of the Socialist Labor Party, with which it would fight the revolutionary battles on two fronts—the industrial and the political.

DeLeon's policy created immediate problems within the SLP. Many of its members, such as Peter J. McGuire of the Carpenters, also belonged to unions affiliated with the AFL. This faction believed in working within the Federation to convert it to socialism. They rejected the idea of dual unionism that DeLeon's new federation represented, on the grounds that it would divide the labor movement. DeLeon won the battle but lost the war.

The disgruntled trade unionists left the SLP and with them went any hope for DeLeon's grand plan for an alliance between a mass labor movement and a revolutionary socialist party. Both the SLP's electoral figures and its union support dropped dramatically.

The split in the SLP led to interest by other groups in the formation of an effective socialist movement. Prominent among these were the followers of Eugene V. Debs and a brilliant Milwaukee socialist by the name of Victor L. Berger. In 1897 Debs dissolved what was left of his American Railway Union after the disaster at Pullman and, along with a number of other labor and political reform groups, started the Social Democracy. At the heart of the new organization was Debs's utopian colonization plan in which social-ists were to emigrate to one state and turn it into a cooperative common-wealth, from which the idea would spread.

The Social Democracy gained support from several quarters. Disen-chanted Jewish SLP members from New York came in with their newspa-per, the *Jewish Daily Forward*. German socialists from Milwaukee, under the leadership of Victor Berger, also joined. Berger had been instrumental in the conversion of Debs to socialism. In 1898, after having discarded the utopian colonization idea, these three groups established the Social Demo-cratic Party of America and proclaimed the trade union movement and independent political action as "the chief emancipating factors of the work-ing class." In 1900, the Social Democrats joined with another anti-DeLeon faction of the Socialist Labor Party and supported Eugene Debs as the socialist candidate for president. This dissident SLP faction was led by Morris Hillquit, a young socialist labor lawyer from New York. The Hillquit group represented the trade unionist faction. It urged cooperation with the AFL and "boring from within" to draw the federation to socialism. The differences among the various factions were largely left behind in the en-thusiasm generated by Debs's showing in the election. Debs collected 97,000 votes, three times more than DeLeon's SLP. Shortly after the elec-tion, the Hillquit faction and the Social Democrats met and formed the Socialist Party of the United States.

The new party's ultimate goal was the establishment of socialism. But, under the influence of Berger and Hillquit, it also supported a strong trade union movement and affirmed the importance of immediate gains for workers in order to promote class consciousness. While there was still no absence of revolutionary rhetoric among the party faithful, the mainstream of American socialism had clearly embarked on a course emphasizing grad-ual reforms achieved through political and trade union action.

THE GOOD YEARS

American socialism made its greatest gains between 1900 and 1915, during a period of reform ferment that historians have labeled the Progressive Era.

Many Americans, not just socialists, had become profoundly disturbed with the effects of unrestrained industrial capitalism on American society. City dwellers, concerned with the desperate conditions of the urban poor, began to echo farmers' demands for governmental regulation of big business. Increasingly, small businessmen and middle-class professionals looked to government to protect them from monopoly capitalism. Distrustful of legislators and courts that they perceived to be under the control of business, these two groups instituted reforms that broadened the direct expression of democracy. Under their prodding, the graduated income tax and the direct election of U.S. senators became part of the Constitution. Urban reformers worked to remove corruption from city and state governments and created institutions, like the settlement houses, to educate the immigrants.

From all of this, socialism benefited. Long identified as an ideology with appeal only to immigrants, socialism began to gain supporters in the Midwest among populists who had long been fighting the power of the great corporations and the banks. By 1912, the party enrolled 118,000 members, most of whom were native-born Americans. Debs rose from a well-known labor leader to a national political figure, beloved by the party faithful and admired by hundreds of thousands more. As the socialist presidential candidate in 1912 he received nearly one million votes, many from the western states. Socialist political success was evident at every level of government. By 1912, more than 1000 socialists served in public office, from Victor Berger in Congress to hundreds of municipal officials. In 1910, Milwaukee became the first city to elect a socialist mayor. In years to come other cities such as Bridgeport, Connecticut, and Reading, Pennsylvania, followed. Of the forty-two socialist weeklies in 1916, one, *The Appeal to Reason*, had a circulation of one-half million. Socialist publishers, schools, and student organizations thrived. Many of the nation's intellectuals— men and women like Sherwood Anderson, Jack London, Carl Sandburg, Upton Sinclair, Helen Keller, and Margaret Sanger—put their talents in the service of socialism.

NO ROOM IN THE HOUSE OF LABOR

The key to the success of socialism lay in its relations with the AFL. Although there were still those in the party who believed that the conservative Federation could never be converted to socialism, the majority felt that the trade unions were valuable agencies for improving labor conditions and that socialists should remain in the AFL, join in fighting labor's immediate battles, and educate the rank and file.

AFL socialists had good reason for optimism. A significant proportion of the Federation's rank and file either belonged to or sympathized with the party. In 1893, the socialists won what seemed like a great victory at the Federation's annual convention. During that depression year the AFL delegates voted overwhelmingly for socialist resolutions calling for independent political action and the collective ownership of the means of production. At the 1899 AFL convention, Max Hayes, a socialist member of the Typographical Union from Cleveland, proposed that the AFL study the possibility of nationalizing major industries. In addition, sixteen national unions, including the Carpenters and Brewery Workers, supported a resolution committing the Federation to the collective ownership of the means of production.

Gompers himself had been an early sympathizer with socialism. As a young man he had been greatly influenced by Marxist theory but gradually came to believe that socialism could not work in the United States. As a young unionist he saw economic action as the means to develop solidarity among the working class which would lead to ultimate political power and social change. But the experiences of the labor movement by the end of the nineteenth century convinced him that the capitalist system was permanent. He perceived labor's best hope in the dilution of the power of big business and visualized a future in which management and labor, by mutual agreement, sought to eliminate evils in the economy through collective bargaining. His fear of concentration of power, which to him meant power over the workers, led him to oppose government intervention in economic affairs. Where the socialists saw unions as transitory institutions that would not be necessary in the workers' state, Gompers saw them as permanent agencies of defense for workers in a pluralistic state.

As long as the socialists in the Federation left their politics out of trade union affairs, they coexisted peacefully with Gompers. But the logic of socialist belief in the role of trade unions in the radical transformation of society inevitably put them on a collision course with Gompers. As early as 1903 the AFL leader lashed out at the socialists, during a convention debate on the nationalization of the means of production, "Economically you are unsound; socially you are wrong; and industrially you are an impossibility." Between 1903 and 1913 the bitterness between Gompers and the socialists grew. It culminated in 1913 when Max Hayes challenged Gompers for the presidency and lost. The high-water mark of socialist influence in the AFL had been reached. There and in society at large, the socialist tide began to recede. With it went the last great hope for the century-old dream of labor reformers, the cooperative commonwealth.

One of the central issues in the AFL-socialist conflict was the old controversy of industrial versus craft unionism. Although there had always been divisions among the socialists on tactics, they all agreed that for any real social and economic change to take place, the mass of industrial workers had to be organized. This sentiment found little sympathy among the leaders of craft-oriented trade unions. It is not surprising then that, blocked in the AFL, industrial unionism, dormant since the defeat of the American Railway Union, rose in particularly militant form on the left in the form of the Industrial Workers of the World (IWW).

INDUSTRIAL UNIONISM AND DIRECT ACTION

The path that led to the formation of the IWW, popularly known as the "Wobblies," began in the gold, silver, and lead mining regions of the West where a series of bitter strikes forged a spirit of radical industrial unionism. In the metal mining regions of Colorado, Montana, and Nevada conditions began to change dramatically in the last ten years of the nineteenth century. Once characterized by small, independent mines, an influx of eastern capital and immigrant workers transformed the industry. Technology intervened with the appearance of the machine drill that did the work of five hand drillers and reduced many of the skilled miners to shovelmen. The inevitable downward pressure on wages followed. Worker refusal to accept the cuts led to a series of lockouts around the mining town of Coeur d'Alene, Idaho, in 1892, where defeat by state militia and federal troops brought home the need for organization. As a result, the miners formed the Western Federation of Miners (WFM) in Butte in 1893.

The WFM was an industrial union. It planned to organize all workers regardless of skill in the metal mining and smelting industries. The appearance of the militant WFM resulted in a series of violent labor-management struggles. Strikes resembling class warfare occurred in Cripple Creek, Colorado; Leadville, Colorado; Coeur d'Alene, Idaho; and Telluride, Colorado, between 1894 and 1901. Somehow the union survived these miniature wars and had a membership of 50,000 by 1902.

Much of the leadership and the rank and file of the WFM was attracted to socialism. From the beginning, the union placed an emphasis on political action. But political attempts to win eight-hour legislation in the state legislatures failed. The union then took its fight to the bargaining table and the picket line. The movement culminated in the second Cripple Creek strike in 1903, a violent confrontation that led to numerous deaths and the arrest and forced deportation of hundreds of miners to Kansas and New Mexico.

With the strike lost, the WFM, now desperate and vulnerable, sought new allies. The AFL remained an option, but the WFM had earlier seceded from the Federation because of its refusal to give financial aid to the Leadville strikers. Reconciliation proved unattractive to the miners' leaders whose militant industrial unionism had become increasingly incompatible with the AFL's ideology. Instead of returning to the house of labor, the WFM moved toward a flirtation with a radical brand of revolutionary unionism called syndicalism, which advocated the organization of workers along industrial lines in order to seize and operate the nation's industries.

In 1905, the WFM and a diverse group of radicals and trade unionists, including Daniel DeLeon, Eugene Debs, Lucy Parsons (the widow of one of the Haymarket martyrs), "Mother" Mary Jones (the legendary United Mine Workers organizer), and others met in Chicago and founded the Industrial Workers of the World. William "Big Bill" Haywood of the WFM called the meeting to order as "the Continental Congress of the working class."

So much myth and exaggeration surrounds the history of the Wobblies that it is difficult to appraise their real importance in American labor history. Historian Patrick Renshaw attributes the fascination with the IWW to the fact that it ran counter not only to the mainstream of the American labor movement and American life, but of the whole of Western society. The IWW were, he argues, a romanticized embodiment of America's revolutionary heritage, a heritage that had long been buried by the inroads of modern industrial capitalism. As a labor organization they were a failure, but as one Italian anarchist poem reads, "Give flowers to the rebels failed." Not surprisingly, many who came after them were eager to give flowers to the "Wobblies," the failed rebels of America's revolutionary heritage.

The fundamental goal of the IWW was to form "one big union" of the working class. Though never long on theory, the Wobblies embraced a mixture of anarchism and syndicalism that rejected political action. They called for continual industrial organization and action, culminating in the total general strike that would paralyze the nation and deliver it into the hands of the workers' organizations.

Any organization founded by so many diverse elements was a prime candidate for internal dissension. Disputes began immediately. DeLeon was expelled when the undisciplined Wobblies refused to accept his brand of Marxist orthodoxy and rejected political action. Debs and the Western Federation of Miners left when the IWW's version of revolutionary syndicalism proved too strong even for their tastes.

What survived after the first few years of bickering was a radical, direct action group of syndicalists and industrial unionists. The IWW turned their attention to the categories of workers that trade unions had practically ignored: agricultural workers, immigrant factory workers, longshoremen, and lumbermen. Under the leadership of a group of colorful radicals like Elizabeth Gurley Flynn and Carlo Tresca, and dedicated organizers like Joe Ettor and Frank Little, the Wobblies waged free-speech fights on the West Coast; colossal strikes in the steel mills of McKees Rocks, Pennsylvania; the textile mills of Lawrence, Massachusetts; the silk mills of Paterson, New Jersey; among the harvest hands of the Great Plains; and against the lumber barons of the Northwest. They employed techniques like the sit-down strike, the slowdown, and the mass rally that would be used effectively in years to come by the CIO and the civil rights movement. They did it all to the spirited songs of Wobbly songwriters Joe Hill, T-Bone Slim, and Ralph Chaplin.

FRANK LITTLE

Though less famous than Bill Haywood, Vincent St. John, Elizabeth Gurley Flynn, and Joe Hill, no one deserves a place of honor in the IWW pantheon more than Frank Little. Born in 1879, the son of a Cherokee Indian mother and a Quaker father, Little was one of the radical faction of the Western Federation of Miners who defected in 1907 and joined the Industrial Workers of the World. He was jailed during the free speech fight in Spokane in1909. One year later in Fresno, California, he organized agricultural and construction workers, including Mexicans and Japanese. When Fresno officials prohibited street speeches, Little called for the Wobblies to pack the jail and after being brutalized and tormented by their jailers, the strikers forced the city to grant them free speech.

Little soon came to be one of the union's most militant and effective organizers. Wherever the need was greatest—among metal miners, lumberjacks, longshoremen, or agricultural workers—Frank Little got the call.

By 1916 he had risen to a position on the IWW executive board from which he led the fight against involvement in World War I. He attacked the war as a capitalist plot in which workers died and the rich prospered. His defiant opposition to the draft worried some in the IWW who feared that an antiwar stance could lead to the destruction of the union. Little responded that it was "Better to go out in a blaze of glory than give in."

In July 1917, he found himself in Butte, Montana, leading a strike of metal miners against the bitterly antiunion Anaconda Copper Company. The local newspapers railed against Little as a radical and a traitor to his country. On the night of August 1, six masked and armed men broke into his hotel room where Little, suffering from a broken leg, was beaten, taken outside, tied to the bumper of a car, and dragged several miles. He was then hanged from a railroad trestle with a note pinned to his pajamas that read, *First and last warning.* Not surprisingly, in the intense antiunion climate of the copper fields, no serious attempt was made to bring Little's murderers to justice.

Although its bark often proved worse than its bite, the IWW's revolutionary philosophy and fiery propaganda struck fear in the hearts of many Americans. Wobblies gained the reputation of violent revolutionaries, but most of the violence was committed against them. Employers used every method—legal and illegal—to crush the Wobblies. When the IWW refused to support American participation in World War I, they were branded as traitors. This brought the full force of the U.S. government down on them and a series of government raids and mass trials led to the crippling of the organization by 1920. Surprisingly, the IWW did have a brief renaissance after the war and even managed, under the most difficult of circumstances, to reach its highest membership ever by 1923. But by that time internal struggles between the syndicalists and Communists for control of the organization had sapped much of its vitality. By 1928 it had been reduced to a tiny band.

What, then, did the IWW contribute to earn it such a revered place in the pantheon of labor's heroes? Perhaps most importantly the Wobblies demonstrated that America's growing industrial working class—its immigrants and dispossessed—could be organized despite ethnic divisions and immense corporate power. Barriers of race, sex, and national origin disappeared in IWW strikes. The IWW, more than any other labor organization up to that time, made a determined attempt to organize black workers. A leaflet addressed to "Colored Workingmen and Women," promised, "if you are a wage earner you are welcome in the IWW halls, no matter what your color. By this you may see that the IWW is not a white man's union, not a black man's union, not a red man's union. All of the working class in one big union." One estimate puts black membership in the Wobblies at around 10 percent. Most of the success in organizing blacks took place among the dock workers of the East and Gulf coasts and the lumber workers of the South. In a number of strikes the union proved that racial differences could be overcome and black and white workers could stand together in solidarity. Throughout the organization's many trials and tribulations, a predominantly black longshoremen's local in Philadelphia provided the most stable source of funds.

The IWW also kept alive the radical spirit in American labor. Theirs was a uniquely American brand of radicalism, long on action and short on theory. The IWW also carried the banner of industrial unionism at a time when the AFL was increasing its craft consciousness. Finally, the Wobblies inspired generations of labor organizers to come with the record of its legendary struggles. Even today, the anthem of the American labor movement remains Wobbly Ralph Chaplin's hymn, "Solidarity Forever."

PART II
Growing Pains

The AFL also benefited from the upsurge of reform spirit in the Progressive Era. In spite of spirited challenges from the left, the Federation, under the steady hand of Samuel Gompers, grew dramatically at the beginning of the century. Unions made great gains in the building trades, railroads, printing, machine shops and coal mining. By 1904 the AFL claimed 1.675 million members, up from 265,000 in 1897. The Carpenters surged to 155,000, making them the largest craft union. Outside the Federation, the independent railroad brotherhoods and a few other independent unions represented 400,000 workers.

Even if the AFL appeared too timid for some socialists and the IWW, it certainly had not given up on militant trade unionism. Between 1900 and 1910, Federation affiliates carried out hundreds of strikes and boycotts. These actions were job-related economic disputes and their intensity sometimes led to violence. The McNamara brothers, leaders of the Structural Iron Workers, confessed to having dynamited the *Los Angeles Times* building in 1910 as a response to the vicious antiunion policies of the newspaper's owner. Twenty died in the bombing. Evidence showed that 150 buildings and bridges had been dynamited by the Iron Workers in their battles with the National Erectors Association over the hiring of nonunion labor.

While responsible labor leaders condemned the violence, a Chicago leader put it in perspective: "If a man says to me that the McNamaras should be condemned, my reply is: all right, we will condemn the McNamaras; but we will also condemn the Carnegies and the steel trust. If a man says to me that the iron workers union should be condemned, I say: all right, but we will also condemn the National Erectors Association. Before the union began to use dynamite their men lived on starvation wages, some of them on less than $400 a year, with families! . . . put on the searchlights and we are willing that our sins should be compared with the sins of the employers."

Amidst the turmoil the labor movement continued to grow. As the big unions, such as the Carpenters and the Machinists, became powerful institutions in their own right, their power in the AFL increased proportionately. The principle of exclusive jurisdiction cut both ways, depending on the power of the unions affected. When technology divided an old craft such as printing into several new crafts, a variety of new craft unions emerged, only, however, because the typographical union permitted it to happen. But when the same process affected a powerful but less tolerant member union, strength prevailed and the new unions were forced to surrender to the old. Behind the principle of craft autonomy lay a healthy dose of pragmatism and a recognition of the reality of power.

This pragmatism could be seen most clearly in the attitude toward industrial unionism. Although craft autonomy remained in the bedrock of the Federation, much of its dramatic growth during this period came as the result of the rise of industrial unionism in the coal mining and garment industries. Indeed, the resurgence of the mine workers was the most tangible symbol of labor's resurgence. Defeat after defeat had not dulled the miners' desire to unionize in the face of the oppressive conditions in the coal fields. "The story of coal is always the same," wrote Mother Jones. "It is a dark story. For a second's more sunlight, men must fight like tigers. For the privilege of seeing the color of their children's eyes by the light of the sun, fathers must fight as beasts in the jungle. That life may have something of decency, something of beauty—a picture, a new dress, a bit of cheap lace fluttering in the window—for this, men who work down in the mines must struggle and lose, struggle and win."

MOTHER JONES

Mary Harris Jones became the most famous woman in American labor history during a career of labor activism that spanned half a century. During coal strikes in West Virginia, Colorado, Ohio, Illinois, and Pennsylvania she challenged deputies, company police, and national guardsmen. Mother Jones's battalions of miners' wives, mothers, and daughters aided the strikers in many ways and were feared by law enforcement and company officials throughout the coal fields. Going to jail for picketing and harassing scabs became a routine experience for Mother Jones.

Although her greatest fame came as an organizer for the United Mine Workers, she also supported steelworkers at Homestead in 1892 and, during the great strike of 1919, and was in Chicago for the Pullman Strike of 1894. Mother Jones helped striking copper miners in Arizona in 1910 and took part in the strikes of New York City streetcar and garment workers during 1915 and 1916.

To dramatize the evils of child labor, Mother Jones led the famous 1903 "march of the mill children" from the strikebound textile mills of Philadelphia to the Oyster Bay, Long Island, home of President Theodore Roosevelt. When Mother's small band of sickly and often maimed child workers reached the president's estate, he declined to receive them. Although the march failed in its main purposes of raising money and bringing public pressure on the textile operators of Philadelphia to settle with the union, the incident did receive tremendous publicity and added to the growing legend of Mother Jones.

Employers and public officials alike feared her sharp tongue. She once characterized antiunion employers as "high-class burglars." When a Pittsburgh judge asked her who had given her the right to speak on behalf of striking steelworkers, she referred him to "Patrick Henry, Thomas Jefferson, John Adams." Accused of not being ladylike on another occasion, Mother Jones advised women, "No matter what your fight, don't be ladylike. God almighty made women and the Rockefeller gang of thieves made ladies."

An immigrant from Cork, Ireland, Mother Jones began her career as a labor organizer at the age of thirty-seven in 1867 when her husband and four children died in a yellow fever epidemic in Memphis Tennessee. Sixty-three years later she died and was buried in the miners' cemetery in central Illinois. At the dedication of her monument in 1936, 50,000 miners stood in silent tribute to Mary Harris "Mother" Jones, the miners' angel.

Ten years after their disastrous defeat in the Long Strike of 1875, the miners began to resurrect their union. Under the leadership of John McBride, the National Federation of Miners and Mine Laborers' success in Ohio led to the founding of the United Mine Workers of America (UMWA) in 1890. Eight years later, with the aid of Eugene Debs and Samuel Gompers, the union made a major breakthrough when operators in Illinois, Indiana, Ohio, and western Pennsylvania recognized the Mine Workers and granted the eight-hour day.

In 1898 a young Illinois miner named John Mitchell assumed the presidency of the union. Notwithstanding the successes in the bituminous fields, Mitchell realized that in order to survive, the union had to crack the antiunion bastion of the anthracite fields of northeastern Pennsylvania where John Siney's Miners National Association had met total defeat. There, scattered throughout the lovely mountain valleys, 145,000 miners toiled in semislavery. The anthracite fields were a hodgepodge of ethnic groups barely able to communicate with one another and kept divided in the dismal "patch towns" by the hated coal and iron police. For an annual wage of $250 they had to dig 4000 pounds of coal a day. Most of their wages returned to the company through the company store or rent for squalid company houses. Few ever saw any real money because payment often came in company scrip, redeemable only in the company store. Many never left the isolated valleys where they lived and worked, cut off by natural barriers and poverty from their brothers and sisters elsewhere in the region.

Mitchell's astonishing success under such difficult conditions gave the lie to those who despaired that the "dagoes" and "hunkies" as they were called could ever be organized. When the call of union rang down the valley's thousands responded. In 1900, 100,000 miners laid down their tools. A general public informed of the awful conditions under which the miners lived and worked gave its sympathy. Republican leaders, fearful of the repercussions of a coal strike in a nation in which anthracite was the major home heating fuel, counseled the operators to settle. Although the union got little of what it wanted, Mitchell accepted a weak settlement and prepared for the next round.

Both sides resented the agreement. The operators because they had been forced to acknowledge, if not recognize, the union, and the miners because there had been little change in their conditions. In 1902, the UMWA made new demands—union recognition, an increase in wages, and the eight-hour day. But this was not an election year and the operators, led by the Philadelphia and Reading Coal Company, were determined to smash the union.

President Theodore Roosevelt, worried about the effect of a winter without fuel, tried to bring the operators together with the union but was rebuked by the president of the Philadelphia and Reading Coal Company, George F. Baer, for "negotiating with the fomenters . . . of anarchy." Enraged, Roosevelt persuaded J.P. Morgan, whose bank had helped to finance the companies, to intervene or the mines would be seized. Under Morgan's direction the operators agreed to impartial arbitration of the strike by a seven-man Anthracite Coal Commission. The Commission's award proved to be a victory for the miners. Although formal union recognition did not come until 1916 in the anthracite fields, the settlement brought the United Mine Workers membership to 200,000 and made it the largest affiliate in the AFL.

The Mine Workers were an industrial union and their admission to the Federation in 1890 illustrated the pragmatism of Gompers and the leaders of the craft unions. Craft autonomy notwithstanding, the Federation saw the folly of turning down the additional revenue the UMWA offered. Had there been a way to divide the various craftsmen who worked around the mines among the existing unions, they would have preferred it. But the UMWA would not come in under any but industrial organization and was clearly strong enough to go it alone. Much the same kind of pragmatism applied in the ladies garment industry.

FERMENT IN THE NEEDLE TRADES

New York City was the center of the women's garment trade at the turn of the century. There, in crowded tenement sweatshops and small, dangerous, and crowded loft "factories," some 30,000 workers, mostly Jewish and Italian, and overwhelmingly women, toiled inhumanely long hours to make garments for American women. The work was seasonal and payment was by piece rate. Pauline Newman, a garment worker and union organizer described the world of the garment workers as one of "incredible exploitation of men, women and children. . . ."

> *The corner of the shop would resemble a kindergarten. We were young, eight, nine, ten years old. It was a world of greed; the human being didn't mean anything. The hours were from 7:30 in the morning to six-thirty at night when it wasn't busy. . . . My wages as a youngster were $1.50 for a seven day week. All shops were as bad as the Triangle Waist Company. When you were told Saturday afternoon . . . "If you don't come in on Sunday, you needn't come in on Monday," what choice did you have? And when the inspectors came around. . . . The supervisors made all the children climb into one of those crates that they ship material in, and they covered us over with finished shirtwaists until the inspector had left, because of course we were too young to be working in the factory legally.*

Conditions for effective unionization did not exist in the industry while garments were mostly made in tenement sweatshops. But a revolution in women's fashion changed all that. As increasing numbers of women began to work in America's offices, they went dressed in white shirtwaists and long, dark skirts. Shirtwaists came on the market about 1895. They were made largely by women working together doing specialized operations in garment factories. The closeness of the stifling working environment and the recognition of their common predicament provided the conditions under which unionization became possible.

Early attempts to organize the industry met with little success. Only a small cutters union, made up of skilled men, had any stability. In 1900, several weak locals of the largely Jewish Cloakmakers Union met in New York and formed the International Ladies Garment Workers Union (ILGWU). For nine years the union languished. But, in 1909, when the ILGWU struck the Triangle Shirtwaist Company because of its policy of firing union members, the frustration of the workers exploded. In response to company brutality against picketing women, 20,000 shirtwaist makers—most of them young Jewish and Italian women—walked off the job throughout the garment district. The "Uprising of the Twenty Thousand" lasted three months and resulted in little or no real improvements for the workers. But it did give expression to the rising working-class consciousness of both men and women on New York's Lower East Side and led to a successful strike by 60,000 cloakmakers in the summer of 1910—a strike that led to the unionization of the garment industry. The settlement, called the "Protocol of Peace," established orderly relations in the industry for a few years and gave the ILGWU security and the stability to grow.

Only one week after the New York settlement in the women's garment industry, the United Garment Workers of America struck the men's clothing firm of Hart, Schaffner and Marx in Chicago. Although the strikers won little, it was the first round of a struggle that led to the establishment of the Amalgamated Clothing Workers in 1914.

Even though the garment workers achieved a great deal, one terrible event showed the nation how much remained to be done. The workers of the Triangle Shirtwaist Company had failed to win their strike during the Uprising of the Twenty Thousand. Conditions in the factory were representative of the nonunion shops in the industry. Workers toiled for fifty-nine hours a week behind doors locked to keep workers in and union organizers out. Fire escapes from the shops located on the seventh, eighth, and ninth floors of the buildings were largely nonfunctional. When fire broke out on March 25, 1911, 146 workers, mostly young women, burned to death or died as a result of leaping from the windows in desperation. The outrage that followed the Triangle fire led to improved safety laws in New York and other states, but the fragmented and marginal nature of much of the industry made them difficult to enforce.

The struggles in the garment industry involved women to a greater degree than any others in labor history. These women were aided by an organization that represented the best of the reform spirit of the period. In 1903, a coalition of women trade unionists, social reformers, and wealthy supporters created the Women's Trade Union League. Women such as Jane Addams, leader of the urban settlement house movement; Rose Schneiderman, garment worker; Mary O'Sullivan, laundry worker; and Mary Kehew, Boston philanthropist worked together to improve the situation of women workers by organizing them into unions, educating them in leadership skills and lobbying for legislation to shorten hours and improve working conditions. The League played a major role in a number of strikes, including the Uprising of the Twenty Thousand. It convinced the Bureau of Labor to carry out an historic study of the conditions under which women and children worked, and its efforts led to the establishment of a women's bureau in the Department of Labor. Through the League the voice of working women was heard in the struggle for the right to vote for women.

BUREAUCRACY AND OPPORTUNISTS

The surge of growth not only gave the large unions more stability than they had ever known, it also changed their internal structures and began to alter the nature of trade unionism. Growth increased complexity and power began to flow gradually away from the locals toward the national headquarters. New labor market realities made this inevitable.

Union Staffs increased as operations became more specialized and complex. Labor leaders were no longer just first among equals. They were becoming administrators of complex organizations, and union hierarchies, like those in business, were becoming places offering regular, if precarious, full-time employment as salaries became common for officers and staff. In this environment, a few opportunists began to see the unions as a place to advance their personal fortunes, sometimes to the detriment of the interests of the members. Of paramount importance to this new breed of professional unionist was stability, not conflict.

The unionists shared this desire for stability and order with a growing number of businessmen who were beginning to see that working out an accommodation with a union could make financial sense. In some industries, mostly decentralized ones such as construction, employers reasoned that unions could act as a stabilizing force to ensure an orderly flow of workers and guarantee equal labor costs among competing firms. But cooperation had its darker side as well. In certain industries, union business agents and local officers had ample opportunity for corruption. Evils such as extortion and "sweetheart contracts," although engaged in by a tiny minority, began to tarnish labor's image. In 1897, the Contractors Association in Chicago entered into an agreement with a business agent for a number of carpenters' locals, granting the closed shop in return for the union's pledge not to supply labor for nonassociation members. The union thus helped to drive contractors who wouldn't join the association out of business whether or not they employed union labor. Pacts similar to this also appeared with plumbers, printers, bricklayers, and steamfitters. Some involved outright corruption. The Stonecutters Union of Brooklyn received 10 percent of the $600,000 in excess profits earned by the employer's association members as a result of the union's policy of striking independent companies which refused to abide by the association's price-fixing policy.

THE LOGIC OF ACCOMMODATION

Opportunities for collusion that led to scattered instances of corruption were part of a larger trend toward cooperation that went beyond opportunism and self-interest. A wider movement among various sectors of society to reconcile the differences between management and labor to reduce the dangers of class conflict provided the framework. Where unions did not exist, management resisted them with all of their resources. Where unions did exist, accommodation was sometimes seen as preferable to conflict. Given a choice between the moderate AFL and the rising threat of labor radicalism, a number of influential corporate leaders opted for conciliation rather than conflict.

Out of this spirit came the National Civic Federation. Founded in 1900 it included business leaders such as Mark Hanna, Republican Party Leader and associate of the Rockefellers and J.P. Morgan. Its goal was to provide a forum where industrial conflict could be settled without resort to strikes.

Hanna brought a number of AFL leaders—including John Mitchell of the Miners and Samuel Gompers—into the organization. Flushed with labor's successes during a period of prosperity and wary of their socialist challengers, these labor leaders accepted the premise that labor and capital had a mutual interest in the stability and growth of a progressive capitalist economy. But it was also likely that Gompers and Mitchell saw membership in the NCF as some measure of protection against the majority of business leaders who refused to recognize, let alone cooperate with, unions.

CONTAINMENT

In spite of experiments like the National Civic Federation, plenty of evidence exists to demonstrate that the great majority of business and political leaders had little time for unions. Instead of accepting labor's right to exist, they counterattacked. A multitude of employer associations sprang up under the banner of the open shop movement. They put forth an image of the employer as a victim of corrupt and radical labor leaders. In 1903, the National Association of Manufacturers (NAM) took command of the movement, attacking the closed shop as un-American. NAM's message flowed from church pulpits, newspaper editorial offices, and university and college classrooms. Lockouts became common. Employers cooperated to hire nonunion labor, employed spies, organized strikebreaking agencies to exploit black and immigrant labor, and offered financial aid to struck companies. Results came quickly. Labor suffered serious setbacks in the building trades, meat packing, and—most importantly—in steel.

A kind of climax of the antiunion campaign came in1914 at Ludlow, Colorado, where state militia in the pay of John D. Rockefeller's Colorado Fuel and Iron Company attacked a tent colony of striking coal miners and killed sixteen, including two women and eleven children.

The courts proved to be the employers' most important allies. They supplied frequent injunctions against strikes and key judicial decisions restricting workers' rights. In particular, they stripped labor of one of its most effective weapons, the boycott. Unions had been able to gain recognition from a number of employers by persuading their members and sympathizers to refrain from buying products that did not carry the union label or, in more immediate circumstances, were made by companies that either refused to recognize unions or were on strike.

In 1902, the United Hatters Union called for a national boycott of the products of the D.E. Loewe and Company of Danbury, Connecticut, in support of a strike by a local union. The company sued for damages charging the union with conspiracy in restrain of trade in violation of the Sherman Antitrust Act. Following fourteen years of litigation, the federal court ruled for the company and assessed the union a quarter of a million dollars in fines and costs. The decision brought secondary boycotts under the ban of the Sherman Act and also made individual union members liable for damages.

Even as the Danbury case dragged through the courts, the AFL became embroiled in an even more significant dispute. In 1906 the AFL placed the Buck's Stove and Range Company of St. Louis on its "We Don't Patronize" list in support of workers striking for the nine-hour day. J.W. Van Cleave, president of the company and also president of the National Association of Manufacturers, secured an injunction restraining the officers and members of the AFL from putting his firm on the boycott list and from calling attention to the strike either orally or in writing. When Gompers refused to comply with such a sweeping limitation on his First Amendment rights, the court found him in contempt and sentenced him to a year in prison. Gompers never served his sentence and ultimately the Supreme Court dismissed the case.

The assault shook the AFL and gave ammunition to Gomper's foes in the Federation, especially the socialists, who argued that the antiunion drive gave proof that American business would never accept the legitimacy of unions and that Gompers's conciliatory approach had been proved a failure. Gompers was able to beat back the challenge, but the business and government assault did cause the AFL to rethink its position on political action.

PROGRESSIVE ALLIANCE

The Federation had never been out of politics, but its nonpartisan policy to reward labor's friends and punish labor's enemies was based on the reality of the decentralized American political system. Allegiance to one party ran against the principle of craft autonomy as well. The various affiliates were deeply involved in politics; but they made their political choices depending on which party could do them the most good at the state and local levels.

But in 1906 the labor movement presented "Labor's Bill of Grievances" to Congress. It called for, among other things, exemption of labor from the antitrust laws, and an end to the use of injunctions in labor disputes.

Congress largely ignored labor's appeal and this rebuff spurred the AFL to take an active part in the 1906 congressional campaign. In 1908, representatives of the Federation made labor's case before the platform committees of both major parties. The Republicans wanted none of it, but the Democrats were receptive and in the presidential campaign labor's unofficial support went to William Jennings Bryan, the unsuccessful Democratic candidate. Labor expanded its role in 1912. Many in the movement argued for Eugene Debs, the Socialist Party candidate, but the hostility between the socialists and the majority of craft unionists precluded any alliance. Instead most Federation unions threw their support behind Woodrow Wilson, the scholarly Princetonian and Democratic candidate. With the Republicans split between the "Bullmoose Party" of Theodore Roosevelt and the loyalists of William Howard Taft, Wilson became the first president in history on whom labor had any legitimate claim.

Of course, the labor movement, in concert with progressive allies, had contributed to significant legislative gains for working people before Wilson's election. Progressives naturally concerned themselves with labor problems because the evils that they identified with had their most visible impact on working people. By 1917, most states had enacted minimum age and maximum hours legislation for children under sixteen. Maximum hours laws for women became common. In the wake of the Triangle Fire, many states strengthened factory safety legislation. In some states, workmen's compensation laws removed the responsibility for industrial accidents from the injured worker. The attempt to pass strong maximum hours legislation for adult men foundered, partly because of the AFL's lack of support.

With Wilson in the White House federal reform came for children, railway workers, and seamen. Despite opposition from the textile companies and the National Association of Manufacturers, Congress passed the Owens-Keating Act in 1916 forbidding the movement in interstate commerce of goods manufactured using child labor. The LaFollette Seamen's Act provided comprehensive protection for workers at sea. In 1916, under the threat of a nationwide strike by the railway brotherhoods, Wilson pushed the Adamson Act through Congress granting the eight-hour day for railroaders. In addition, the president showed his gratitude for labor's support by implementing legislation passed during his predecessor's administration and establishing the Department of Labor with William B. Wilson, a member of the miners union, as Secretary of Labor.

Labor's top legislative priority remained relief from injunctions in labor disputes. What appeared to be a great victory came with the passage of the Clayton Antitrust Act. Gompers called it labor's Magna Carta because it seemed to exempt unions from injunctions issued by federal courts under the nation's antitrust laws. Time proved, however, that this had been a false hope. Loopholes in the law ultimately rendered it of little value to labor.

PART III
Gentlemen Carpenters

Two major ideas dominated the organization of the American labor movement from the beginning. One called for a unionism that would transform American society into some form of cooperative commonwealth. The other strain saw the labor movement as a more limited weapon. It stressed protection of workers on the job and concerned itself with immediate gains that could be measured in the worker's pay envelope, in his or her occupational safety, and in the number of hours he or she toiled.

It would be wrong to see these ideas as distinctly separate. They were never mutually exclusive and for the most part they coexisted to one degree or another. Yet by the first decade of the twentieth century, the organization of the American labor movement reflected this division more than at any other time in history.

Because of study by historian Robert Christie, it is possible to view this drama as it was played out in one union, the United Brotherhood of Carpenters and Joiners. The conflict came to a head amid the widespread technological and social change that transformed the United States in the late nineteenth and early twentieth centuries. The protagonists were Peter J. McGuire, founder and historic leader of the Carpenters—a first-generation Irish American and a lifelong socialist—and the pragmatic young professional trade unionists emerging in the carpenters.

In many ways, the carpenter was the aristocrat of workers. Part engineer, part architect, and proud of his status, he treasured his skills and the traditions of his craft. He worked in an unstable industry vulnerable to speculative financing, marginal operators, the weather, and the uncertainty of the business climate. Without permanent employers to give him security, his union provided stability and to it he gave his first loyalty.

Before 1915 the union consisted of a collection of proud, autonomous locals. Collective bargaining took place at the local level and the national union concentrated on protection of the trade's jurisdiction. To the members, jurisdiction meant simply that anything made out of wood was carpenters' work.

Historian Christie paints a compelling portrait of these singular crafts-men.

There appeared in The Carpenter *of July, 1914, a picture of the carpenters who had erected the L.C. Smith Building. They stood on the roof of the completed building, a score or so of walrus-mustachioed old-time carpenters, glowering at the camera. Almost without exception, they had on under their overalls, stiff collars, ties and tie pins. They all wore white shirts, suit coats, and bowlers, derbies, or slouch felt hats. Those without overalls had gold watch chains and fobs stretched across their abundant middles. Their day, perhaps has passed. The attire certainly has. But it goes a long way toward symbolizing the old-time carpenter's craft pride and character; he came to work attired like his boss. He took pride in neither wearing gloves nor getting his hands very dirty. He worked with his hat on—at the day's end he took off his overalls, folded them atop his tools in the toolshed, washed his scarcely dirty hands, straightened his tie, tipped his bowler a bit more jauntily, and sought out the nearest bar.*

These men were Peter J. McGuire's carpenters. Symbols more of what had been, than what was to be. Even as they posed, the world of work they knew had largely passed away.

As early as the 1870s new technology began to alter the trade. Some jobs of carpenters began to disappear from the construction site as doors, windows, and other fixtures began to be manufactured in factories by "green hands" operating the new sanders and compound carvers. At the job site, the standardized fixtures could be installed by "outside green hands" who worked on piece rates. The carpenters saw their trade divided into a number of simplified tasks. To counter this threat they organized their union.

Standardization and piecework changed the industry. Where earlier the carpenters worked for the independent contractor directly, now the middleman entered the scene. He bid on the entire job and then subcontracted the specialized tasks to others who in turn hired "green hands" at low wages. The old-line carpenters directed their anger not at the exploited pieceworkers but at a system directed by speculators, middlemen, and capitalists that had little regard for craftsmanship and dignity—only for speed and profit. The carpenters saw their plight as no different from that of other workers who were being ground down by the same inexorable process. Their solution, and the solution of Peter J. McGuire, was the radical transformation of society.

As a socialist McGuire saw the union's role as organization, agitation, and education. Collective bargaining served only to protect the interests of workers and to bring them to an understanding of their common problems. Once this class consciousness developed, the union would provide the organizational framework for revolutionary change. Consequently, the day-to-day operations of industrial relations could be left to the locals. For the national union, whose chief responsibility was education, no elaborate bureaucracy was necessary.

But all of McGuire's pronouncements about the evils of capitalism did nothing to protect the carpenters from piecework and the middlemen. Only union control of the job site could ensure that only carpenters did carpenters' work. This required full-time union representatives who could keep watch over construction and who had the power to call strikes when they discovered the presence of "green hands." Such was the beginning of the "walking delegate," later known as the business agent.

But no one local could afford such service. The solution lay in the creation of district councils of locals. Banded together the various locals could afford the services of a full-time business agent. The district council added something else to the union—an intermediate administrative level between the members and the national. By 1890 there were twenty-six district councils, and the increased complexity of the industry required that more and more power gravitate away from the locals to the districts.

The business agent became the personification of this new power. Increasingly, he took on a variety of duties. He negotiated contracts, acted as liaison with the other building trades, and became the central figure in regulating the labor market. The agent alone possessed comprehensive information about the many jobs scattered throughout the district's jurisdiction. Almost out of necessity he served as a labor contractor. By ensuring contractors a stable labor force and by doing away with piecework, the business agent took the place of the middleman. In the process he became indispensable to management and labor alike.

McGuire saw the evils of piecework, but he did not perceive that someone had to perform the role of middleman in the industry. The union's survival depended on its control of that key function. Rather than transforming the system, the carpenters were becoming an integral part of it. The result was business unionism.

The business agent differed from traditional trade union leadership in an important way. He was a professional—a far cry from the old timers who had served their unions and often broke their health for little or no financial reward. He represented the first of the permanent trade union administrators. The agent built his career in the union and although he came from the ranks, he saw his new position as a step up the career ladder, not a temporary assignment from which he would one day return to the trade.

Consider the gulf between these modern trade unionists and the old, radical McGuire. As late as 1891 he still saw the role of unions as educating the working class "to prepare it for the changes to come, to establish a system of cooperative industry in place of the wage system, to emancipate the workers from subjugation to the capitalists. . . ." According to Christie, when McGuire stood on a platform with the new professionals, "nineteenth and twentieth-century trade unionism met. Like oil and water, they did not mingle."

McGuire resisted the growth of a union bureaucracy because he believed it would dampen the activism of the workers. He feared that they would lose their self-reliance and turn into passive dues payers who would soon surrender their historic role as leaders of the working class. The old leader consistently blocked the growth of the union's administrative structure. He continued to run the executive office of the largest union in the AFL as if it were still a small, loose amalgamation of autonomous locals. "Workmen have no use for complicated machinery with intricate cogs and wheels in labor organizations," he said. "The simpler it is the better [it is] understood."

But McGuire's creaky, small administrative structure did not provide the career opportunities to which the new professionals aspired. More importantly, the structure was no longer functional because of rapid technological change in the woodworking industry. Increasingly factory workers did what carpenters once had done. They did it in factories outside the cities where they were beyond the reach of the union's district councils. These mill workers could only be organized through cooperation between a number of district councils. This required more administrative centralization and coordination, not less.

Centralization in the industry also spurred the union to centralize its operations. Alarmed by union gains, contractors in the heavily unionized big city markets began an antiunion offensive. In 1887 the National Builders Association assumed control of the movement and the union began to see its eight-hour strikes go down to defeat. A weak federation of local unions could not hope to match the combined power of a national federation of employers.

Those who urged professionalism and centralization faced a painful dilemma. In order to carry out the necessary changes they had to attack McGuire, and to many of the rank and file, McGuire *was* the union. While McGuire had sentiment and loyalty on his side, technological developments proved to be his worst enemy. In the space of a few years the appearance of structural steel, reinforced concrete, new riveting processes, the elevator, and new engineering advances ushered in the era of the skyscraper. This revolution in construction affected the carpenters in several ways. It changed the major employers from small contractors to large regional or national construction companies because of the cost involved in building the huge new structures. By 1911, Samuel Gompers estimated that only a dozen or so large construction companies built the majority of modern office buildings in the United States. Because skyscrapers were standardized buildings, they created a demand for specialized carpenters. Out of this came a number of new unions, such as the ceiling woodworkers. Entirely new crafts such as sheet metal work appeared, some of which involved new materials that replaced wood. Finally, the importance of the woodworking mills increased because the standardized fixtures used in skyscrapers could be mass produced cheaply. As the number of mill workers grew, a new union, the Machine Wood Workers International Union, claimed jurisdiction.

All of these problems were national problems and required a national solution. No amount of rhetoric about the cooperative commonwealth could make them disappear. Present in all of the problems were threats to the United Brotherhood's jurisdiction. McGuire responded to these challenges without undue alarm. First, he did not necessarily think it a good thing that the Carpenters Union should grow. A bigger union meant a bigger bureaucracy, which would lead to a watering down of the union's real purposes—agitation and education. His opponents argued that if the Brotherhood did not aggressively protect its jurisdiction against the new unions, it would die. McGuire did not fear this. He did not see the survival of one particular union as overly important. He cared only that the new categories of workers were unionized, no matter what the union. What was important to McGuire was the labor movement—the solidarity of all workers in a class conflict with the owners of capital. Over the objections of the professionals then waging an organizing battle with the Machine Woodworkers, McGuire signed an agreement giving jurisdiction over the planing mills to the new union.

The struggle between McGuire's idealistic brand of reform unionism and the needs of the modern business union lasted for ten years. In the end, the pure and simple unionists triumphed, and McGuire was ousted by the Carpenters in 1902.

The Carpenters Union emerged with a centralized administrative structure with paid, full-time staff and organizers, a convention system which placed power in the hands of large locals, and a rigid and aggressive jurisdictional philosophy that concentrated on the survival and growth of the Carpenters union first, and the interests of the labor movement second.

WILLIAM HUTCHESON

The man who dominated the Carpenters Union after McGuire came to symbolize orthodox and successful craft unionism more than any other AFL leader. "Big Bill" rose through the ranks as an organizer, business agent, and second vice-president. He later admitted that his election to the latter office in 1913 was rigged. Hutcheson moved up to first vice-president later the same year when the incumbent resigned. Hutcheson's good fortune continued when two years later the president, James Kirby, died of food poisoning, leaving "Big Bill" with the top spot. Hutcheson held the post for thirty-six years.

Under Hutcheson's leadership the Carpenters prospered. He built his power in the union on the bedrock of jurisdictional protection. Under his direction the Carpenters did little organizing of their own. "Big Bill" preferred to claim jurisdiction after other unions had done the organizing. He fought with the Amalgamated Woodworkers over lumbering and sawmills, with the Sheet Metal Workers over metal trim, with the

Machinists over heavy machinery, and with the Iron Workers over piles, docks, and window frames. To the old-time carpenters, anything made out of wood had been carpenters' work. Under Hutcheson everything *ever* made out of wood was carpenters' work. "God created the forests," went one saying, "and he gave them to Bill Hutcheson."

After establishing unchallenged control over the Carpenters, Hutcheson became the leader of the building trades unions that made up the most powerful element in the AFL. As the leading Republican in the house of labor, he was labor's bridge to the conservative presidents of the twenties. His obsession with defending the Carpenters' jurisdiction made him a bitter foe of industrial unions. Indeed, according to one observer, "Only one aspect of the United Brotherhood changed after 1920. That was Hutcheson's power, which grew in almost geometrical progression." As a successful man he joined the Elks and Masons and the Chamber of Commerce, bought a farm in Ohio and wintered in Florida. When he retired in 1952 he passed the presidency of a strong and thriving union on to his son who held it for twenty years.

DISCUSSION QUESTIONS

1. Consider why socialism achieved its greatest influence in the United States from 1890 to 1914.
2. How did the syndicalism of the Industrial Workers of the World (IWW) differ from the ideas of both the socialists and the pure unionists?
3. As unions grew larger and more successful, their bureaucracies grew as well. This led to an increase in professionalization in the labor movement. Discuss the implications of this for the nature of trade union leadership.
4. How did craft union emphasis on control of the labor market sometimes create opportunities for the rise of corrupt union officials?
5. Why did the business agents of the carpenters union challenge Peter J. McGuire's conception of the union? What does the controversy reveal about the transformation of the labor movement at the turn of the century?

KEY WORDS AND PHRASES

Progressive Era
Socialist Labor Party
Socialist Party of the USA
Eugene V. Debs
Industrial Workers of the World

International Ladies Garment
  Workers Union
Triangle Fire
Women's Trade Union League
Business Unionism

William Haywood
McNamara Brothers
Mother Jones
United Mine Workers
John Mitchell
Anthracite Strike of 1902
Uprising of the Twenty Thousand

National Civic Federation
Danbury Hatters Case
Bucks Stove and Range Case
Labor's Bill of Grievances
Clayton Antitrust Act
Peter J. McGuire
William Hutcheson

BIBLIOGRAPHY

The material for this section was drawn largely from:

Christie, Robert. *Empire in Wood: A History of the Carpenters' Union.* Ithaca: The New York State School of Industrial and Labor Relations, 1956.

Green, Marguerite. *The National Civic Federation and the American Labor Movement, 1900–1925.* Washington: Catholic University of America Press, 1924.

Jones, Mary (Harris). *Autobiography of Mother Jones.* Chicago: Kerr, 1925.

Kenneally, James. *Women and American Trade Unions.* St. Albans, Vt.: Eden Press, 1978.

Laslett, John M. *Labor and the Left: A Study of Socialist and Radical Influences in the American Labor Movement, 1881–1924.* New York: Basic Books, 1970.

Ligenfelter, Richard. *The Hardrock Miners.* Berkeley: University of California Press, 1974.

Lipset, Seymour Martin, "Trade Unionism and the American Social Order" in Seymour M. Lipset, *The First New Nation.* New York: Basic Books, 1963.

Morris, James O. *Conflict Within the A.F. of L.: A Study of Craft versus Industrial Unionism, 1901–1938.* Ithaca: Cornell University Press, 1958.

Quint, Howard H. *The Forging of American Socialism: Origins of the Modern Movement.* Indianapolis: Bobbs-Merrill, 1964.

Renshaw, Patrick. *The Wobblies: The Story of Syndicalism in the United States.* Garden City: Anchor Books, 1968.

Selvin, David. *Sky Full of Storm: A Brief History of California Labor.* Berkeley: University of California Center for Labor Research, 1966.

Taft, Philip. *The A.F. of L. in the Time of Gompers.* New York: Harper & Row, 1957.

Van Tine, Warren R. *The Making of the Labor Bureaucrat.* Amherst: University of Massachusetts Press, 1973.

Wertheimer, Barbara. *We Were There: The Story of Working Women in America.* New York: Pantheon, 1977.

For additional reading see:

Brody, David. *Steelworkers in America: The Non-Union Era.* Cambridge: Harvard University Press, 1960.

Cornell, Robert J. *The Anthracite Coal Strike of 1902*. Washington, D.C.: Catholic University Press, 1957.

Dubofsky, Melvin. *We Shall Be All: A History of the Industrial Workers of the World*. Chicago: Quadrangle Books, 1969.

Henry, Alice. *Trade Union Woman*. New York: D. Appleton, 1915.

Kornbluh, Joyce. *Rebel Voices: An I.W.W. Anthology*. Ann Arbor: University of Michigan Press, 1968.

Seretan, Glen. *Daniel DeLeon: The Odyssey of an American Marxist*. Cambridge: Harvard University Press, 1979.

Stein, Leon. *The Triangle Fire*. Philadelphia: Lippincott, 1962.

SECTION
FIVE

PART I
War on Two Fronts

The period from the turn of the century to American entry into World War I was, on balance, a good one for the labor movement. Membership grew, as did labor's political influence. Most important, labor's central institution, the AFL, achieved stability. Continued employer hostility notwithstanding, the old pattern of constant defeat seemed a thing of the past.

Much of this new climate reflected the fact that, since the turn of the century, critics of big business had been relentlessly attacking corporate America as impersonal, monopolistic, greedy, and amoral. Out of this criticism grew the basic framework for increased government participation in the management of the twentieth-century American economy. The financial panic of 1907 had demonstrated the need for a central banking system, and, in response, Congress created the Federal Reserve System in 1913. Few at the time realized its potential to affect the direction and functioning of the economy. The adoption of the Sixteenth Amendment in the same year gave the government a new income-taxing power with a similar potential. In 1914, Congress established the Federal Trade Commission to police unfair business practices.

However, effective as these reforms were, they did not reflect anything like a serious disillusionment among the majority of Americans with the economic system. On the eve of the great war, most Americans had a great deal of confidence in the system's ability to adapt and meet new challenges. They took considerable pride in the fact that the Ford Motor Company had developed a revolutionary assembly-line technique for mass producing automobiles, and that its enlightened management had inaugurated an unprecedented forty-hour week and a $5-a-day-wage. Farmers, too, were enjoying relative prosperity. The only negative sign was the mild recession that plagued the economy during 1913 and 1914.

A heightened government role in the economy had largely occurred because of a desire to curb the excesses that had resulted from the tremendous private economic power of big business. But the intensification and spread of World War I soon changed the relationship between big government and big business. Defense preparation and then-active participation in the hostilities brought government and business into partnership.

Well before American entry into World War I, the United States had become the "Armorer of the Allies." War orders pulled the economy out of the slump of 1913 and 1914 and initiated a decade and a half of business growth and prosperity. Military expenditures during the four years of war approached $80 billion. In all, the United States bore one quarter of the cost of the Allied war effort, but profits more than balanced the account. Indeed, while the government called on all segments of society to sacrifice during the period of American involvement, business declined the responsibility. Profits soared to an all time high. Even *The Wall Street Journal* felt compelled to scold the steel industry for "utterly indefensible" profits, and the president of the McKinney Steel Company candidly stated that he was "making more money out of this war than the average human being ought to."

The magnitude of wartime production transformed a number of industries. Electricity and chemistry led to technological breakthroughs resulting in more efficient machinery. Whole new industries such as motion pictures, radios and telephones, and household appliances assumed major importance as the result of scientific research carried on during the war.

Technological innovation and the increase in size and complexity of industry accelerated the change in the nature of work. New machinery led to simplified, standardized operations. By war's end, the most numerous group of workers in the major metal working industries were specialized, semiskilled machine operators. Between 1915 and 1920 this category increased by 40 percent a year in the automobile industry. A 1923 survey of the industry found only 9 percent in the skilled trades and less than that performing common labor.

For some of these new workers, the war provided a step up the occupational ladder. Women flocked into jobs once reserved for men. They became telegraphers and messengers, elevator operators, and factory workers. For a woman, welding paid a great deal more than domestic service or the drudgery of the garment factory. As white women were drawn to the better-paying jobs, black women began to replace them in the traditionally female occupations.

The war also brought black workers to the industrial centers of the North. The slowing of immigration and the draft created tremendous labor shortages. This movement of rural blacks constituted one of the great internal migrations in the nation's history. The migration had begun before the war because of depression and hard times in southern agriculture, but it accelerated with the outbreak of hostilities in Europe. Between 1910 and 1920 the black population of Chicago increased from 44,000 to 109,000. Similar statistics applied for Philadelphia, Cleveland, Detroit, and other cities. The largest increase of black workers took place in steel, automotive, mining, shipbuilding, and meatpacking. By 1920 there were 901,181 black industrial workers, nearly double the 1910 figure.

DECADE OF CHANGE

Rapid changes in technology and business organization were perfected during the postwar decade. The application of electricity to production allowed for the even distribution of power through the great plants, and productive capacity expanded enormously as a result. The continuous processes of the conveyor belt and the assembly line became cost efficient. The resulting standardization provided the perfect conditions for the application of the techniques of scientific management, especially time and motion studies and incentive pay schemes. This led to an increase in factory discipline and a dramatic increase in supervisory personnel.

Electricity also permitted the transmission of power over long distances leading to the beginning of a dispersal of American industry to the outskirts of the city and to rural areas now that factories no longer needed to be near the traditional sources of water and coal power. This, along with electrified trolly lines and the growing popularity of the automobile, had the effect of breaking down the sense of community that had developed in the working-class neighborhoods of the old industrial cities and towns. Dispersal also changed the working class in another significant way: workers not familiar with unionism, and who came out of the conservative setting of rural and small-town America, moved into the factories.

Indeed, the movement from farm to town was another of the striking demographic changes of the 1920s. Between 1920 and 1929 some twenty million Americans left the land as a result of depressed conditions in agriculture and the mechanization of the farm. This influx of new workers held down wages and retarded unionization. Ideal conditions existed to use these new workers. The shortage of skilled labor during the war created a situation in which technology became cheaper than skilled manpower. Great wartime and postwar profits provided a pool of investment capital that was used to finance the frenzied mechanization of the 1920s. Results were dramatic. Output per man-hour, or productivity, rose 72 percent in manufacturing during the decade. While it is true that this resulted in a rise in national income of approximately 6 percent a year, the real gains showed up in salaries and dividends, not in wages.

Not only was there a dramatic change in the personnel of American industry, but also in the distribution of occupations. While manufacturing employment remained stable, and even declined in industries such as mining and lumbering, white-collar employment surged ahead by 45.7 percent. The dramatic increase in the service sector brought millions of women to work. By 1930, some 10.6 million workers, almost one in four, were women. This represented an increase of 20 percent over 1920.

While all of these factors put pressure on the traditional white male force, and especially on the unionized portion, there were also trends in the other direction. Child labor declined and by 1930 had dropped to 667,000, 53 percent below the 1920 figure. As skills declined and experience counted for less, older workers became expendable.

It has already been noted that immigration slowed to a trickle during the war. After a brief surge in the immediate postwar years, this traditional labor supply was permanently reduced by restrictive immigration laws in 1921 and 1924. The total number of immigrants dropped 70 percent between 1914 and 1925. With the end of mass immigration, ethnic divisions began to break down, English became more widespread, and foreign-born and American workers began to draw together.

For the most part, real hourly wages remained stable during the 1920s, but there were marked differences between skilled and unskilled workers. Women, immigrants, and blacks continued to suffer severe income discrimination. One manufacturing survey in 1929 placed the average hourly earnings of male, skilled, and semiskilled workers at 67¢, of male unskilled, 50.3¢, and of all females, 40.1¢. There also existed a significant difference between union and nonunion wages. Stability did not signify prosperity. According to a Brookings Institution study, 21 percent of all families had incomes of less than $1000, and 70 percent had less than $2500. This came at a time when the estimated poverty level for a family of four was $1000 to $1100. The seeming disparity between these figures and the general overall prosperity of the period can be explained by the extraordinary imbalance in the distribution of income. By 1929 the combined incomes of the top 1 percent of Americans equalled those of the bottom 42 percent.

Still, for those who had stable jobs in the 1920s, the standard of living improved. It was the growing white-collar class and the elite of the working class who fueled the consumption of automobiles, motion pictures, radios and telephones, refrigerators, and stoves, which gave the "Roaring Twenties" their popular image. The explosion of consumer goods symbolized the good life to an increasing number of Americans; as the producers and purveyors of these new technological wonders, the businessman, the industrialist, and the financier became the high priests and pied pipers of American life.

DEFENDERS AND DISSENTERS

The vehicles carrying the business elite to its dominant position in American society were the great corporations. While mechanization led to economies and a soaring rate of productivity, the maldistribution of income meant that markets did not expand at the same rate. Workers could not consume at a rate to match productive capacity because employers had taken the opportunity to lower labor costs as a factor of production. This led to the threat of ruinous competition. Under this pressure a great wave of mergers took place and many markets that had once been competitive became monopolistic.

The new corporate goliaths grew tremendously in the 1920s and, as they grew, they came to dominate most areas of American life. New technologies that the big corporations had made available, such as radio and motion pictures, brought Americans everywhere under the influence of the business community. So effective were their public relations that Frederick Lewis Allen, the social historian, wrote that "the overwhelming majority of the American people believed with increasing certainty that businessmen knew better than anybody else what was good for the country." Small wonder then that when a president of the United States declared that "the business of the United States is business." many saw nothing odd about the statement.

Nevertheless, there remained skeptics and outright dissenters. If American business triumph appeared complete by 1929, it did not come without opposition. There were those on the radical left and in the trade union movement who gave battle for other versions of the American dream. American business turned its attention to the task of eliminating these bothersome critics.

As soon as American industry assumed the role of supplier to the Allied war effort, American radicals, most of whom opposed the war, became exposed to charges of being unpatriotic. As American involvement grew and led to direct participation in the war, attacks on the radicals grew more intense and the charges were expanded to include treason. The main victim was the IWW, which was systematically harassed and destroyed by a coalition of government and business. But antiwar socialists and advocates of industrial unionism also suffered grievously.

On July 22, 1916, during a "preparedness parade" sponsored by the antilabor San Francisco business community and patriotic societies to encourage the strengthening of American military power, a bomb exploded, killing ten people and leaving scores injured. Arrested for the crime were Tom Mooney, a molder and leader of the left wing in the California labor movement, and Warren Billings, a radical member of the Boot and Shoe Workers Union. Both were convicted in a trial shot through with suspicions of unfairness, if not outright rigging, by employer associations. Radicals, the AFL, and others concerned with the impartial administration of justice, mounted a protest campaign that became one of the key struggles of the epoch. Even though later findings discredited the trial, the two remained in prison until 1939, when they were pardoned by Culbert Olson, the governor of California.

The high point of the government's antiunion campaign came with the arrest of Eugene Debs for publicly stating that "The master class has always declared the war, the subject class has always fought the battles. The master class has had nothing to lose, while the subject class has had nothing to gain and all to lose—especially their lives." Debs entered prison in April 1919, well after the end of the war he had so determinedly opposed. Despite appeals for clemency from the great and humble alike, Woodrow Wilson refused to free him. Ironically, Debs had to wait for the action of a conservative Republican president, Warren Harding, to regain his freedom. Debs proved that he still spoke for a significant number of Americans when he ran for the presidency from Atlanta Federal Penitentiary in 1920 and captured almost one million votes.

POSTWAR UPHEAVAL

The repression of dissent during the war created a surface calm that barely lasted past the armistice. The confluence of two more or less unrelated circumstances led to an industrial explosion that shook the nation to its very foundations. The first occurred in Russia where the Bolshevik revolution turned the czar's empire into the world's first socialist state. The events in Russia were to have a profound effect on the relation of forces everywhere, but their immediate effect in the United States was twofold: they pumped new life into the battered and beleaguered socialist movement, and they threw a scare into the leadership of the world's leading capitalist nation.

The second circumstance had little to do with events in Russia, but was rather the result of the frustrations of American workers brought on by the inequality of sacrifice during the war. This led to an outbreak of strikes on an unheard-of scale; almost eight and one-half million workers struck in 1919 alone. For the radicals who believed they were no longer condemned to utopian theorizing but rather were riding an irrepressible historical tide, the discontent of the industrial working class appeared to be the first shot in the long-predicted revolution. Many businessmen and government officials read the signs in a similar way, but with quite a different conclusion. They saw no inevitable historical tide and they were determined to smash this challenge to their power ruthlessly. Although these leaders talked a great deal about the threat of revolution for public consumption, the real threat they perceived was the threat of the unionization of the industrial workers in the heart of American corporate power—the mass-production industries. In an important sense, the Bolshevik revolution and the resurrection of American radicalism that followed it gave business a convenient justification to crush the industrial uprising. The efforts of labor organizers could automatically be discredited in the eyes of a jittery American public by labeling them Communists, or more commonly, Bolsheviks.

The turbulent year began shortly after the armistice when 60,000 Amalgamated Clothing Workers, led by Sidney Hillman, struck for three months and won the forty-four-hour week and a 15 percent raise. Hard on the heels of the garment strike, a radical-led general strike paralyzed Seattle when 60,000 workers walked out in support of striking shipyard workers. Carried away with their brief taste of power, the leaders of the Seattle strike, many of whom were socialists and Wobblies, created a workers' council of striking unions and unwisely called it a "soviet." Although the strike lasted only four days, news of the "revolution in Seattle" captured the attention of the country. The fact that similar "soviets" appeared briefly in several other cities did nothing to calm the fears. Soon, events in Boston, although in no way connected with any radical movement, convinced many Americans that the warnings of impending conflagration were to be taken seriously.

On September 9, 1919, the Boston police, dissatisfied with low wages and poor working conditions, and forbidden to form a union and affiliate with the AFL, went on strike. It was the first widely reported police strike in American history and it received an overwhelmingly hostile reception from the public. President Wilson blasted the walkout as a "crime against civilization." But the man who made the most capital out of the strike was the obscure governor of Massachusetts—Calvin Coolidge—whose ringing statement that "there is no right to strike against the public safety, by anybody, anywhere, anytime," launched him on the road to the White House.

Boston, Seattle, and a score of other strikes in other cities created the environment of hostility for the labor movement in which the great steel strike of 1919 took place. Important as they were, the other strikes were sideshows compared to the confrontation in steel. It was there that the battle lines were drawn between capital and labor, there that the pattern of industrial relations for the next decade or more was set. And it was there that the forces of unionism would battle United States Steel, the largest financial colossus that the world had ever seen. The conflict in steel was the first battle in a war that continued for over twenty years—the climactic phase of the old struggle to organize the workers created by the Industrial Revolution.

Elbert Henry Gary led the corporate legions in the steel strike from his position as Chairman of the Board of U.S. Steel. As early as 1901, Gary had proclaimed U.S. Steel's determination to run an open shop. He believed, along with many of his business contemporaries, in the divine rights of employers. Workers' interests, in the opinion of Gary, were best left in the hands of "the employers, the capitalists, those having the highest education, the greatest power, and influence." With Gary's paternalistic philosophy as its guideline, U.S. Steel took the lead in instituting welfare capitalism. Stock options, bonuses, improved safety, and recreation gave the company a progressive image. But the gloss of paternalism could not hide the fact that steelworkers toiled twelve-hour days for wages that an impartial study showed left 38 percent of them below the subsistence level in postwar America.

The man chosen to lead the strike was a young AFL organizer named William Z. Foster. Foster came out of the IWW, but a trip to Europe had exposed him to the tactics of the French syndicalist unions that had discarded independent action and "bored from within" to capture their country's General Confederation of Labor. In order to translate this tactic into American terms, Foster had to come to grips with the AFL.

As an industrial unionist, he realized that the cautious craft unions of the Federation could not be persuaded to support the organization of industrial workers unless their own jurisdictional interests were protected. Without AFL support he thought little would be possible because the only money for organizing industrial workers lay in the treasuries of the large craft nationals. In order to overcome this problem he fashioned an organizing strategy called "amalgamation." He proposed that a variety of unions claiming jurisdiction in the industry cooperate in a joint organizing drive, then divide the workers into separate craft locals. The key to Foster's plan rested on a new level of union organization. For purposes of collective bargaining, the separate craft locals would be federated into an industry council, with its own executive board and staff. In essence, during collective bargaining, strikes, or organizing drives, the industry council would act as an industrial union. But for membership purposes, the workers could still belong to the appropriate craft unions.

Foster had earned the opportunity to try his plan in steel because of his dramatic success along with John Fitzpatrick, president of the Chicago Federation of Labor, in organizing the Chicago packinghouse workers in 1917. It was the first real victory in a mass-production industry. The steel campaign began slowly using the universal appeal of the eight-hour day to rally support. Soon the industry became aware of the activities of the small, underfunded National Committee for Organizing Iron and Steel Workers. Company officials in league with handpicked city and county officials banned organizers and suspended free speech in the steel towns. Constitutional guarantees were so flagrantly disregarded that Mother Jones felt compelled to ask "whether Pennsylvania belongs to Kaiser Gary or Uncle Sam?" "Jesus himself could not speak in Duquesne for the AFL," according to the mayor of that Pennsylvania town. Thousands of union sympathizers received discharge notices. As the momentum built the companies prepared for a strike as if they were going to war. By the day of the walkout, 25,000 coal and iron police, deputized by local authorities, ranged the Monongahela River from Pittsburgh to Clarion.

But these were old tactics, and while they slowed the union drive, they did not stop it. The issue that the company skillfully used to discredit the movement was communism. Already uneasy because of the events in other cities, the public took heed when company propaganda warned that this was no ordinary labor dispute, not just a struggle for the eight-hour day, but the beginning of a Bolshevik revolution in the United States.

Yet with all of the obstacles, 350,000 steelworkers were on strike by the end of September. Company repression intensified. Strikers and their families were terrorized. Particular attention was paid to sowing dissension among the myriad of ethnic groups that made up the workforce. Forty thousand black strikebreakers were imported and put to work. State police openly sided with the companies against the "red menace."

In the campaign for the hearts and minds of the American people, the companies had full reign. By and large, the press became little more than an arm of the industry's public relations effort. Scare stories about the activities of Bolsheviks appeared regularly. *The New York Times* justified the illegal arrest of hundreds of aliens as a way to ensure that the strike would not be used as a means of "advancing bolshevism."

Against this onslaught, the organizers had only the lukewarm support of the AFL unions. To wage a battle that Foster estimated required $2 million a week for relief payments alone, they had less than $\frac{1}{2}$ million for the entire strike. The twentyfour unions officially involved in the drive gave just one-fifth of that total. Significant support came only from the International Ladies Garment Workers, the Amalgamated Clothing Workers, and the Furriers. As Christmas approached, it became clear that the strike was failing, and in January the National Committee called off the strike and told the men to return to the mills if the companies would have them.

RED SCARE

With the industrial conflict as background, the anti-Communist, anti-foreign hysteria began to spread to the larger society in a brief rampage historians have labeled "The Red Scare." On November 7, 1919, Department of Justice agents raided the headquarters of IWW and Marxist groups in a number of cities. Almost 2000 were arrested in New York alone. Two months later another wave of raids netted thousands of Wobblies, Communists, Socialists, and hapless aliens. At the peak of the hysteria, 556 aliens with radical connections, no matter how tenuous, were summarily deported without protection of due process aboard a ship the press dubbed the "red ark."

The coordination of the mass raids lay in the hands of A. Mitchell Palmer, Attorney General of the United States. It is no wonder that lower officials such as J. Edgar Hoover, future director of the FBI, showed so much zeal for radical hunting if the nation's chief law enforcement official could write that "like a prairie fire the revolution was sweeping over every American institution of law and order."

NICOLA SACCO AND BARTOLOMEO VANZETTI

All the antiradical, antilabor, and antiforeign sentiment of the period of the Red Scare came to be symbolized by the fate of two immigrant Italian radicals. Sacco and Vanzetti, one a shoe cutter and the other a fish peddler, lived in the Boston area. Vanzetti has been blacklisted after leading a successful strike of rope and twine workers. Both men proudly proclaimed their revolutionary anarchist views.

On May 5, 1920, just before holding a rally in Brockton, Massachusetts, to protest the suspicious death of an anarchist friend while in the custody of federal department of justice agents, the two anarchists were arrested and charged with the murder of a paymaster and guard during a payroll robbery at South Braintree three weeks before.

In a trial in which the judge characterized the defendants as "conscious of guilt as murderers or as slackers and radicals"—a reference to their antiwar views during World War I, the jury brought in a verdict of guilty and the judge imposed the death sentence. "By systematic exploitation of the defendants' alien blood, their imperfect knowledge of English, their unpopular social views, and their opposition to the war," wrote future Supreme Court Justice Felix Frankfurter, "the district attorney invoked against them a riot of political passion and patriotic sentiment; and the trial judge connived at—one had almost written cooperated in—the process."

For the next six years the case became an international *cause celebre*. Demonstrations and strikes in support of the condemned men took place in many American cities and in Warsaw, Cairo, Havana, Rome, and Moscow, to name just a few. When the men were executed in August 1927, a quarter of a million protesters marched in Boston, and 150,000 paraded in front of the American embassy in Paris.

The two immigrants immortalized themselves with their last words:

Only two of us will die—our ideas, you, our comrades will live by millions. We have won. We are not vanquished. Just treasure our sufferings, our sorrows, our mistakes, our defeat, our passion, for future battles for the great emancipation. We embrace you all and bid you an extreme good bye. Now and ever, long life to you all. Long live Liberty.

WAR ON THE LEFT

The Red Scare dealt an almost fatal blow to American radicalism. It is doubtful if the left could have resisted successfully even if it had been strongly united, but fratricidal warfare among the radicals rendered them helpless in the face of the massive assault. The split among American radicals followed the Russian revolution. After the early euphoria American radicals, like Marxists everywhere, began to define their positions according to their attitudes toward what lessons the Bolshevik revolution held for their country. Although personal ambition and pride played a role in the argument, simply stated the basic issue was whether the best road to socialism lay in the revolution or electoral activity. This was an old conflict in the American left, but events in Russia sharpened the issue. The supporters of revolutionary action, always a minority in the socialist movement before 1919, could now point to the success in Russia to support their position. Claiming to be in the vanguard of history, the revolutionaries made many converts. The moderates, while generally supportive of the Soviets, argued that conditions in the United States were vastly different from those in Russia, a semifeudal country with an absolute monarch, and that here education of the masses for political action offered the best hope.

Crucial to the debate were the two factions' attitudes toward the labor movement. Seeing the revolution as close at hand, the Communists advocated a militant, revolutionary labor movement under the tight control of the Party. The moderate socialists held to the old goal of winning the unions to an electoral alliance with the Socialist Party in a broad social democratic movement. In the emotional atmosphere of the time, their differences proved irreconcilable and after a strident and often violent fight, two new parties—the Communist Labor Party, with the famous journalist John Reed as one of its leaders, and the Communist Party of the United States—were formed in 1919 by advocates of the revolutionary path who split from the Socialist Party. Eventually the groups, both of which rejected what they considered the timid reformism of the Socialist Party, were brought together in 1921 under orders from the Communist International (COMINTERN) in Moscow.

With these massive defections, the Socialist Party, already battered during the war and decimated during the Red Scare, ceased to be a major factor on either the industrial or political scene. Eugene Debs' death in 1926 seemed to symbolize the decline of what only a decade before had appeared to be a robust and viable political movement. For the next thirty years the Communists held sway as the main organizational expression of Marxist thought in the United States.

By the early 1920s, it became clear that the Communists had made a major error in their evaluation of the chances for revolution. Everywhere in Western Europe the tide of revolution was turned back and Russia, instead of being the first of many socialist states, turned out to be an encircled outpost. Reaction, not revolution, seemed everywhere as fascism, not socialism, came to Europe. Surrounded by hostile neighbors, their economy in shambles, the leaders in the Kremlin changed directions and sent out the word that Communist parties everywhere in the world were to forge alliances with other progressive groups, no matter how moderate. For

American communists this meant reevaluating their antagonism toward the AFL.

Under these circumstances, circumstances that had little to do with events in the United States, the Communists resurrected William Z. Foster's strategy of "boring from within." Disillusioned with the defeat in steel and impressed with the Bolshevik revolution, Foster had cast his lot with the Communists in 1921. Foster brought with him the Trade Union Educational League (TUEL), which he had formed to work within the AFL to convert it to industrial unionism. At the time this did not seem an entirely hopeless undertaking. Foster's idea of "amalgamation" as a back door to industrial unionism had supporters in the Federation, most notably among the garment workers. There were other hopeful signs as well. At the 1920 AFL convention, the railway unions pushed through a resolution, over Gompers's objection, calling for nationalization of the railroads.

But the leaders of the Federation soon began to realize that the real target of the zealous radicals was pure and simple unionism. TUEL activities led to rank-and-file movements in a number of affiliates. In 1923 Samuel Gompers unleashed the full force of the AFL against the Communists. The affiliates expelled thousands of TUEL members. The fiercest fight took place in the socialist-led garment unions, where the larger struggle between Communists and socialists increased the bitterness. Everywhere the Communists were routed. In the United Mine Workers, John L. Lewis "red baited" a progressive challenge to his leadership and drove both Communists and progressives out of the union.

The defeat of the Communists had larger implications for the AFL. It put a stop to the growing sentiment for industrial unionism which, through guilt by association, became identified as a Communist-led movement and was thus easy to discard. Even industrial unions like the International Ladies Garment Workers, which had fought off a Communist-led rank-and-file movement of their own, gave anticommunism a higher priority than preaching industrial unionism to the craft unions. TUEL did lead several major strikes in which Communist organizers displayed their skill and courage battling bitterly antiunion employers in places like Passaic, New Jersey, and Gastonia, North Carolina, but once expelled from the house of labor, the organization had no real purpose anymore. Another change of position in Moscow simply gave theoretical justification to what in the United States was already an accomplished fact. "Boring from within" was dead and buried.

In 1929, world communism went on the offensive again. Old allies were discarded and the emphasis returned to dual unionism. TUEL was replaced by the Trade Union Unity League, a proposed federation of independent industrial unions that was to compete with the AFL. It existed largely on paper, and only one affiliate—the Furriers—achieved any stability and permanence. Isolated and weak, cut off from any practical influence with the working class, the Communist movement in the United States became more and more dependent on fraternal direction from the Soviet Union. Decisions in Moscow based on conditions in Europe made little sense when applied in the United States. In the process, the Communist Party lost the independence of thought and action that might have made it more able to adjust its strategy to the realities of the American scene. This proved to be a fatal flaw that would haunt it for most of its history.

THE AMERICAN PLAN

The antiunion campaign of 1919 had relied primarily on the tactic of smearing union activities as alien attacks on the American way of life. But during the 1920s this rather crude tactic was refined in a number of ways. A mixture of the old and the new, it emerged in more sophisticated form as the American Plan. The content of the American Plan was not new, but the method of selling it was. A revolution in advertising and public relations techniques began before the war, but never had propaganda been so skillfully employed as it was by the government to win the public's support for the war effort. "The war taught us the power of propaganda," said one businessman. "Now when we have anything to sell to the American people we know how to sell it. We have the school, the pulpit and the press."

What the American Plan sold was the old argument that collective bargaining and the closed shop were un-American because they limited the worker's right to contract individually for the sale of his or her own labor and because they interfered with the rights of private property. American Plan associations spread throughout the nation under the leadership of the National Association of Manufacturers and the Chamber of Commerce. Propaganda flowed to ministers, teachers, newspapermen, politicians, and judges. Scores of lobbyists fought proworker legislation and supported the use of injunctions. Emphasis on the one side was placed on the theoretical rights of workers. The American Bankers Association announced that every man should be allowed to "work out his salvation and not . . . be bound by the shackles of organization to his own detriment." On the other side labor leaders were depicted as either radical or corrupt. In a flight of hyperbole, John E. Edgerton, president of the National Association of Manufacturers, denounced "The palatial temples of labor whose golden domes rise in exultant splendor throughout the nation, the millions of dollars extracted annually by the jewelled hand of greed from the pockets of wage earners and paid out in lucrative salaries to a ravenous band of pretenders." He bemoaned this "pitiful story of a slavery such as this country never knew before," and urged his fellow industrialists to "break the shackles that have been forged upon the wrists of those who labor with you by showing them in your daily contact and attitude that you are their best friends and that it is not necessary for them to follow the false leadership of designing pirates who parade in the guise of workingmen's friends."

Industrialists had no compunction about helping their workers to resist the blandishments of unionism. Yellow dog contracts flourished. A.M. Glassbrenner of the Indiana Manufacturers Association voiced the general sentiment when he declared that "we will not employ an individual that does not sign an individual contract in which it is expressed that he is not and will not become a member of a labor organization in our employ." Business did not hesitate to use the boycott for its own purposes. Bethlehem Steel refused to sell steel to contractors in New York and Philadelphia who hired union labor.

Where unions existed, companies allocated whatever resources they felt were necessary to defeat them. Strikebreaking agencies did a booming business. The Erie Railroad paid one agency $2 million to break the 1920 switchmen's strike, and one AFL estimate put the number of company spies active in 1928 at 200,000. The director of one labor espionage agency outlined their functions:

> First: *I will say that if we are employed before any union or organization is formed . . . there will be no strike and no disturbance. This does not say that there will be no unions formed, but it does say that we will control the activities of the union and direct its policies. . . .*
>
> Second: *If a union is already formed and no strike is on or expected to be declared . . . we could—and I believe with success—carry on an intrigue which would result in factions, disagreement, resignations of officers and a general decrease in membership; and, if a strike were called, we would be in a position to furnish information. . . .*

The other side of the American Plan involved the flowering of welfare capitalism. Improvements in safety and working conditions accompanied stock options and profit sharing. Personnel departments expanded and psychological testing of prospective employees became commonplace. Employee social clubs and sports teams, company-sponsored classes in homemaking and English, and other manifestations of welfare capitalism proliferated. All were used to reinforce the idea that the workers' interests could best be cared for within the "family" of the firm.

Welfare capitalism, the American Plan's benevolent side, did nothing to address the issue of power. There were people who recognized the contradiction of the authoritarian organization of business enterprise in a society based on popular rule. These reformers, largely outside the ranks of labor, supported the industrial democracy movement that began during World War I. The movement's goal did not differ fundamentally from those other attempts to make the worker part of the industrial "team." Its professed aim was to turn the workplace into a model of the larger democratic society, to enfranchise the workers and provide for real codetermination of rules and policies. Even President Woodrow Wilson, caught up in the need for labor and management cooperation during the war, called for "a genuine democratization of industry." In fact, much of the impetus for industrial democracy grew out of the government's intervention in the economy during the war. Wartime cooperation between management and labor in various special agencies, such as the War Labor Board, seemed to herald a change in the old pattern of industrial relations. The characteristic form for industrial democracy was modeled after the plan developed by the Colorado Fuel and Iron Company after a strike in the Colorado coal fields in 1914. Called Employee Representation, it consisted of works committees on which management and elected representatives of the workers discussed common problems and grievances. Such plans existed in more than 200 firms by the end of 1921. Enthusiasts called the experiments nothing less than a revolution in industry.

But if one looks closely at industry's acceptance of the reform, it becomes apparent that they had other motives as well. The greatest application of the idea came during World War I, after the government required war-related industries to bargain collectively with their employees. In order to comply with the letter of the order, rather than its spirit, General Electric and some 125 other companies created Employee Representation Plans, or as labor called them, company unions.

Company unions had no independence. Their bylaws prohibited bargaining for wages and working conditions. Company grievance procedures did not provide for impartial arbitration. Indeed, for all issues considered by the Employee Representation Plans, management remained the final authority.

In the final analysis, whatever the positive goals of reformers who were searching for a means to bring harmony to industry, the fundamental purpose of employers was to prevent the growth of independent trade unionism.

PATRICK HENRY McCARTHY

McCarthy epitomized the tough craft unionists who rose to prominence as leaders of the building trades in the first quarter of the twentieth century. Born in Ireland on St. Patrick's Day in 1863, McCarthy arrived in the United States in 1880 as a carpenter's apprentice. Along with Peter J. McGuire he played a role in founding the United Brotherhood of Carpenters and Joiners. He then moved on to San Francisco where he became president of the Carpenters local and in 1898, president of the San Francisco Building Trades Council, a job he held for the next twenty-four years.

McCarthy wielded the Council into a powerful force in the political life of San Francisco. He was elected mayor in 1909 on the Union Labor Party ticket. Under his leadership, the Building Trades Council was able to impose its own code on the city's construction industry. Only union men worked construction in the city and they handled no materials that had not been prepared by other union men.

The system held until wartime inflation drove wages up substantially. In the midst of the antiunion drive after the war, the employers went on the offensive. Employer associations presented a united front. When McCarthy refused to accept an arbitrator's decision on a union demand for higher wages, the employers replied with a lockout and told the men they could only return under the open shop. Backed by business pledges of a million dollars, the employer associations enthusiastically backed the "American plan."

Beaten and demoralized, McCarthy urged acceptance of the employers' terms, but a rank-and-file referendum rejected it. When a general strike failed, the men returned to work at lower wages and under the open shop. The employers maintained their hold for more than a decade by hiring nonunion men and by setting up their own system of trade schools to train new craftsmen.

Patrick McCarthy, his power gone, resigned and used his talent to become a successful contractor and investment banker. He died in 1933.

PART II
Under Siege

After the optimism of the Progressive Era, the decline of the 1920s came as a shock to the labor movement. All the more so because the first world war seemed to signal the entry of labor as a full partner in American economic life. According to historian Simeon Larson, the war offered labor the opportunity to convince employers that trade unions, "far from being a liability to business, could aid in increasing productivity and . . . act as a preventative to the rise of more radical elements among the workers."

For Samuel Gompers, winning the war took precedence over everything else. Gompers viewed the war in Wilsonian terms, as a struggle to make the world safe for democracy. He rejected economic determinism as a cause of the conflict and blamed it instead on German militarism. Victory, he believed, would lead to an increase of political democracy everywhere. Gompers saw no connection between American involvement and the interests of American business. To him the war, after American entry, became "the most wonderful crusade ever entered by men in the whole history of the world." Gompers believed that cooperation would lead to legitimacy and increased power for unions. Above all, labor would be judged by its role in the war effort.

But there were those who did not share his idealistic assessment. Many on the American left interpreted the war as a capitalist struggle for world markets. American industrialists, they argued, were no different from their counterparts abroad in their willingness to shed workers' blood to further their interests. This difference in assigning blame for the war increased the tension between the socialists and Gompers within the Federation, as well as with the independent and antiwar IWW. The increased isolation of the radicals on the war issue helped Gompers to defeat them in the AFL. Thus, he hoped, further legitimizing the Federation in the eyes of the business community. As for the IWW, Gompers urged the War Department to crush the Wobblies because of their "arrogant disregard of constitutional and common law."

DREAMS OF PARTNERSHIP

Although the AFL's enthusiasm for cooperation was not shared by much of the business leadership, the determination of the Wilson administration to eliminate industrial conflict during the war gave labor hope that there existed a new willingness on government's part to balance the scales. The establishment of the War Labor Board seemed to confirm this judgment. It included equal representation for business and labor, supported the right of workers to form unions, protected unions where they already existed, and prohibited lockouts. In return, labor surrendered the right to strike for the duration.

Much has been made by historians of labor's cooperation during the war. But the record shows that labor was at best a junior partner in the business-labor-government trinity. Labor representation was limited to those wartime agencies dealing with labor disputes. Agencies controlling the awarding of contracts lay firmly in the hands of business and finance. While AFL membership rose from 2.37 million on January 1, 1917, to 3.26 million one year later, most of the increase resulted not from organization but from the growth of already unionized companies. Indeed, the steel companies let it be known that they had counted on AFL assurances to the government that no attempt at organization would occur while the war lasted.

Nor did unions uniformly adhere to the agreement to forego the closed shop in return for government acceptance of union wages and hours. This ran into considerable opposition from the building trades for which the closed shop, according to William Hutcheson of the Carpenters, was the "foundation upon which all other conditions rested." These unions disregarded the no-strike pledge in order to seize the opportunity to increase craft control of jobs. Five citywide general strikes took place during the war, most of which involved building tradesmen.

In truth, there was no labor peace in the period. More strikes occurred than in any previous period of similar length. During the years of American participation in the war, 4 million workers struck. Although many were in nonunion shops, the majority were not. Clearly a number of workers and local labor leaders did not totally accept the bargain with the Wilson administration.

These strikes did not imply a rejection of Gompers's stand on the war. They were economic and job control strikes involving issues such as the enforcement of work rules, union recognition, and the regulation of layoffs and dismissals.

There were also significant changes in the goals of the strikes and their organization. Many took place in the mass production industries. Shop committees developed in the metals industries in order to coordinate action by the various trades. Particular resentment surfaced to incentive pay systems and time-and-motion studies. The tight labor market gave workers the leverage to assault these pillars of the industrial efficiency movement. Workers demanded wage standardization according to job classification instead of piece rates. Employers resisted, preferring individualized pay systems like the one at the H. H. Franklin Company of Syracuse, which set "scientific" wages on an individual basis by evaluating each worker's output, attendance, spoiled work, "cooperation and conduct," and fourteen other behavioral variables.

After the rash of lost strikes in the immediate postwar period, labor militancy declined dramatically. Much of this can be attributed to the rising unemployment that accompanied the depression of 1920 and 1921, but after recovery, the old pattern of labor's resurgence in times of prosperity did not follow. In part, this happened because of the success of the American Plan and welfare capitalism. But it also reflected labor's reluctance to give up on cooperation long after it had become functionally obsolete.

The AFL's conscious decision to try to extend the wartime spirit of cooperation to the postwar period left them few weapons with which to resist the business onslaught. Even the Federation's historic refusal to link wages to productivity was laid aside. The *American Federationist* admonished its readers that "Trade unions must cooperate actively with management to promote high productivity, elimination of waste and lower cost of production in organized establishments."

In the midst of the travail of the 1920s, Samuel Gompers died. The selection of William Green as his successor demonstrated that there would be no break with the more conservative Gompers's line of the later years. Green, out of the United Mine Workers, was a compromise candidate acceptable to the two most powerful affiliates—the Miners and the Carpenters. He was a humane and honest man whose personal habits and tastes reflected the middle-class respectability that the AFL sought. Above all, Green was an organization man, a team player, and a master of what John L. Lewis called the policy of "anxious inertia." His selection as successor to the dynamic and decisive Gompers meant that power would flow away from the presidency to the Executive Council dominated by the strong craft unions. Green signaled his adherence to the policy of cooperation soon after his election by declaring that "More and more organized labor is coming to believe that its best interests are promoted through concord rather than by conflict."

To be sure, there were several examples of successful cooperation. The Baltimore and Ohio Railroad and the Railroad Brotherhoods established joint management-worker shop committees to improve efficiency, grievance handling, working conditions, and wages. In 1925, the Amalgamated Clothing Workers and Hart, Schaffner and Marx agreed to permit the union to take over shop discipline in order to increase efficiency. The plan worked well and a number of nonunion shops were organized as a result, but as efficiency increased the number of workers declined. A particularly interesting experiment took place in the Rocky Mountain Fuel Company where a progressive company president—Josephine Roche—recognized the United Mine Workers, established a cooperative productivity plan, and appointed a union official as vice-president of the company.

RESTLESS RANK AND FILE

But cooperation had few successes largely because business had little use for it at a time when the heart of American industry remained unorganized. Nor were the new realities of the labor market reflected in the AFL. Black workers remained largely unorganized. For the most part, they found work in the mass production industries where they were relegated to unskilled jobs. According to one steel mill foreman, "They [blacks] are well fitted for this hot work, and we keep them because we appreciate this ability in them. . . . The door machines and the jam cutting are the most undesirable, it is hard to get white men to do this kind of work." No institution—be it government, union, or business—did anything during the period to ease racial discrimination. Even during the skilled labor shortage of the war years, the number of black craftsmen actually declined. Much of the responsibility for this lay with the unions, which kept blacks out of apprenticeship positions, with the concurrence of management.

The explosive conditions created by the friction between black and white workers became all too clear in the race riots in East St. Louis, Illinois, on July 2, 1917. The use of black strikebreakers set off the trouble. Instead of attempting to organize the new workers, the St. Louis trade unions mounted an antiblack campaign to restrict further migration to the city. The resulting riot left thirty-nine blacks and eight whites dead.

Events in East St. Louis brought the gravity of the situation home to the leaders of the AFL, and the Federation went on record in support of the organization of blacks at its 1917 convention. But very little happened, causing blacks to organize several short-lived unions of their own during the war.

The crux of the problem of the admission of blacks to the ranks of organized labor lay, as it always had, with the AFL's member unions. Gompers had frequently reaffirmed the necessity of organizing black workers, but after the turn of the century he was reluctant to try to force the affiliates to conform to the Federation's policy on the issue. By 1930 the National Association for the Advancement of Colored People (NAACP) estimated black trade union membership at only 50,000; half of those were in the all-black Brotherhood of Sleeping Car Porters founded by A. Philip Randolph in 1925.

A. PHILIP RANDOLPH

In 1925 a small group of black sleeping car porters in New York City decided they needed a union. Previous attempts had failed because the

Pullman Palace Car Company had always managed to discover and fire the prounion porters. This time they decided to look outside of their ranks for a leader. They found a thirty-six-year-old Harlem socialist and accomplished street corner orator named A. Philip Randolph, who at the time was also the editor of the *Messenger,* a radical journal supporting black civil rights.

Randolph was born in Crescent City, Florida, in 1889. Like many southern blacks of his generation, Randolph moved north to escape the oppressive environment of legal segregation in the South. He arrived in New York City in 1911 and set out in search of an acting career. In 1917, after studying economics at City College and the Rand School and becoming a socialist in the process, he started the *Messenger* with another young black radical named Chandler Owen. His experiences in New York taught him that the *de facto* segregation of the North was little better than what he had left behind in Florida.

Burning with the desire to improve the condition of blacks, Randolph accepted the offer from the sleeping car porters. In August 1925, he called the first public meeting and began the Brotherhood of Sleeping Car Porters with himself as general organizer and the *Messenger* as the union's official publication. Handsome and dignified, Randolph was, in spite of his age, a majesterial figure. His oratorical skills were legendary and he became the most eloquent spokesman for the aspirations of black Americans. Over the years Randolph made the Sleeping Car Porters, a small union of several thousand workers, into the keystone of a movement for racial equality in America.

In 1941, he organized the March on Washington that led to the creation of the Fair Employment Practices Committee. He became a vice-president of the AFL-CIO in 1955, was one of the founders of the Negro-American Labor Council, and its president from 1960 to 1966. As the principal black spokesman within the AFL-CIO, he frequently clashed with George Meany and other labor leaders over the discriminatory practices of some unions, but he always remained loyal to the AFL-CIO. When the black civil rights movement emerged in the 1950s and 1960s, Randolph held an honored place as an elder stateman of the long struggle for black equality.

Much the same attitude applied to women. The influx of women into the wartime industries did not alter the Federation's basic attitudes shared with virtually every other institution in the United States. The Executive Council endorsed equal pay for equal work and urged that women be organized, but the chief motivation was to prevent low women's pay from undermining wage rates.

Labor's record of organizing women can be seen from the fact that while the female labor force increased 27.4 percent to 10.4 million in the 1920s, the absolute number of women in unions declined. And where women were organized in large numbers, as in the garment unions, men invariably held most of the leadership positions. The Womens Trade Union League took the lead in organizing women. With League encouragement, a summer school for women workers began at Bryn Mawr College under the direction of Hilda Smith. In addition, the League led or aided several strikes in the 1920s, some of them in the bitterly antiunion South.

But very little change came. Women operated under many of the same handicaps as blacks. They labored in industrial and service jobs that were most resistant to organization. They also had to fight a stereotype. Where blacks were considered fit only for backbreaking and menial jobs, women were considered above labor. James J. Davis, Secretary of Labor, expressed this attitude in 1924 when he wrote that "all will agree that women in industry would not exist in an ideal social scheme. Women have a higher duty and . . . I personally prefer to see a woman guiding the destiny of the nation in the home."

BACK TO INJUNCTION LAW

Bad as its internal problems were in the period, they were nothing when compared to the beating the courts gave the labor movement in the 1920s. Many of the gains of the progressive era were swept away in a series of court cases that left labor little better off legally than it had been a century before. Limitation of child labor and minimum wage laws for women fell by 1925. It also quickly became evident that the antiinjunction provision of the Clayton Antitrust Act provided no protection at all. The courts consistently held that the loophole that permitted injunctions to prevent irreparable injury to property or property rights applied to most strikes and boycotts. Most of the trouble developed out of a decade of decisions concerning the Hitchman Coal and Coke Company of West Virginia and the United Mine Workers. In 1907, Hitchman sought an injunction to stop the union from interfering with the individual employment contracts its employees had signed. Up to then, courts did not consider these agreements contracts at all because, aside from the fact that workers had no choice but to sign them, either party could break them unilaterally, the worker by quitting or the company by dismissal. But in the Hitchman case, a federal judge ruled that yellow-dog contracts were legally binding and issued an injunction against a UMWA organizing drive. The Supreme Court upheld the ruling in 1917, but government policy during the war restrained other companies from taking advantage of the ruling. After the war, however, a sweeping injunction in the Red Jacket Coal case gave protection to the contracts and virtually eliminated anything the union could do to organize the mines.

The assault continued in 1921 when the Supreme Court found in the

Duplex case that the Machinists Union's attempt to have its locals refuse to install equipment made by a company whose workers were on strike constituted an illegal secondary boycott and was in violation of the Clayton Act. By the end of the 1920s it was difficult to say with any certainty just what was legal for unions to do.

CHANGING POLITICAL LANDSCAPE

The intensity of the antiunion campaign led many activists in the labor movement to look to independent political action again. Out of the diverse grievances of midwestern farmers, socialists, survivors of Progressivism, and trade unionists, a new political movement developed. Labor parties appeared in New York and Chicago and more widely in several industrial states. Farmer-labor coalitions appeared in North Dakota and Minnesota. In 1922, largely through the initiative of the independent railway brotherhoods, representatives of these groups met in Chicago and formed the Conference for Progressive Political Action. The Socialist Party, seeing the movement as the embryo of a new labor party, threw its energies into the new movement. The Communists, initially favorable because they were still in their popular front stage, were once again caught by a change in the line from the COMINTERN in Moscow that viewed the Progressives as largely an agrarian movement. After a disasterous attempt to form their own third party movement, the Communist Party withdrew from any attempt at coalition building and ran its own slate of candidates.

The Federation resisted the movement at first, but when it came together on a national level as the Progressive Movement in 1924, the AFL Executive Council broke with its nonpartisan position and endorsed the Progressive presidential candidate, Robert LaFollette. Sentiment for LaFollette was by no means unanimous in the Federation, which included staunch Republicans like John L. Lewis and William Hutcheson, and ardent Democrats like Daniel Tobin, and when the movement began to crumble after a promising start in the election, the AFL pulled back into nonpartisanship.

The brief rise of the Progressives masked an even more important political drift in the 1920s. Urban and industrial workers moved increasingly toward the Democratic Party, particularly in support of Alfred E. Smith, the Roman Catholic, pro-labor governor of New York. The trend was especially evident among urban ethnic voters who were beginning to come to political maturity. This shift did not signify any change in labor's position since most of these working class people were not in trade unions. But it was the beginning of a fundamental realignment of the two major political parties that would be finalized in the 1930s when a new kind of labor movement and a radically different Democratic Party would find mutual advantage in close alliance.

In sum, during the 1920s labor's hopes for growth and acceptance as a legitimate partner in the free enterprise system came to little. Craft unionism was not functional in the bitterly antiunion new industries: automotive, chemical, rubber, and electrical manufacturing, nor in the great corporate mergers such as steel. In industries characterized by local product markets such as construction and printing, unions held on and even advanced. But overall the figures were dismal. Sixty percent of the AFL unions either barely held their own or declined, and some—like the Seamen and the Mine, Mill and Smelter Workers—almost disappeared.

many unions
lost hold
in 1920 end

PART III
The Agony of the Miners

The fate of the powerful United Mine Workers in the 1920s stands as a case study of the forces, both internal and external, which brought the labor movement to the edge of disaster. Hostile employers, injunction law, internal dissension, and a changing industry stripped the "shock troops" of labor of most of the gains they had made during fifty years of struggle.

By the end of World War I, the bituminous coal industry had experienced the end of three decades of growth during which annual tonnage increased fivefold and the number of operating mines rose from 2500 to 9000. Six hundred thousand men labored in and around the mines and almost 500,000 had memberships in the United Mine Workers. A semblance of order had been achieved in the chronically chaotic industry as early as 1898 when the union succeeded in establishing more or less uniform wage rates in the Central Competitive Field, which included Ohio, Indiana, Illinois, and western Pennsylvania. The tactic proved only partially successful because a large part of the industry did not subscribe to the minimum wage agreement. For the most part, these were the nonunion mines of the southern Appalachian fields. Attempts by the union to organize these West Virginia and Kentucky mines failed dismally in the face of violence, intimidation, and the explosion of injunctions following the Hitchman case. But as long as the demand for coal to fuel America's industrial expansion continued to increase, the union mines maintained wage rates in spite of southern competition.

During the 1920s the industry's economic prospects took a turn for the worse. Demand, which had been artificially inflated during the war years, began to level off. High coal prices and new technologies encouraged a trend toward economy in fuel consumption. This—coupled with increased competition from other fuels like oil, natural gas, and hydroelectricity—meant that the great expansion of industry that took place between 1920 and 1929 required virtually the same quantity of coal as had been produced in 1920. "Next to a scab," lamented a UMWA organizer, "the lowest form of life is an oil burner salesman."

The relative decline in the demand for coal increased the effects of competition from the nonunion mines. Southern operators—benefiting from excellent geological conditions, lower wage costs, and preferential freight rates—increasingly captured markets once dominated by northern producers. By 1926 the capacity of American mines stood at one billion tons, the need was half of that, and the nonunion mines had seized almost half of the market.

The man who led the miners during this dark period was John L. Lewis, son of a Welsh immigrant who had come to the Iowa coal fields and become a staunch member of the Knights of Labor. Lewis was an impressive figure with an imposing, almost theatrical appearance and a flair for the dramatic to match. Loved and hated with an intensity rarely accorded to public figures, he dominated the labor scene for thirty years. Possessed of little formal schooling, Lewis was aggressive, ambitious, and highly intelligent—qualities that served him well in an America that revered the ethic of achievement at almost any cost. Throughout his adult life his consuming interest was personal power, and as the son of a coal miner, he chose the union as the means to satisfy his ambitions. Through hard work and a sharp political sense Lewis rose through the ranks from the pits to the presidency of the most powerful union in the country at the age of thirty-nine.

Although he was the leader of the militant miners, Lewis was no radical. A lifelong Republican, he firmly believed in competition and conflict as the basis of a free society. To him the strike was not a weapon of class struggle—only an essential component of a capitalist system. He saw unions as the reverse side of the corporate coin. Both had similar functions. Each was organized to monopolize sales—goods in the one case, labor in the other. Fundamentally conservative, Lewis was anti-Communist and he used "red baiting" to crush challenges to his power from within the union as skillfully and ruthlessly as his corporate counterparts used them to crush unions.

Challenges came regularly as Lewis moved to consolidate his power in the rough-and-tumble union he had inherited. Using his constitutional authority to unilaterally revoke the charters of rebellious districts, subdistricts, and locals so that he could place them in the hands of loyal subordinates, he systematically drove his enemies out of the union. An army of staff representatives answering only to Lewis kept the monolithic machine under control.

One of Lewis's challengers, the idealistic and humane John Brophy, characterized Lewis as "concerned solely with his own political ambition. . . . Ethical and human considerations were brushed aside if they interfered with his ambition. On many union matters I agreed with him and should willingly have worked with him, yet again and again the ruthlessness and extreme egotism of the man drove us apart." Brophy had good cause to understand Lewis' qualities, both good and bad. He would later join him in the great industrial organizing drives of the 1930s, when Lewis seized the opportunity and led the transformation of the American industrial relations scene. But in the 1920s, Brophy posed the chief threat to Lewis's control of the union. "Slowly but inexorably," Brophy wrote, "I was driven to the conclusion that Lewis's power had to be challenged by a candidate for the presidency of the UMW who would offer a constructive program for rebuilding the union." The heart of Brophy's campaign was nationalization of the mines, a position Lewis had once paid lip service to for tactical reasons, but had by then discarded. Lewis beat back Brophy's 1926 "Save the Union" campaign by attacking his opponent as a dual unionist and a Communist sympathizer. The bitterness of the campaign and the numerous irregularities in the vote count eventually led to a split in the Miners and the creation of a dual union (the Progressive Miners of America) in the important Illinois fields.

The factionalization in the UMWA also led to the decline of a promising worker's education movement. In the early 1920s, the AFL supported the creation of the Workers Education Bureau. Among the prime movers in the movement were James Maurer, socialist president of the Pennsylvania Federation of Labor; A.J. Muste, a prolabor minister and advocate of industrial unionism; Hilda Smith, founder of the school for women workers at Bryn Mawr; and John Brophy. The Bureau had a close, although unofficial, relationship with Brookwood Labor College. At first the AFL gave unqualified support and soon came to dominate the Bureau's executive committee. But events in the Miners undermined the movement. A core of Brookwood graduates and staff formed the nucleus of Brophy's anti-Lewis organization in 1926. That year Lewis rose at the AFL convention to denounce the campaign against him as a Bolshevik plot. Under the urgings of the miners' leader, the AFL conducted an investigation of Brookwood and charged that the school was teaching communism and attacking the principles of the AFL, meaning pure and simple unionism. By 1928 the AFL blacklisted Brookwood and instructed its affiliates to do the same.

Distracted and weakened by internal dissension, the Mine Workers faced the struggle with the coal operators at considerably less than full strength. Operators in the Central Competitive Field blamed their problems on the only factor over which they had any control—the relatively high wage rates in the union mines. Attempts to impose significant wage reductions, in some cases up to 50 percent, met bitter resistance in the 1922 strike, during which nonunion mines made serious inroads in the market. The conflict set the stage for the Jacksonville Agreement of 1924 in which the operators agreed to keep wages at $7.50 a day.

As the southern penetration of the market continued, the operators, many of whom were now operating on a halftime basis, asked for relief. Lewis refused. He identified the industry's problem as overproduction. As a believer in the natural law of survival of the fittest, Lewis argued that strict adherence to the Jacksonville Agreement would drive the inefficient operators out of business, leaving fewer mines and fewer miners and a more stable and prosperous industry. The only alternative would have been to organize the southern mines, but, in a series of miniature wars in Mingo and Logan Counties, West Virginia, in 1920 and 1921, the UMWA had been virtually exterminated south of the Mason-Dixon line.

Lewis's hard line in the face of the disaster confronting the industry gave little solace to the operators. Their solution was to crush the union. In 1925, the Pittsburgh Coal Company broke ranks, discarded the contract and opened nonunion. After that came the deluge. Company after company followed Pittsburgh Coal's lead and by Christmas of 1925, more than two-thirds of the bituminous coal was mined nonunion. Hard times descended once again on the coal fields.

When the companies and the union met to negotiate a new agreement in 1927, their positions were diametrically opposed. The operators insisted on a significant reduction of wages, and Lewis vowed "no backward step." On April 1, 1927 he ordered his depleted legions to lay down their tools. Thus began the terrible coal strike of 1927. From the beginning the miners endured intense hardship. The operators used strikebreakers, private police, and injunctions—the whole range of antiunion weapons. Evictions from company houses became commonplace. Striking miners were housed in tent cities and crudely constructed barracks. Union relief and private charity rarely amounted to more than a few dollars a week. Senator Frank Goodling of Idaho reported to the Senate Interstate Commerce Committee that "conditions which exist in the strike-torn regions . . . are a blotch upon American civilization. . . . The Committee found men, women and children living in hovels which are more unsanitary than a modern swinepen."

A New York reporter venturing into the coal camps of western Pennsylvania saw "thousands of women and children literally starving to death," and "hundreds of destitute families living in crudely constructed bareboard shacks." He claimed to have discovered "a system of despotic tyranny reminiscent of czar-ridden Siberia at its worst," in which the "weirdest flock of injunctions that ever emanated from American temples of justice" were enforced by police brutality and "industrial slavery."

Company police wielded all the powers of public police officers in the states where they were authorized to serve. The violence they provoked led to counterviolence from the miners. Especially hated were the strikebreakers, often hapless unemployed men recruited from among miners put out of work by the combination of the mechanization of the mines and the depression in the industry. These factors had struck particularly hard at black miners who were traditionally last hired and first fired. Although blacks were no more frequently used as strikebreakers than whites, racism combined with the hatred of scabs frequently led to violence. Although the total number of black workers exploited in this way is difficult to estimate, one Pennsylvania company increased its black workers from 586 in 1924 to 3704 in 1927, out of a total work force of 9000.

The strike proved to be a disaster for the union. Lewis reluctantly surrendered the principle of industrywide bargaining and instructed the various districts to make the best deal they could. Agreements in Indiana and Illinois resulted in 18.7 percent wage cuts and Ohio miners saw their wages reduced by one-third. The United Mine Workers' only remaining strength lay in the dissension-ridden Illinois and Indiana bituminous fields and in anthracite. By 1929 only about 84,000 dues-paying members remained— just 20 percent of the nation's working miners.

Lewis emerged in absolute control of the husk of a once-powerful union. Few would have predicted a resurrection, but that was to underestimate the considerable abilities of John L. Lewis. When conditions changed dramatically in the next few years, few men in American labor were as well equipped to take advantage of the new opportunities.

DISCUSSION QUESTIONS

1. Rapid changes in technology and business organization during and after World War I created ideal conditions for the application of the techniques of scientific management. What were those conditions?
2. How did the combination of the postwar strike wave and the Bolshevik revolution in Russia contribute to the antiunion backlash in the United States in the 1920s?
3. Why can William Z. Foster's "amalgamation" strategy in the drive to organize the steel industry be seen as a "back door" to industrial unionism in the AFL?
4. How did the AFL's reluctance to attempt industrial unionism put them in a position of weakness during the twenties? Why did the AFL leadership prove to be so resistant to the idea of industrial unionism?
5. How did business leaders justify the "American Plan" and what do you think its real purposes were?

KEY WORDS AND PHRASES

Assembly Line	The Open Shop Campaign
Mooney and Billings	Yellow-dog Contracts
Bolshevik Revolution	Welfare Capitalism
Seattle General Strike	Employee Representation Plans
Boston Police Strike	William Green
Steel Strike of 1919	A. Philip Randolph
William Z. Foster	Hitchman Coal Company Case

Amalgamation
The Red Scare
Sacco and Vanzetti
Communist Party of the
United States
The American Plan

Conference for Progressive
Political Action
John L. Lewis
Brookwood Labor College
Coal Strike of 1927

BIBLIOGRAPHY

The material for this section was drawn largely from:

Bernstein, Irving. *The Lean Years: A History of the American Worker, 1920–1933.* Baltimore: Penguin Books, 1966.

Brody, David. *Workers in Industrial America: Essays on the 20th Century Struggle.* New York: Oxford University Press, 1980.

Cantor, Milton. *The Divided Left: American Radicalism, 1900–1975.* New York: Hill and Wang, 1978.

Cochrane, Thomas C. and William Miller. *The Age of Enterprise: A Social History of Industrial America.* New York: Harper & Row, 1961.

Cumbler, John T. *Working Class Community in Industrial America: Work, Leisure, and Struggle in Two Industrial Cities, 1880–1930.* Westport, Conn.: Greenwood Press, 1979.

Dubofsky, Melvyn and Warren Van Tine. *John L. Lewis: A Biography.* New York: Quadrangle, 1977.

Edwards, Richard. *Contested Terrain: The Transformation of the Workplace in the Twentieth Century.* New York: Basic Books, 1979.

Filippelli, Ronald L. "Diary of a Strike: George Medrick and the Coal Strike of 1927 in Western Pennsylvania," *Pennsylvania History,* vol. 43, no. 3 (Fall 1976): 253–256.

Foner, Philip. *Organized Labor and the Black Worker, 1619–1973.* New York: Praeger, 1974.

Howard, Sidney. *The Labor Spy: A Survey of Industrial Espionage.* New York: Republic Publishing Co., 1921.

Kenneally, James J. *Women and American Trade Unions.* St. Albans, Vt.: Eden Press, 1978.

Larson, Simeon. *Labor and Foreign Policy: Gompers, the AFL, and the First World War, 1914–1918.* Rutherford, N.J.: Fairleigh Dickinson University Press, 1975.

Lens, Sidney. *Radicalism in America.* New York: Thomas Crowell, 1969.

Lunt, Richard. *Law and Order vs. the Miners: West Virginia, 1907–1933.* Hamden, Conn.: Archon Books, 1979.

Montgomery, David. *Workers' Control in America.* New York: Cambridge University Press, 1979.

Nelson, Daniel. *Origins of the New Factory System in the United States, 1880–1920.* Madison: University of Wisconsin Press, 1975.

Spero, Sterling and Abram L. Harris. *The Black Worker*. New York: Atheneum, 1972.

Taft, Philip. *The A.F. of L. from the Death of Gompers to the Merger*. New York: Harper & Row, 1959.

Weinstein, James. *The Decline of Socialism in America, 1912–1925*. New York: Monthly Review Press, 1967.

For additional reading see:

Brandes, Stuart. *American Welfare Capitalism, 1880–1940*. Chicago: University of Chicago Press, 1976.

Brody, David. *Labor in Crisis: The Steel Strike of 1919*. Philadelphia: Lippincott, 1965.

Draper, Theodore. *The Roots of American Communism*. New York: Viking Press, 1957.

——— *American Communism and Soviet Russia*. New York: Viking Press, 1960.

Feurlicht, Roberta S. *Justice Crucified: The Story of Sacco and Vanzetti*. New York: McGraw-Hill, 1977.

Gordon, David, Richard Edwards and Michael Reich. *Segmented Work, Divided Workers: The Historical Transformation of Labor in the United States*. New York: Cambridge University Press, 1982.

Murray, Robert K. *Red Scare: A Study in National Hysteria, 1919–1920*. New York: McGraw-Hill, 1964.

Noble, David F. *America by Design: Science, Technology and the Rise of Corporate Capitalism*. New York: Alfred A. Knopf, 1977.

Preston, William, Jr. *Aliens and Dissenters: Federal Suppression of Radicals, 1903–1933*. New York: Harper and Row, 1966.

Russell, Francis. *A City in Terror, 1919: The Boston Police Strike*. New York: Viking Press, 1975.

SECTION SIX

PART I

New Deal for Americans

By the time the "Roaring Twenties" ended, the decade had produced a confidence and optimism among the vast majority of Americans. The United States stood as the richest and most secure nation on earth. So promising did the future appear in the spring of 1929 that the president of the United States, Herbert Hoover, could confidently boast that "we in America today are nearer to the final triumph over poverty than ever before in the history of our land." "The poorhouse," he added, "is vanishing from among us."

Only eight months later those words had a hollow, ironic ring for millions of Americans. "Black Thursday," the stock market crash of October 29, 1929 signaled the descent of the United States into the worst depression in the history of the modern industrial world. By mid-November the standard statistical index of common stock prices had declined 39 percent from its September peak, and the value of all shares on the New York Stock Exchange had fallen by nearly $26 billion.

The Depression took a catastrophic toll of total national income, which dropped 54 percent between 1929 and 1933, a period during which the business failure rate soared by 50 percent. Corporate profits before taxes declined by two-thirds in 1930 and turned into huge losses by 1932. Although iron and steel, construction, mining, automotive services, railroads, and retailing were the hardest hit, few sectors escaped the impact of the Depression of the 1930s.

Attempts to soften the impact on workers through shorter hours and share-the-work schemes failed. Soon wage cuts became widespread. By 1933 almost 87 percent of businesses had lowered wages by an average of 18 percent from the 1929 level. Total money income in the form of wages and salaries dropped 42.5 percent between 1929 and 1933. Construction workers lost 75 percent, those in mining 55 percent, and workers in manufacturing as a whole suffered a 51 percent loss. Much of this reflected part-time employment. A March 1932 survey of more than 6500 companies in all branches of industry revealed that less than 26 percent of the firms were operating full time.

Still, fewer hours and lower wages were better than none at all. Those still working were the lucky ones. By 1933, 24.9 percent of the labor force, one in four, had no work at all. The unemployment rate declined only slowly throughout the 1930s. It remained above 20 percent in 1934 and 1935, and in no year before 1941 did it fall below 14 percent. In 1932, out of 108,000 Birmingham, Alabama, wage earners, only 8000 were earning their normal incomes. Some 25,000 had no work at all. In Cincinnati, one out of four were unemployed and 40,000 others worked only part time. Detroit, center of the hard-hit automobile industry, suffered an unemployment rate approaching 50 percent. Unemployment struck particularly hard at the young and the elderly, while those in the middle bracket fared somewhat better. Indeed, the widespread unemployment and suffering among older Americans and the burdens placed on their families resulted in mounting pressure for the establishment of old-age insurance and more liberal relief for the elderly.

Along with economic dislocation, the Depression had a profound psychological impact on the young. By the end of the 1930s, large numbers of young people who had entered the labor market in the preceding years had never had a steady job, and even more had never held a job worthy of their abilities and education. Lack of work led to postponed marriages, loss of purpose, boredom, and discontent. Juvenile delinquency and minor crime increased. Millions of young Americans underwent a crisis in values and a loss of confidence in the institutions of society.

Of course, the Depression had a catastrophic impact on those groups that had the worst problems even in the best of times. Black workers experienced unemployment rates dramatically above those of whites. In Philadelphia in 1931 the figure was 10 percent higher. In Baltimore, where blacks constituted 17 percent of the population, they made up 32 percent of the unemployed. Women became, according to Senator Robert Wagner of New York, "the first orphans in the storm." Female unemployment far exceeded the rate for men. Unskilled women were increasingly driven into "gypsy" industries that took advantage of the glutted labor market; work standards were abandoned and the sweatshops revived. The desperate competition for employment increased male resentment of working women. In Woonsocket, Rhode Island, men in the spinning mills struck against the hiring of women, and President A. Lawrence Lowell of Harvard admitted firing scrubwomen and replacing them with men in order to avoid paying the Massachusetts minimum wage that applied only to women.

Married women with working husbands felt especially strong pressure to withdraw from the workforce. The 1931 convention of the AFL urged "preference in employment to those upon whom family or dependency rests," and repeated its old position that "married women owed primary obligation to the home." In order to make jobs available for men, the city of Syracuse fired 170 married women in December 1931. All married women were laid off by the New England Telephone and Telegraph Company, and the city of Akron, Ohio, requested the school board, department stores and rubber companies to discharge women with working husbands. Interestingly, the Akron city fathers not only expected this to help the unemployment rate, but to reduce the divorce rate as well. Sentiment against married working women resulted in the introduction of legislation in twenty-four states to limit or prohibit their employment in public service jobs. Even the federal government dismissed some women whose husbands also worked for the government. The myth that married women worked for "extras" that were not essential to the maintenance and security of their families penetrated even into the highest councils of the Roosevelt administration. Frances Perkins, Secretary of Labor during the 1930s, the nation's first women cabinet member, and a champion of the rights of workers, scolded married women who worked for "pin money" and urged those who did not need jobs to devote themselves to home and family.

Although unemployment hit hardest those people with less education and skills, those from less privileged social and economic groups, for the first time on a large scale the Depression also had a severe impact on the middle class. These were the people who had most enthusiastically embraced the business ethic of competition and individual initiative. So when growing numbers of middle-class workers found themselves unemployed, it led to a crisis of values of major proportions. According to the chairman of the California Labor Camp Committee, most of the jobless and destitute who drifted into the camps were laborers, but "there were also businessmen and tradesmen. There were many professional men and many high school and college graduates . . . . We have quite a number of small tradesmen and businessmen who have gone broke . . . . We have men who had been bankers and brokers. They listed themselves as clerks, and after that they came in to get a job, many of them giving a false name, as a matter of pride."

As workers despaired of finding work in their own communities, great numbers of them took to the road, hitchhiking and riding freight trains. By the end of 1931, even before the great droughts struck the Midwest and created another wave of refugees, there were 100,000 nonresident jobless, homeless, and penniless men in California. Railroad officials in Kansas City estimated that 1,500 a day passed through on freight trains. Boys and young men predominated, but there were also many women and even entire families. When asked why she was on the road and where she was headed, one girl spoke for millions when she replied, "Going? Just going."

Other symbols of the Depression became commonplace. Hobo jungles sprang up along the tracks as stopping-over points for the drifters. Communities of homeless people living in cardboard, tin, and wooden shacks—called "Hoovervilles" as a bitter comment on Herbert Hoover—appeared in most major cities. Long bread lines of somber, dejected men and women symbolized the collapse for which no one seemed to have an explanation.

THE CRISIS OF THE SYSTEM

Under such conditions the morale of Americans plummeted. Fear replaced hope for many and millions called the old ethic of self-reliance into question. No amount of individual initiative would produce a job. Signs of the changing mood were everywhere. Business, which had held an unchallenged position of leadership only a few years before, came under increasing attack.

As the national mood changes from fear to anger, the old fear of revolution surfaced again. "The leaders of our organization have been preaching patience," one AFL representative told a Senate Committee in the spring of 1932, ". . . if something is not done and starvation is going to continue, the doors of revolt in this country are going to be thrown open."

In the face of the crisis, American institutions, both public and private, found themselves philosophically, politically, financially, and administratively unprepared to cope with the massive unemployment, loss of income, and poverty that the Depression caused. No federal program to assist the jobless existed. State unemployment insurance programs were nonexistent and private industry plans covered only a tiny fraction of the labor force. The absence of government assistance reflected the deeply ingrained belief that it was a disgrace to be poor in the land of opportunity. Relief, according to this justification, would only reinforce the shiftlessness that led to poverty, and should only be given to the truly helpless. Responsibility for caring for the destitute lay first with family and then with private charity. Poorhouses run by local governments still constituted the basic system of tax-supported poor relief. This general attitude found expression in the White House as well. President Herbert Hoover believed that direct relief undermined self-sufficiency and initiative and under his administration the federal government provided no funds for direct relief of the unemployed before July 1932, and then only on a small scale in the form of loans to the states.

The failure of the prevailing ideology to correspond with reality led a number of people to take matters into their own hands, further contributing to the general fear that law and order was breaking down. In 1932, 20,000 World War I veterans camped in Washington demanding early payment of $50 and $100 bonuses due them in 1945 under a 1924 act of Congress. The "Bonus Army" created an impression of the nation's capital under seige from its own citizens and was finally driven from the city by U.S. Army regulars under the command of Army Chief of Staff Douglas

MacArthur. The image of homeless veterans and their families being assaulted by American troops contributed to the growing perception of the Hoover administration as heartless and cruel.

RETURN OF THE RADICALS

The vacuum created by the lack of action on the part of the responsible authorities led to a reemergence of the left. The Socialist Party, dormant since the early 1920s, had a surge of growth. But the real gainers were the Communists. To an increasing number of Americans, particularly the intellectuals, the Russian experiment, with which they had no firsthand experience, began to look better and better when contrasted with the chaos in the United States. Many turned to communism and the U.S. Communist Party's strength increased from 7000 members in 1930 to 55,000 by 1938. Outside of formal party membership, but in sympathy with its goals, were thousands more people. Communists organized the unemployed and led huge unemployment demonstrations in a number of cities in the early years of the depression. In 1930, they organized unemployed councils, as did the socialists and Musteites, who led protests, stopped tenant evictions, and supported labor's organizing drives. The unemployed councils did not turn into a revolutionary movement, however. The unemployed supported them not out of any understanding of or real interest in Marxism or the Communist political line. They were interested in immediate relief and reform, not revolution, and they turned for help to whomever offered it. But the converts that communism made in this period and the organizational skills they acquired prepared them for the key roles they were to play in the great industrial union drive that was to follow.

A.J. MUSTE

Abraham Johannes Muste emigrated to the United States from his native Holland in 1891. His career as a minister began in 1909 when he was ordained in the Dutch Reformed Church. Muste held pastorates in several cities but soon became dissatisfied with the harshness of Calvinist dogma and increasingly drifted toward Quaker thought and Christian pacifism. In 1916 he joined the Fellowship of Reconciliation and embarked on a life of activism during which he flirted with most varieties of radical thought, but rarely swerved from his devotion to nonviolence.

His involvement with labor began in 1919 when he led a strike of textile workers in Lawrence, Massachusetts. The strike led to the formation of the Amalgamated Textile Workers of America, which Muste served for two years as general secretary. From 1921 to 1933 he was educational director, fund raiser, and teacher at Brookwood Labor College, leaving finally because of an idealogical schism within the faculty.

In 1924 Muste campaigned for Robert LaFollette Sr., the presidential candidate of the Progressive Movement. In 1929 Muste helped found the Conference for Progressive Labor Action, and its successor the American Workers Party. Those clustered around Muste in support of independent political action and industrial unionism came to be known as Musteites. They led strikes in the North Carolina textile industry, including the great strike in Gastonia in 1929 where they cooperated with the Communists, and in support of West Virginia coal miners.

From 1929 to 1936 Muste temporarily abandoned pacifism for revolutionary socialism and threw his support behind the attempts to organize industrial unions in the mass-production industries. During the depression the Musteites organized the National Unemployed League, which was particularly strong in Ohio and which helped lead the 1934 Auto-Lite Strike in Toledo and the 1936 Goodyear Tire strike in Akron.

After 1936, Muste returned to Christian pacifism and the Fellowship of Reconciliation, which he served as executive secretary from 1940 to 1953. After the late 1930s, he ended his close association with the labor movement and devoted his time and attention to the civil rights and peace movements. When he died in 1967, Senator Robert F. Kennedy called him "one of those rare men of whom it can be said that our inability to follow his example speaks more to his excellence than to the limitations in ourselves."

If the revolutionary potential of the unemployed never materialized, the Communists were not the only ones who read the signs the wrong way. "There'll be a revolution sure," a banker declared in the fall of 1932. "The farmers will rise up. So will labor. The Reds will run the country—or maybe the Fascists. Unless of course, Roosevelt does something."

Franklin Roosevelt's rise to power took place in as chaotic a political decade as the country had ever seen. During the 1930s, millions moved in and out of various radical and reform movements. Political candidates from right to left attracted large, if temporary, followings through various combinations of personal charisma and radical political appeals. Senator Huey Long's "Share the Wealth" program offered everyone a guaranteed income of $2500 a year. "Every man a king," was Long's slogan. L.W. Allen's "Ham and Eggs" movement promised $30 every Thursday for every unemployed or retired person over fifty. Dr. Francis Townsend's National Recovery Plan presaged social security by promising $200 a month for the aged, all to be financed by a national transaction tax. The "radio priest," Father Coughlin, attracted millions of listeners to his strange combination of fascist and populist preachings. Most of these appeals were directed to the working class, the poor, and the unemployed. But, in the end, the dramatic rise of political consciousness among these groups flowed into massive popular support for Franklin Delano Roosevelt and his "New Deal" programs. Roosevelt came to the presidency in 1932 and, through his personal leadership and his bold relief and recovery programs, allied his administration and the Democratic Party with the masses of Americans who had never before had an administration in Washington with which they identified.

RELIEF AND REFORM

Franklin Roosevelt was an unlikely candidate to give political expression to the needs and concerns of the mass of American workers. A Hyde Park, New York, aristocrat with a term as governor of New York behind him, there was little in his record to indicate a penchant for wide-ranging experimentation and social and economic reform. But Roosevelt was above all a pragmatist, and he realized that something must be done if the American political and economic systems were to survive. Because of the shifting voting alignments brought on by rising urbanization, Americanization of the immigrants, and the impact of the Depression, he was also less dependent on business than any president since the Civil War. This freedom to maneuver in the face of crisis led him to declare that "The country needs and demands bold persistent experimentation." "Above all," he urged, "try something."

What Roosevelt tried was not radical, although it had an almost revolutionary impact on the way Americans interpreted the role of government in American society. The New Deal proved to be an innovative, reformist response to the Depression, an extraordinary example of crisis management. Roosevelt's critics accused him of destroying the free enterprise system. While this was a gross overreaction, it is true that implicit in the New Deal was the recognition that unregulated capitalism had failed and that the market did not, as the classical economists had argued, provide an automatic, foolproof mechanism that kept the economy in balance. The government had a major role to play.

The New Deal rejected the old belief that poor people were responsible for their own condition, and replaced it with the idea that the poor and the unemployed were victims of social and economic forces over which they had no control. Fueled by this belief, the New Deal's programs stressed assistance for low-income groups in general and wage earners in particular. Recovery, relief, and employment programs such as the Works Progress Administration (WPA), Public Works Administration (PWA), the Civilian Conservation Corps (CCC), and the National Youth Administration (NYA) provided jobs and dignity to millions of workers ranging from unskilled laborers to concert pianists. Three fundamental principles guided the application of unemployed relief: that providing work was better than the dole, that when the private sector could not provide jobs the government should act as employer of last resort, and that people have a right to a job, whenever possible, commensurate with their skills and training.

But the relief programs of the New Deal were viewed as temporary, lasting only until the economy could be brought back. As more permanent structural changes, the Roosevelt administration introduced a more progressive income tax structure, a system of social insurance that included federal welfare assistance, old-age pensions, unemployment compensation, and low-income public housing. For workers came federal protection of the right to organize into unions of their own choosing, the right to bargain collectively with their employers, and a federally mandated minimum wage and maximum hours.

Although it did not solve the problems of the Depression, the New Deal did attack the problems, provided relief for millions of Americans, pulled the nation out of its debilitating and dangerous mood of despair, and gave people hope again. In the process, it preserved the fundamental political and economic institutions of the nation.

PART II
Something Fresh Is Stirring

The labor reforms of the New Deal could not have come at a better time for organized labor. Already reeling from the successful antiunion campaign of the 1920s, the labor movement suffered a further decline of 469,000 members between 1929 and 1933. Unions that had managed to remain strong in the previous decade, largely in construction, communications, and transportation, took the full impact of the blow. Membership in the building trades dropped by 336,000 in the four years following 1929. The Bricklayers alone lost almost half of their membership. Unions everywhere reduced officers' salaries and cut staffs. Organizing activity virtually stopped, and the incidence of strikes declined dramatically. Strikes that did occur, usually in response to wage cuts, had little chance for success. By 1931 the Teamsters union ordered its locals not to call strikes to increase wages and reduce hours. Union-management cooperative schemes, such as those on the Baltimore and Ohio Railroad and the women's garment industry, became inoperative in the face of massive unemployment.

The vulnerability of the weakened unions also led to another, more insidious effect. With the end of Prohibition in 1933, organized crime, searching for an activity to replace its lucrative liquor business, increased its penetration of a number of unions. In several cities, such as Chicago and New York, unions in the laundry, restaurant, baking, hotel supply, trucking, and building materials industries fell under mob control. "Sweetheart" contracts as well as the extortion of both workers and employers became commonplace. The AFL took no action against this penetration, largely because of the strength of some of the affiliates involved. Only the Amalgamated Clothing Workers successfully drove the gangsters out.

The condition of the United Mine Workers graphically illustrates the depths to which labor had fallen. Already only a shell of its former self by the end of the 1920s, the UMWA was nearly overwhelmed by the Depression. The industry collapsed as production dropped to the level of 1904. Because labor made up two-thirds of mine costs, company survival depended on eliminating union wage scales where they still existed. Conditions in the mine fields became desperate. The average number of days worked annually declined to 146 in 1932, down from 219 in 1929, while average hourly earnings in bituminous dropped from 68¢ to 50¢ in the same period.

The plight of the coal miners had a great deal to do with the quickening pace of reform that began even before Roosevelt's election. Senator George Norris of Nebraska toured the coal fields and spoke with miners and their families. He came away profoundly moved by the experience. He returned to Washington determined to help the miners. What emerged in 1932 was the Norris-LaGuardia Act. The law as finally passed removed the threat of federal injunctions and yellow-dog contracts. For the first time a federal statute recognized that liberty of contract was a cruel hoax for the individual worker. Norris-LaGuardia signaled the beginning of an historic turn. Although Norris-LaGuardia was substantially a triumph of the AFL's traditional laissez-faire goal of keeping the government out of industrial relations, it breathed life into a devastated labor movement and heralded the beginning of a changing legislative direction that would soon make the government a major actor on the industrial relations scene—no longer as just an enforcer of employer interests but as a protector of working people.

DECLINE OF VOLUNTARISM

The severity of the Depression had a profound impact on the philosophical underpinnings of the AFL. Its loss of membership and bargaining power undermined the Federation's confidence in its ability to take care of itself. It also shook the leadership's faith in the ability of an unregulated, free-market capitalism to muddle through. The old policy of self-reliance came under increasing attack. The Federation's first reaction to the Depression had been that the government should let the decline run its course and allow industry to work out the problem by itself. But as the Depression deepened, pressure built for a new policy. Respected AFL leaders like George Berry of the Printing Pressmen argued that the capitalist system required a radical reorganization if the economic crisis was to be overcome.

The philosophical debate crystallized around the issue of unemployment insurance. Samuel Gompers had always considered the evils of unemployment preferable to government involvement, which he believed would limit "the freedom of workers to strive and struggle for their own emancipation through their own efforts." His attitude had governed AFL policy toward unemployment insurance since 1919 when Gompers rejected the idea as socialism. Opponents argued that the responsibility for unemployment insurance lay with the employers. Self-reliance was fine in the abstract, they argued, but workers could not eat rugged individualism.

The tide turned decisively against voluntarism when Dan Tobin of the Teamsters and John L. Lewis of the Miners, both previously devout believers in the law of the jungle, changed sides. At its 1932 convention the AFL supported the idea of unemployment insurance. "There are rather definite indications," noted one observer, "that this depression marks the end of an era in the history of American trade unionism. . . . A narrow labor philosophy formulated in the eighties loses its validity . . . something fresh is stirring."

The confirmation of this prediction came with the AFL response to the whole range of New Deal legislation. No issue better illustrates this than the Federation's ultimate support for the Fair Labor Standards Act of 1938 establishing minimum wages and maximum hours. As early as 1932 the AFL called for "an immediate reduction in the hours of labor as a condition . . . essential to the restoration and maintenance of prosperity." That year's convention instructed the Executive Council to draft legislation to present to the first New Deal Congress. Although the Executive Council had some reservations about the law as it emerged in 1938, it fell into line when Congress included a provision that made it clear that the wage-and-hour provisions would not interfere with collective bargaining. Looking back in 1939, William Green summed up the transformation of the AFL. "The labor movement has had to adapt itself to changed conditions," he wrote. "For many years its chief emphasis was on the use of its economic power, the united effort of the workers, to add to the sum of human happiness. . . . We now seek benefit for the workers and all our fellow men by the use of either direct economic strength or legislation as the situation demands. Neither alone can suffice."

HISTORIC OPPORTUNITY

If anything Green gave too little credit to the role of legislation in the dramatic resurgence of the labor movement in the 1930s. That role was decisive, beginning with the National Industrial Recovery Act (NIRA).

Franklin Roosevelt signed the NIRA on June 16, 1933. It marked a bold step toward replacing competition with cooperation in the nation's economy. Clearly a piece of crisis legislation, the act relied on voluntary action by industry to draw up codes of fair competition in each industrial sector in order to regulate prices and wages and to maintain employment. The National Recovery Administration (NRA) was empowered to administer the law. Of paramount significance to labor, Section 7(a) of the act required that all approved codes of fair competition must include provisions guaranteeing the right of workers to organize and bargain collectively through representatives of their own choosing, and that they be free from interference, restraint, or coercion on the part of employers or their agents while exercising these rights. *The New York Times* noted that labor had "jumped into . . . sudden power." As it turned out, that judgment proved premature, but labor was clearly on the verge of becoming politically powerful and the stage had been set for labor's greatest advances.

The degree to which the passage of the NIRA, the Depression, and the militancy of industrial workers combined to put some industries on the defensive was illustrated by events at the Philco plant in Philadelphia. In June 1933, company officials established an employee representation plan to comply with the letter, if not the spirit, of Section 7(a) of the NIRA. The plan failed because of the presence in the plant of a small group of young industrial unionists. A company order requiring employees to work ten hours a day, temporarily, to make up for a Fourth of July holiday, produced a spur-of-the-moment walkout by some 350 testers, assemblers, and repairmen. The committee of young activists found themselves negotiating with one of the corporate giants of America. Only a few days after the strike began, Philco signed a contract calling for an eight-hour day, forty-hour week, time-and-one-half for overtime, and wage increases of up to 30¢ an hour. A grievance procedure and seniority system were included for good measure.

Barely a month after signing the first agreement, Philco agreed to the union shop. When a question arose as to whether the union shop violated Section 7(a), the union sent a delegation to Washington to get the opinion of General Hugh Johnson, Director of the National Recovery Administration. With only a photo of Johnson to identify him, the workers located him in a conference with top management of the automobile industry. They interrupted the conference and got Johnson's hurried approval of the union shop proviso. With such haste, the largest radio plant in the country was unionized. The Philco local later became one of the founding unions of the United Electrical Workers, one of the major CIO unions.

No labor leader perceived the significance of Section 7(a) as acutely as did John L. Lewis. Organizers fanned out through the coal fields telling the miners that the president wanted them to join the union. They pointedly neglected to say which president, Franklin Roosevelt or John L. Lewis. The Central Competitive field became solidly union again. Antiunion strongholds like West Virginia and Kentucky fell to the onslaught. One Kentucky UMWA organizer wrote to headquarters that "the people have been so starved out that they are flocking into the union by the thousands. . . . I organized 9 locals Tuesday." In a matter of months the union regained its old strength. In the Appalachian Agreement, which covered 70 percent of the industry, *The New Yorker* commented that "The defeated mineowners agreed to all the things that deputy sheriffs usually shoot people for demanding."

His old base secure, Lewis turned his attention to the "captive mines" owned by the steel companies. To Lewis, miners were miners wherever they worked, but to the steel industry, miners in the captive mines were steel company employees and bore no relationship to those in the independent mines. Behind this argument lay the fear that unionization of their mines would serve as a Trojan horse for organization of the mills and the end of the open-shop policy. With the help of a strike and presidential intervention, the union captured some of the mines. A breach had been driven into the steel industry, the citadel of the open shop.

Not all of the AFL leadership shared Lewis's enthusiasm for NIRA. Conservative craft unionists like Matthew Woll and John P. Frey feared centralized governmental economic planning. But William Green recognized the significance of Section 7(a) and urged unorganized workers to form unions. A flood of applications for AFL charters followed from workers who had spontaneously organized. The hope of NIRA and the festering discontent of the Depression had produced a renewal of energy. "Hunger and hurt," wrote the poet, Archibald MacLeish, "are the begetters of brotherhood." In 1934, the AFL issued 1300 federal charters—charters that affiliated the new locals directly with the Federation rather than with any of the international unions. Enthusiasm for organization led to a strike wave in which over one million workers participated during 1933 and 1934. "The country is full of spontaneous strikes," wrote labor journalist, Benjamin Stolberg, "wherever one goes one sees picket lines."

At the Toledo Auto-Lite plant, a strike led by the radical socialist A.J. Muste and supported by the unemployed councils proved to be one of the first steps toward organization of the auto industry. In Minneapolis, Farrell Dobbs and the three Dunne brothers, followers of the exiled Bolshevik leader, Leon Trotsky, led a citywide truck drivers strike that revitalized the Teamsters union. The young radicals developed an innovative strategy when they divided the city into sections under the surveillance of "flying squads" of roving Teamsters in automobiles. Nonstriking truckers were pursuaded to leave the road by whatever means necessary. The strikers responded to police wiretaps aimed at discovering the whereabouts of the flying squads by setting up dummy garages and bogus patrols. The strikers won the right to union recognition, but only after a pitched battle with 2000 deputies left two persons dead.

West Coast longshoremen—under the leadership of a young Australian immigrant, Harry Bridges, and with the organizational support of the Communists—shut down West Coast ports from British Columbia to southern California. When police tried to open the San Francisco docks, two strikers were killed and hundreds on both sides wounded. After three months, the longshoremen won a limited, but important, victory.

The rash of organizational activity proved to be a mixed blessing for the AFL. Charters were often issued reluctantly because the Federation still had not come to grips with the issue of industrial unionism. The Building Trades unions made up the heart of the AFL and controlled the Executive Council. Most of the newly organized federal locals were organized along industrial lines, and included many workers who fell under the traditional jurisdictions of the craft unions. The question of what to do with the workers held in the federal locals could not be avoided. Craft leaders insisted that they be divided among the existing unions. John L. Lewis led the faction that pressed for the issuing of industrial charters. When it became clear that William Green would not cross the powerful craft unionists, Lewis became convinced that industrial organization of the basic industries would never come out of the AFL. While the conflict between industrial and craft unionism grew inside the house of labor, industry began to regain its composure and turn the tide against Section 7(a). Soon the National Industrial Recovery Act was being referred to by workers as the national runaround.

NATIONAL RUNAROUND

The problem lay in the lack of any enforcement agency with power to force industry to comply with the labor provisions of the law. In order to deal with the increasing number of strikes, Roosevelt had established the National Labor Board with Senator Robert Wagner of New York as chairman and equal representation from labor and industry. But the Board, and its immediate successor, the first National Labor Relations Board, could only make recommendations. As business began to revive, opposition, led by the National Association of Manufacturers, hardened. Henry Ford refused to sign the automobile code and William Randolph Hearst spoke for many in the business community when he blasted NIRA as "a measure of absolute state socialism."

While many employers did comply with code provisions in all respects, others welcomed the chance to fix prices and divide the market but bitterly resisted the wage-and-hour provisions. Compliance boards that had been established to oversee the codes, became stacked with businessmen who at best gave enforcement of Section 7(a) the lowest priority. The experience of the textile workers illustrated the problems. Employers took every opportunity to ignore the labor provisions of the industry code, which called for a forty-hour week and $13 a week in wages. In reality the companies paid a good deal less, instituted a speedup, and fired nearly 4000 workers for union activities. When workers responded with an industrywide strike, employers used police violence and 11,000 national guardsmen to keep the union out. The textile industry was not unique either. Disregard of 7(a) led to violence. From August through October 1933, fifteen strikers died as a result of incidents on picket lines. Another forty died in 1934 and forty-eight more followed during the next two years. In the eighteen months between the middle of 1933 and the end of 1934 state militia put down strikes in sixteen states.

The major tactic employed by industry to thwart Section 7(a) was company unionism. In the first four months after passage of the NIRA, 400 company union plans were put into operation. Especially prominent in the steel, rubber, petroleum, and chemical industries, company unions enrolled one-fourth of all industrial workers by the spring of 1934.

Section 7(a) had other defects as well. The stipulation that employees should be free to choose their own representatives was interpreted by many companies to mean that employees had the right to elect to deal individually with their employers even if the overwhelming majority of workers desired union representation. A final flaw involved the lack of any mechanism to force employers to bargain with the elected representatives of the workers.

HISTORIC TURN

Senator Robert Wagner saw these flaws clearly. He identified the company union as contradictory to the reform ideology of the New Deal. He recognized that businessmen were being allowed to pool their information and experience in vast trade associations in order to reduce the destructive effects of competition. If employees were denied the same right, Wagner pointed out that they could not uphold their end of the labor bargain. He hoped that employers would see that their own interests would be served by an orderly system of labor relations, one that rested on the equality of bargaining power. To Wagner such a system, based on cooperation among equals, would allow responsible labor leaders "to preserve order" and to "restrain the wayward acts of irresponsible groups." There is little doubt that Wagner feared an escalation of class conflict that might threaten the very foundation of the system.

When the Supreme Court ruled the NIRA unconstitutional in 1935, few in either business or labor mourned its passing. Even before the decision, Wagner had begun to press for legislation to remedy the flaws in Section 7(a). Wagner's bill emerged without much support from Roosevelt, but with the firm backing of Secretary of Labor Frances Perkins. When the courts struck down the NIRA, an angry Roosevelt embraced the bill. When the bill became law on July 5, 1935, the Wagner Act, or the National Labor Relations Act, signaled a shift on the part of Roosevelt away from the carefully balanced bipartisanship of the NIRA toward firm support for organized labor. No concessions were made to management. The bill implicitly recognized that only government help would allow labor to meet management on anything like equal terms. Every unfair labor practice banned by the Wagner Act applied to employers. Labor's right to organize was reaffirmed, and all employer interference was forbidden. To correct the weakness of Section 7(a), the Wagner Act created a new National Labor Relations Board with authority to determine the appropriate bargaining unit and to order and supervise elections for union representation. The Board also heard complaints of unfair labor practices, issued cease-and-desist orders, and could petition the courts for enforcement of its orders.

WAR IN THE HOUSE OF LABOR

The impact of the Wagner Act was immense. Once again the burden of seizing the opportunity lay with the leaders of the increasingly divided American Federation of Labor. Where many of the cautious craft union leaders saw complications as well as possibilities in the Wagner Act, John L. Lewis and his close associates saw only opportunity. Armed with the abundant treasury of the rejuvenated miner's union, Lewis raised the specter of radicalism to press the AFL leadership to seize the initiative and charter industrial unions in the mass-production industries. Federal local charters continued to be issued at a rapid rate and hundreds of thousands of restive workers remained second-class citizens, posing a threat to the stability of the Federation. While the federal locals agitated for industrial charters, the craft unions were lost in a byzantine maze of complex jurisdictional squabbles. Lewis supported requests for industrial charters for the auto, rubber, cement, radio, and aluminum industries, but his most persistent demand was for the organization of the steelworkers, whose jurisdiction lay in the hands of the leadership of the Amalgamated Association of Iron, Steel and Tin Workers. The craft union leadership of the AFL met this rising tide of sentiment with little more than vague endorsements of industrial unionism. As time passed and the opportunities threatened to elude their grasp, Lewis and his associates grew increasingly impatient to move, with or without the AFL's approval.

Lewis's chief associate in the industrial union movement was Sidney Hillman, leader of the Amalgamated Clothing Workers. Hillman also had seized the opportunity provided by Section 7(a) to rebuild his union, all the while solidifying his power. He had come out of the socialist tradition of the Jewish needle trades but by 1935 pragmatism, not socialism, underlay his attitude toward union organization. An activist with little time or inclination for theory, Hillman had tamed his leftist opposition in the Clothing Workers much as Lewis had done in the Miners. He had no fundamental objection to craft unionism, but, like Lewis, he presided over an industrial union and realized that in no other way could unionism be functional in the mass-production industries. In addition to these qualities, he brought to the alliance with Lewis a genius for public relations, a skill in political maneuvering, and the ability to instill loyalty in his subordinates.

Another industrial unionist, David Dubinsky, president of the International Ladies Garment Workers Union, became the third key figure in the braintrust. He also had revived his union during 1933. As a socialist he had played a decisive role in the defeat of the communists in his union during the 1920s. Although his socialism had become largely *pro forma* by 1935, Dubinsky retained a strong belief in industrial democracy and industrial unionism. His great talent was for mediation and compromise. A scrupulously honest man, Dubinsky presided over a union of tremendous ethnic diversity. Like Hillman he believed unions had a larger role to play in the welfare of their members and he remained a lifelong supporter of progressive causes.

It was no accident that the rebuilding of the Miners, Clothing Workers, and Garment Workers provided the foundation for the industrial union movement. All were industrial unions in a craft-union-dominated AFL. All had dynamic and unchallenged leaders, and all possessed newly fattened treasuries.

As the battles on the picket lines captured the most attention between 1933 and 1935, the battle for the heart and mind of the AFL raged out of public view in conventions and Executive Council meetings. The struggle came to a head in Atlantic City in 1935 where a stormy AFL convention rejected a resolution supporting industrial unionization. Soon after, at a meeting on November 9, 1935, Lewis, Hillman, and Dubinsky, along with other sympathetic union leaders such as Charles P. Howard of the Typographers, Thomas McMahon of the Textile Workers, and Max Zaritsky of the Hat, Cap and Millinery Workers formed the Committee for Industrial Organization (CIO). Lewis, as CIO chairman, demonstrated his ability to put organizational priorities above personal feelings when he named John Brophy, his old antagonist whom he had ruthlessly driven out of the Mine Workers, as the first CIO director. The new organization set out to build the financial and organizational resources to organize industrial unions in the mass-production industries.

The AFL Executive Council moved quickly to counter the threat of the CIO. They instructed the federal locals of radio workers to turn over their charters to the International Brotherhood of Electrical Workers which had offered them second-class status. The Mine, Mill and Smelter Workers, an industrial affiliate, was ordered to give up its skilled members to the appropriate craft unions, and the small AFL auto workers union found its jurisdiction severely limited. In response Lewis withheld the Mine Workers' per capita tax to the Federation. As events built to a climax, the AFL moved hastily to suspend the CIO unions, violating its own constitution and its fundamental principles of autonomy. Of this internal bloodletting historian Philip Taft concluded, "there is no evidence that the members of the CIO wanted to secede. . . . Green instead of seeking some method for solving the crisis, sought the advice of his lawyer . . . on how the CIO unions might be legally suspended." It was according to Taft, "a failure of leadership that has no equal in the history of American labor."

CIO

Following formal expulsion of the CIO unions by the AFL, the Committee for Industrial Organization met in Pittsburgh and transformed itself into the Congress of Industrial Organizations (CIO).

Between spring 1936 and summer 1937, armed with the Wagner Act and under the leadership of the CIO, workers in the mass-production industries found the initials CIO a rallying cry with almost magical significance. Everywhere there seemed to be militant organizing drives, sitdown strikes, mass picketing, and company union takeovers. By autumn of 1937 the CIO boasted of four million members. Although undoubtedly somewhat inflated, the actual figures remained impressive. The United Auto Workers claimed 375,000, the United Electrical Workers had 137,000, the Textile Workers Organizing Committee and the Steel Workers Organizing Committee both enrolled nearly 500,000.

The CIO's first major strike came in the rubber industry in 1936. In response to the firing of 137 workers for staging a sitdown to resist layoffs, 14,000 workers strung eleven miles of picket lines around the huge Goodyear Tire and Rubber Company property in Akron, Ohio. Labeled as outside agitators, the strikers responded by identifying the true agitators in the strike as Goodyear hours and wages, which they claimed were "native products." The Akron strike proved to be a testing ground for tactics that were to become commonplace in CIO strikes. The union set up tents and shacks to provide some protection for pickets from the raw Ohio winter. Workers' wives served 5000 meals a day from improvised commissaries. Akron's citizens generally supported the CIO, which skillfully used the radio to counter the hostile local newspaper coverage of the strike. When the company employed the time-honored tactic of demanding the help of the national guard, Ohio's governor saw no compelling reason to comply with the request. Attempts to form a Law and Order League to break the strike failed. After five weeks, the company surrendered and the CIO had gained its first great victory—a victory attributable primarily to the rank-and-file militancy of the rubber workers.

On Sunday, July 5, 1936, the CIO's Steel Workers Organizing Committee (SWOC) held a rally of steelworkers and coal miners at the graves of the union men who had fallen during the great Homestead Lockout of 1892. Pat Fagan, then president of District Five of the United Mine Workers, promised the crowd of several thousand that "The blood of the martyrs of the '92 strike would be the seed of the organization in 1936." The final drive to organize the steel industry had begun.

For the CIO, victory in steel held the key to success for the industrial union movement. For the Miners, it would guarantee their claim to the captive mines, but even more importantly, if steel fell then no mass production industry could be considered unorganizable. To win so important a victory Lewis was willing to commit all of the Mine Workers' resources. At the head of the drive he placed Philip Murray, his most trusted lieutenant.

Murray was to win a special place in the pantheon of labor's legendary heroes. The son of immigrants, union blood ran deep in his veins. His father had been a strong trade unionist in the Scottish mines to which he had emigrated from his native Ireland. Young Philip first entered the mines at the age of ten as his father's helper. He shared the hardships of several strikes and absorbed the militant traditions of the Scottish miners. After immigration to western Pennsylvania in 1902, Murray resumed his trade and developed a lifelong commitment to helping his fellow miners by bringing them the benefits of unionization. He rose quickly through the ranks from local to district office and in 1920, John L. Lewis, who quickly recognized his talents, brought him in as vice-president of the UMWA. A close relationship developed between the two men, and Murray remained loyal to Lewis throughout the factional struggles that scarred the union. Although they were close allies, the leadership qualities of Murray and Lewis rested on vastly different foundations. Where Lewis was charismatic, shrewd and often ruthless, Murray had a humanity and warmth about him, a compassion and love for working people that Lewis lacked. Historian Irving Bernstein aptly called Murray the good man of the labor movement. "It was Murray's special quality," one observer wrote, "to touch the love and not the fear of men." Murray was more than humble and compassionate; he was also intelligent, dedicated, and decisive—necessary qualities for waging industrial war with the masters of the steel industry.

Under Murray's direction, and with the largest war chest in labor history at its disposal, the Steel Workers Organizing Committee sent 400 organizers into the steel towns of Pennsylvania, Ohio, Illinois, and Alabama. Clearly this was not to be another understaffed, underfunded drive like the ones that had failed before. This time there was no AFL involvement. The CIO had seen to that by capturing control of the weak Amalgamated Association of Iron, Steel and Tin Workers from its ineffective leadership and from the AFL.

Steelworkers flocked to the CIO banner. Lewis, with his characteristic flair for dramatic language, warned the antiunion forces that they were either madmen or fools if they believed "that this river of human sentiment . . . can be dammed or impounded by the erection of arbitrary barriers of restraint." Soon the citadel of the open shop began to crumble from the force of the CIO assault. Company denunciations of SWOC organizers as "Emissaries of Moscow" fell on deaf ears. These were different times. Company unions fell into the hands of SWOC activists like ripe fruit, as did some of the steel towns with the election of union sympathizers. By the close of 1936, SWOC counted 100,000 dues-paying members. A momentous conflict seemed inevitable. But suddenly, on March 1, 1937, a surprised nation learned that as a result of secret negotiations between Lewis and Myron Taylor, chairman of the board, United States Steel had agreed to recognize SWOC as bargaining agent for its members, granted a 10 percent wage increase, and accepted the eight-hour day and forty-hour week. The greatest prize in the American economic system had fallen without a fight.

In spite of the surrender of United States Steel, the leaders of "little steel," that constellation of companies that included Bethlehem, Republic, Youngstown Sheet and Tube and Inland, did not consider the triumph of the CIO as inevitable. Led by Tom Girdler of Republic and Eugene Grace of Bethlehem, they chose to resist with all of the considerable resources at their command. The most savage conflict of the 1930's, the Little Steel Strike of 1937, resulted from their decision.

In late May and June, after months of hard organizing, 70,000 steel workers struck the nonunion companies. On first impression SWOC seemed equal to the task. It was heir to the growing CIO myth of invincibility and by early 1937 it boasted 300,000 members in 140 firms. But in truth SWOC was over-extended, its resources spread thin. Nor had it ever been truly tested in battle.

And battle was what the companies had in mind. All of the old repressive tactics reappeared in the Little Steel Strike, newly packaged in what came to be called the Mohawk Valley Formula. The Remington Rand Typewriter Company had perfected the strategy in 1936 against striking office equipment workers. It was a judicious blend of the old and the new. In time-honored fashion the company branded union organizers as outside agitators and subversives. A company front organization, usually called a citizens committee, soon appeared claiming to represent the interests of the community and of the "loyal majority" of workers. If a strike developed the call went out for law and order to quell imaginary or company instigated violence. Sympathetic local officials, often on the company payroll, were expected to raise an armed force of local police, company agents, and vigilantes. When the security force was in place, the puppet organization of "loyal employees" staged a widely publicized march to the plant gates in a back-to-work movement. Throughout, the tightly controlled local press acted as a conduit for company propoganda. Everything was aimed at breaking the morale of the strikers and creating doubts in their minds concerning the ability of the union to succeed. The Little Steel companies employed this strategy in textbook fashion.

With all of its theatricality and sophisticated public relations techniques, the heart of the Mohawk Valley Formula remained the company's willingness to employ naked force. Republic Steel had prepared for the strike by arming its 370-man police force with 552 pistols, 64 rifles, 245 shotguns, 143 gas guns, 2707 gas grenades, and 232 billy clubs. Other companies took similar precautions. The results were predictable. During the strike 18 workers were killed, 160 fell wounded, and thousands found themselves in local jails. In Ohio the National Guard swept the steel towns of picket lines. In Johnstown, Pennsylvania, Bethlehem Steel paid the mayor for paramilitary and other assistance. The spiral of terror climaxed on Memorial Day 1937, at the gates of Republic Steel's South Chicago plant, where Chicago police fired repeatedly into a peaceful crowd of striking steelworkers and their families. Ten steelworkers died and over 100 suffered wounds in the Memorial Day massacre. Most had been shot in the back. In the end, old-fashioned terrorism had been decisive. Not until 1941 under pressure from the government and through victories in National Labor Relations Board elections under the provisions of the Wagner Act, were the Little Steel companies unionized.

SITDOWN

As the drama in steel unfolded, an equally important struggle took place in the greatest of America's mass production industries—the auto industry— symbol of the triumph of the Industrial Revolution. There the application of advanced technology to work processes had found its fullest expression. Auto workers spent their days performing monotonous tasks geared to the constant demands of the assembly line. "Where you used to be a man," one auto worker told a Senate investigating committee in 1937, "now you are less than their cheapest tool . . . ."

Auto workers participated in the flurry of organizing activity that marked the passage of the NIRA and a number of small unions developed. But company resistance and the AFL's paralysis took the steam out of the drive. By August 1935, the Federation had reluctantly bowed to the inevitable and chartered what remained of the auto locals as the United Auto Workers. But by then the CIO had captured the attention of the workers and in the summer of 1936, after a rank-and-file revolt against AFL leadership, the young auto union threw in its lot with John L. Lewis's Committee for Industrial Organization.

A monumental task faced the small union. Although organization had been moderately successful in scattered plants, the question of how to organize huge, multiplant companies like General Motors, Ford, and Chrysler remained unanswered. The solution adopted by the union's leaders was the sitdown strike. The tactic had been used in the United States by the IWW at General Electric in 1906 and European workers, particularly the French and Italians, had employed it with some success. The sitdown at Goodyear in Akron had also given a hint of the potential of the weapon. Indeed the action of the rubber workers had led to a rash of sitdowns in 1936 and one year later, when the auto workers used it successfully, the tactic became a national mania. Novelist Upton Sinclair expressed a widely held view when he wrote that "for seventy-five years big business has been sitting down on the American people, and now I am delighted to see the process reversed."

The sitdown gave the initiative to the workers in a way that no other union tactic had. In a large, integrated manufacturing operation, such as the automobile industry, a small group of workers could stop the entire process by shutting down one key operation. The sitdown also eliminated the employer's ability to operate with strikebreakers. The need to rely on picketing, which was vulnerable to police or company attack, was greatly reduced as well. Any assault on sitdowners also ran the risk of damaging expensive equipment. It was no accident that the rash of sitdown strikes resulted in no deaths and very little property damage.

To its critics, and there were many after the first fascination with the phenomenon began to fade, the sitdown appeared to be a radical, even revolutionary tactic, aimed at undermining the sanctity of private property. John L. Lewis replied that the tactic was a reaffirmation of the property rights of workers in their jobs and in their tools.

Unlike the old craft unionists whose power lay in their ownership of their tools, which they took with them when they struck, the mass-production workers had no possibility of owning the machinery. Since they could not exercise their property rights by removing their tools, they exercised them by staying in control of the machinery. It is significant that seizure of the machinery during the sitdowns was not followed by any attempt to operate the factories, as some European workers had done. Although the tactic was innovative and potentially revolutionary, American workers used it only to gain limited ends.

Even with this limited use, labor leaders were reluctant to endorse the tactic. Most sitdowns occurred without formal union sanction. The CIO leadership, which never formally approved sitdowns, grasped the opportunity that they presented and turned it to their advantage. In 1939 the Supreme Court outlawed sitdowns as a trespass on private property, but by then the tactic had brought General Motors to the bargaining table.

Scattered groups of auto workers began to use the sitdown toward the end of 1936. It had worked at Bendix Products in South Bend, Indiana, and at Kelsy-Hayes in Detroit. The trick was to figure out how to use the sitdown to paralyze an entire company, not just isolated plants. For its main target, the United Auto Workers picked General Motors, the nation's richest and most powerful corporation, and, according to UAW organizer Wyndham Mortimer, "the citadel of power and the maker of policy for the auto industry." As was the case for United States Steel, for a struggling union to take on General Motors at any other time in history would have been suicidal. But these were not ordinary times. The Wagner Act was law, Roosevelt had tilted decidedly toward labor, and a progressive governor, Frank Murphy, had ridden the New Deal tide to victory in Michigan, the heartland of the auto industry.

Fortune magazine called General Motors "the highest techno-organism of our technological age." The company operated 110 plants, was the world's largest producer of automobiles, and in 1937 alone it grossed $1.6 billion, equal to the combined budgets of Michigan, Minnesota, California, Pennsylvania, and New York. In all, a quarter of a million people worked for General Motors. To ensure that unionism did not disrupt this colossus, the company operated an espionage system on which it spent $1 million between 1934 and 1936.

The sitdown began at the Fisher Body Plant Number One on December

30, 1936. The plant was the Achilles heel of an almost totally integrated company. Only two sets of body dies had been made for the 1937 models, one for Fisher One and the other for a Fisher plant in Cleveland. The Cleveland plant had been shut down two days earlier. News of the sitdown at Fisher One spread quickly, and soon most of General Motors' operations lay silent, either because of strikes or lack of parts.

The Flint sitdown lasted forty-four days. Determined to keep order, the strikers organized themselves into units of fifteen. Union patrols kept the peace and particular care was taken not to damage the machinery. Fisher One took on all the aspects of a small community. An elected "mayor" and council coordinated a variety of activities, including a makeshift barbershop. Local theatres sent in entertainment. Friendly merchants donated food supplies, and UAW field kitchens, with help from volunteers from the Cooks and Chefs' Union (AFL), prepared three hot meals a day for 5000 strikers.

From the beginning of the organizing drive General Motors had resolutely opposed the union. When the sitdowns began the company's public relations experts labeled the strikers as radicals, trespassers, and lawbreakers. John L. Lewis noted the irony in the fact that a corporation engaged in violating the Wagner Act could speak so forcefully about law and order. After its espionage system and an attempt to use the Mohawk Valley Formula failed, and under intense pressure from Lewis, Roosevelt, Secretary of Labor Perkins, and Governor Murphy of Michigan, the company agreed to recognize the union. But before it did, company agents and Flint police fought several pitched battles with strikers and their supporters in the Women's Emergency Brigade. In one, the so-called "Battle of the Running Bulls," thirteen strikers suffered gunshot wounds.

Victory over General Motors ended a brilliant organizing campaign. Together with the triumph in steel, it guaranteed the survival and influence of the CIO. But, as in steel, there was no domino effect. While Chrysler succumbed shortly thereafter to a sitdown by its Detroit workers, Ford did not fall into line without a bitter battle.

WYNDHAM MORTIMER

Mortimer, the son of a miner who belonged to the Knights of Labor, was born in Clearfield County, Pennsylvania, in 1884. He left school at the age of twelve and went to work in the mines as a "trapper boy," joining the United Mine Workers four years later. After several years in the mines, Mortimer moved on to work in the steel, auto, and railroad industries, all the while becoming active in radical labor circles.

He became well known as a labor organizer after the passage of the National Industrial Recovery Act in 1934. Taking advantage of Section 7(a) of the act which permitted unionization, Mortimer organized the workers of the White Motor Company in Cleveland into the AFL. He headed the left-wing caucus in the AFL auto union in the mid-1930s that led the fight to take the union out of the AFL and in to the CIO.

Mortimer's greatest fame came when he slipped quietly into Flint, Michigan, in June 1936. At the time he was fifty two and one of the CIO's most experienced organizers. He was, according to historian Irving Bernstein, both a dedicated trade unionist and a confirmed Communist. He shared these attributes with scores of other leftists who played such an important role in the organization of the industrial unions during the 1930s. Mortimer planned the strategy for the organization of the Flint strike and worked tirelessly to secretly build the union. His success was his undoing. When then United Auto Workers president, Homer Martin, began to fear him as a potential rival, Mortimer agreed to leave Flint only if he could name his successor, a fellow Communist named Robert Travis, who carried on Mortimer's work to its successful conclusion.

In 1940 Mortimer once again drew public attention when the UAW sent him to California to organize the aircraft industry. He was one of the principal leaders of the 1941 strike against the North American Aviation Company, a strike that most of organized labor and President Roosevelt condemned as part of a Communist strategy to hinder American rearmament.

Although he identified himself as a militant socialist, Mortimer continued to deny ever having been a member of the Communist party until his death in 1966. He is remembered as one of the great organizers of the greatest period of union growth in American history.

Unlike General Motors, Ford had not entrusted its antiunion operations to outside agencies. Instead, Henry Ford, the patriarch of the family-owned number two automaker, assigned the task to an ex-boxer, Harry Bennett, who headed Ford's special "service department." Composed of several hundred thugs and a network of spies, Bennett's department kept Ford union free through espionage, systematic intimidation, and violence. Bennett's men severely beat UAW leafleteers near the Ford assembly plant in South Chicago, and in a famous incident on May 29, 1937 in Detroit, five UAW organizers, led by Walter Reuther and Richard Frankensteen, suffered a similar fate at the hands of service department agents in full view of reporters and photographers. Bennett's methods had the full support of Henry Ford, who had denounced the UAW and all unions as the "worst thing that ever struck the earth" and vowed never to deal with them.

Ford's resistance and the temporary weakening of the union by internal dissension led to the failure of early attempts to duplicate General Motors' triumph at Ford. But, in 1940, a revitalized UAW, with a generous donation of CIO funds, tried again. The fact that Ford, once the leader in the auto industry, had fallen behind General Motors and Chrysler in hourly wage rates began to tell. A series of sitdowns over work-related grievances broke out in the huge River Rouge plant in Detroit. The drive climaxed on April 1, 1941 when the company discharged the entire UAW grievance committee. A spontaneous walkout paralyzed the world's largest auto plant. The role of black workers proved to be crucial in the strike because blacks were more heavily employed at Ford than in any other auto company. Prior to the strike the UAW leadership had made efforts to gain the support of skeptical black workers and community leaders. This effort paid off as nearly all of the black auto workers left the plant with the white workers and most refused to cross the union's picket line. Black UAW organizers played a key role in the strike and black community leaders supported the UAW. Yet a significant number of blacks remained in the plant, and soon violence broke out between these workers and the strikers and threatened to grow into generalized racial conflict. As the situation deteriorated, the intervention of black community leaders and pressure from the governor of Michigan led to a settlement. There were undoubtedly other reasons for Ford's decision. Harry Bennett had come to believe that the strike was lost, and the opportunity for lucrative defense contracts no doubt also played a role in Henry Ford's decision to agree to an immediate National Labor Relations Board election in which the union won an overwhelming victory.

The Ford workers won the best contract in the auto industry, including the union shop and the dues checkoff, a concession for which they had not even asked. On the question as to why Ford gave in so completely, Henry Ford's reasoning is enlightening. Speaking of the dues checkoff, under which the company collects union dues, Ford remarked, "That will make us their bankers, won't it? Then they can't get along without us. They'll need us just as bad as we need them."

AFL REVIVAL

By 1937 the CIO posed a challenge to the supremacy of the AFL without parallel in its half century of existence. Along with the successful drives in steel, auto, and rubber, the CIO also made enormous gains in electrical manufacturing, longshoring, and meatpacking. Under this intense competition, the AFL unions abandoned their strict adherence to the principles of craft unionism and committed themselves to industrial organizing. The old ideological war which had weakened American labor from the beginning now seemed little more than an anachronism. The Carpenters organized lumber and sawmill workers, the Machinists led vigorous campaigns among aircraft and other metal workers, and the International Brotherhood of Electrical Workers moved in on electrical manufacturing. As competition between the two rival federations intensified, the CIO mounted a counterdrive in the building trades by forming the Construction Workers

Organizing Committee—a challenge that spurred the AFL building trades unions to extend their membership to the smaller cities and into highway and industrial construction.

Ironically, the success of radicals in the Northwest had a lot to do with the AFL recovery. Following their 1934 victory in Minneapolis, Trotskyist Teamster organizers Farrell Dobbs and Associates organized the long-haul, over-the-road truckers in eleven northwestern states. By 1938 they had created a district council and negotiated a master agreement covering 2000 companies and 250,000 workers. Jimmy Hoffa in Detroit and Dave Beck in Seattle followed the same strategy and organized midwestern and western Teamster Councils, adding huge numbers to the AFL ranks.

To wage the organizational war with the CIO, the AFL amassed a huge war chest and by 1938 the Federation had seized the initiative and maintained its position as the larger of the two organizations, more than recovering the numbers lost by the expulsion of the CIO unions. AFL and CIO rivalry also spilled over into the political arena. During the 1938 elections the AFL opposed CIO-supported candidates in a number of states, including Pennsylvania, where the Federation opposed Lieutenant Governor Thomas Kennedy, a United Mine Workers official, for the Democratic gubernatorial nomination.

The competition, frequently bitter and sometimes violent, drove the competitors farther apart and replaced the earlier philosophical differences with personal animosities that made labor solidarity impossible and limited labor's ability to take full advantage of the opportunities presented by its remarkable membership gains.

HOPE FOR BLACKS AND WOMEN

The CIO challenge to the AFL also had great significance for minorities and women. Until the rise of industrial unionism AFL racial policies showed little sign of change. The fight to change those policies was led by the outstanding black trade unionist, A. Philip Randolph. Randolph played a major role in the formation of the Brotherhood of Sleeping Car Porters in 1925. In 1928, with the help of William Green and over the jurisdictional claims of the Hotel and Restaurant Employees Union, the AFL granted a federal local union charter, but not full membership as a national union to the Brotherhood. A second attempt at a Federation charter failed in 1934 when the Executive Council granted jurisdiction to a small, white-only union, the Order of Sleeping Car Conductors. Randolph then threatened to pull out unless the decision were reversed, and in 1938 the Federation, after several years of sorting out complex jurisdictional claims, awarded a national union charter to the black union.

Randolph never ceased in his attempts to rid the AFL of institutional racism, and he emerged as an eloquent spokesmen for the hopes and aspirations of all black Americans, the vast majority of whom were working class. His efforts in the AFL largely failed, resulting in little or no action. Randolph realized the promise of industrial unionization for black workers. "The craft union invariably has a color bar against the Negro workers," he said, "but the industrial union in structure renders race discrimination less possible, since it embraces all workers included in the industry, regardless of race, creed, color or craft, skilled or unskilled." Although he was sympathetic, Randolph did not join the CIO exodus from the AFL, believing it his duty to remain and carry on the fight. But he was correct in perceiving that the structure of industrial unions would greatly reduce discrimination. Blacks averaged 8.5 percent of all iron and steel workers nationally, and as much as 68 percent in Alabama, and some 17 percent of all semiskilled and unskilled in the slaughter and packinghouse industries. Some companies like Ford had especially heavy concentrations of blacks. The story was the same in all areas of mass production.

Given these circumstances the CIO pursued a nondiscriminatory policy from the beginning. SWOC appealed to "every Negro worker in the steel mills for the sake of his fellow men, his family and his country to join immediately with all others . . . in building the union," and the CIO regularly reaffirmed its open policy. Black leaders reacted cautiously, but soon the pleas of Randolph and others galvanized them into support for the CIO. They had little choice as black workers responded enthusiastically to the CIO organizing drives. Black organizations such as the National Negro Congress and the NAACP encouraged blacks to support the CIO and, along with the black press, played major roles in the drives in steel, auto, meat packing, and rubber. As the craft unions responded with their own industrial organizing, racial barriers began to fall in AFL unions as well, although not to any great degree in the building trades. Nevertheless, with all of the progress brought by industrial unionism, many of the old problems remained. CIO contracts left hiring entirely up to employers who frequently excluded blacks or kept them in menial jobs. Seniority clauses, a breakthrough in terms of job security, had the unintentional effect of freezing existing inequities and kept white workers ahead of blacks in line for skilled and semiskilled jobs. For most black workers the curse of last hired, first fired continued to apply. Blacks did not achieve leadership positions in the CIO unions in anything like their numbers warranted.

What applied for blacks also applied for women in most particulars. Where women were already present in mass production, their involvement was essential. Throughout the 1930s, they played a militant role. In industries where they were heavily represented, such as retailing, pharmaceuticals, food service, and hotel, women spearheaded organizing drives with the help of the Women's Trade Union League and prominent women such as Cornelia Bryce Pinchot, wife of Pennsylvania's governor, and the first lady, Eleanor Roosevelt. Female union organizers compiled an outstanding, if largely overlooked, record. Bessie Hillman and Dorothy Bellanca of the Amalgamated Clothing Workers led successful organizing drives in the runaway shops of Pennsylvania that had been established to capitalize on the cheap labor of miners' wives, sisters, and children. Rose Pesotta of the ILGWU organized garment workers on the West Coast, rubber workers in Akron, and automobile workers in Michigan.

In addition thousands of wives, daughters, and mothers of workers helped in CIO drives as part of women's auxiliaries. They picketed everywhere with striking workers and were frequently gassed and beaten. During the Memorial Day massacre and other violent confrontations the billy clubs, tear gas, and bullets did not discriminate according to sex. The Women's Emergency Brigade, led by Genora Johnson, mobilized thousands of women in the United Auto Workers' strike against General Motors and played a major role in the success of the Flint sitdown strike where they picketed, fought police, maintained relief services, and displayed a degree of courage equal to any in labor history.

By the end of the 1930s women had achieved significant representation in the labor movement. But as for blacks, inclusion proved to be only a first step. Few women gained access to leadership positions and traditional job categories affected them adversely as well. Although the CIO had opened the door, the struggle for equality was far from over.

ROSE PESOTTA

Rose Pesotta is representative of the many women, most of them lost to history, who played important roles in the organization of the CIO. She emigrated to the United States from Russia in 1913 at the age of seventeen. Like many Jewish girls who came to New York City, she searched for work in the garment industry and found it in a shirtwaist factory. There she joined Waistmakers Local 25 of the International Ladies Garment Workers Union.

Pesotta was one of those intelligent and committed unionists who benefited from the growing network of workers schools that sprang up in the United States during the 1920s. She received a scholarship to attend the Bryn Mawr College Summer School for Women in Industry in 1921, 1922, and 1923, moved on to the Brookwood Labor College from 1924 to 1926, and later attended the University of Wisconsin Summer School for Industrial Workers.

The combination of her experience in the garment shops and her workers education turned Pesotta into a militant trade unionist and a skilled organizer. When the upsurge of industrial unionism hit in the 1930s, she traveled across the country organizing workers in and out of the garment industry. In 1937 she played a role in the first great CIO victory of the rubber workers in Akron. That same year she was in Flint for the sitdown strike against General Motors.

Rose Pesotta's talents brought her recognition in her own union and she served as a national vice-president of the ILGWU from 1934 to 1944. Her organizing skills earned her the position of general organizer for the United States, Canada, and Puerto Rico. In 1942, she voluntarily returned to the rank and file, working as a sewing machine operator on the production line in a New York City garment factory.

THE DEMOCRATIC CONNECTION

The importance of government support to labor's organizational successes in the 1930s cannot be overemphasized. Roosevelt's second election in 1936, and the restructuring of the Democratic Party that accompanied it created new possibilities for the growth of labor's influence. As a result of the alliance with the Democrats, labor's voice began to be heard in Congress, state legislatures, and city halls across the nation.

Until the advent of the New Deal, both major parties depended on the same economic groups for the bulk of their campaign funds. This dependency on business support prevented either party from taking liberal positions. But the crisis of the depression brought the industrial working class into the political process as an influential participant. Roosevelt understood the changing nature of American society and he made the urban workers the cornerstone of his New Deal coalition. National elections were now decided in the urban areas of the big industrial states with large blocs of electoral votes. These were the same areas in which the CIO's strength lay. Indeed, urban workers had been moving in the direction of the Democratic Party since 1928. The Depression accelerated the process. The Republican Party had its roots among rural and small-town voters and among white Anglo-Saxon Protestants in the business and professional classes. As immigrants and blacks populated the cities, their needs had largely been ignored by the Republicans. City dwellers most needed government help in the form of relief, unemployment insurance, old-age pensions, and minimum wages. When the Roosevelt Democrats offered them this help, a dramatic transformation of American politics occurred and the Democrats became the majority party. Both labor and the Democrats benefited from the increased political awareness and power of the urban masses and in much the same way. In this setting, labor moved into the political mainstream of American politics as a powerful interest group.

The new labor movement did not discard the old policy of rewarding its friends and punishing its enemies whatever their party, but in the 1930s this clearly meant a close alliance with the Democratic Party. It can be said that Roosevelt's primary interest was not union security, but rather the welfare of individual workers. Roosevelt supported labor legislation when he recognized its widespread political support among his new constituency. It did not escape him that the chief organizational voice for that constituency—the industrial unions—were becoming an important and potentially powerful interest group in the Democratic Party.

Labor's political potential became apparent in the 1936 election with the creation by Lewis and Hillman of Labor's Non-Partisan League. Nonpartisan in name only, the League's overriding goal was the reelection of Roosevelt and a Democratic congress. Ostensibly independent—it did include some AFL unions—the League was in reality an arm of the CIO. It became the largest contributor to Roosevelt's campaign, giving $1 million, half of which came from the Miners. In New York, where independent socialist politics had been a tradition among the garment workers, the League created the American Labor Party, but everywhere else it supported the Democrats.

Labor's role in the Roosevelt coalition did not go unchallenged by its traditional enemies. Probusiness organizations such as the Liberty League attacked the New Deal as socialist, frequently citing Roosevelt's labor allies as proof. Sidney Hillman and other League leaders were attacked as Soviet agents and one pamphlet warned workers not to join the CIO and "Help build a Soviet America." But "red baiting" had lost much of its effectiveness in the 1930s and workers strongly supported not only the CIO but its protector, the Democratic Party, as well.

After Roosevelt's smashing victory in 1936, Lewis looked to the White House for a return on labor's investment. When the unqualified support the CIO leader demanded was not forthcoming, relations with Roosevelt began to cool. Angry at what he saw as a lack of support by the President during the General Motors strike of 1937, Lewis told the press that when the "economic royalists" attempted to drive Roosevelt from office, the President asked for help and labor gave it. "The same economic royalists now have their fangs in labor," he continued, and "the workers of this country expect the administration to help workers in every legal way and to support the workers in the General Motors plants." The gulf between the two men widened during the Little Steel Strike when an exasperated Roosevelt called down "a plague on both your houses." Lewis responded by lecturing Roosevelt that "It ill behooves one who has supped at labor's table and who has been sheltered in labor's house, to curse with equal fervor and fine impartiality both labor and its adversaries when they become locked in deadly embrace."

Other matters also strained the relationship between the two proud men. Rumors that Lewis wanted to be secretary of labor or even vice-president on the Roosevelt ticket in 1940 appear to have little substance. It was no doubt insulting to an egotist like Lewis that Sidney Hillman, not Lewis, has become Roosevelt's chief labor advisor. Certainly personal pique between two such powerful personalities played a role in the split. But there were substantive differences as well. Lewis believed that Roosevelt had not delivered the appropriate degree of support to labor.

With all of the innovative programs, mass unemployment still plagued the nation and defeats at the hands of Little Steel and Ford had slowed the CIO juggernaut. The two men also differed on foreign affairs as Lewis objected to Roosevelt's drift toward involvement in the war in Europe. Whatever the cause, Lewis broke with Roosevelt in 1940 and supported Wendell Willkie, the Republican candidate. Few leaders of CIO unions followed his lead and when Roosevelt won, Lewis resigned as president of the CIO and was replaced by Philip Murray. Several years later Lewis pulled the United Mine Workers out of the CIO and took the Non-Partisan League with him.

PART III
CIO: An Assessment

The changes in the industrial relations system that occurred during the Depression were so significant that it is possible to misinterpret the real nature of those changes. Workers were moved by a powerful, if temporary, class solidarity and outrage at the failures of the capitalist system. And in some ways the events of those years raised the CIO's struggle to a symbol of revolt against an economic order that had failed. Because of brilliant leadership and the presence of a friendly government in Washington, the CIO matched this new rank-and-file spirit with organizational skill. "For the first time in the history of the United States," according to *Barron's Magazine*, industrial management faced a labor movement which was "smart and courageous, wealthy and successful," a movement which was "winning its battle by applying a shrewd imitation of big business organization and techniques."

This new, efficient and confident labor movement made real gains for workers in the areas of wages, seniority, grievance procedures and the like. Perhaps more importantly, it gave them a sense of dignity and control over their lives. But while it significantly reduced management's power, there were important business leaders who preached the gospel of accommodation, men such as Gerard Swope of General Electric and Myron Taylor of United States Steel. They recognized that industry could benefit from encouraging strong national union leadership and emphasizing the sanctity of the collective agreement. In return for a guarantee of union security, such men envisioned orderly industrial relations carried out at the top, a system that would reduce the influence of local leadership and control shop floor militancy. Carefully handled, the union could discipline the workers. In cooperation, not conflict, lay the best hope.

For revolutionary unionism, such an accommodation would have had little appeal. But for all of its militant trappings, there was nothing revolutionary about the CIO. Certainly its demands went beyond higher wages and shorter hours, and through collective bargaining and political action it asked for a voice in determining the conditions under which men and women worked and lived. But the leaders of the CIO were practical men who did not question that capital or management should receive a reasonable and generous return, but argued that labor's rights and incomes provided the foundation of true social stability. Lewis believed that if the law guaranteed the right to organize and bargain, secure unions could cooperate on an equal basis with management toward more constructive goals, goals like "a voice in the determination of those policies that affect the human element in industry . . . . that affect the amount of food that the family of a worker may eat, the extent of education of his children, the kind and amount of clothing they shall wear, the few pleasures they may enjoy." Important as these factors were, they were far from the far-ranging social and economic changes championed by earlier union movements, such as the Knights and Wobblies. Indeed these factors were well within the goals and objectives of the AFL.

The disagreements between the AFL and the CIO had always been structural rather than philosophical, having to do mainly with the viability of one form of organization over another. Like the AFL, the CIO pursued job-oriented, rather than class-oriented, unionism. This is not surprising considering that even though the Depression had created a rise in working-class consciousness, by the 1930s most workers had become increasingly wage and consumer oriented. The Industrial Revolution had taken its toll and for most, work had become only a way of acquiring an income, a necessary evil. The old working-class communities where shared work experiences, craft traditions, and ethnic bonds had reinforced class consciousness had been greatly weakened by technology, the dispersal of the factories, and the spread of the suburbs. The industrial worker, feeling little sense of definite social location or class membership, looked to the unions primarily as agencies to better his or her economic position.

These factors also accounted for the failure of the left to capitalize on the historic opportunity that organization of the industrial working class presented. In one sense, the triumph of the CIO marked the high-water mark for American radicalism. The Communists in particular achieved a degree of power in the labor movement greater than at any time in history. The CIO needed experienced organizers by the hundreds, and the Communist, and to a lesser extent, socialist movements, were the most likely sources. Communists or those sympathetic to their cause held leadership positions in unions with as much as one-fifth of CIO membership well into the 1940s. But the top leadership remained firmly anti-Communist. When asked about his reliance on Communist organizers, Lewis responded, "Who gets the bird, the hunter or the dog?" Lewis' remark illustrates the fact that rather than the Communists capturing the CIO, the CIO captured the Communists. Where Communists did achieve leadership positions in CIO unions, they did so because of outstanding work as organizers and trade unionists. Whatever attention they paid to their ideological interests had little impact on their day-to-day performance as trade union leaders.

Just as the CIO's adherence to a combination of traditional economic unionism and reform politics precluded the emergence of revolutionary unionism, so did the CIO's alliance with the Democratic Party end prospects for independent Marxist working-class politics among industrial workers. There is no denying that both the Socialist Party and the Communist Party grew during the 1930s. But increasingly their leaders, like Norman Thomas of the socialists, a Princeton-educated minister, appealed more to segments of the disaffected middle class and the intellectuals. Marxism's historic base, the working class, chose the Democrats. Even the old socialist base that had existed among the garment workers, the brewery workers, the machinists, and the miners defected to Roosevelt and the New Deal.

Much of the credit for channeling the discontent of the depression in a reform direction must go to Roosevelt. His alliance with the moderate leadership of the labor movement strengthened their control and brought order to a volatile labor relations scene. That the New Deal revived the faltering capitalist system was of little concern to the majority of workers. Its elimination of the worst aspects of the depression made Roosevelt the champion of the common man. In the words of socialist Norman Thomas, "What cut the ground . . . out from under us was this. It was Roosevelt, in a word."

DISCUSSION QUESTIONS

1. How did the impact of the Great Depression on the middle class help to pave the way for massive government involvement in relief and reform policies for the first time? Why could this be termed a crisis of values?
2. Discuss why the political changes during the Depression led to the reform of existing institutions rather than to revolution.
3. What circumstances during the 1930s led the AFL to reject its traditional "voluntaristic" positions on government involvement in such things as unemployment insurance, minimum wages, and maximum hours? Why had the AFL previously rejected these programs?
4. Why was government involvement—in the forms of legislation such as the NIRA, the Wagner Act, and the Fair Employment Practices Act—so crucial to the success of the CIO? Discuss the meaning of this for the CIO's activist and partisan political role as part of the Democratic Party.
5. Consider both the similarities and the differences between the AFL and CIO unions at the end of the 1930s. Was the CIO really a radical break with the mainstream of American trade unionism?

KEY WORDS AND PHRASES

Black Thursday
Bonus Army
Unemployed Councils
Franklin Roosevelt
The New Deal
Norris-LaGuardia Act
Voluntarism
National Industrial Recovery Act
Wagner Act
John L. Lewis
Sidney Hillman

David Dubinsky
CIO
Philip Murray
Steel Workers Organizing
  Committee
Little Steel Strike
Mohawk Valley Formula
Sitdown Strikes
United Auto Workers
A. Philip Randolph
New Democratic Coalition

BIBLIOGRAPHY

The material for this section was drawn largely from:

Anderson, Jervis. *A Philip Randolph: A Biographical Portrait*. New York: Harcourt Brace Jovanovich, 1973.

Auerbach, Jerold S. *Labor and Liberty: the LaFollette Committee and the New Deal*. Indianapolis: Bobbs-Merrill, 1966.

Bernstein, Irving. *The Turbulent Years: A History of the American Worker, 1933–1941*. Boston: Houghton Mifflin, 1970.

Brody, David. "The Expansion of the American Labor Movement: Institutional Sources of Stimulus and Restraint" in Stephen E. Ambrose, ed. *Institutions in Modern America*. Baltimore: The John Hopkins University Press, 1967.

————. *Workers in Industrial America: Essays on the 20th Century Struggle*. New York: Oxford University Press, 1980.

Brooks, Thomas R. *Picket Lines and Bargaining Tables: Organized Labor Comes of Age, 1935–1955*. New York: Grosset and Dunlap, 1968.

Cantor, Milton. *The Divided Left: American Radicalism, 1900–1975*. New York: Hill and Wang, 1978.

Chandler, Lester V. *America's Greatest Depression, 1929–1941*. New York: Harper & Row, 1970.

Clayton, Horace and George Mitchell. *Black Workers and the New Unions*. Chapel Hill: University of North Carolina Press, 1939.

Derber, Milton and Edwin Young. *Labor and the New Deal*. Madison: University of Wisconsin Press, 1957.

Dubofsky, Melvyn and Van Tine, Warren. *John L. Lewis: A Biography*. New York: Quadrangle, 1977.

Fine, Sidney A. *Sitdown: The General Motors Strike of 1936–1937*. Ann Arbor: University of Michigan Press, 1969.

Galenson, Walter. *The CIO Challenge to the A.F. of L.: A History of the American Labor Movement, 1935–1941.* Cambridge: Harvard University Press, 1960.

Gordon, David, Richard Edwards and Michael Reich. *Segmented Work, Divided Workers: The Historical Transformation of Labor in the United States.* New York: Cambridge University Press, 1982.

Greenstone, J. David. *Labor in American Politics.* New York: Vintage Books, 1969.

Higgins, George G. *Voluntarism in Organized Labor in the United States, 1930–1940.* Washington: Catholic University Press, 1944.

Jacobson, Julius, ed. *The Negro and the American Labor Movement.* Garden City. N.Y.: Doubleday and Co., 1968.

Kenneally, James J. *Women and American Trade Unions.* St. Albans, Vt.: Eden Press, 1978.

Lens, Sidney. *Radicalism in America.* New York: Thomas Crowell, 1969.

Lynd, Alice and Staughton Lynd. *Rank and File: Personal Histories by Working-Class Organizers.* Boston: Beacon Press, 1973.

Michigan Labor History Society. *Sit Down.* Detroit, 1979.

Tomlins, Christopher L. "AFL Unions in the 1930s: Their Performance in Historical Perspective," *Journal of American History,* vol. 65, no. 4 (March 1979): 1021–1042.

For additional reading see:

Dobbs, Farrell. *Teamster Rebellion.* New York: Monad Press, 1972.

Grubbs, Donald H. *Cry from the Cotton: The Southern Tenant Farmers Union and the New Deal.* Chapel Hill: University of North Carolina Press, 1971.

Huberman, Leo. *The Labor Spy Racket.* New York: Modern Age Books, 1937.

Preis, Art. *Labor's Giant Step: Thirty Years of the CIO.* New York: Pioneer Publishers, 1964.

Stein, Walter J. *California and the Dust Bowl Migration.* Westport, Conn.: Greenwood Publishing Company, 1973.

Terkel, Studs. *Hard Times: An Oral History of the Great Depression.* New York: Pantheon Books, 1970.

SECTION
SEVEN

PART I
From Hot War to Cold War

War, not the relief programs of the New Deal, brought the Great Depression to an end. When Hitler's Nazi legions marched across Europe, American industry began to step up defense production. After Pearl Harbor, the Roosevelt administration followed the example set in World War I and created many special agencies to oversee the war effort on the home front.

An uninterrupted flow of armaments to the theaters of war required the organization and control of the nation's labor force. To this end, Roosevelt created the War Manpower Commission to deal with the strain that military and civilian manpower needs placed on the nation's human resources.

Stressing voluntary acceptance of its policies, the Commission undertook the massive job of getting the right workers to the right place at the right time. It encouraged stepped-up industrial training programs and discouraged the hoarding and pirating of skilled labor. Programs were established to facilitate the hiring of women with children and handicapped workers.

The crisis also changed the employment picture for groups traditionally relegated to marginal occupational status. At the war's beginning, blacks, three-fourths of whom lived in the South, worked overwhelmingly in agriculture. Those in other occupational sectors were found primarily in unskilled and service jobs. Most of the gains black workers had made between 1910 and 1920 disappeared during the Depression, and by 1940 their percentage of the workforce was lower than it had been in 1910.

Determined that blacks would not be left behind this time, A. Philip Randolph mobilized the black community and threatened a march on Washington to protest discriminatory hiring policies. Roosevelt, conscious of the potential effect of racial conflict on the war effort, responded by ordering nondiscrimination in all defense work and created the Committee on Fair Employment Practices (FEPC) in 1941 to investigate claims of discrimination in training and employment in defense plants. Although the FEPC held public hearings and investigated thousands of complaints, its impact was moral because it had no legal enforcement powers.

Indeed, although blacks had forced the establishment of the FEPC, the agency itself demonstrated the importance of racism in American society. On the presumption that they would be more effective in dealing with white employers and labor leaders, most of the committee members were white, as were all the chairmen except for a brief period when a black served as acting chairman.

The committee faced several obstacles. Organized labor gave only half-hearted support. Southern congressmen tried continually to kill the FEPC. In May 1943, Roosevelt strengthened the committee by increasing its budget and placing it administratively in the Executive Office of the President. In addition, unions were included as institutions forbidden to discriminate on the basis of race, sex, or creed. Randolph had demanded but failed to get this provision when the FEPC had been created in 1941. By turning up evidence of massive discrimination on the part of unions and companies, such as on the railroads and in the west coast shipbuilding industry, the committee contributed to a rise in the militancy of black workers.

Wartime pressures and a new assertiveness on the part of black Americans created explosive social tensions. Blacks noted the discrepancy between the crusade for freedom overseas and their own conditions at home. In a number of cases, the introduction of blacks into what had been largely white jobs resulted in wildcat strikes by protesting whites. In industrial cities disputes arose over housing, employment, and transportation. On February 28, 1942, a riot took place in Detroit over an attempt to move black families into a public housing project. In June of the same year 3000 rioters attacked blacks and Mexican-Americans in Los Angeles. Similar outbreaks followed in Texas and Harlem. Yet despite continuing difficulties, blacks and other minorities moved steadily into industry as the critical demand for labor continued. By April 1944, nearly 5 million blacks worked in civilian jobs—1 million more than in 1940. The number employed in manufacturing and processing increased from 500,000 to 1 million. Much the same was true in transportation, public utilities, and communications. Even more dramatic increases took place in government service.

But the gains of the war years were difficult to maintain when the fighting stopped. In the immediate postwar period, blacks returned to unemployed status in far greater numbers than white workers. The economic condition of blacks improved again in the early 1950s under the impetus of renewed defense production for the Korean War and increased consumer spending. In 1951, earnings of black males averaged 64 percent of those of white males, compared to 54 percent in 1947, and by 1953 the black unemployment rate for men and women hit post-World War II lows of 4.4 percent and 3.8 percent, respectively. But even with the gains, by 1955 blacks still found themselves concentrated at the bottom of the occupational ladder in jobs that were increasingly being eliminated by automation.

Women also gained access to jobs in unprecedented numbers during the war. By 1944, the peak year of war production, just over 9 million women worked, up nearly 6 million since 1940. Old barriers crumbled as women flooded into the nation's shops and mills. The aircraft industry alone employed more than a third of a million women. As a result of this influx, child care centers began on large scale.

A massive advertising campaign extolling the patriotic virtues of "Rosie the Riveter" encouraged women to take employment in occupations formerly closed to them. But the large number of women in traditional male jobs raised issues that underlined the handicaps women faced in improving their occupational status. The Office of War Information (OWI) declared that sweater-clad women posed a threat to war production. "It isn't just a rumor," said the OWI, "that a tightly sweatered working companion takes a man's eyes off his machine." The agency also warned women not to "trade on their femininity" by dating the boss, flirting with the foremen, or trying to get male workers to do the heavy or unpleasant tasks.

While the Office of War Information went on treating them as temporary curiosities at the workplace, the women had other ideas. Of the almost 6 million new women workers, 75 percent hoped to continue working after the war. Indeed, as one CIO official told a Los Angeles Chamber of Commerce meeting at the war's end, "Rosie the Riveter isn't going back to emptying slop jars."

His statement proved prophetic. Even though the propoganda machinery turned around at the end of the war and encouraged women to return to their "natural" roles as homemakers and mothers in order to make room for the returning GI's, by 1947 the percentage of working women still exceeded that of 1940 by a healthy margin and was growing. There was no mystery about the reasons for this. A 1946 study by the Census Bureau discovered that one-fifth of all women workers in nonfarm families were either the sole support of their families or the major wage earner. In the nation as a whole, women earned at least half of the total income in one family in eight. Clearly the great majority of married women worked because their husbands' income was not sufficient. In all, one-half of the female labor force either supported themselves entirely or provided the main support for their families.

Nevertheless women still worked under many of the old handicaps. They found themselves disproportionately represented in the lowerpaying industries. Even in the heavily unionized manufacturing sector, women's pay lagged considerably behind that of men.

Old social conventions did not crumble easily. Alice Leopold, President Eisenhower's director of the Women's Bureau in the Department of Labor, insisted that "the most important function of a woman is to run a home, be a mother, and contribute to the life of the family and community." The director of staff studies for the National Manpower Council's study on working women, warned that the families of working women suffered from psychological strain, and that working women risked mental illness later in life.

The increased presence of women in the workforce led to a dramatic increase in the number of women in unions. But as in the case of blacks, there was little penetration into the policy-making positions. At the 1957 convention of the AFL-CIO, only 13 of the 676 delegates were women.

QUID PRO QUO

While the task of dealing with the influx of new workers fell to the War Manpower Commission, the War Production Board and the War Labor Board were the linchpins of the government's labor policy. The War Production Board, formed in 1942 as the replacement for the Office of Production Management and the Council on National Defense, was charged with increasing productivity. Labor had representation on the board but little real influence. Most of the productivity schemes sponsored by the War Production Board had little discernible success. The majority of the 4000 labor-management production committees established under its auspices degenerated into a method for handling minor activities. Management refused to surrender its prerogatives and unions also lacked a strong interest in participatory schemes.

War Labor Board activities proved to be of much greater significance. Shortly after Pearl Harbor representatives of management and labor pledged to refrain from strikes and lockouts for the duration. An emergency union-management conference also recommended the creation of an agency to oversee industrial relations in critical industries.

Roosevelt responded with a program designed to protect against inflation. He called for an even-handed approach to guarantee equality of sacrifice. In addition to a wage freeze, the plan called for a ceiling on incomes and a rigid price freeze. But the New Deal tide had waned and the 1942 congressional elections placed a conservative coalition of Republicans and southern Democrats in control. Congress promptly discarded any ceiling on incomes and through constant harassment of the Office of Price Administration made the price freeze only partially successful. Only the War Labor Board and the wage freeze remained of the president's program. At first, the War Labor Board's authority rested on voluntary cooperation, not compulsion, although it could request the president to use his wartime powers of plant seizure to bring noncooperators into line. The board could intervene only in cases referred to it as labor disputes. Voluntary wage agreements remained outside of its jurisdiction. But it soon became clear that voluntary settlements in the tight labor market were fueling an inflationary spiral. As a result, Congress passed the Wage Stabilization Act on October 2, 1942 enabling Roosevelt to quickly place authority for all wage changes, voluntary or otherwise, under the War Labor Board's control.

During the war and immediately after, the board intervened in thousands of labor-management disputes and compiled an admirable record of labor peace. The pillars of its policy emerged as "maintenance of membership" and the "Little Steel Formula" to ensure labor peace by dealing with the problems of union security and an equitable wage policy. Unions that had given a no-strike pledge wanted assurance that management would not take advantage of the influx of new workers to break the unions. The maintenance-of-membership plan gave employees fifteen days after employment or after a contract settlement to decide whether or not to join the union. After that all union members were obligated to retain membership for the length of the contract. As a bonus to the union, the company collected union dues through the dues check-off and remitted them to the union.

In dealing with a dispute between the United Steelworkers and the Little Steel companies, the board rejected the idea of a total wage freeze and instituted a formula under which any group of employees who had failed to receive a general increase of 15 percent in average straight-time hourly earnings between January 1, 1941 and May 1942, a figure that represented the rise in the cost of living, would be permitted an increase necessary to reach that figure.

Of the two policies, the reasoning behind maintenance of membership was the most significant. In creating the plan, the War Labor Board recognized labor's right to exist, but in the context of a severely limited role. "By and large," the board stated in explaining its decision, "the maintenance of stable union leadership and responsible union discipline, makes for keeping faithfully the terms of the contract, and provides a stable basis for union-management cooperation for more efficient production."

With the aid of maintenance of membership and the dues checkoff unions grew. Most of this growth came in already organized industries, but unions also took advantage of wartime pressures on industry to make significant gains in the textile, meat packing, shipbuilding and aircraft industries. After World War II, union membership stood at fifteen million, a fivefold increase since 1933.

REACTION

In spite of labor's gains, business took advantage of its role in the war effort to resume its customary position of dominance in American life. Before undertaking the risks of conversion to defense production, business demanded no limitation of profit on defense contracts, general tax write-offs for new plants and equipment, and no excess profits tax. Not until a Senate committee approved a tax bill satisfactory to industry leaders in 1940 did war contracts begin to flow.

Once the matter of tax legislation had been satisfactorily attended to, industry rushed into conversion. Between 1940 and 1945 the federal government added 200 billions to the national debt. "To the Americans war is a business, not an art," observed a British official. Profits of $10¾ billion after taxes in 1944, up $6½ billion from 1940, supported his argument.

Only business management possessed the skills and know-how to deal with the organization of industrial production to fight a war on a global scale. Droves of "dollar a year" men on loan from business came to Washington to staff the wartime agencies and oversee the organization of men and material. Enemies of the New Deal came to dominate the civilian war command, the wartime agencies, and the War and Navy Departments.

This new business influence in the executive branch combined with the new conservative Congress to change the direction of American politics. The Justice Department shelved a number of pending antitrust suits because of the wartime emergency. Congress molded tax legislation to fit the needs of business to such an extent that Roosevelt vetoed one bill for "providing relief not for the needy, but for the greedy." When the critical issue of legislation to provide for reconversion to a peacetime economy arose, business was granted handsome cash allowances in the termination of defense contracts. Workers, on the other hand, were left to state unemployment systems in which compensation was often low and of short duration.

Unquestionably, by the end of the war business leaders had turned the tide. They sat confidently astride the greatest economy the world had ever seen. A system with a gross national product of around $80 billion in the 1930s emerged from the war doing business of over $153 billion in constant 1939 dollars.

NEW RED SCARE

As business solidified its dominance, industrial workers whose grievances and frustrations had been left unattended during the war began to stir. Strikes increased noticeably in the last months of fighting and exploded after VJ Day in one of the greatest strike waves in American history. Unemployment began to rise as defense industries wound down and the inflation rate climbed. For a people who had undergone fifteen years of strain and sacrifice at home, and who had watched nervously as the Soviet Union extended its control in eastern Europe, the strike wave offered one more sign that somehow things had gone wrong.

A change in national mood is difficult to describe, but as early as 1945 one perceptive observer, historian Bernard DeVoto, noted a spread of reaction in the country led by business that equated the New Deal with communism. "The Communists," according to DeVoto's perception of what people were thinking, "were responsible for the New Deal and they intend to inflict a labor dictatorship on us . . . . they want to destroy initiative and profit, business and freedom, the individual and the United States."

Liberals, no matter how anti-Communist, soon found themselves on the defensive. Just as the Bolshevik revolution had provided the basis for the Red Scare of the post-World War I years, a new Red Scare rolled across the country between 1946 and 1952. Republicans seized the issue and linked the Democrats, the New Deal, and labor with communism. Democrats were blamed for the "loss" of eastern Europe and China. Richard Nixon of California announced that the Communists had infiltrated the very highest councils of the Truman administration. The U.S. Chamber of Commerce demanded that all "Communists, fellow-travelers and dupes" be barred from jobs in newspapers, radio, television, book and magazine publishing, and research institutions, as well as from libraries, schools and "large manufacturing plants." Thirty states established loyalty oaths for teachers, while congressional and state committees investigated unions, the motion picture industry, and many other American institutions.

The great purge began among conservative politicians who used the anti-Communist issue to flay their opponents. The trend was evident as early as the 1946 congressional elections that turned out to be a disaster for the Democrats who lost 54 seats. The election taught Truman and the Democrats, who had already launched the anti-Communist crusade abroad, that they faced disaster if they didn't get on the popular side of the issue at home as well. Responding to pressures from his opponents, Truman launched the federal loyalty program on March 25, 1947. In addition to establishing a loyalty review procedure in the Civil Service Commission, the order authorized the Attorney General to compile a list of organizations that he considered to be "totalitarian, fascist, communist or subversive, or as having adopted a policy of approving the commission of acts of force or violence to deny others their constitutional rights."

Current membership in an organization on the Attorney General's list came to mean almost automatic dismissal for federal employees. Evidence of past membership, even if the employee had publicly repented, was almost as damaging. But the loyalty program went beyond evidence of actual membership and applied the vague concept of "sympathetic association" as well. Such a fundamental threat to the civil rights of federal workers received no opposition from the federal employees unions. According to its president, the American Federation of Government Employees (AFL) was "confident" that the Civil Service Commission and the FBI would carry out the program in a "truly American fashion." There was no reason for the "notion" that this was to be a "witch hunt." The independent National Federation of Government Employees went even farther. "Federal employees who have nothing to conceal," said the Federation's president, "are not those who are crying out most passionately against the loyalty program and raising the bogey of persecution."

The loyalty program turned out to be a good deal more than a "bogey." By the mid-1950s one out of five workers had to take a loyalty oath or receive a security clearance as a condition of employment.

In the loyalty review procedures, the burden of proof fell to the accused. Past association with organizations on the attorney general's list, or an even larger list of the House Committee on Un-American Activities (HUAC), resulted in a presumption of guilt. Only a tiny fraction of those accused were ever confronted by prosecution witnesses.

According to the best available estimates, the federal loyalty program resulted in about 2700 civilian dismissals and 12,000 resignations between 1947 and 1956. During the same period, loyalty boards at the state and local levels dismissed about 500 employees for political reasons. In the private sector some 4 million workers in about 21,000 different plants were required by the government to have security clearances between 1947 and 1956. A total of 5312 workers reviewed under the Industrial Personnel Security Program, the Port Security Program, and the Atomic Energy Commission loyalty program were denied security clearance. The majority lost their jobs.

Companies also created their own security programs and company personnel had ready access to the files of congressional and state investigating committees and local police departments. Figures for private security programs are nonexistent, but one scholar estimated that they resulted in the dismissal of some 700 workers through 1956.

CONTAINMENT

The first Republican Congress since 1928 reflected the conservative mood. It turned down federal aid to education, aid for public housing, price controls, and an extension of social security benefits. Organized labor came in for special attention. During 1946 and 1947 a host of antilabor bills appeared, and in 1947 the Taft-Hartley Act amended the Wagner Act in favor of Business.

With all of the malaise and paranoia, the unchallenged world economic dominance of the United States and the growth of a huge peacetime defense industry provided the framework for the general prosperity that characterized the postwar period. Despite several short recessions, these were years of rapid growth, increased demand for labor, and low inflation.

Workers shared in this new prosperity, and those in mass-production industries, most of which were unionized, benefited the most. Mass-production techniques and the mechanization of agriculture had created a consumption-oriented society. Signs abounded that the average American was living better. Widespread improvements in diet and housing testified to the fact that many unionized workers had moved into the middle-income bracket. In this environment, unions continued to grow, largely because of the growth of the labor force in the mass-production industries. Still, the labor movement, while immeasurably stronger than before, was largely contained. An effort to organize in the mostly nonunion South

foundered on rivalry between the AFL and the CIO, and on the unwilling-
ness of both federations to confront the racism that divided southern workers. In sum, business held the line, and while it made no real attempt to
break unions where they already existed, it successfully resisted their
spread to other sectors of the economy.

While business resistance retarded union growth, there were other factors as well. Automation began to make inroads at the workplace during
and after World War II. For the most part economic growth minimized its
impact on workers. But in the early 1950s, a pattern began to develop that
showed that automation reduced the percentage of production workers
and increased the percentage of clerical and professional employees, although often not enough to offset the number of skilled and semiskilled
jobs displaced.

Automation created work processes that were less dependent on workers, thus making it more difficult for unions in certain highly automated
industries to use the strike weapon effectively. In a 1954 strike of operating
and maintenance workers at atomic energy plants in Kentucky and Tennessee, a small number of supervisory employees were able to maintain
operations throughout the three-day walkout. Joseph Bierne, president of
the Communications Workers of America, argued after a less than successful strike against the Bell Telephone Company in 1955 that unions would
increasingly have to deemphasize strikes and turn instead to political
action to gain a share in the economic and political decisions of the nation.

Perhaps even more important; automation and rising consumer demand
changed the nature of the workforce and posed serious organizing problems for unions. Growth in the number of clerical, professional, technical,
and other service workers meant that in order to grow, unions would have
to organize among categories of workers that had always proved most
difficult to unionize. By 1955, white-collar workers made up over one-third
of the total workforce, and only about one in five belonged to unions.

PART II
Politics and Purges

The war brought significant increases in earnings for unionized workers. The Little Steel formula provided a buffer against inflation; and although the increase in straight hourly rates lagged behind the 50 percent cost-of-living increase during the war, take-home pay increased substantially because six- or seven-day work weeks and nine- and ten-hour days were common.

For the first time, the relative prosperity of union workers began to create something of a backlash among workers without union protection. Few of the millions of white collar and salaried workers received as much as the 15 percent increase which the Little Steel formula gave most union workers. An Office of War Information press release in 1943 declared that 20 million Americans received inadequate incomes. Not surprisingly many in these circumstances had trouble seeing unions as in need of their sympathies. The fact that companies were making the highest profits in history was generally overlooked.

In part, the attitude that unionized workers in the building trades and in the mass-production industries had become a privileged group led to a close scrutiny of labor by the politicians, press, and public during the war. Wartime strikes, justified or not, brought the full force of public opinion down on the unions. In truth, most of those strikes were without formal union sanction and resulted from tensions over working conditions and the arbitrary use of management power. The push for war production had made the American workplace even more dangerous. The combination of the neglect of safety precautions and tired workers led to a staggering accident toll. From Pearl Harbor to January 1, 1945, accidents in wartime industry took a toll of 6725 million casualties. In the first two years of the war, 37,600 workers were killed on the job—7500 more than the American military dead for the same period. Wartime industrial accidents permanently disabled more than 200,000 workers. Under such conditions, a significant number of wildcat strikes causing tensions between labor leaders and the rank and file did occur, yet in the entire wartime period only 36.3

million workdays were lost to strikes, a tenth of one percent of available working time.

Nevertheless any wartime strike gave the growing antilabor coalition in Congress an opportunity to press its advantage, and none more so than the miners' walkout in 1943. Once again John L. Lewis figured prominently in a changing of mood toward organized labor when he refused to accept the decision of the War Labor Board as well as an appeal from President Roosevelt. Although the miners won important concessions, the impact of their action on unions as a whole was ominous. Although most labor leaders condemned Lewis, Congress moved quickly to pass the War Labor Disputes Act, or Smith-Connally, over Roosevelt's veto. The law proved to be the first step in a legislative campaign aimed at containing the power of organized labor.

Smith-Connally included presidential seizure powers, a ban against political contributions by unions, a provision for a thirty-day "cooling off" period before a strike in a defense industry could take place, and the provision for a secret strike ballot by the workers.

Although the law turned out to be the only important labor measure enacted by Congress during the war, a raft of antilabor legislation was proposed that dealt with strike limitations, the closed shop, Wagner Act amendments, and requirements for the filing of financial data by unions. Just as ominous were the large number of antilabor bills passed in the state legislatures.

The CIO responded to the attack with the formation of the Political Action Committee (CIO-PAC) in 1944 under the direction of Sidney Hillman of the Amalgamated Clothing Workers. CIO-PAC developed into an efficient, practical political organization. It taught workers on a vast scale the workings of practical politics, such as voter registration, door-to-door canvassing and the use of phone banks. CIO-PAC used large sums of money to educate its members and the wider electorate on the significance of a Roosevelt defeat.

The effort contributed to Roosevelt's reelection and a more progressive Congress, and labor received much of the credit for the victory. But the visibility of CIO-PAC during the election also made it a symbol for attack by the Republicans and antilabor forces. Some were anti-Semitic attacks on Sidney Hillman, but more damaging were charges by the House Committee on Un-American Activities that CIO-PAC's efforts were nothing more than a "subversive Communist campaign to subvert the Congress of the United States to its totalitarian program." Republicans less inclined to "red baiting" stressed that labor had taken over the Democratic Party and that Roosevelt had cleared the selection of Harry Truman as his vice-presidential candidate with Hillman. "Clear it with Sidney," became a popular Republican campaign refrain.

The 1944 campaign also reinforced the ties between the labor movement and the Democratic Party—a party which by that time was moving steadily away from the progressive New Deal tradition toward the broad middle of the political spectrum. This shift reflected the whole movement of American politics to the right. In these circumstances most unions rejected non-partisanship because of the increasingly conservative caste of the Republicans. The Democratic Party also came to realize that most unions had nowhere else to go, and this reality led eventually to a reduction in labor's influence in the high councils of the party. Philip Murray made this dependence clear when he turned back suggestions for a third party in 1944. "We are opposed to the organization of a third party," said the CIO leader, ". . . because it would divide the forces of progressives throughout the nation."

TAFT-HARTLEY

The measure of labor's political vulnerability became clear in the immediate postwar years. The federal government had enormously expanded its role in the economy during the New Deal and World War II. Both business and labor recognized that increasingly the critical economic battles would be waged on the political front.

As we have seen, the political balance tipped toward business during and after the war. Probusiness lobbies chipped away at the "dangerous" power of unions and the "one sidedness" of the Wagner Act. The 1946 strike wave deepened the antilabor sentiment. When the coal miners struck in that year a fury of antilabor feeling, intensified by the memory of the coal strike during the war, swept the country. Virginia's conservative Senator, Harry Byrd, damned John L. Lewis on the Senate floor as "drunk with power." Even more ominously, Senator Scott Lucas of Illinois, a union sympathizer, lamented that "If this government has not the power to outlaw strikes of this character, then this government has no power of self preservation." Clear as it seems in retrospect, both the AFL and the CIO underestimated the scope of this sentiment among the American people for "reform" of the nation's basic labor law.

In 1946 the Case Bill passed Congress. The act, vetoed by President Harry Truman, was a punitive piece of legislation that went too far toward disturbing the equilibrium for moderates who wanted reform but not reaction. But the Case Bill contained much on which there was widespread consensus.

Truman's veto did not dissuade the conservative coalition from pushing ahead. The Taft-Hartley Act, which emerged in 1947, proved more temperate than the Case Bill, though it included some of its provisions, but threatening enough to cause labor to refer to it as the "slave labor bill." Labor's strategy to stop Taft-Hartley reflected its misperception of the mood of the country and of the Congress. Certainly the main thrust of the legislation was antilabor, but many moderates, whether out of conviction or political expediency, had come to accept that amendment of the Wagner Act was inevitable. By refusing to accept some of the less offensive amendments in the hope of staving off more serious changes, labor's lobbyists undertook a battle they could not win. This put Truman in the position of having his veto of the bill that he called "bad for labor, bad for management, and bad for the country," overridden by a hostile Congress.

There is no question that Taft-Hartley was a creature of the business lobby. The National Association of Manufacturers spent a fortune supporting it, and the Republican National Committee paid corporation lawyers to draft it. It did not, however, fundamentally threaten the rights labor had gained in the Wagner Act. The fact that many viciously antilabor amendments were left out indicated that its sponsors understood that they could only go so far. What emerged reflected the widespread sentiment in the country, and in the business community, that unions had to be restrained, but not destroyed. Even Truman agreed with the prohibition of secondary boycotts and jurisdictional strikes, and limitations on strikes in vital industries.

Taft-Hartley matched the unfair labor practices for business embodied in the Wagner Act with a list of unfair labor practices for unions, and it threatened union security by banning the closed shop and allowing states to ban the union shop. As a result the number of states having right-to-work laws increased to twenty-one, all in areas where there were few union members. This hindered the CIO's southern organizing drive, but in the industrial states, such as Ohio, labor beat back attempts to outlaw the union shop.

The act also required labor leaders to sign a non-Communist affidavit in order for their unions to use the National Labor Relations Board. The requirement was highly insulting to labor leaders who believed they had amply demonstrated their loyalty to the country during the war. Most of the union leaders in the strongly anti-Communist AFL signed without hesitation. For the CIO, which included a significant Communist minority, it was a more delicate problem. But when noncompliance exposed them to raids by AFL unions as well as to the congressional witch hunters, Murray and most of the CIO leaders quickly fell into line. In the entire labor movement, only the United Mine Workers and the International Typographical Union, neither with Communist leadership, stood on principle and refused to sign.

Taft-Hartley also resurrected the emergency strike provision of the wartime Smith-Connally Act. It enabled the president to ask Congress for permission to use an eighty-day injunction against strikes that in his judgment threatened the national health and safety.

Experience with the national emergency strike provision demonstrated the difficulty of imposing legislative restrains on free collective bargaining in a democratic society. Truman first used the injunction power in the 1950 coal strike. But when the union told the miners to comply, they refused to return to the mines. With the union in compliance and the workers not, Truman asked Congress for authorization to seize the mines. While Congress vacillated, the operators and Lewis reached a settlement. Taft-Hartley had little effect.

When in 1952, during the Korean War, the steel industry refused to accept the recommendations of a new Wage Stabilization Board, pressure grew on Truman to invoke the emergency strike provision. He refused because the United Steelworkers, who had already worked three months without a contract, had accepted the Board's proposal. Instead Truman seized the steel mills. The Supreme Court promptly ruled the seizure unconstitutional. With the mills back in private hands the union carried out the long-delayed strike and won a settlement on the lines of the Wage Stabilization Board's original recommendations. It remains problematic if all of the government activity produced anything better than would have resulted from free collective bargaining.

A third test came on the New York waterfront in 1953. There deadlocked negotiations between the International Longshoremen's Association (ILA), an AFL union, and the New York Shipping Association led to a strike that closed the nation's most important port. The factor that rendered government intervention of little use in this case turned out to be interunion warfare resulting from corruption.

Serious penetration by organized crime into a few AFL unions occurred in the 1920s and 1930s. Mob influence was most pervasive in the building trades, trucking, on the waterfront, and in the garment trades—all industries characterized by a number of small competitive businesses in which union control of available labor made both companies and workers vulnerable to extortion and intimidation. Only the garment unions had significant success in driving the racketeers out.

In the hostile climate of the postwar period, negative publicity about union corruption added to labor's problems. In 1953 the New York Crime Commission publicized the sordid details of union corruption on the docks. International Longshoremen's union officials were found to have taken payoffs from stevedoring and shipping companies, employed thugs and the infamous "shape up" system to terrorize the workers, looted the union's treasury, and shared in loan sharking and cargo theft operations. George Meany, the new AFL president, moved decisively to clean up the situation and the 1953 AFL convention expelled the ILA and chartered a new longshoremen's union.

In the midst of the controversy, President Eisenhower invoked the emergency provisions of Taft-Hartley to end the strike, but warfare between the two rival unions led to a series of wildcat strikes that kept the port of New York in turmoil. Although the eventual settlement led to several years of labor peace on the docks, little credit belonged to Taft-Hartley. And after fruitlessly spending nearly $1 million to defeat the ILA, the AFL abandoned the effort.

TOWARD UNITY

The defeat on Taft-Hartley and the rising tide of conservatism demonstrated the need for a unified political effort on labor's part. The presence of a minority of Communist-led unions in the CIO continued to retard cooperation with the strongly anti-Communist AFL, but events leading up to the 1948 election were to bring this problem to sharp resolution.

Other factors drew the two federations closer together. By 1948 the AFL had almost totally abandoned nonpartisanship in national politics, although it still refrained from endorsing a presidential candidate. The AFL had come to strongly support expanded social insurance programs, higher minimum wages, and the beginnings of national health insurance; and most of its affiliated unions were, for all intents and purposes, in the Democratic camp.

A crucial factor in the 1948 election proved to be the emergence of two new political parties, The Dixiecrats and the Progressive Party, both of which threatened to appeal to sections of the normal Democratic constituency. The Progressive Party and the presidential candidacy of its standard bearer, Henry Wallace, grew out of disagreements among American liberals and leftists with the foreign policy of the Truman administration. The Progressives rejected the Democrats' strategy of confrontation and containment in relations with the Soviet Union through the Marshall Plan and military aid to Europe. Instead they argued for a continuation of the World War II alliance in order to forestall the division of the world into two armed camps. As the movement developed, American Communists assumed an important, some have said dominant, role in the Progressive campaign. The left-wing or Communist leaders of a minority of CIO unions urged the CIO to remain neutral. But the CIO Executive Council, fearing the election of a Republican president, endorsed Truman.

Throughout the 1948 campaign, CIO-PAC and the AFL's new political action committee, Labor's League for Political Education, cooperated on Truman's behalf. So critical did their contribution appear to the President that on learning of his upset victory, Truman exulted, "Labor did it." The statement contained some, but not all of the truth. Labor overwhelmingly supported Truman, but so did blacks and most white minority groups as well as a significant percentage of small farmers and the new middle class, precisely the segments of the population that had benefited most from the New Deal. The election proved that while the nation might have drifted to the right, any predictions about the disappearance of the Roosevelt coalition were premature.

But the surprising victory, satisfying as it was, was not overwhelming. Although the Democrats retained control of Congress, the coalition of conservative Democrats and Republicans remained strong enough to turn back labor's chief legislative goal, repeal of Taft-Hartley. Labor could not be ignored, but neither could it collect full measure from the Democrats for its campaign contributions.

PURGE

Although the issue of support for the Progressive Party in the 1948 presidential election brought the issue to a head, pressure on the CIO to deal with its Communist minority had been building for several years. Most of this pressure came to rest on the person of Philip Murray. There was no question of Murray's patriotism. As a devout Catholic, communism held no attraction for him. But Murray was no ideologue. Above all a practical man, he placed no faith in isms of any kind. If he had a philosophy of labor, it was one that viewed trade unions as an important part of a just society based on cooperation between labor and management in the public interest. This corresponded to a strong belief in the essentially economic functions of trade unions. For the political beliefs and non-trade-union activities of the CIO leaders, Murray had remarkable tolerance. But he demanded absolute loyalty on what he considered trade union matters.

Murray came slowly to his decision to purge the Communist-led unions. When he finally acted he did so in the belief that he had no other choice. The serious defeat of the Democrats in the 1946 congressional elections convinced him that the alliance between the CIO and the Democrats was critical to the interests of American workers. The political loyalty necessary to maintain that alliance had, in Murray's mind, become a trade union issue. Thus when the Communist labor leaders defected to Henry Wallace and the Progressive Party in 1948, Murray moved ruthlessly against them.

Murray presided uneasily over the CIO while the conflict between the anti-Communists and the Communists simmered. For the most part the old animosities remained beneath the surface during the popular front of the war years. Indeed, during the war the urge for unity became so great that the Communist Party dissolved itself and became the Communist Political Association. So taken were the Communists with their newfound respectability as part of the win-the-war effort that they became the most vociferous supporters of the no-strike pledge, no premium pay for overtime, and other productivity programs. For many in the anti-Communist camp, Communist enthusiasm for the war, which came only after the German invasion of the Soviet Union in 1941, often sacrificed the legitimate interests of the workers.

As long as the alliance between the Soviet Union and the United States endured, the Communist-led unions were not vulnerable. But the development of the Cold War and a change in the Moscow line from cooperation to conflict caught the Communist union leaders in a trap. When they quickly fell into line with Soviet policy and attacked the anti-Communist foreign policy of the Truman administration, they became dangerously exposed.

For a time Murray's principled refusal to comply with the non-Communist affidavit requirement of the Taft-Hartley Act continued to provide a measure of protection to the Communists inside the CIO. Unions whose officers did not sign could not be certified as a bargaining agent by the

NLRB, could not insert a union-shop clause in any contract, and could not file unfair labor practice charges. But, as we have seen, external and internal pressures became too strong, and Murray gave permission to sign. For the Communist leaders, this posed a painful dilemma. If they did not sign, their unions became vulnerable to raids from complying unions and their inability to use the NLRB machinery severely hindered new organization. If they did sign, they became liable to federal prosecution for perjury.

By 1947 Murray's direction had become clear. He had come out strongly in favor of the Marshall Plan and the Truman Doctrine of containment of the spread of communism. In his own union, the United Steelworkers, Murray had always limited left-wing influence. But the CIO presented a bigger problem. The Communist-led unions accounted for approximately one-quarter of CIO membership. Most were small, but a few, like the United Electrical Workers; the Mine, Mill and Smelter Workers; and the International Longshoremen's & Warehousemen's Union were large and militant affiliates. In addition, several other unions, most notably the United Auto Workers, had important left-wing factions that could be expected to be unenthusiastic about any purge.

But as anti-Communist sentiment spread rapidly in the nation, several events altered the balance of power in the CIO. Most significant was Walter Reuther's rise to the presidency of the Auto Workers, the CIO's largest affiliate, in 1946. Reuther had defeated R.J. Thomas, a moderate who had considerable left-wing support in the union. Soon after, Michael Quill of the Transport Workers and Joseph Curran of the National Maritime Union, both left wingers, broke with their former allies and added their unions to the anti-Communist majority in the CIO.

When the Progressive Party emerged to challenge the Democrats in 1947, all of the elements necessary to crush the Communists were in place. The issue came to a head in January 1948, when the CIO Executive Board voted by 33 to 13 to condemn the Progressive Party and support the Marshall Plan. In August the board endorsed Truman after another bitter debate. Soon after, high-level left wingers, including Murray's close advisor, General Counsel Lee Pressman, resigned from the CIO's administrative staff. Murray had taken the critical step and imposed a political loyalty test in the CIO. Loyalty to the Democrats has become a trade union issue. Maurice Travis, a Communist official of the Mine, Mill and Smelter Workers union, asked: "I would like to know where in . . . the constitution of the CIO it says that we have to support the Marshall Plan or . . . conform to the foreign policy of the Democratic Administration."

In fact only the Mine, Mill and Smelter Workers and three small Communist-led unions formally endorsed Wallace. Although a number of left-wing leaders took an active part in the Progressive Party campaign, most realized that they were not leading radical constituencies.

Fresh from their participation in Truman's victory, the anti-Communist unions came to the 1949 CIO convention eager to complete their victory over the Communists. Secretary of State Marshall and the Chairman of the

Joint Chiefs of Staff were the featured speakers. The United Electrical Workers (UE), whose leaders could read the handwriting on the wall, had already stopped paying per capita, and did not bother to send a delegation. With Murray, Reuther, and George Baldanzi of the Textile Workers leading the anti-Communist forces, the convention expelled UE and the small Farm Equipment Workers Union, which was locked in a jurisdictional dispute with the Auto Workers. A new union, the International Union of Electrical Workers (IUE), was immediately chartered to assume UE's jurisdiction.

The convention also amended the CIO constitution to bar members of the Communist Party or those who consistently pursued "policies and activities directed toward the achievement of the program or purposes of the Communist Party," from serving as CIO officers or members of the Executive Board. In addition the Executive Board was given the power to expel any union whose policies followed the Communist Party line. Membership in Fascist and other totalitarian organizations was also forbidden.

In the following year, charges were brought against the remaining Communist-led unions. A committee of CIO vice-presidents conducted hearings that tried to establish that the accused unions had neglected their members' interest as a result of their pro-Communist activities. Much was made of poor organizing records of the small unions, but the same criticism could have been applied to a number of the smaller anti-Communist unions. With regard to the larger unions, the charge had even less credibility. In the end, the committee justified the expulsion of the unions by demonstrating that they had publicly supported the Communist Party line through two or more changes.

The CIO's action led to a surge of anticommunism in the labor movement. By 1954, fifty-nine AFL and CIO unions had constitutional provisions barring Communists from holding office. Forty-one unions barred advocates and supporters as well as party members. Forty unions barred communists from membership as well as office. Nor were these provisions mere formalities. Expulsions occurred frequently and were almost always upheld by the courts.

Throughout the ensuing struggle the anti-Communist unions had the full support of the government. When, under the pressure of raids, Communist leaders decided to sign the non-Communist affidavits, they were charged with perjury. After Ben Gold, president of the Fur Workers, was convicted of perjury, the Amalgamated Meat Cutters (AFL) carried out a raiding campaign with the aid of government officials and the press.

The NLRB canceled the exclusive bargaining rights of the Mine, Mill and Smelter Workers and kept most of the union's leaders tied up in the courts for years. In 1955 the attorney general petitioned the Subversive Activities Board to declare Mine, Mill "Communist infiltrated." Through it all the Steelworkers raided Mine, Mill and reduced its strength to barely one-third of its postwar peak.

Congressional investigating committees played an important role in the labor civil war. In the Senate, the Internal Security Subcommittee, the Permanent Subcommittee on Investigations, the Subcommittee on Labor and Labor-Management Relations, and the Subcommittee on Immigration all used their subpoena powers to harass the expelled unions. On the House side, the Committee on Education and Labor and the House Committee on Un-American Activities (HUAC) took an especially active interest.

HUAC, claiming that it had discovered a communist plan to "colonize America's basic industries," intervened repeatedly in the civil war. As early as 1947 the Committee became involved in the struggle between the anti-Communist insurgents and the Communist leadership in UE. At that time, the HUAC counsel told insurgent UE witnesses that if others would follow their example, "we wouldn't have to pass some of the labor laws we are passing today." In 1949 HUAC carried out highly publicized interrogations of UE's three top leaders at the same time that union members were electing delegates to the upcoming UE convention. A convention in which the anti-Communist forces were prepared to mount their most serious challenge.

After the expulsion of the Communist-led unions, congressional committees repeatedly subpoenaed their national and local leaders and scheduled hearings to coincide with NLRB elections. When accused labor leaders invoked the Fifth Amendment, a number of companies automatically dismissed them. At General Electric during the UE-IUE conflict, HUAC activities resulted in the dismissal of twenty-eight workers and the loss of seniority and pension rights for others. A similar story unfolded at Westinghouse in Baltimore.

Under the Port Security Program the federal government, the National Maritime Union (CIO) and the Seafarers International Union (AFL) undertook a joint campaign to wipe out Communist influence on the waterfront, and to crush the International Longshoremen's Union and the Marine Cooks and Stewards, a largely black union.

Frequently, employers encouraged the purge and aided the raiding unions. But this was not always the case. Once the Communist-led unions were on the defensive, some employers reasoned that a weak union, whatever its politics, would be a more docile bargainer. According to anti-Communist labor historian David Saposs, "Employers . . . were influenced primarily . . . by immediate, practical considerations of plant harmony, advantageous labor relations, and effect on business prospects, rather than by the principle or ethics of having dealings with communists." Where unions had little strength, such as in the South and West, employers did not make fine distinctions between "good" unions or "bad" unions. They red baited them all.

The CIO purge removed the last obstacle to the entry of the labor movement into the bipartisan reshaping of the postwar world. Government officials, corporate executives and labor leaders agreed that continued prosperity depended on the unfettered expansion of the free enterprise system.

When Communist expansion seemed to threaten the desired world order the United States assumed the role of protector. Truman persuaded Congress to provide billions to rebuild the shattered economies of Western Europe on the American model. These policies and the new American defense commitment in Europe and Asia created a bonanza for American business and workers, but they also created a permanent defense establishment and solidified the power of what came to be known as the "military-industrial complex." Between 1945 and 1970 the country spent $1000 billion, 60 percent of its total budget on defense. With the Cold War providing a rationale acceptable to both business and labor, the bulk of the money went to the largest corporations, in many of which the unions were most strongly entrenched.

The cooperation of a procapitalist, anti-Communist labor movement was essential to the carrying out of America's new world responsibilities. It was seen as essential that the world's free-enterprise economies be integrated into a global, free-market system so that the devastation of war would not result in social disintegration and revolution. For the orderly transition to take place, European labor movements, which had been crushed by the Nazis, had to be rebuilt. American policy makers soon realized that the historic mainstream of European labor lay on the left, with the socialists and Communists. In Italy, France and Greece dominance had shifted to the Communists as a result of their role in the resistance movements. When the Cold War began, the presence of these Communist-led labor movements posed a serious threat to American goals. In order to counter this threat and attempt to rebuild European unions free of Communist influence, the government turned to the American labor movement for help.

At first rivalry between the AFL and CIO hindered the program, but that stopped after the CIO withdrew from the World Federation of Trade Unions, an international labor body created by the labor movements of the allies during the war that included Soviet representation, and purged its Communist-led affiliates. Agents of American labor, in close cooperation with the U.S. government, played an active role in attempting to channel the reconstruction of European labor in a pro-American direction. AFL representatives in Europe nourished existing divisions and helped finance splits in the Communist-dominated labor movements of France, Greece, and Italy.

The goal of American labor was the creation of unions for which economic, not political, considerations were of primary importance. But government and business enlisted American labor in the struggle against communism not because of any real interest in the creation of strong, independent unions of European workers, but in order to give stable market economies time to grow. In Europe where Catholic and social-democratic labor traditions existed, American labor representatives supported pro-American Catholic and social-democratic unions against the Communists with whom they already had old and deep divisions. The results were weak, internally divided labor movements that posed few problems for the remarkable resurgence of private enterprise in Europe.

Labor's involvement expanded beyond Europe as American economic interests as well as the Cold War spread to the underdeveloped and developing world. In those parts of the world where few labor traditions existed, and where any bona fide labor movement was seen as a threat to traditional ruling classes, American union representatives often found themselves asked to subvert struggling labor movements with left-wing leadership even though no viable alternatives existed. For labor the proclaimed goal was to train anti-Communist labor leaders in developing countries to run effective unions free of communist political domination. For government and industry the goal was to preserve friendly relations with anti-Communist and frequently totalitarian regimes. The results were often weak, government-controlled labor movements that offered no resistance to the penetration of their countries by American business. No matter what the motives, the overall effect, according to UAW official Victor Reuther, was "an exercise in trade union colonialism." The exercise ultimately backfired on many American workers, most of whom knew little or nothing of this aspect of union activity. Weak labor movements abroad, although perhaps non-Communist, contributed to low-wage labor markets that American companies increasingly took advantage of to export American jobs.

Perhaps the purge of 1949 was inevitable in the framework of the postwar years. The CIO never challenged the American economic system. It could not gain maximum benefits from that system as long as it harbored a radical minority that undercut its legitimacy in the eyes of the nation. From the beginning the CIO had depended on government support from the Democratic Party. When the Democrats became dependent for political survival on a hard-line, anti-Communist policy, the logic of the CIO's position gave Murray little choice but to expel the left-wing unions. But that decision had larger ramifications. It signaled the effective end of political diversity in the leadership of the labor movement. For the first time in history the radical voice was gone from the mainstream of organized labor.

MICHAEL QUILL

Mike Quill was called "the man who ran the subways" and the short, round Irishman with the cherubic face and the heavy brogue came to personify the big city labor leader of the 1950s and 1960s. By that time, few people remembered that at an earlier period the appelation had been "Red Mike" and many viewed Quill as an agent of the Soviet Union with the vital arteries of America's greatest city at his mercy.

Born in Ireland in 1905, Quill attended school for six years and then served in the Irish Republican Army during the Irish rebellion of 1919–1923. He came to New York in 1926 and took a job as a gateman in the New York subway. In 1934, he put the militant socialism he had learned in Ireland to use when he helped found the Transport Workers Union of America. One year later, he was the union's president and when the CIO began, Quill, like other leftists, took his union in.

Although Quill always denied Communist Party membership, the TWUA was one of the few CIO unions to have been created almost from scratch by Communists. With Quill as a colorful front man who enjoyed the spotlight, the Communist Party provided the money and organizational skills to build the union. Quill's activities ranged far beyond the union. He ran successfully for New York City Council on the Communist-supported American Labor Party ticket in 1936, and from then on became a fixture in the city's politics.

When Quill decided to break with the Communists, he had the support of the Association of Catholic Trade Unionists (ACTU). The ACTU had for many years been one of the major forces supporting attempts in various unions to rid the CIO of Communist influence. When the break finally did come, Quill's personal popularity with the mostly Irish rank and file, and his support by the Roman Catholic Church hierarchy proved too much for the Communists, who controlled a majority of the Union's executive council.

Philip Murray rewarded Quill for his move into the anti-Communist camp with CIO support in his battle with the Communists for control of the TWUA. In New York City, Mayor William O'Dwyer let it be known that were it not for the Communists the city would be willing to work out a pension plan with the union. He also announced that a purge of the Communists in the TWUA was a precondition for city approval of a new plan for collective bargaining on the New York transit system—a plan favorable to the union.

Quill became one of the labor movement's leading anti-Communists, but never lost his militancy. Alone among the top leaders of the CIO, he opposed the 1955 merger with the AFL as a betrayal of the CIO's social philosophies. He finished his volatile career as a labor leader in 1965 while leading a transit strike that paralyzed New York City. Jailed for refusing to obey a court order, Quill suffered a heart attack. He died soon after in 1966.

A GROWING CONSENSUS

Republican Dwight Eisenhower's election to the presidency in 1952 confirmed the swing to conservatism that had occurred in the country since

World War II. Eisenhower's cabinet, although it included Martin Durkin of the Plumbers Union as Secretary of Labor, reflected just how much business had reasserted itself. "Eight millionaires and a plumber," the *New Republic* called it.

Yet business dominance did not lead to an onslaught against unions. Unquestionably there were those in the business community who had never accepted the reforms of the New Deal, but they were a small minority in terms of power. Most leaders of big business had made their accommodation with the welfare state.

This relatively benign use of its power by big business reflected a recognition of the realities of American society. The nation emerged from World War II as an organized society of contending interest groups. Most Americans looked to one association or another to protect their interests. Workers increasingly found themselves employed by large-scale enterprises, and the typical businessman was an employed manager, not an independent entrepreneur.

Increased government involvement in many areas of life made Americans more dependent on government at all levels. Life in an increasingly urban, complex and in many ways frightening society, led to a decline of individualism. Whatever the nostalgia to return to a less complicated time, there was no inclination to dismantle the welfare state. Nor had most Americans forgotten the Depression. In this setting, business had no desire to disturb the equilibrium and return to the old days of the jungle. Even if it had wanted to, labor's very real power, although restrained, made the risks too great. Accommodation rather than conflict made good sense to both sides.

PART III
A Tolerable Accommodation

Labor-management skirmishes in the political arena and a great strike wave immediately following the war obscured the development of a broad community of interest among labor leaders and the management of big business. This community of interest had its roots in the wartime cooperation between business and labor, but it blossomed in the long period of economic growth following the war, a period in which American economic dominance in most of the world went unchallenged. To find the real nature of the relations between labor and capital, one had to look beyond politics to the collective bargaining process, the heart of the institutional relationship between companies and unions.

Both labor leaders and management faced an increasingly restless membership in the shops at the war's end. In the last four months of 1945, man-days lost to strikes soared to double the wartime peak of 1943. Immediately after the war, at the urging of the AFL and the CIO, President Truman authorized wage increases through collective bargaining that did not affect prices. At this point the War Labor Board still existed. But a number of factors came together after the war and made a return to free collective bargaining inevitable. Workers who had become used to overtime found themselves cut back to forty hours during reconversion. For the average manufacturing worker, this meant a 20 percent reduction in take-home pay. Millions who had been upgraded to better paying jobs were downgraded to prewar classifications. To make matters worse, there were two million unemployed one month after VJ Day.

All of this occurred against a background of inflation resulting from the end of wartime price controls. When industry argued that it could not grant wage increases without raising prices—in spite of wartime profits two and one-half times the prewar average—an epidemic of work stoppages struck the economy. By the beginning of 1946, 2 million industrial workers in auto, meat packing, electrical manufacturing, and steel walked the picket lines. Settlements came in mass production after the government allowed industry to raise prices. Soon after, the strike in the soft coal mines almost brought the nation to its knees.

An angry Truman seized the mines under the provisions of the Smith-Connally act, but soldiers could not mine coal and sporadic walkouts continued for most of the year. Finally, a court injunction that resulted in massive fines against the United Mine Workers broke the strike. But by the time the mines returned to private management in June 1947, Lewis had negotiated a new contract that included nearly everything the miners had struck for.

In the midst of the coal strike, the beleaguered Truman faced the threat of a nationwide rail strike. In May 1946, the railroad brotherhoods threatened to close down the nation's entire rail system. Frantic negotiations conducted by a special emergency board led to a tentative settlement, but the Trainmen and Engineers rejected it and sent out strike orders. Truman once again used his wartime emergency powers and seized the railroads; once again the workers paid no heed despite threats to draft them into the armed forces. Just as Truman was asking Congress for these special powers, word came that the strike had been settled. But the crisis had added to the momentum for new restrictive labor legislation that had been building in Congress since 1943.

Yet even with over 4 million workers on strike in the twelve months since the war, the economy stabilized and surged ahead. The postwar strike wave taught everyone a valuable lesson. Organized labor was here to stay and any attempt to disregard that reality would be met with the full force of its political and economic power.

Not that anyone of any importance in the business community had any such designs. Employers made no significant attempts to duplicate their tactics in 1919. Whereas in the old days the confrontation had taken place in the streets, now the real action moved to the bargaining tables. An air of friendliness prevailed on the picket lines. *Fortune* noted that the strikes had produced almost no violence and that even though labor leaders sounded off in public with the old militant rhetoric, privately they, like the strikers, "were calm, cool, even friendly warriors."

The differences between 1919 and 1946 could be attributed to a number of factors. In the first place, strong unions led the strikes of 1946, and they had a stake in maintaining control of the situation. Labor leaders had become industrial statesmen. No longer outlaws as in the old days, their new status depended on their ability to keep the bargains they had struck with industry and government.

Government too assumed a different role. Through the centralized planning of the New Deal and World War II, it had become a major factor on the industrial relations scene and from that time forward would play a major role in bargaining in critical industries.

Industry had also changed. A return to the old tactics of naked power now carried with it unacceptable political and social risks. Management too had a stake in not undermining the authority of labor leaders who understood the mutual benefits of orderly industrial relations.

Another difference with 1919 lay in the fact that rather than being attacked as radical threats to the free enterprise system, most unions after World War II had enlisted as partners in the global war of containment against communism.

Just as significantly, there had been a change among the workers. Sacrifices during the Depression and the war had made them anxious to become consumers again. New Deal programs like unemployment insurance gave them some security against total loss of income. Most important of all, union protection gave them a say in wages and working conditions, and their new political power provided some assurance against the dismantling of the welfare state. Workers might gripe about their leaders but they went right on paying dues.

THE COLLECTIVE BARGAINING MODEL

The relatively benign course that postwar industrial relations were to take was not entirely predictable in 1945. In November of that year, on the eve of the great postwar strike wave, the National Labor-Management Conference took place in Washington. The conference's main promoter, Republican Senator Arthur Vandenburg of Michigan, testified to organized labor's new status when he noted that "responsible management" knew that collective bargaining was a reality and he urged that they wholeheartedly accept it.

Although the conference's purpose was to extend the wartime spirit of cooperation between management and labor, business leaders were far from as optimistic about the possibilities as Senator Vandenburg. In fact, labor refused at the conference to agree to a list of specific management prerogatives. For business this seemed to signal further labor inroads into the management function.

There was evidence that management had good reason for anxiety. At the end of the war union membership totaled fifteen million, five times more than in 1933. Even more unsettling to business was where those members were. Two-thirds of all production workers in manufacturing industries and a like number in transportation, the heart of the American economy, came under collective bargaining. Industries such as auto, steel, railroading, electrical manufacturing, and rubber were virtually all union.

Many of these members, particularly the shop stewards and other activists, had learned their trade unionism during the organizing struggles of the 1930s. Tight labor markets and production speedups during the war had deepened their militancy.

Considering the horrible wartime working conditions and the size of the labor force, the frequency of strikes remained low. But many strikes did occur, and the vast majority were wildcats, unauthorized stoppages over shop floor issues such as safety and the speed up. Although of shorter duration than prewar strikes, the average number of strikes between 1941 and 1945 topped the average in the peak depression strike years of 1933 to 1938 by 60 percent. The turmoil in the shops signified two things: rank-and-file dissatisfaction with the bargain their leaders had struck with management for the duration of the war and the erosion of management authority that had taken place on the shop floor.

So demoralized were foremen in many basic industries that companies worried that they would fall prey to the lure of unionism. A key management demand at the Labor-Management Conference was assurance that there would be no unionization of foremen—a provision that they succeeded in having included in the Taft-Hartley Act of 1947.

Nor did it appear to management that the challenge to their control was restricted to shop floor militants. In the early years of the war, CIO leaders Walter Reuther of the Auto Workers, Clinton Golden of the Steelworkers, and John Brophy of the CIO staff put forth a plan for industrial councils through which management and labor could cooperate to manage war industries. They envisioned the industrial councils as prototypes of an "industrial democracy" based on national planning that would make labor a "coequal with management." Fear of this kind of thinking later led General Motors president Charles Wilson to urge that collective bargaining be legally contained within "its proper sphere" so that the "American System" could be spared a social revolution "inspired from east of the Rhine."

Management's fears proved to be exaggerated. Industrial councils were an interesting topic for academic debate, but few important labor leaders had any real sustained interest in them. In fact, the union chiefs had anxieties similar to their management counterparts. They were only slightly less apprehensive about losing control in the shops.

In a provocative essay on postwar collective bargaining, labor historian David Brody has argued that the leadership of both management and labor had an interest in containing shop floor militancy that predated the end of the war. Soon after the war began, management made the battle for control of the shop floor a top priority. Protected by the no-strike pledge and wage controls, companies moved to recapture some of the prerogatives they had unofficially ceded during the upsurge of industrial unionism. They used grievance procedures, largely initiated during the war as a quid pro quo for the no-strike pledge, in such a way as to remove resolution of disputes from the workplace and the influence of the militants. They increased the ratio of supervisory to nonsupervisory personnel dramatically in an attempt to shore up a demoralized first-line management. By 1944 management had begun to turn the tide. In that year, a wave of work stoppages against disciplinary actions by management hit the economy. In the rubber industry, 18.5 percent of the workers struck at some point during the year. The figure in steel was 20.3 percent, and for auto, an astounding 50.3

percent. General Motors, one of the hardest hit, attributed over one-half of the strikes and 83 percent of all manhours lost to worker reaction to "necessary disciplinary action."

The CIO leadership also took measures to contain wildcat strikes and militant union activity. Organized labor benefited from its cooperation in the war effort. Through the maintenance of membership and dues check off provisions granted by the War Labor Board, union membership grew dramatically. Labor also bartered its cooperation for grievance procedures and seniority systems. The smooth working of the system depended a great deal on union control of the shop stewards and local officers whose acceptance of the greivance process was essential to give it legitimacy.

According to Brody, this shared interest in containing shop floor militancy drew labor and management into closer collaboration at the top. The legal system of collective bargaining that had emerged from the New Deal required that union leaders be able to fulfill the bargains they struck with management. Contentious local leaders and activists made this more difficult. It weakened the union's representative function and disrupted the contract, the cornerstone of the American industrial relations system.

Management understood this need for union leaders to exercise control. A National Planning Association study of a number of major firms in 1953 concluded that management was frequently willing to make concessions in order to not undercut the prestige and influence of the incumbent union leaders. Conversely, union leaders recognized this and used it to extract concessions in bargaining.

One journalist summed up the emerging labor relations scene as early as 1948 by describing the collective bargaining behavior of George Humphrey, a coal executive, and Charles Wilson of General Motors. "Wilson and Humphrey," he wrote, "have about as much resemblance to the Republican big businessmen of the Coolidge-Hoover era as the Indian elephant has to the hairy mammoth—the general outline is the same, but there are vital differences in detail . . . . These two performances were neither 'conservative' nor 'liberal.' They were, however, practical."

Five years later Benjamin Fairless, chairman of the board of United States Steel, spoke at a testimonial dinner for David J. McDonald, Philip Murray's successor as president of the United Steelworkers. Fairless praised McDonald as a labor statesman and argued that industrial peace could be accomplished very easily if both sides could rid themselves of "the utterly false idea that our economic interests are in conflict and . . . . that we must always try to take something away from each other." "Our interests are identical," he continued, "For better or worse, we are inseparably bound together in a state of economic matrimony."

The postwar accommodation between labor and the large corporations rested on mutual advantage. Most unions ceded almost total power over the organization of production and the direction of the enterprise to management, except for the critical personnel function. These management prerogatives permitted corporations, through the application of new technology, the reorganization of work, and the location of plants to segment work and divide workers, all of which served to weaken the bargaining power of workers and their unions.

Unions extracted a price for this management freedom by securing rising real wages, reliable employment security, and improved working conditions. Until the mid-1960s, real average weekly wages of workers in mass-production industries increased substantially. At the same time, unemployment rates between 1946 and 1953 averaged about 4 percent, while rates among adult male workers, the most heavily unionized group, fell below 2 percent by the mid-1960s. After 1948, cost-of-living escalator clauses gave large numbers of workers automatic safeguards against increases in the cost of living.

The history of postwar collective bargaining clearly shows that companies placed a higher value on control issues than on immediate economic issues. It also shows that unions had little quarrel with this definition of their role. Unionized workers made substantial gains beyond wages. Supplemental benefits, so called "fringes," such as paid holidays and vacations became part of most contracts. Beginning with the Mine Workers in 1946, negotiated employee health plans proliferated.

Pensions were harder to win but although companies resisted them just as they had resisted Social Security, by 1952 practically every sector of basic manufacturing had a pension plan worth at least $100 per month. Gains like these led Walter Reuther to praise the trade union movement for creating a "whole new middle class" through collective bargaining.

In exchange for these important concessions, companies received protection against violations of the contract. When Taft-Hartley made union leaders responsible for contract violations by any part of the union, they responded by seeking contract language that placed the liability directly on the members involved. Companies also won multiyear contracts, a feature that gave them time to plan in an environment of predictable labor costs and industrial peace.

All of this and more was included in the collective bargaining agreement—what David Brody has called the "workplace rule of law." In the postwar period, its net came to include nearly every aspect of formal workplace life. Through the grievance procedure, the contract provided for the orderly resolution of workplace conflict. So effective was this feature that by the 1950s it could be found in the overwhelming majority of union contracts. Although a considerable bargaining achievement, few noted that the initiative lay with management until the final step of impartial arbitration. Even nonunion employers realized its value by implementing similar systems to keep unions out.

The contract and the grievance procedure gave the worker due process in the polity of the workplace. It gave the company a reasonable assurance of stable production for the life of the contract. It made union officers responsible for the enforcement of rules to which they had agreed. And finally, argues Brody, the data on labor problems provided through the grievance procedure became an invaluable part of management's information system.

THE PATTERN IN THE AUTOMOBILE INDUSTRY

The accommodation that emerged in postwar labor relations was intimately bound up with collective bargaining in the greatest of American industries, the automobile industry. Events that occurred in auto, particularly in General Motors, proved critical in the establishment of the pattern of collective bargaining that persisted into the 1960s. The guiding force on the union side in this evolution was Walter Reuther.

Walter Reuther entered the world, appropriately enough, on Labor Day 1907 in the minor industrial metropolis of Wheeling, West Virginia. His father, a brewery worker, infused Walter and his brothers Roy and Victor with the democratic socialist vision of Eugene V. Debs. Young Walter dropped out of high school to become an apprentice tool and die maker and a union activist. By 1932, his union activities had cost him his job with the Ford Motor Company. Always one to turn misfortune into opportunity, Walter and brother Victor set out on a sort of grand tour of the European working class. The trip climaxed with an up-close look at the Communist system during fourteen months of work in a Soviet auto plant. The experience left the Reuther brothers fond of Russian workers and less enthusiastic about the Soviet political and economic system. After a leisurely return trip via India and Japan, they arrived home in time to throw themselves into the great CIO organizing drives in the auto industry. Walter played a minor role in the Flint sitdown and came to public notice after his beating by Harry Bennett's thugs at the "battle of the overpass" during the Ford organizing campaign. Using his leadership of the big west-side Detroit local as a springboard, he became UAW vice president in charge of General Motors during the war and a spokesman for shop floor dissatisfaction with the speedup and the no-strike pledge. In the faction-ridden UAW, this placed him in a strategic position from which to challenge for the top post.

Reuther burst into the front ranks of labor leadership during the General Motors strike of 1946 when he demanded a 30 percent wage increase and the right to examine the company's books to determine if the demands could be met without price increases. Company president Charles Wilson rejected the demands out of hand and proposed instead a 5 to 8 percent increase and the extension of the work week to forty-five hours.

After lengthy negotiations General Motors offered 10 percent, but only if accompanied by the right to raise prices. On the issue of open books, the company remained adamant. A surrender on that issue would have undermined General Motors's total control over policy making. It would, the company claimed, have been the first step toward a system of industrial codetermination, and General Motors stood firmly against it as the defender of unfettered management prerogatives for all American business enterprise. Company advertisements appeared in newspapers across the country asking, "Is the Union Seeking Facts or New Economic Power. . . . a Look at the Books or a Finger in the Pie?" Power, not wages, was the central issue.

With negotiations deadlocked, 180,000 auto workers struck 96 General Motors plants on November 21, 1946. Truman, worried about the effect of the strike on the reconversion program, appointed a fact-finding panel with authority to examine the company's books, but General Motors refused to cooperate. To yield, said General Motors's attorney, "would mean the end of free enterprise." When the President's panel recommended a 19½¢ settlement without a price increase, General Motors rejected it. By now the strike had dragged for six weeks and the company had the initiative. Reuther, who had earlier rejected any compromise, accepted the panel's recommendation enthusiastically. The episode gained the auto workers much public support, but an increasingly confident General Motors continued to resist.

Events began to overtake Reuther at this juncture. The UAW's Ford and Chrysler departments settled for 18¢ an hour without mentioning price increases or open books. Another blow came when Truman relaxed his opposition to price increases to end a strike of 750,000 steel workers. Assured of their right to raise prices, the steel companies settled with Phil Murray's United Steelworkers of America for 18½¢ an hour. Soon after the United Electrical Workers, who were also on strike against General Motors, followed the steel pattern and settled.

But still Reuther and his members held out. By now it had become a matter of principle. Reuther had already signaled his willingness to accept 19½¢, only one penny above the pattern set by Murray. General Motors, now determined to teach the union a lesson, offered the steel pattern with no strings on price increases. The two sides spent the last month haggling over a penny an hour. An agreement finally came when Phil Murray and Charles Wilson agreed to 18½¢ and added benefits in vacations and overtime. There was no mention of the company's pricing policy or the open books issue in the settlement.

Everyone could claim victory in the General Motors strike. The company had partially turned back the union's wage demands, maintained the right to increase prices to make up for higher labor costs, and defended its management prerogatives. The UAW withstood a long strike against the most powerful corporation in the world and forced the 18½¢ settlement and the beginning of pattern bargaining. Reuther was the biggest winner of all. Only two weeks after the settlement, he was elected president of the UAW and assumed the leadership of the progressive wing of the labor movement.

Successive UAW contracts pioneered new benefits for workers, but it is questionable whether they resulted from the UAW's militancy or as a result of the new accommodation between the union and the company. General Motors came out of the 1946 strike confident that it held the line and determined to avoid costly confrontations in the future. During the 1948 negotiations, the company, not the union, proposed tying wages to the cost of living and productivity increases. In 1950, the proposals were included in a new five-year contract, the longest on record. General Motors had bought labor peace and *Fortune* noted that while it cost the company $1 billion, it was a bargain. In 1955, Reuther achieved a breakthrough with the Big Three auto makers when he negotiated the beginnings of a guaranteed annual wage that gave laid-off auto workers supplemental company unemployment benefits, which, when coupled with state benefits, amounted to twenty-four weeks at 60 percent of normal wages. The provision became a model for other major industries and was an historic milestone in American collective bargaining.

The supplemental unemployment benefits plan, as significant as it was, confirmed the direction of postwar collective bargaining. When the UAW addressed the problem of unstable employment in the auto industry, it had two choices. On one hand, it could have attempted more of a say in the operation of the company so as to create more stable employment. On the other hand, it could place its emphasis on protecting its members from the consequences of management decisions. By choosing the latter, according to David Brody, the union conceded away its interest in the former. The Ford Motor Company specifically conditioned its agreement on the supplemental unemployment benefits plan on gaining greater flexibility over the organization and rate of production.

The nature of the union's approach to unstable employment demonstrated the triumph of a unionism that made no fundamental challenge to corporate control. By the postwar years Reuther had become a blend of idealist and realist. Like Hillman and Dubinsky before him, his socialism had been transformed into a mixture of business unionism and a social unionism concerned with the needs of all workers. But the main thrust of the postwar era was not to be social unionism, but the narrower vision of Philip Murray. A vision in which the arena was the industry or the shop, not all of society, and the primary role of unions was to represent the interests of their members and the industries that paid them. In return, Murray expected an economic statesmanship from management that recognized labor's contributions to an orderly industrial system and rewarded it accordingly.

For labor to provide this stability, union leaders needed firm control of their organizations. Reuther—no less than Murray—recognized this. He stamped out factionalism in the UAW and orchestrated what could best be described as democratic centralism. His leadership was highminded and honest, and he drove the union to a leading position in the labor movement.

CENTRALIZATION OF BARGAINING

The kind of collective bargaining relationship that developed between the Auto Workers and General Motors typified what sociologist Daniel Bell called the "subversion of collective bargaining." Rather than an adversarial relationship in which one side's gain was the other's loss, bargaining in the big manufacturing and transportation sectors had become a no-lose situation. Each party knew in advance the price it would have to pay, and pretty much got what it set out to get, with the corporation usually the greater gainer.

By the 1950s, corporations had learned how to turn collective bargaining and strikes to their advantage. After Truman removed price controls in 1946, companies traded impressive wage concessions for union silence on even larger price increases. Company ability to pay came to depend on the ability to pass on higher labor costs by raising prices on one hand, or on the unrestrained right to increase productivity through new technology on the other.

Government played a key role in this process. A shared interest in the containment of communism brought government, unions, and management together in support of large defense budgets. It did not hurt that the by-products of national vigilance were higher wages and higher profits. Increased defense spending fueled prosperity and expansion. Defense firms benefited from cost-plus government contracts in which they received a guaranteed rate of return in spite of cost overruns. Union negotiators demanded that part of this largesse be passed on to workers.

Government regulation of certain industries also served to keep wages and profits high. In the transportation sector, federal state and local subsidies to air, rail, and bus systems combined with regulated prices allowed bargainers to partially disregard market factors. In interstate trucking the combination of government licensing of long-distance carriers and the Teamster Union's almost complete organization of the industry led to a situation whereby labor cost increases could be passed on to shippers and ultimately to the consumers in the form of regulated freight rates. The ability of the Teamsters to extract uniform industrywide wage increases enabled the carriers to use the collective bargaining agreement as a link in the process through which they could secure government approval of rate increases. Regulated rates had a similar effect on bargaining in public utilities.

The stable accommodation between management and labor also resulted from the growth and centralization of America's basic industries. The dual advantages of almost unrivaled access to the world's markets and effective control over raw material and energy prices provided the preconditions for one of the great merger waves of American history. This resulted in the rise of a characteristic kind of large corporation after World War II—one that combined vast size with industry concentration or oligopoly—a market condition in which a handful of producers are dominant.

By the end of the 1950s, this kind of market concentration had come to characterize most of American manufacturing including auto, steel, rubber, electrical manufacturing, chemicals, petroleum, aircraft, and transportation. As in the case of General Motors, their sheer size and their market control allowed corporations in these circumstances to set prices by executive decision and not by competitive market conditions. In setting such prices, due allowance was made for higher labor costs without disturbing desired profit levels.

In the expansionary economic environment of the postwar period, the negative effects of this process were mitigated somewhat by the process of pattern bargaining. After 1946 "rounds" of negotiations in several key industries such as auto and steel came to set wage and benefit rates that varied by only a few cents. These were followed by other bargainers in other large industries and, to a lesser extent, also affected wages throughout the economy for union and nonunion workers alike. By the mid-1950s, wage patterns came to become the justification for wage increases that began to outstrip productivity gains for the first time since 1946.

Unions had to have an industry effectively organized in order to extract their share from this process. As we have seen, the success of the CIO had created this condition in the mass-production and transportation industries. This enabled the unions to take wages out of competition by negotiating industrywide settlements while at the same time narrowing pay differentials between high- and low-wage workers.

Centralized bargaining on an industrywide basis thus made sense for both management and the unions. However, the sheer size and complexity of bargaining at this level put a premium on centralized expertise, authority, and decision making. In this process, power gravitated to the top, further reducing the influence of local factors and local leaders. This raised the question of the compatibility of centralized bargaining and union democracy.

Some argued that industry centralization forced a corresponding centralization on unions and that this led to dependence on experts, the rise of professional union officers, and a decline in union democracy. In this environment, a premium was put on internal union loyalty and unified support for national negotiating policies and objectives. Dissenters were attacked as disloyal for weakening the union and giving aid to the "enemy."

Clark Kerr, a noted industrial relations expert, admitted that union democracy and local autonomy suffered from centralized bargaining, but that the collective bargaining process makes an important contribution to a democratic society by creating a two party legislative system governing the life of the workplace. Others argued that union survival depended on labor leaders having maximum authority and flexibility to deal with management, and that any resulting loss of democracy in the union was a necessary trade off. In a debate over the centralization of authority in the Teamsters Union in 1966, a local officer gave a concrete example of the latter argument:

> (Local autonomy) is a beautiful thing, but we cannot afford it if in fact we are giving it up. We cannot protect the big city local . . . if Sealtest or Borden's or Beatrice (Foods) or anyone else can come within 150 miles of Louisville . . . and build a brand-new automated plant out in the country area that is not organized or is poorly organized and back ship (dairy products) to my town, it doesn't matter what my contract says. It doesn't matter if everybody has autonomy. . . we've got voting machines all over the damned hall (but) if nobody is working, then we are dead.

Whatever the merits of this argument, events in the Teamsters demonstrated the potentially dangerous side effects of centralized bargaining structures. Partly as a result of the growth of large national trucking companies, Teamster Union policy from the mid-1950s on was to standardize terms and conditions of employment throughout the industry. The consolidation of metropolitan and regional contracts began to accelerate after the 1957 election of James Hoffa to the union's presidency. Over the next decade Hoffa succeeded in gaining control over all internal union policy-making bodies. By 1967, national contract negotiations and an industry-wide master contract covered all major economic issues.

For Teamster truckers, this resulted in a wage increase of 40 percent between 1958 and 1967, well above increases in most other industries. But in the process, the union became riddled with corruption, internal democracy atrophied, and rank-and-file movements aimed at unseating the incumbent leadership were effectively, and sometimes brutally, suppressed.

Although corruption and dictatorial control resulted in a small number of cases, most unions emerged during the postwar years as honest, efficiently run, and disciplined organizations that carved out secure positions in the economic system and won steadily increasing benefits for their members. Through stable collective bargaining, unions traded long-term contracts and orderly labor relations for higher wages, cost-of-living escalator clauses, supplemental unemployment benefits, health plans, vacations with pay, and pensions. The vast majority of Americans, union and non-union alike, benefited from the role unions played in American life.

DISCUSSION QUESTIONS

1. Why did cooperation between business and labor during World War II not disintegrate after the war to anywhere near the degree that it had after World War I?
2. Why was General Motors willing to make substantial concessions in wages and fringe benefits in bargaining with the UAW, but not willing to allow the union to see the company's books?
3. What was Philip Murray's concept of the role of unions? What implications did this have for the collective bargaining model that developed after the war?
4. Why was the left-wing unions' support for the Progressive Party in 1948 such a crucial factor in Murray's decision to purge them from the CIO?
5. Discuss the motivation behind labor's cooperation in the anti-Communist policies of the government at home and abroad after the war.

KEY WORDS AND PHRASES

Fair Employment Practices
   Committee
Rosie the Riveter
War Labor Board
Little Steel Formula
Maintenance of Membership
New Red Scare
Loyalty Program
Automation
Smith-Connally Act
CIO-PAC
Taft-Hartley Act

Collective Bargaining
Fringe Benefits
Grievance Procedures
Management Prerogatives
Pattern Bargaining
Supplemental Unemployment
   Benefits
Walter Reuther
Centralization of Bargaining
Union Democracy

BIBLIOGRAPHY

The material for this section was drawn largely from:

Barbash, Jack, "The 1980s—A New Era in Industrial Relations" in Michel Brossard, *Les Relations de Travail en Periode de Crise Economique*. Montreal, 1983.

Brody, David. *Workers in Industrial America: Essays on the 20th Century Struggle*. New York: Oxford University Press, 1980.

Brooks, Thomas R. *Picket Lines and Bargaining Tables: Organized Labor Comes of Age, 1935–1955*. New York: Grosset and Dunlap, 1968.

Bell, Daniel, "The Subversion of Collective Bargaining," *Commentary*, vol. 29 (1960): 185–197.

———. *Work and Its Discontents*. Boston: Beacon Press, 1956.

Caute, David. *The Great Fear: The Anti-Communist Purge Under Truman and Eisenhower*. New York: Simon and Schuster, 1978.

Cochran, Bert. *Labor and Communism: The Conflict That Shaped American Unions*. Princeton: Princeton University Press, 1977.

———, ed. *American Labor in Mid-Passage*. New York: Monthly Review Press, 1959.

Craypo, Charles. *Economic Bargaining Power: Case Studies in the Private Sector* (unpublished manuscript).

Derber, Milton, "Labor-Management in World War II," *Current History*, vol. 48 (1965): 340–345.

Foner, Philip S. *Organized Labor and the Black Worker, 1619–1973*. New York: Praeger, 1974.

Foster, James C. *The Union Politic: The CIO Political Action Committee*. Columbia: University of Missouri Press, 1975.

Goldman, Eric. *The Crucial Decade: America, 1945–1955*. New York: Alfred A. Knopf, 1956.

Goodman, Jack, ed. *While You Were Gone: A Report on Wartime Life in the U.S.* New York: Simon and Schuster, 1946.

Greenstone, J. David. *Labor and American Politics*. New York: Vintage Books, 1970.

Jacobson, Julius, ed. *The Negro and the American Labor Movement*. Garden City, N.Y.: Anchor Books, 1968.

Jensen, Vernon. *Strife on the Waterfront: The Port of New York Since 1945*. Ithaca: Cornell University Press, 1974.

Kenneally, James. *Women and American Trade Unions*. St. Albans, Vt.: Eden Press, 1978.

Lader, Lawrence. *Power on the Left: American Radical Movements Since 1946*. New York: W.W. Norton and Co., 1978.

Lubell, Samuel. *The Future of American Politics*. New York: Harper and Row, 1952.

Pierson. *Unions in Postwar America: An Economic Assessment*. New York: Random House, 1967.

Radosh, Ronald. *American Labor and United States Foreign Policy*. New York: Random House, 1969.

Reuther, Victor. *The Brothers Reuther, and the Story of the UAW: A Memoir*. Boston: Houghton Mifflin, 1976.

Seidman, Joel. *American Labor from Defense to Reconversion*. Chicago: University of Chicago Press, 1953.

Serrin, William. *The Company and the Union*. New York: Vintage Books, 1974.

Warne, Colston E., ed. *Labor in Postwar America*. Brooklyn: Remsen Press, 1949.

For additional reading see:

Cormier, Frank and William J. Eaton. *Reuther.* Englewood Cliffs, N.J.: Prentice-Hall, 1970.

Flynn, George Q. *The Mess in Washington: Manpower Mobilization in World War II.* Westport, Conn.: Greenwood Press, 1979.

Godson, Roy. *American Labor and European Politics: The AFL as a Transnational Force.* New York: Crane, Russak and Company, 1976.

Kampelman, Max M. *The Communist Party vs. the CIO: A Study in Power Politics.* New York: Praeger, 1957.

Larrowe, Charles P. *Harry Bridges: The Rise and Fall of Radical Labor in the United States.* New York: Lawrence Hill and Company, 1972.

McClure, Arthur F. *The Truman Administration and the Problems of Postwar Labor, 1945–1948.* Rutherford, N.J.: Fairleigh Dickinson University Press, 1969.

SECTION
EIGHT

PART I
Changing Work, Changing Workers

To most Americans of the mid-1950s, the future seemed filled with promise. Weaned on the belief that progress could be equated with continued economic expansion, they looked forward to increased job security and expanded economic opportunities.

In the belief that a rising tide raises all boats, the nation counted on economic growth to bridge the social and economic divisions that separated rich and poor, black and white, without requiring sacrifices from privileged groups in American society.

For most of the period to the end of the 1960s, these economic expectations were more or less satisfied. True, there was an overall increase in unemployment between 1955 and 1979, but the real growth in that statistic took place near the end of the era. Most benefited from government spending in the defense and space programs, which helped spur industrial production and contributed to an increase in real incomes from the late 1950s through the 1960s.

Yet the relative prosperity masked profound changes in the American economic system. Reliance on government contracts dulled the competitive edge of American industry. Foreign economies such as the Japanese and German, unburdened by massive and wasteful defense expenditures, grew at a much faster rate than the American. This competition from abroad struck hard at America's aging mass-production facilities and helped spur a steady decline in the heart of American industry.

Government jobs (particularly at the local and state levels) and not private employment provided the major new employment opportunities during the 1950s and 1960s. Total federal outlays increased from $68.5 billion in 1955 to $493.7 billion in 1979, an increase of over 700 percent. The Federal deficit increased from $3 billion in 1955 to $27.7 billion in 1979. Yet federal employment levels rose only slightly.

The dramatic increase took place in state and local governments, which were spending $322 billion a year by 1977, up from $40 billion in 1955. As in the case of the federal government, spending far outpaced revenues and by 1977 all outstanding local and state debt had soared to $260 billion. However, unlike the federal level, this increase resulted in a rise in public sector jobs from just over 5 million in 1955 to 13 million by 1978.

The burgeoning deficits at all levels were based on the assumption that future economic growth would generate the tax revenues to manage the debt. But massive spending for the Vietnam war fed an inflation rate that continued after the war in spite of recessions in 1973/1974 and 1981/1982, which sent the unemployment rate to the highest level since the Great Depression.

Cracks began to appear in the system and social conflict began to undermine the confidence of many Americans even during the relative prosperity of the 1960s. For the first time since the Depression malaise struck deep into the heart of the American middle class. Many of their children, strangers to depression or economic deprivation, grew alienated from a society that seemed to place its highest values on unrestrained materialism. Infused with the egalitarian myth of America, the young noted the discrepancy between the dream and the reality for millions of minorities and poor whites. Freed from economic responsibility for their own support by the very system they were criticizing, and searching for meaning in their lives, the young learned the tactics of mass protest from the civil rights movement and used these tactics to unsettle the nation when the Vietnam war drove many of them into fundamental opposition to the system.

BLUE-COLLAR BLUES

As middle-class youth became alienated from the institutions closest to their lives, so too did increasing numbers of workers. Concern about "the blue-collar blues" became a familiar refrain as sociologists, business leaders, politicians, and labor leaders debated whether the so-called work ethic was finally breaking down. In fact, dissatisfaction with the conditions of the American workplace was not new. What was new was the concern for the impact of alienation on the competitive position of American industry in the face of competition from abroad.

As investigators began to open the window on the American workplace, they found the failure of the dream of Frederick Taylor, Henry Ford, and all the rest who had put their faith in technology, discipline, fragmentation, and routine. True, for many, especially those with union protection, the system had led to greater efficiency, higher production and better wages. But, by the 1960s, the trade-off no longer appeared to be enough; a new generation of workers seemed less willing to trade boring, repetitive, powerless, and dangerous work lives for the financial ability to seek fulfillment in consumption. In the widely publicized report, *Work in America*, the U.S. Department of Health, Education and Welfare noted that worker dissatisfaction "as measured by absenteeism, turnover rates, wildcat strikes, sabotage, poor quality products, and a reluctance by workers to commit themselves to work tasks" was crippling productivity and profits.

Concern with the quality of work life led to a reassessment of the nature of work in America. Part of that concern focused on the long-neglected problems of occupational safety and health. Workers and their unions had long been aware of the dangers of the workplace. By the late 1960s that realization had spread to other sectors of society caught up in the reform spirit of the times.

WAR ON POVERTY

Along with the old problems of worker alienation and occupational safety, another perennial surfaced during the 1960s. Because of the intense focus on social inequality, large numbers of Americans became aware of just how unequally Americans shared the nation's wealth. Figures showed that between 1947 and 1969 the poorest 20 percent of all families consistently received less than 6 percent of total personal income, while the richest 20 percent received over 40 percent. Even more striking was the fact that during the same period the top 5 percent received over twice as much total family income as the bottom 20 percent. Not surprisingly, in 1969, according to the Bureau of Labor Statistics standard, 20 percent of all American families fell below the subsistence level.

The increased militance of minority groups that suffered most from poverty and the concentration of the media and the academic community on the problem raised the consciousness of millions of Americans. Under the leadership of Lyndon Johnson and the Democratic Party, Congress enacted a spate of legislation in a "war on poverty" aimed at eliminating the paradox of poverty in America and creating a "Great Society" of "abundance and liberty for all." Direct aid for the poor came in the form of food stamp programs and rent supplements. Federal funds to help the poor flowed to the states and cities in a variety of programs and medical care for the elderly and the poor became part of the Social Security system. It was an explosion of government involvement in the solving of social problems rivaled only by the New Deal. Yet, in the end, the war on poverty could not coexist with the war in Vietnam. Both cost enormous amounts of money and the Johnson administration's attempt to do both led to a steady inflation, which limited real growth, a growth that was essential if both the war in Vietnam and the war on poverty were to be fought simultaneously.

BLACK POWER

For minorities, the two decades after World War II were years of struggle and turmoil. In 1954 the Supreme Court ruled that legal segregation in public education was unconstitutional, thus striking down the myth of "separate but equal." Three years later in Montgomery, Alabama, Rosa Parks refused to obey the law and move to the back of the bus. Her arrest led to a spontaneous mass protest and boycott by Montgomery blacks in which Martin Luther King, Jr., a Baptist minister, emerged as the historic leader of the civil rights movement. The movement, which brought the plight of black Americans to the consciousness of the nation, climaxed in Washington in 1963 in a massive march for jobs and freedom.

As legal barriers fell, it became clear that there could be no social and political equality, without economic equality. Blacks had always been at the bottom of the income ladder, but for most of their history, they had been largely an agricultural people, subsisting in rural isolation away from the centers of political and economic power. However, the steady movement of blacks to northern cities, a movement that had begun during World War I and accelerated during World War II, exploded after 1950. Cities like New York and Detroit saw their black population double and sometimes triple.

In 1970 half of all blacks lived in the North, mostly in urban areas. By that time, job opportunities for blue-collar workers, particularly the unskilled, were declining. A million and a half factory jobs disappeared between 1950 and 1960 as production became more automated. As the racial composition of the cities changed, industry followed the exodus of white Americans to the suburbs.

By 1970, nearly three-quarters of all Americans lived in urban areas, and most of the growth had taken place in the overwhelmingly white suburbs. In fact, nearly 40 percent of the 153 cities with 100,000 or more inhabitants suffered population losses between 1960 and 1970. The influx of poor blacks and other minorities and the flight of the middle class and industry placed a heavy burden on the cities' resources. When New York faced near collapse in 1975, there were one million people on the welfare rolls, while there were some 400,000 fewer jobs in the city than in the previous five years.

The urbanization of blacks, the relocation of industry, and the inroads of automation resulted in a black unemployment rate double that of whites throughout most of the period. For black teenagers the situation was worse, reaching a catastrophic 50 percent during the recession of 1973 and 1974, and remaining there for the rest of the decade.

Behind the drama of the civil rights movement lay a disturbing reality. In 1959, 56 percent of blacks fell below the official poverty line. Seven years later, as a result of economic growth and the war on poverty, that figure had declined to 41.8 percent. Yet in spite of the progress, black unemployment remained twice the rate for whites. In addition, blacks, who comprised 11 percent of the population, made up only 6 percent of professional workers, 3 percent of managers and proprietors, and 6 percent of crafts workers and foremen.

The combination of dismal economic and social conditions and the frustration of the hope held out by the war on poverty led to terrible rioting in the cities in the mid-1960s. Black power, not integration, became the rallying cry as the movement began to focus on jobs and economic justice. Radical groups like the Black Panthers urged revolution. Other militant organizations such as the Student Non-Violent Coordinating Committee began to compete with the more conservative civil rights organizations for the allegiance of black Americans, pushing the entire movement toward an emphasis on economic and political power. It was symbolic of this new direction that Martin Luther King, Jr. was supporting a strike of black sanitation workers when he was assassinated in Memphis, Tennessee, in April 1968.

The upheaval caused by the uprising of blacks led to some change. In addition to the war on poverty, President Johnson maneuvered a Civil Rights Act through Congress in 1964, which banned racial and sexual discrimination in public accommodations and employment. It was an historic breakthrough and put the force of the federal government behind equal opportunity for all Americans.

The enforcement of the act had a positive effect on discrimination at the workplace. Many employers, faced with the possible loss of lucrative government contracts, entered into legal consent decrees or conciliation agreements with the Equal Employment Opportunity Commission. These affirmative action agreements included goals, timetables, and seniority override provisions aimed at accelerating the advancement of minorities and women. Affirmative action had implications for union negotiated seniority systems. In an historic agreement, the United Steelworkers and the steel industry agreed to replace departmental seniority systems with plantwide systems—a move aimed at removing the handicaps that minorities and women faced in moving up the occupational ladder because seniority accumulated in segregated departments was not transferrable. The central question became how to balance the rights of past victims, at a disadvantage due to pre-Civil Rights Act job discrimination, with those of advantaged white males. While the issue is far from settled at this writing, the Supreme Court in 1979, in the case of *Weber* v. *Kaiser Aluminum*, ruled that voluntary, race-conscious, affirmative action plans initiated by an employer and union are generally legal under Title VII of the Civil Rights Act. Although affirmative action became a fact of life for many employers and unions, in the period of economic decline that began in the early 1970s, there were few jobs available for anyone, particularly in the old urban and industrial areas where many working-class blacks lived. For many of those who did find work during the Vietnam war-inspired boom of the late 1960s, the principle of last hired-first fired operated during the recession of 1973/1974.

Blacks were not alone in challenging the existing distribution of power. Mexican-Americans followed their example. Conditions for Chicanos, while generally better than those of blacks, were decidedly inferior to those of whites. In 1970 the median income of Mexican-American families, while 113 percent of black family income, was only 70 percent of the median income of white (including Mexican-origin) families. In the Southwest and West, where most Chicanos lived, they enjoyed little or no political power. But during the 1960s, *La Raza* (the race) became the rallying cry for a political, cultural, and economic movement among Mexican-Americans. Since the vast majority were working class, the trade union movement became a central institution in their struggle.

THE WOMENS' MOVEMENT

As racial and ethnic minorities began to assault the citadels of privilege, a broad-based protest developed among another disadvantaged group—women. Like blacks, women had made great gains in both blue- and white-collar jobs during World War II and had watched many of those jobs slip away in the postwar period. In 1961, Esther Peterson, director of the Women's Bureau in the Department of Labor, persuaded President John F. Kennedy to establish the President's Commission on the Status of Women to recommend programs to "demolish prejudices and outmoded customs" impeding full realization of women's rights. The Commission uncovered enormous inequities in the treatment of women and recommended the extension of equal pay protection, increased minimum wage, the equalization of employment opportunities, paid maternity leaves, and state legislation to extend equal pay and to protect the rights of workers to join unions.

One factor that increased the consciousness of women about their second-class status was their increased presence in the workplace. The number of families headed by women increased from 10.9 percent in March 1970 to 14.6 percent in March 1979. By 1970, more than half of all mothers worked, and the number of single women in the workforce was also increasing steadily. According to the Bureau of Labor Statistics, by 1975 68 percent of the female labor force was single, widowed, divorced, or separated or married to husbands who earned less than $10,000 a year. In other words, they were either sole providers for themselves and their families, or essential to the family's financial security. By 1979, for the first time, a majority of all women sixteen and over were working, including one-half of all married women.

During the past quarter of a century more women have moved into nontraditional jobs as truck drivers, plumbers, and welders. In 1972 women were first accepted as apprentice painters and carpenters and by 1979 they made up 2 percent of all workers in the building trades. Most dramatic of all, 5000 women worked in the coal mines, where there had been none a decade before.

Nevertheless, in 1979 women still earned only 59 percent as much as men, a differential the same as in 1959. One obvious reason for this was occupational segregation. As late as 1977 almost 80 percent of working women could still be found in low-paying or low-skilled jobs. Women represented 98 percent of all secretaries, 94 percent of all typists, 64 percent of all service workers, 78 percent of all clerical workers, 95 percent of all household workers, and less than 5 percent of all managers.

As it had for blacks, the Civil Rights Act of 1964 provided the framework in which to attack the problems. But progress was painfully slow. A 1970 study by the American Society for Personnel Administration and the Bureau of National Affairs found that one-half of all companies disqualified women from certain jobs. The 1973 Economic Report of the President concluded that there had been no drastic change in occupational segregation by sex and expressed the belief that the amount of job segregation by sex exceeded that by race.

For women and minorities the years between 1955 and 1980 proved frustrating. Their relative positions changed little, but higher expectations resulting from the fluid social and political conditions of the 1960s made disappointment all the more bitter. In the final analysis, the ability of the economic system to absorb new workers at living wages was the key to real improvements for all disadvantaged groups. But by the 1960s the American economy was changing in ways that made that an increasingly unlikely prospect.

THE CHANGING ECONOMY

The percentage of blue-collar workers as a proportion of the total economically active population remained relatively stable between 1900 and 1970 and then began to decline. But even in the period of stability, the least-skilled laborers category declined from just over one-third to approximately 12 percent, while craft workers, supervisors, and operatives—the middle groups in skill level—gained significantly. This meant that the manufacturing sector, where new workers without skills had traditionally been absorbed, offered fewer jobs overall, with an even greater decline in unskilled jobs.

In fact, by 1970 the typical American worker wore a white collar. Where the 1900 census found only 134,000 stenographers, secretaries and typists in the nation, by 1970 their number had grown to 3.92 million. The business world of 1900 got along with one clerical worker for every 20.6 nonfarm workers. By 1970 it required one clerk for every 5.4 nonfarm workers.

Growth in the clerical occupations provided opportunities for women and—especially in the public sector—minorities. But most of the other white-collar growth sectors did not. By 1970 the growth of science and technology had resulted in the employment of $11\frac{1}{2}$ million professional, technical, and related workers, including 1.23 million engineers, more than double the number in 1950. These jobs overwhelmingly went to white males who had benefited from their access to higher education. Much the same applied to the explosion of growth in the health professions in which, by 1970, 1.66 million people found employment.

With all of the turmoil and change in the number and kinds of occupations, profound changes in the organization and location of business enterprise also took place. Between 1948 and 1968, the nation's 200 largest manufacturing corporations acquired 3900 companies having combined assets in excess of $50 billion. This enormous merger movement made up part of a broader movement toward concentration and centralization in the American economy. Increasingly manufacturing corporations acquired large, nonmanufacturing subsidiaries. Firms in retail distribution, insurance, broadcasting, newspapers, and utilities also diversified. The holding company, a vehicle by which nonindustrial corporations, especially railroads and banks, extended their influence and control over major industrial activities, returned to prominence.

By the end of 1974, the largest 200 manufacturing corporations, consisting of one-tenth of 1 percent of all manufacturing firms, had two-thirds of all assets used in manufacturing and more than three-fifths of all sales, employment, and net income. At the end of 1974, the largest 200 firms had a greater share of all manufacturing, sales, employment, and assets than the largest 500 firms had in 1955.

Such enormous combinations of economic power were threatening enough to a democratic society, but size was not the only problem with these new corporate giants. Of equal concern, particularly to organized labor, was their conglomerate form of organization.

Conglomeration was a new form of corporate diversification in which a parent firm acquired companies that produced unrelated goods and services. In this diversified structure, no single product line accounted for more than a small part of annual profits. Where in the old integrated firms the unions could match business structure though industrial unionism and companywide bargaining, the conglomerate made this all but impossible. In addition, the complex corporate structure and accounting methods of the diversified firms made it almost impossible for union or government to find out what was really going on.

The trend toward conglomeration and centralization carried absentee ownership to its logical conclusion. As locally owned firms disappeared into the conglomerates, management's responsibility and concern for given communities went with them. Conglomerates closed companies or moved them at will. In the United States, this often meant leaving the heavily unionized Northeast and Midwest, the so-called "frost belt," for the right-to-work states in the southern and western "sunbelt."

The impact of this trend became increasingly clear during the 1960s and 1970s. Capital investments and jobs moved south and overseas. Between 1970 and 1975, more than 2.5 million northerners moved to sunbelt states.

Since 1960, manufacturing jobs in the Southeast rose by 43.3 percent, and in the Southwest by 67 percent. By 1979 manufacturing jobs in the South outnumbered those in the Northeast. It was clear where many of them had come from. Between 1960 and 1975 manufacturing employment declined by 9.9 percent in New England, and 13.7 percent in the Middle Atlantic states. In Massachusetts alone, the textile, leather, and food processing industries lost more than 200,000 jobs since World War II. Akron, Ohio, rubber companies eliminated over 24,000 manufacturing jobs between 1950 and 1975. Between 1970 and 1978, New York City lost 647,000 jobs of different kinds, and in less than five years, Philadelphia watched nearly one-quarter of its factory jobs disappear.

Among the primary reasons for this movement were preferential tax rates and, frequently, tax exemptions for a number of years for incoming industry. But fewer unions, fewer strikes, and lower wages also loomed large in the corporate decision-making process. Only 13% of southern workers belonged to unions by 1979. In North Carolina, the most heavily industralized state in the South, only 6.9 percent of all workers were unionized, compared, for example, to 38 percent in New York. In fact, according to the Bureau of Labor Statistics, unions actually declined as a percentage of the labor force in eight of eleven southern states between 1964 and 1974.

Of course the lure of cheap labor could not be contained within the borders of the United States. The new mobility of industry was part of a larger movement on a global scale. Between 1950 and 1974 American companies invested more than $100 billion abroad. This meant that by 1970, 33 percent of the total assets of the chemical industry, 33 percent of the pharmaceutical industry, 40 percent of the consumer goods industry, and 75 percent of the electrical industry were located abroad. Cheap Asian labor produced almost all television sets and radios produced by American companies. It could not be denied that a substantial portion of the imports that had displaced American workers by the 1970s were produced in American-owned foreign factories. Exports to the United States by American firms that had moved a few miles across the Mexican border to find cheap labor increased from $7 million in 1966 to $350 million by 1972. The impact was most pronounced in labor-intensive industries like textiles and apparel that started to feel the competitive effects of American financed imports long before the auto and steel industries. In the early 1960s, U.S. manufacturers began moving their plants overseas or buying clothing from foreign contractors. By 1983, imports made up at least 45 percent of all garments sold in the United States, twice the percentage of 1972. In Pennsylvania alone, 70,000 garment and textile jobs disappeared between 1966 and 1983.

In carrying out this massive relocation, American multinational firms created the global factory and the global payroll. The largest firms—such as Ford, ITT, Kodak, and Proctor and Gamble—employed more than one-third of their workforce outside of the United States. The impact on the

American branch of the global factory was dramatic. The AFL-CIO estimated that the United States lost just under one million jobs to American-owned foreign subsidiaries between 1966 and 1971. One AFL-CIO official lamented that the transfer of production overseas was making the United States "a country stripped of industrial capacity and meaningful work. . . a service economy . . . a nation of citizens busily buying and selling cheeseburgers and root beer floats."

PART II
Holding On

Approximately 35 percent of the nonagricultural labor force in the United States belonged to unions in 1955. These millions of workers had used their unions to win wages unrivaled in the world. Not only were wages at historic highs, but an increasing number of workers enjoyed protection from arbitrary dismissal and discipline. Seniority systems and grievance procedures, won in collective bargaining, brought a large measure of equity to the workplace. Fringe benefits such as pensions, paid vacations, and medical insurance provided a measure of security for millions.

Their unions belonged to a labor movement more unified than at any time since the heyday of the Knights of Labor. By 1955, most of the important differences between the AFL and CIO had disappeared. The issue of craft versus industrial unionism, once so important, lay largely forgotten. The divisive issue of Communist influence had been removed from the CIO and the AFL had begun to clean out the corruption that plagued a few of its affiliates. Personal bitterness had also faded with the years. John L. Lewis, an old man leading a weakened union, no longer possessed the resources to hinder unity. Both Philip Murray and William Green had died in November 1952. The men who replaced them—Walter Reuther of the CIO, and George Meany of the AFL—carried no deep personal scars from the civil war between the two rival federations.

In these circumstances, and in the face of the legislative challenge to union gains, the two federations merged in 1955. The new AFL-CIO included unions representing 16 million workers, over 85 percent of union membership in the United States. The impulse toward unity also extended beyond the bounds of the AFL and CIO to the independents. In the two years after the merger, the Brotherhood of Locomotive Firemen and Enginemen, Railroad Trainmen, Train Dispatchers, and Railway Supervisors came in.

At the head of the biggest organization of unions in the nation's history stood a new leader for new times—a New York City plumber named George Meany. Meany's selection as the first president of the merged organization reflected the numerical superiority of the AFL unions. Meany was born into a union family in New York in 1894. His father had risen to the presidency of a large plumbers' local and young George left high school after one year to apprentice in the trade. In a union where a combination of family connections and talent meant a great deal, Meany rose from jour-neyman plumber to business agent by his twenty-eighth birthday. By 1930 he was president of the New York State Federation of Labor. He moved on to Washington to become secretary-treasurer of the AFL in 1939 and at William Green's death, he assumed the presidency.

Meany wore the AFL's leadership mantle well. He grasped the fact that the pragmatic federation that he headed could only thrive if it could main-tain its place among the countervailing interest groups that had come to dominate American political and economic life. Meany understood that there existed no fundamental differences of philosophy between the craft and industrial unions, and more than anyone else he deserved credit for the merger.

Meany believed firmly that a free enterprise economy operating in a pluralistic political system offered the best environment for independent trade unions to function. Consequently he remained a bitter anti-Commu-nist all of his life. No inevitable class struggle existed in Meany's mind, nor did he see the need for one. "I never went on strike in my life, never ordered anyone else to run a strike in my life, never had anything to do with a picket line . . . . ," he told the convention of the National Associa-tion of Manufacturers in 1956. "In the final analysis," he continued, "there is not a great difference between the things I stand for and the things the NAM leaders stand for. I stand for the profit system; I believe in the profit system. I believe it's a wonderful incentive. I believe in the free enterprise system completely." Although the two were to develop serious differ-ences, Walter Reuther had no real quarrel with Meany on this point. "We don't believe in the class struggle," he said in 1958.

INTERNAL PROBLEMS

From the beginning, the new federation had its share of internal problems. In 1957, a special committee of the U.S. Senate—the McClellan Commit-tee—made dramatic revelations of widespread corruption in the labor movement. It became clear once again that unions that accepted the busi-ness ethic were as susceptible to corruption as their counterparts in the corporate boardrooms. But in the midst of the conservative years of the 1950s, revelations of corruption threatened the institutional legitimacy that labor had worked so hard to achieve. Under the leadership of Meany and Reuther the AFL-CIO expelled the Teamsters, Bakery Workers and Laun-dry Workers in 1957. One year later, varying degrees of supervision over the Operating Engineers, Carpenters, Jewelry Workers, Hotel and Restau-rant Workers and Meat Cutters went into effect.

The willingness to take on the Teamsters—the AFL-CIO's largest affiliate—indicated Meany's determination. But the dilemma in which the federation found itself after expelling the Teamsters illustrated how little pressure the Federation could actually exert on a strong affiliate. New unions were chartered for the bakery and laundry industries, but no such attempt could be made against the Teamsters. Many affiliates depended on the support of the truckers when carrying out strikes. Whether or not the teamsters crossed the picket lines often spelled the differences between success and failure. Under these circumstances local cooperation between the expelled union and AFL-CIO unions went on as before.

Nor did the AFL-CIO's stand on principle have much effect on the attitude of the Teamsters toward their leaders. Revelations of corruption brought no upsurge of democratic sentiment. After Teamster president Dave Beck was jailed, he was promptly replaced by Jimmy Hoffa, a Detroit union leader with strong ties to organized crime, who soon followed Beck to prison. The members of the Teamsters belonged to a union whose primary purpose was to gain the greatest financial reward for its members. Corrupt or not, its leaders accomplished this with remarkable success.

Of course, in such an environment union democracy sometimes disappeared. When challenges to union autocracy did appear in the form of rank-and-file movements, they often met with apathy among the members as well as charges from the incumbents that they were led by outside agitators or radicals.

The AFL-CIO was ambivalent to any challenge to existing leadership in unions, either inside or outside of the Federation. The reasons for this were complex. In the first place the Federation had no authority to interfere in the internal affairs of unions. Its only recourse was to use the extreme weapon of expulsion. When Meany did so in the case of the Teamsters, Bakery Workers and Laundry Workers, it was little short of a revolutionary move.

A second reason was the historic reluctance of unions to attack one another for fear of giving ammunition to antiunion forces. This corresponded to a strong belief that only the members, as part of a voluntary organization, had the right and responsibility to judge their elected leaders. Any outside interference, especially on the part of the government, was seen as opening a Pandora's box of government interference that could just as easily be used against unions in the legitimate exercise of their rights.

One can clearly see the "voluntaristic" legacy of Samuel Gompers in these arguments. But as in Gompers' time, an argument based on principle can also serve to cloak self-interest. By the 1960s, highly bureaucratized, authoritarian administrations had come to characterize many unions. While usually high minded and honest, many leaders came to wield near absolute control over their organizations. Few unions had contested elections for the top leadership posts. When challenges did arise, they were often treated as signs of disloyalty rather than indicates of democracy.

Yet despite the difficulties, rank and file movements did occur. Revelations of union corruption may have spurred some of them, and the passage in 1959 of the Landrum-Griffin Act provided safeguards for union electoral procedures, thus making challenges easier. Surely the rebellious tone of the turbulent 1960s, the generational change in the labor force, and the resentment against the oppressive working conditions on the shop floor were also factors. By the late 1960s, rank-and-file militance, largely dormant during the 1950s, was on the rise again. In 1967 the Federal Mediation and Conciliation Service reported that workers had rejected nearly 15 percent of the year's contracts. The incidence of strikes occurring with a contract in effect doubled between 1960 and 1969, indicative surely of the growing importance of shop-floor issues. As the struggle for control of the workplace heated up again, union leaders were often blamed along with management. The effect of all of this on internal union politics was an increase in challenges of incumbent officers. During the 1960s, the Teamsters, Steelworkers, Painters, Seafarers, Longshoremen, and others experienced bitter internal battles for control.

The struggle for control of a union that received the most publicity occurred in the United Mine Workers. There, the political machine built by John L. Lewis had passed to his heir, Tony Boyle, who ran the union in the dictatorial fashion established by his mentor. In 1969 a United Mine Workers executive board member, Jock Yablonski, challenged Boyle for the presidency. Three weeks after his defeat in a rigged election, Yablonski, his wife, and daughter were found murdered in their Pennsylvania home. The murder shocked the nation and threw a spotlight on the corruption and authoritarianism which characterized the Boyle administration. A new movement—the Miners for Democracy—picked up Yablonski's standard and in 1972, with Arnold Miller as its candidate, and with government supervision of the election, defeated Boyle. Soon after, Boyle was implicated in the Yablonski murders and was later convicted for ordering the murder of his rival.

The tragedy of the miners, long years in coming as a result of the autocratic nature of the union's leadership, did not end with the election of Arnold Miller. With the disintegration of the old Lewis machine, factionalism ran rampant in the union. The Mine Workers drifted like a rudderless ship. Weakened internally, they could not move to seize the organizational opportunities presented by the resurgence of the coal industry as a result of the growing energy shortage. In 1977 and 1978, the crippled union carried out a long and tortuous strike. Internal factionalism restricted the UMWA's ability to bargain. Miller seemed to speak for no one but himself as his members rejected two settlements to which he had agreed. Only under the threat of a Taft-Hartley injunction, ninety-two days after the strike had begun, did the two sides reach agreement. In the process, the coal operators, now dominated by huge corporations, made significant headway in reversing gains the union had made in previous contracts. Yet the internal strife in the United Mine Workers had not been in vain. When Arnold Miller stepped down for health reasons there was an orderly transfer of power to Sam Church. In 1983, the internal democracy that the miners had fought for functioned well as a young Pennsylvania miner and lawyer named Richard Trumka defeated Church for the presidency.

SCHISM

Almost from the beginning of the merger, the shaky alliance between George Meany and Walter Reuther began to break down. Vastly different styles of leadership undoubtedly contributed to the growing split, but there were substantive differences as well. Reuther had become increasingly skeptical of the value of the AFL-CIO's partnership with the State Department and the Central Intelligence Agency in foreign affairs. Although he was also anti-Communist, Reuther wanted American labor's international activity channeled through the International Confederation of Free Trade Unions (ICFTU). Meany, on the other hand, distrusted the ICFTU bureaucracy, and wanted a free hand. Reuther came to believe in the possibility of détente with the Soviet Union. Meany never wavered from his hard line anti-Soviet beliefs. When Meany ordered the AFL-CIO representatives to walk out of the International Labor Organization meetings in 1966 because of the election of a delegate from Communist Poland as presiding officer, Reuther openly challenged the action. Finally, Reuther's disenchantment with the AFL-CIO's strong support for American involvement in Vietnam brought the foreign policy differences of the two men into sharp relief.

On the domestic front there were quarrels as well. When Reuther finally pulled the United Auto Workers out of the AFL-CIO in 1968, he charged that the Federation had failed to organize, particularly among farm workers and the "working poor," that it had become complacent and a supporter of the status quo, that it lacked social vision and a crusading spirit. Yet with all of the rhetoric, the differences between the two men were really more a matter of emphasis than kind. While it was true that Meany as a leader was more the business agent representing his members than the captain of a social movement, Reuther, in his dealings with the auto industry, was also firmly in the business unionist mold.

Shortly after withdrawing from the AFL-CIO, the Auto Workers joined with the Teamsters to form the Alliance for Labor Action. The Teamsters union was a strange partner for the socially conscious Reuther to pick to "revitalize the labor movement." Few were surprised when the Alliance died a quiet death in December of 1971.

The schism did alter the role of the American labor movement in international labor matters. In 1969 Meany pulled the AFL-CIO out of the ICFTU because it failed to reject the Auto Workers' petition for membership to the world labor organization. In fact, Meany had long been interested in severing his relationship with the organization the AFL had been instrumental in founding as part of the anti-Communist effort after World War II. By 1969 many of the leaders of non-Communist European labor movements in the ICFTU no longer believed that total quarantine was the most effective way to deal with the Communist world. But Meany's position had not changed, and he had long ago begun to carry out a foreign policy independent of the ICFTU.

THE POLITICAL CHALLENGE

Internal divisions did nothing to enhance labor's political influence. Much of the impetus for merger had come from the antilabor shift in Congress, which led to the passage of Taft-Hartley. Yet in the face of the revelations of union corruption by the McClellan Committee, not even a unified labor movement with a Democratic congressional majority could turn back Landrum Griffin, officially named the Labor-Management Reporting and Disclosure Act of 1959. The law provided safeguards for the rights of union members; required filing reports describing the organization, financial and business practices of unions, their officers, and employees; safeguarded union election procedures; set standards for the handling of union funds, closed existing loopholes in the prohibition of secondary boycotts; and limited organizational and jurisdictional picketing. Labor fought the law but the public sentiment for reform swept aside all opposition.

Labor's major legislative goal—the repeal of Taft-Hartley—became little more than a *pro forma* exercise. As we will see, later attempts to affect relatively minor reforms in the nation's basic labor law also failed.

The major successes came in the area of health and safety. After years of effort, reasonably strong coal mine safety legislation became law between 1969 and 1977. In 1970, President Nixon signed the Occupational Safety and Health Act (OSHA). The bill, which had been lobbied through Congress by the labor movement, authorized the Department of Labor to investigate hazardous working conditions, establish safety standards in the nation's workplaces, and enforce compliance with them. OSHA marked the first serious attempt by the federal government to make the workplace safe. In its first decade OSHA resulted in reductions in the rates of work-related injuries and illnesses. In addition, a start was made in identifying and regulating the use of hazardous substances, such as vinyl chloride, asbestos, and other carcinogens, which had long been hidden killers of workers.

Labor lobbied to push through the Employee Retirement Income Security Act of 1974 (ERISA). The act was passed because of a growing problem of default by employee pension and welfare funds. ERISA required disclosure of pension plan provisions and financial information, and established funding and vesting requirements along with standards of conduct for trustees and administrators of pension plans, and provided for government guarantee of the pension.

Yet even though there were scattered victories, and some consistent successes such as periodic increases in the federal minimum wage, unions were unable to convert their overwhelming support for the Democratic Party, the majority party in Congress for all but a few years since 1932, into legislation to help unions organize in a period when industry began to take the offensive. Both the Common Situs Picketing Act—a piece of legislation aimed at helping the building trades organize in an increasingly open-shop industry—and the even more significant Labor Law Reform legislation were defeated in the 1970s.

Labor's political strength was most effective when used in coalition with other groups in support of the Great Society anti-poverty programs of the Johnson administration. Yet the AFL-CIO's support for Lyndon Johnson's Vietnam policies seriously undercut its relationship with its traditional liberal allies. Indeed the conflict between the antiwar Democrats and the regular Democrats, including organized labor, led to serious splits in the party in 1968 and 1972. Differences on the war resulted in 1972 in the AFL-CIO withholding its endorsement from George McGovern, the Democratic candidate, even though McGovern had a good labor record as a senator and his opponent was the traditionally antilabor Richard Nixon. After eight Republican years, the Watergate scandal, and the end of the Vietnam War, organized labor returned to the Democrats in support of Jimmy Carter in 1976.

Some of labor's political problems stemmed from the perception by many of labor's traditional friends that the AFL-CIO had become a status quo organization. This was true of the split between the antiwar and the labor movements. It also arose over the issue of the role of minorities and women in the labor movement.

LABOR AND BLACK POWER

When the Civil Rights movement began in the 1950s, the AFL-CIO called on Eisenhower to enforce the Supreme Court's decision on school desegregation, but it remained silent on the Montgomery bus boycott of 1956. Much of this hesitation reflected the fact that the Federation allowed itself to be held hostage by its small minority of white southern members. Not only was the policy morally questionable, but it was shortsighted as well. Fear of the southern reaction led to the shelving of a planned southern organizing drive after the merger. But, as one scholar, Ray Marshall, later pointed out, blacks were among the most forthright union supporters in the South and in organizational drives their support frequently meant the difference between victory and defeat. In fact, it could be argued that organized labor's weakness in the South stemmed more from its lack of organization among black workers than among white workers.

Throughout the late 1950s and early 1960s the AFL-CIO maintained something of a split personality on the race issue. Its increasingly strong support for civil rights legislation was frequently coupled with a reluctance to push the issue of discrimination with the affiliates.

A 1961 report by the National Association for the Advancement of Colored People (NAACP) took note of the progress made in the reduction of racial barriers in some unions, most notably the recently admitted Brotherhood of Railway Trainmen, but lamented that in its first five years the AFL-CIO had failed to eliminate "the broad pattern of racial discrimination and segregation in many important affiliated unions. . . ." This was especially true, according to the report, in the building trades where traditional anti-black practices remained in effect.

George Meany reacted angrily to the NAACP indictment, calling it a "distorted picture" of labor's efforts in civil rights. The fact that the newly formed Negro American Labor Council, headed by A. Philip Randolph, also supported the NAACP report seemed like a betrayal to Meany. Soon after, the AFL-CIO executive council censured Randolph, blaming him for "the gap that has developed between organized labor and the Negro community." Embarrassingly, one day later the U.S. Commission on Civil Rights documented the extent of discrimination in organized labor and pointed out that the AFL-CIO had largely been ineffective in curbing racism.

By 1963 the issue became part of the growing split between Meany and Reuther. As the March on Washington led by Martin Luther King, Jr., approached, a number of unions took an active role in support of the civil rights movement. When the AFL-CIO Executive Council withheld support for the march, the federation's Industrial Union Department, under Reuther's control, denounced the decision. Reuther and Randolph were among the unionists who took part in the march. The events of 1963 proved to be a turning point. AFL-CIO lobbyists threw their wholehearted effort behind the Civil Rights Act of 1964 and, in the words of the NAACP's Clarence Mitchell, "Organized labor gave unfailing and massive support where it counted most . . . . the members of organized labor were always present at the right time and in the right place." In fact, the inclusion of the section on discrimination in employment in the law occurred largely because of George Meany's efforts. Aware of the AFL-CIO's lack of authority to force the affiliates to change, he saw the law as one way to force reluctant unions to lower the racial barrier.

Still the problem continued, and by 1968 the pressures building in the unions and on the national political scene could not be ignored. "Black power" in the union context meant a share in running the unions at every level. Soon black caucuses began to appear in a variety of unions, some of them espousing revolutionary goals.

Of all the black insurgent movements, none received as much attention in the press as those in the United Auto Workers, a union with a progressive image on the race issue. The first sign of incipient rebellion came at Ford's Mahwah, New Jersey, plant where 500 black workers shut down the line after a foreman used a racial slur in reprimanding a worker. Soon black caucuses began forming in a number of auto plants. Many asked only for affirmative action to ensure proper representation of blacks in the union's hierarchy. Others, like the Dodge Revolutionary Union Movement, organized in the factories around a Marxist line that identified both the companies and the union as enemies. The UAW responded by increasing the number of blacks on its staff and by encouraging blacks to run for local offices.

Events in Memphis, Tennessee in 1968 and Charleston, South Carolina in 1969 symbolized the coming together of the civil rights movement and the labor movement. Both strikes illustrated the degree to which the black movement had shifted its emphasis to economic power. Both the sanitation workers of Memphis and the hospital workers of Charleston were poorly paid service workers in cities in which organized labor had little strength. But with the support of the American Federation of State, County and Municipal Employees (AFSCME) in Memphis, and Hospital Workers Local 1199 in Charleston, both groups were able to prevail against the combined strength of the business, political, and media communities in their respective cities. Local labor councils gave what help and solidarity they could. National unions with no direct stake in the battles contributed funds. When Martin Luther King was killed while helping the Memphis strikers, labor increased its pressure until a settlement was reached.

As stirring as the events in Memphis and Charleston were, they did not eliminate criticism of the AFL-CIO's racial policy. Most of this criticism centered on the building trades unions which, unlike the industrial unions, had no large black memberships to mount challenges from the inside. Pressure for change, therefore, came from outside, most importantly from the government.

The fact that the insignificant percentage of blacks in the building trades—as in most other selective institutions in American society—was due in large measure to racism was undeniable. Yet the nature of unionism among these skilled workers made it difficult to correct. The building trades unions had always restricted membership to limit competition for jobs and increase wages. "We don't take *any* new members, regardless of color," said one Philadelphia building trades leader. The chief lever with which to control entrance to the trade was apprenticeship—a system that, by design, could not produce journeymen overnight. In addition, the building trades, operating in an unstable industry, maintained control over the trade by controlling the hiring hall. The system had the potential for favoritism, kickbacks, and racial exclusion.

Another widely criticized, and not very well understood, aspect of the building trades unions was their tendency to reserve space in the limited apprenticeship programs for sons and other relatives of union members. On first glance this obvious nepotism seemed unfair. But, to the craft worker, his trade and access to it were his most valuable possessions. Unable to provide his son with a sizable monetary inheritance, the worker could instead provide him with a valuable trade and a place in the union. The worker saw this as no different from the businessman who brought his child into the business, or the doctor who used his influence to insure that his child gained admittance to medical school. When told of the effects of his actions on minorities and women, the worker asked why he should be singled out as the only one who could not dispose of his legacy as he saw fit. But for blacks the closed system perpetuated a white-only policy and had the effect of excluding blacks from opportunities in the best-paying and most prestigious blue-collar occupations.

To deal with this the Nixon administration, in 1969, implemented the Philadelphia Plan, which established minority group quotas for six building trades unions working on federally funded construction jobs in the Philadelphia area. The unions argued that the plan discriminated against white workers and undermined the crafts, and that it was a politically motivated attempt by Nixon to embarrass unions. Similar plans appeared in a number of other cities, but the charge of political motivation seemed justified when Nixon backed off on enforcement in exchange for building trades support for his Vietnam policy. This alliance of convenience resulted in several confrontations between construction workers—"hard hats" as the media dubbed them—and antiwar demonstrators; as well in as the appointment of Peter Brennan, a New York building trades official and a supporter of the war, as Secretary of Labor.

Meanwhile a voluntary, "hometown approach" in which union, minority, and business leaders worked out local goals and timetables, replaced the quotas of the Philadelphia plan. But by 1975 the worst recession in the postwar era had so devastated the construction industry that real progress became difficult no matter what the approach.

Yet with all the disappointments, blacks made gains. In 1960, nonwhites made up only 2.5 percent of those enrolled in registered apprenticeship programs. By 1968 7 percent of new apprentices were nonwhites.

For unions as a whole, the approximately 2.5 million black members in the mid-1970s constituted roughly the same proportion as that for blacks in the total population, and represented substantial progress from 1956 when only 8.6 percent of black workers held union cards. There is no question that blacks benefited from union membership; their economic status was higher in unionized industries. Income differentials with whites were dramatically less for unionized blacks. When in 1971, Bayard Rustin, an associate of A. Philip Randolph, argued that the labor movement had all but eliminated racism, he was no doubt exaggerating. But when he added that for all its faults the labor movement was the most integrated major institution in American society, he spoke the truth.

WOMEN IN UNIONS

For women much the same proved to be true. When the Women's Trade Union League disbanded in 1952, it did so because most of its functions had been assumed by the labor movement. Soon after the merger, the AFL-CIO spent over $2 million on a successful organizing drive in the Miami hotel industry, and women benefited a great deal from the upsurge of public employee unionism that occurred in the 1960s. In 1957 George Meany pointed with pride to the 200 women who held full-time administrative positions in unions, not to mention thousands of regional and local officials.

The Federation's shifting position could be seen in its attitude toward the Equal Rights Amendment (ERA). ERA, supported in both the Republican and Democratic party platforms since 1948, did not pass the House of Representatives until 1970, and even then the Senate failed to act on it. The long delay was attributable in large measure to the AFL-CIO's opposition to the amendment. The Federation took the position that ERA would endanger existing protective legislation for working women. It urged women to depend on their own strength in unions, not on a constitutional amendment.

Even as late as 1970 many female representatives of unions such as the Communications Workers, Amalgamated Clothing Workers, Ladies Garment Workers, and the Hotel and Restaurant Workers lobbied against the amendment. Yet by that time a shift had begun to develop on the issue. Under pressure from their female membership, unions such as the Steelworkers, Chemical Workers, Teamsters, and the American Federation of Teachers came out in support. When the measure finally passed both houses of Congress in 1972, the AFL-CIO endorsed its ratification and put forth the strongest profeminist program in its history.

The need for an organized voice for women inside the labor movement resulted in the formation of the Coalition of Labor Union Women (CLUW) in 1974. The creation of CLUW coincided with a female membership of 25 percent in the AFL-CIO, the highest in history. However, few of the policymaking positions in the Federation or its affiliates were held by women. In 1978, when a Bureau of Labor Statistics study showed that while approximately 27 percent of the members were women, female representation in elected and high appointed office amounted to a far smaller percentage.

The need to organize women workers was also apparent. In five of the nine industries in which women made up more than 40 percent of total employment, less than 25 percent of the workers belonged to unions. The potential of this membership pool was demonstrated by the fact that women accounted for more than half of the total growth in union membership between 1966 and 1976. By 1979, the 6.7 million female members of labor unions earned wages more than one-third higher on average than their nonunion sisters, not to mention vastly better fringe benefits.

Finally, in the spring of 1980, the AFL-CIO Executive Council recognized the critical importance of the contributions of women and minorities to the labor movement and voted to waive the tradition that executive council members be required to be presidents of affiliated unions. Immediately thereafter, Joyce Miller, vice-president of the Amalgamated Clothing and Textile Workers Union and president of CLUW, became the first woman named to the AFL-CIO Executive Council.

PUBLIC WORKERS, PUBLIC UNIONS

The explosion of public employee unionization after 1960 had a great deal to do with the rise in importance of women and minorities in the labor movement. Both groups benefited from the growth in the white-collar categories of public employment that marked the postwar period. Public employee unions increased their membership by more than 2 million between 1956 and 1976 and the percentage of public workers in unions jumped from 12 percent to 20 percent. When schoolteachers who bargained through the National Education Association were included in this group, the percentage climbed to 39 percent.

Several factors accounted for this dramatic increase. The general prosperity of the 1960s made public employees less willing to overlook undesirable aspects of their jobs in exchange for security. With the steady inflation of the period, public employees became concerned with the methods used to determine their wage increases. Because of the growth in the number of public workers, both politicians and union leaders began to look on the workers with considerable interest—politicians saw that the workers constituted an important vote bloc, and union leaders saw the new numbers as justifying the cost of a major organizing effort. Of considerable importance were the large numbers of young and minority workers, people on whom the general militancy of the 1960s had an effect, and for whom the new unions offered a means to status and power.

Whatever the reasons, changes in public policy provided the legal framework in which public workers could unionize. President Kennedy's Executive Order 10988 issued in 1962 gave federal executive branch employees the right to join unions and bargain collectively. Prior to the Kennedy order, only Wisconsin had granted its public workers the right to unionize. A number of states followed the federal example, and by 1977 twenty states had enacted legislation conferring such protection upon state and local employees.

For postal workers, the 1970 Postal Reorganization Act established the postal corporation and placed its labor relations under private sector labor law. The first mass work stoppage in the 195-year history of the Post Office Department began in the same year with a walkout of postal workers in New York City, a walkout that spread quickly to Detroit, Philadelphia and other major cities. Agreement came after two bitter weeks, and then only when President Nixon declared it a national emergency strike and assigned military units to New York City post offices.

The postal strike symbolized the militancy of public employees. By 1975, the number of strikes reached an all-time high of 428, involving 2.2 percent of public employees, a figure equal to the private sector. The largest strike by far took place in Pennsylvania, which witnessed the first statewide strike of public employees in American history. More than 80,000 members of the American Federation of State, County and Municipal Employees (AFSCME) took part.

The overwhelming majority of public sector strikes occurred at the local level where the issues were often sharply drawn and highly volatile—none more so than those that involved public safety personnel. Fireman and policemen increasingly used the strike weapon in spite of laws forbidding it. Seventy firemen's strikes occurred between 1966 and 1977, while police struck ninety-three times between 1972 and 1975.

Public employee strikes—especially those involving police, teachers, and sanitation workers—created something of a backlash against unionized public workers. This backlash, coupled with the recession of 1973 and 1974, slowed the twin spirals of organization and strikes. When New York City was on the brink of economic collapse in 1975, much of the blame was laid on the city's public employee unions which were charged with bringing the city to bankruptcy through excessive contract demands. The municipal unions found themselves forced to help rescue the city by pledging their pension funds as security for bank loans to the beleaguered city and by moderating their contract demands. Public officials in other cities used the New York example as justification for resisting demands by their own municipal workers.

Nevertheless, by the end of the decade the public employee unions were well established and one, AFSCME, with nearly one million members, had grown to be one of the largest affiliates of the AFL-CIO. Half of its membership was female or nonwhite. In its racial, sexual, and occupational mix it represented the future of the labor movement, just as the craft and industrial unions had at earlier times.

JERRY WURF

In the 1950s and 1960s, a young person's rise to prominence in the labor movement was increasingly likely to occur through a union of public employees. One such shooting star was Jerry Wurf, the man who guided the American Federation of State, County and Municipal Employees (AFSCME) through the period of explosive growth of public sector unionism.

Wurf began his union career in 1940 when he took a job in a New York City cafeteria in order to organize the workers. By 1943, the young activist had helped to create Food and Cashiers Local 448 of the Hotel and Restaurant Employees Union. As a reward, the union gave him a staff organizer's job, a job that ended when the volatile Wurf came out on the losing side of an internal union dispute. Soon after, in 1947, he found a position as an organizer for a small public employees union with practically no membership in New York. One year later he became director of AFSCME for the entire city. From that position he built the union in New York into a political base that enabled him to win the presidency of AFSCME in 1964.

In his first years as president, Wurf's challenge was to achieve public acceptance of the rights of public workers to collective bargaining. By the end of the decade this had been largely accomplished. Now a new challenge loomed. Many American cities were hit with severe financial crises in the early and mid-1970s. Politicians blamed unions of city workers, of which AFSCME was the largest. During New York's near bankruptcy, AFSCME and other municipal unions made great sacrifices to help the city, including the use of billions in pension fund money to buy city bonds. According to Wurf, the unions "did a hell of a lot more than any of the banks. Yet we still ended up the villain."

During his career Wurf kept AFSCME in the forefront of progressive and liberal causes. When Martin Luther King Jr. was shot in Memphis, he was supporting an AFSCME strike of black sanitation workers. Wurf was one of the first leaders of an AFL-CIO union to break with the federation's support of American involvement in the Vietnam war. In 1968 when George Meany succeeded in withholding the AFL endorsement from Democratic presidential candidate, George McGovern, Wurf and AFSCME were among the first to endorse the antiwar candidate independently.

THE ORGANIZATIONAL CHALLENGE

Success in the public sector obscured the relative, but significant, decline in more traditional union strongholds. In fact, union membership as a percentage of all employees dropped sharply between 1956 and 1976. In the heart of unionization—the manufacturing sector—unions lost more than 350,000 members in the twenty-year period and saw the percentage of manufacturing workers in unions fall from 51.3 percent to 44.6 percent. It is true that organized labor added 1.2 million members after 1956 in the rest of the private sector, but because the labor force grew much more rapidly, the percentage of nonmanufacturing workers in unions fell almost 10 percent.

To be sure, there were notable organizational successes and signs of militancy. The 1959 steel strike lasted 116 days, the longest ever in steel. But, like many modern disputes, it was hard to tell which side had won. Although the steelworkers turned back an attempt by the company to alter work practices, their numbers continued to dwindle. And the longshoremen continued to close down the docks periodically, causing presidents to resort to the national emergency strike provisions of Taft-Hartley every few years.

Much more satisfying to those who cherished the labor movement's role as protector of the underdog was the struggle of the Mexican-American and Filipino farm workers of California. Part of the upsurge of Chicano consciousness in the West and Southwest, the cause of the United Farm Workers inspired support from trade unionists, college students, and others across the nation. Its leader, Cesar Chavez, whose brand of unionism mixed Catholicism and pacifism with ethnic pride, became something of a secular saint to a large number of Americans who were searching for an authentic hero in decidedly unheroic times. In 1970, after a four and a half year boycott of California table grapes, Chavez' union finally reached an agreement with most growers. Similar tactics led to breakthroughs in the lettuce fields. When the Teamsters began to raid the Farm Workers, George Meany used his influence to bring about a jurisdictional agreement between the two unions. Through it all, the AFL-CIO unions and the United Auto Workers gave substantial financial support to the struggling union of migrant workers.

CESAR CHAVEZ

The son of migrant workers, Chavez grew up during the depression. He remembered that "strikes were everywhere" during the 1930s when the Communists tried to organize California migrant workers into a union, and that the Chavez family was one of the "strikingest." As his family followed the crops around the southwestern United States, Chavez attended thirty different schools until he dropped out at the end of the seventh grade. He left the fields for service in the navy in World War II, but returned afterward to the migrant life.

At the age of thirty-five, Chavez moved his family to Delano in California's great Central Valley where he began to develop his concept of a union for farm laborers. After several years of organizing, Chavez merged his small National Farm Workers Association with the heavily Filipino Agricultural Workers Organizing Committee in a strike against the Delano grape growers. Chavez' nonviolent tactics attracted national attention. He dramatized the plight of the migrants through his twenty-five day march from Delano to Sacramento in 1966, and his long fast to rededicate the movement to nonviolence. Chavez viewed the strike as more than a labor dispute. To him it was part of a broad movement for social justice and human dignity among the most oppressed sector of the American work force. He used the Spanish words, *la causa*, to describe it, and it grew into one of the main pillars of a movement among Mexican Americans for equal rights and opportunities.

After five years of struggle, including a nationwide boycott of table grapes, the United Farm Workers Organizing Committee obtained contracts with twenty-six growers. Chavez then turned his attention to the lettuce fields where similar tactics had only limited success, in part because of competition from the Teamsters Union. Chavez and associates like Dolores Huerta, and Fred Ross, brought a revolution to the "factories in the fields."

One of the most significant labor victories took place in 1978 at the Newport News Shipbuilding and Drydock Company of Virginia. The breakthrough by the United Steelworkers took place at the largest shipyard in the world (among 19,000 production and maintenance workers, many of whom were black) in a stridently right-to-work state. Steelworkers' president Lloyd McBride called it "a significant advance for the cause of trade unionism in the South."

Undoubtedly it was, but unfortunately the advance was not typical. More in line with the norm was the long struggle between the Textile Workers Union and the viciously antiunion J.P. Stevens Company. The Textile Workers had been trying with little success to organize J.P. Stevens for a number of years. In June 1976, the workers merged with the Amalgamated Clothing Workers and the new union committed itself to a full-scale drive to organize the 40,000 workers in the firm's 85 southern plants.

J.P. Stevens met the drive with a systematic policy of labor law violation. It was a campaign of lawbreaking so flagrant that in March 1978 the National Labor Relations Board asked a federal court to issue a nationwide injunction against J.P. Stevens to bar the company from violating the law. In the first request for a nationwide injunction since the passage of the Wagner Act, the Board accused Stevens of engaging in a fifteen-year "massive, multistate campaign to deny its employees their rights" under federal law. The Board added that the injunction was necessary to "restrain Stevens from a nationwide program of illegal activity and its contumacious conduct toward the National Labor Relations Act." Pointing out that Stevens had committed "unfair labor practices of unprecedented flagrancy and magnitude," the Board noted that the firm had been found guilty fifteen times of violating labor laws and had paid $1.3 million in fines and back wages since the early 1960s.

In July 1978, the Board and Stevens reached an agreement whereby the Board dropped its request for an injunction and the company agreed not to use tactics that would have been banned by the injunction. A Textile Workers union spokesman pointed out that the agreement demonstrated the need for labor law reform because it showed "that a lawless company can escape punishment by making an empty promise to a powerless NLRB which is charged with enforcing a toothless law."

The highly publicized frustrations at J.P. Stevens were only the tip of the iceberg. The union victory rate everywhere in the private sector declined between 1956 and 1976. By the latter year, unions were winning less than half of the representation elections in manufacturing, a drop of more than 20 percent in twenty years. In construction, an even more dramatic decline occurred, from 82.6 percent to 47.8 percent.

Labor's declining ability to organize could be explained by a number of factors. Certainly the occupational mix was of paramount importance. Of the 45 million nonagricultural employees in 1950, 28 percent were production workers. By 1976, the total nonagricultural labor force had grown to 79 million, but the production sector proportion had declined to 17 percent. Obviously, the growth area of the economy lay outside of labor's traditional strongholds.

Perhaps of equal importance was the changing location of jobs. As we have seen, production and technical jobs had been progressively moving to the antiunion South and West or overseas. In the right-to-work states, unions had to deal with a strong antiunion coalition of business, government, and the media. Overseas the problems became even greater. Any attempt to successfully deal with American-based multinational companies required cooperation with trade union movements abroad, an enormously complex undertaking considering the many cultural, idealogical, and legal differences that divided unions across national boundaries. According to Richard Barnet and Ronald Muller:

Nothing is better calculated to weaken the bargaining power of labor than management's prerogative to divide and shift tasks at will on a global scale. . . . Corporate organization on a global scale is a highly effective weapon for undercutting the power of organized labor everywhere. Capital, technology, and marketplace ideology, the bases of corporate power, are mobile; workers, by and large, are not. The ability of corporations to open and close plants rapidly and to shift their investment from one country to another erodes the basis of organized labor's bargaining leverage, the strike. . . . Management finds that its power to close an entire operation in a community and to transfer everything but the workers out of the country produces a marvelously obliging labor force.

As bad as the threat from the multinational corporations was, the diversified conglomerate corporations, whether domestic or multinational, provided an even greater challenge. The structure of one of the biggest—International Telephone and Telegraph (ITT)—illustrated the problem. By

1970, the firm had acquired or was in the process of acquiring over 100 corporations with combined assets approaching $4 billion dollars. These acquisitions transformed ITT's product mix. It no longer depended on any one activity for the major share of its income. This diversity had important implications for collective bargaining. No one subsidiary was essential to the company. Many of the firm's employees were located overseas, where 45 percent of its income came from. Of its American workers, a substantial number were nonunion. Those who held union cards belonged to at least fourteen different unions. Obviously a strike by any one union against any particular subsidiary brought very little pressure on the parent company.

When a company had an antiunion pattern of behavior, the problem became critical. Litton Industries, the sixty-eighth largest corporation in the world in 1983, had 60,000 American employees. But only 10,000 of Litton's workers, who made dozens of different products in eighty-nine different divisions, belonged to unions. Even more indicative of union vulnerability was the fact that this relatively small group of union members was scattered among eight different unions in thirty different locals. Litton argued that the company had no central labor policy and that these matters were left to the individual subsidiaries. But the company's record of getting rid of unions in fifteen subsidiaries after it had acquired them, and the fact that the National Labor Relations Board had issued 50 complaints against Litton for unfair labor practices between 1952 and 1983 cast doubts on the conglomerate's assertion. According to William Winpisinger, president of the International Association of Machinists, by the 1980s Litton had earned the dubious distinction of being America's number one labor law violator. According to Winpisinger, "although Litton operates under many names in many locations, its pattern of union busting is the same everywhere."

The AFL-CIO attempted to balance the power of the diversified companies through the development of joint bargaining among various unions that represented workers in a single company. The strategy had some success when a coalition of unions led by the United Steelworkers carried on a coordinated strike and bargaining against the major copper companies in 1967, and when General Electric in 1966 negotiated a new agreement with the International Union of Electrical Workers in the presence of representatives from ten other unions representing General Electric's workers. But union attempts to cooperate in bargaining ran into serious legal roadblocks. The NLRB ruled that collective bargaining must be restricted to a specific bargaining unit, meaning a specific subsidiary of a diversified firm. Furthermore, the Board held that changing the scope of the bargaining unit was not a mandatory subject for collective bargaining. Although the Supreme Court in the 1972 Phelps-Dodge Case offered the unions some room for cooperation in bargaining with a diversified employer, the basic handicaps remained in place.

In the 1970s, deregulation of the airline, bus, and trucking industries made regulatory rate setting less of a source of employer ability to pay higher wages by passing on the costs to the consumers, as did increased consumer resistance to regulatory rate increases in urban mass transit, energy, and other regulated industries. The impact of deregulation could be clearly seen in the trucking industry. The deregulation bill of 1980 opened the market to smaller, nonunion truckers who drove many larger, unionized operations out of business. This undercut the master freight agreement, the source of the Teamsters' strength. Even though the union signed a thirty-seven-month agreement in 1981 that gave major concessions to unionized trucking companies, hundreds of companies ignored the agreement and made separate agreements with Teamster local unions. The Teamsters' national leadership has been unable to counter this threat to industrywide collective bargaining, nor has it been able to organize the new nonunion trucking companies.

The combination of new technology, business diversification, the relocation of industry, deregulation, and a general economic decline badly disrupted the rough balance that had prevailed in collective bargaining from the end of World War II to the early 1960s. In these circumstances, the quid pro quo between management and labor began to unravel. Up to that time, workers had enjoyed a trend toward rising real wages, employment security, and improved working conditions. But the early 1970s witnessed the reversal of these trends. Real wages declined, unemployment increased, and work-related accidents began to climb.

Unions were sometimes able to protect existing workers from the ravages of automation, but only at the expense of future employment of new workers. In 1960, the Pacific Maritime Association and the International Longshoremen's and Warehousemen's Union agreed on a formula to permit the increased use of labor-saving machinery on the waterfront. In buying their way out of union manning rules, the companies agreed to contribute $5 million a year to a fund to provide each of the 15,000 registered longshoremen with $7920 on retirement at age 65 with twenty-five years of service, to guarantee union members minimum weekly earnings, and to forego layoffs as a result of decreased work opportunities. Along the same lines, the Southern Pacific Railroad and the Order of Railroad Telegraphers negotiated an agreement in 1961 that guaranteed each telegrapher a job or equivalent wages for life. And in 1972, the major railroads and the United Transportation Union, which had been created out of the merger of five railroad brotherhoods, settled one of the longest-running labor disputes in American history when they agreed on a formula to phase out firemen's jobs on diesel freight locomotives without jeopardizing current workers.

Concessions on manning rules in return for lifetime security for current employees became fairly common in industries, such as newspaper publishing, heavily affected by new technology. Such compromises often resulted in immediate gains for union members in the form of retirement bonuses and retraining opportunities. But in industries in economic decline—industries that often had not kept up with new technology—unions often found themselves forced to make immediate concessions in order to protect jobs—concessions that brought no quid pro quo. In the early post-war years, secure domestic markets had enabled the giants of American business enterprise to pass on labor costs to consumers without reducing profit margins. But, as competition from abroad increased, some of it in international transfers by American based multinational companies, pressure became intense on domestic industry to make up for diminished profits in product markets by realizing cost savings in labor markets. This frequently came to mean take-it-or-leave-it bargaining, with companies threatening to close down and relocate if the union rejected the offer. In such a setting, industrywide bargaining, wage patterns, and the union shop began to lose their effectiveness as protective devices for organized production workers. Indeed, by the early 1980s concession bargaining had become the pattern.

With their relative power at the bargaining table reduced, unions looked to the government for relief. They lobbied in Congress, along with their employers, for high tariffs or quotas on imports, domestic content legislation, and for legislation providing adjustment assistance for workers who lost their jobs because of competition from abroad. The Trade Act of 1974 provided workers displaced by imports with up to 52 weeks of payments and assistance in retraining, placement, and relocation. That same year, with unemployment at the highest rate since 1941, the United Auto Workers requested special benefits for 70,000 unemployed workers under the trade adjustment assistance provisions of the act.

While Unions looked to Congress for relief, many companies pressed their advantage and demanded concessions at the bargaining table. In the early phases, unions granted concessions to companies in serious economic trouble in order to protect jobs. But, by the early 1980s, management in healthy industries, realizing union weakness, began to press for concessions because they could get them, not because they needed them. This created a collective bargaining environment unimaginable only a few years before. The AFL-CIO *Federationist* compared it to "swimming upstream in high water," and union strategy in many industries shifted from the historic pursuit of "more" to an orderly retreat in defense of existing terrain.

In the early 1980s the structural problems that had weakened labor's bargaining power were complicated by the effects of the deepest economic recessions since the 1930s. In the first nine months of 1982, unions were able to negotiate percentage increases in wages only half the level of two years before. Even more ominous, about 45 percent of the 2.7 million workers covered by contract settlements in that same year received no wage increases in the first year of their contract.

A clear indication of labor's weakened bargaining position was union willingness to forego the strike weapon to help ailing companies or to keep them from relocating. The National Maritime Union offered a no-strike pledge in an effort to keep some American-owned shipping under the American flag. In an experimental negotiating agreement signed by the United Steelworkers and the big steel companies in 1974, the union agreed to forego the use of the strike in advance of bargaining in exchange for arbitration of any unsettled issues that developed during negotiations for a new contract. This was done to help the sick steel industry, an industry that had been badly managed, slow to modernize, and that was busily buying up subsidiaries in unrelated product markets at the same time that it was asking its workers to sacrifice in order to protect their jobs.

Even the no-strike pledge and union cooperation in lobbying for a limit on foreign steel imports did not prevent United States Steel in 1979 from threatening to close fabricating subsidiaries in Pennsylvania unless the union locals involved agreed to a three-year wage freeze and a limit to their cost-of-living adjustment. Faced with the ultimatum, the locals agreed. Similar concessions followed at Wheeling-Pittsburgh Steel and other companies.

Once underway, the demand for "give-backs" in steel continued to gain momentum. At company request, the Steelworkers agreed to reopen their contracts and bargain early with the leading steel firms in 1982. On two occasions, local union leaders, reflecting a non-concessions mood on the part of the rank and file, rejected contract proposals approved by top union bargainers. By early 1983, however, soaring unemployment led the same local officers to accept a concession package that, while less onerous than those rejected earlier, still amounted to a loss of approximately $12,000 for the average steelworker over the forty-one-month life of the contract.

In addition to gaining wage concessions, the companies avoided any restrictions on the use of new technology, a right that appeared to give them extensive freedom to make substantial cuts in employment as new equipment is introduced. In return, the union was able to extract little more than a vague promise that savings resulting from wage concessions would be reinvested in basic steel—a promise that many observers viewed with some skepticism because only a year or so before negotiations began, the United States Steel Corporation had borrowed huge amounts of money to purchase the Marathon Oil Company.

The reality of the bargaining environment in which the union negotiators had to operate was illustrated by the situation in Midland, Pennsylvania. There, in the fall of 1982, the Crucible Steel Company closed a plant putting 4500 workers out of jobs. Jones and Laughlin Steel Company soon bought the plant, but only with the guarantee that substantial labor savings would be realized through major wage and benefit cuts.

The Midland case also included the right of the company to alter long-standing work and manning rules. This trend was evident in a number of other industries, and management's success in breaking down union resistance to work rule changes was an even more important indicator of the dramatic shift in bargaining power than wage concessions. It signaled that management no longer took unions as a given, and that included companies with long-standing bargaining relationships—companies with whom, it seemed, the argument for the value of collective bargaining had been made long ago.

Concession bargaining was not limited to the private sector. In the 1977 agreement between the New York City Board of Education and the United Federation of Teachers, the union agreed to defer some salary increases, and to extend the conditions of the existing contract by one year. Similar concessions were evident elsewhere. While it is true that wage settlements in the public sector held up better than in the private sector, by 1982 it was becoming clear that management was paying for wage increases with retrenchment. For the first time since World War II, employment in state and local governments shrank.

While concessions appeared to be everywhere, they were not the entire story. Some unions resisted, with mixed results. Members of the United Electrical Workers Union (UE) struck the Westinghouse Air Brake Company near Pittsburgh for seven months in 1981 and 1982 rather than agree to concessions. Two pipe mills operated by Interlake, Incorporated in Newport, Kentucky closed in 1980 after union workers voted 803 to 1 against a wage-and-benefit freeze. In Milwaukee, union workers at the Schlitz brewery not only refused to accept a wage freeze, even though it was obvious that the brewery might otherwise be shut down, they struck for higher wages. Early in 1983 members of the International Association of Machinists resisted demands by Eastern Airlines for concessions and won significant pay increases, but Eastern laid off thousands of workers after the contract went into effect. The United Auto Workers maintained quarterly cost-of-living adjustments and a profit sharing plan after a bitter 205-day strike against the Caterpillar Tractor Company, but had to agree to a freeze on wages.

These examples of resistance to concessions—and there were many more like them—gained considerable media attention, but they obscured the fact that concession, not conflict, had become the rule rather than the exception. By the end of 1982, strike activity was at its lowest level since the 1940s, whether measured by the amount of work time lost or the number of workers involved—a sure sign of union weakness.

PART III
Open Shop

In the early 1960s, it began to appear that business enterprise was reevaluating the benefits it received from détente with labor. At the same time that management asked unions to sacrifice to preserve jobs, and unions cooperated with industry lobbyists to demand congressional curbs on imports and the relaxation of environmental standards, many companies took the offensive against a labor movement that was more vulnerable than at any time since the beginning of the Great Depression.

To be sure, business attempts to test the power of the unions had never been entirely absent. In the 1950s a strategy of take-it-or-leave-it bargaining developed, called "Boulwarism" after its main proponent, vice-president in charge of industrial relations for General Electric, Lemuel Boulware. Under this strategy the company's first offer, supposedly based on perfect balance among the interests of workers, shareholders, and consumers, was its last offer. The NLRB called the tactic a violation of the requirement to bargain in good faith.

In place of Boulwarism a new generation of managers began to employ many of the time honored antiunion techniques in a newly sophisticated manner. A new wave of welfare capitalism surfaced based on the ideas that only disgruntled workers wanted unions and that good managers could convince workers that a union could do nothing for them that the company wasn't already doing. When coupled with the use of sophisticated strategies to frustrate the intent of the nation's labor laws, the new antiunion offensive made impressive headway.

Between 1960 and 1977 employer violations of the National Labor Relations Act increased by 115 percent. Most of these took place outside of the huge manufacturing corporations that had long accommodated the union presence and that, operating in oligopolistic markets, were able to pass on increased labor costs to the public through administered prices. But these industries—such as steel, auto, rubber, and electrical manufacturing—were in relative decline. Smaller companies in the growing service sector of the economy, most of which were nonunion, and manufacturing companies operating in highly competitive markets increasingly fought union organization with the help of antiunion consultants.

Delay became the chief weapon of business resistance to union organizing campaigns—delay of hearings, elections, appeals, and negotiations. By 1977, the huge backlog of petitions before the NLRB was creating median delays of eight months from the time a union requested a representation election until it took place. In cases of unfair labor practices, with company attorneys employing every stalling tactic, the median delay from the filing of a complaint to court enforcement of an NLRB order was two years. Nor was a union victory in an election a guarantee that the workers would ever secure a contract.

The United Auto Workers' experience with the Monroe Auto Equipment Company illustrated what was becoming a familiar story. The union began its organizing campaign in 1964 when Monroe was located in Michigan. The company subsequently moved to Georgia, but the union followed and won an NLRB election in 1966. However, legal appeals by Monroe succeeded in frustrating union attempts to bargain. In fact, between 1964 and 1977, the NLRB ordered three separate elections at Monroe, each of which the Auto Workers won. The NLRB upheld the election results nine separate times and Monroe appealed five times to federal court. One appeal ended in the Supreme Court which upheld the NLRB ruling. Still, no break came until 1977 when a conglomerate acquired Monroe and agreed to recognize the union. One year later the two sides agreed to a contract, fourteen years after the union had won the first NLRB election.

Established union shops were not immune. By 1976 decertification of unions had risen to more than double the 1962 level. In 1978 the National Labor Relations Board conducted a total of 807 decertification elections, and in 73.6 percent of them the unions lost. While it is true that more than half of such elections took place in bargaining units with 19 or fewer members, the trend was ominous.

These figures probably reflected not so much a spontaneous rejection of unions on the part of American workers as a return to prominence of the antiunion employer associations and the reemergence of labor breaking agencies. During the 1970s the chief executive officers in several sectors of the economy moved to pool information and resources in an effort to rid their industries of unions. Organizations like the Master Printers Association and the Associated Builders and Contractors were representative of this phenomenon. At the top of the employer association pyramid rested the National Association of Manufacturers Council on a Union Free Environment, and the prestigious Business Roundtable.

For expertise, business enterprise turned to law firms and consultants specializing in maintaining a "union free environment." The rise of the antilabor consultants during the 1970s paralleled the soaring abuse of the nation's labor laws. In 1979, AFL-CIO records showed that out of 6000 organizing campaigns, two-thirds involved some form of outside antiunion expertise. By some estimates, more than 1000 firms and 1500 individuals were engaged full or part time in preventing unionization in 1979. Antiunion consulting had become a major industry with annual sales of well over one-half billion dollars.

These new union breakers were a far cry from their predecessors who relied on intimidation, espionage, and recruitment of strikebreakers. The modern approach involved a sophisticated blend of psychology, law, and personnel relations. While intimidation remained, it was carefully camouflaged. Where no unions existed, management was advised to develop psychological profiles of employees in order to weed out potential union supporters. When an organizing drive developed, unfair labor practices became common and legal obstructionism was practiced to delay the NLRB election in the knowledge that delay worked to the company's benefit. Even if the company ultimately lost in the courts, the cost in fines and reparations to illegally dismissed workers was outweighed by the benefits of staying nonunion. In 1979, one major consulting firm claimed a 98 percent victory record using similar tactics.

Where a union already existed, consultants coached businesses on how to encourage workers to file decertification petitions without technically violating the law. As we have seen, the number of such elections tripled in the 1970s.

ASSAULT ON THE BUILDING TRADES

The far-reaching implications of the antilabor offensive could be seen in its impact on the building trades. More than any other category of workers, building tradesmen had succeeded in controlling their working lives through their unions. The foundation of this strength was control of the labor market processes of the construction industry. Wages and other forms of compensation were determined through negotiations in which the union, dealing with a number of contractors in a given market area, had a preponderance of bargaining power because of its control of the available labor force. Access to the trade and thus to the labor force lay in apprenticeship programs to which the union locals controlled entrance. Because of the decentralized and irregular nature of the industry, the contractor relied on the union-administered hiring hall to secure workers for a particular job. Most important, the allocation of the work force on the job was governed by various contractual rules relating to work assignments, crew sizes, the ratio of apprentices to journeymen, and other manning and job classification matters. In addition, foremen and lower supervisors were required to belong to the appropriate craft union. Thus unlike most industries, first-level supervision owed first loyalty to the union.

For the contractors, this arrangement worked because it relieved them of responsibility for training and recruitment and because they passed labor costs on to the consumer. And the costs were substantial. Construction costs rose dramatically between 1955 and 1979. Much of this had to do with the general inflationary spiral, a spiral in which building costs, which constituted over 10 percent of the nation's economic activity in 1974, played an important role. In 1969, unionized construction workers won an average 14 percent increase, and in 1970 that soared to 20 percent. In the meantime the wage differential between union and nonunion workers widened considerably between 1965 and 1975. This proved to be the period of the greatest growth of the open shop.

In 1979, *Fortune* magazine estimated that nonunion firms captured 60 percent of the construction industry's dollar volume, up from 20 percent in 1968. Open-shop contractors, always strongest in residential construction, made their most serious inroads in commercial construction, mainly office and retail buildings. Industrial construction remained largely in union hands because only a few open-shop builders could challenge the resources of the unionized members of the National Constructors association in the largest projects. But even in this sector, the few huge open-shop companies had all the work they could handle by the end of the decade.

It is difficult to find authoritative figures on the impact of the use of the open shop on union membership. Nevertheless, at the 1978 convention of the Carpenters, the union's president pointed out that since 1974 the United Brotherhood had lost 68,687 members. He placed the chief blame for the loss on the growth of the "new right" in cooperation with big business in an offensive to create a "union-free environment."

There is little doubt that the sophisticated antiunion techniques played an important role in the rise of open-shop construction. The formation of antiunion employer associations in the early 1950s signaled the new approach. First on the scene was the Associated Builders and Contractors of America (ABC), formed in 1950. By 1979 the organization had 13,000 members among general and subcontractors. While most of ABC's activities were designed to help its affiliates stay union free without actually breaking the law, its Ohio chapter published advice for its members on how to conduct electronic surveillance of union meetings.

The Associated General Contractors, many of whose members have dealt with unions for years, published booklets on operating without unions and held conferences across the nation in which members were advised to "bargain on your own behalf, discharge the obligation to bargain in good faith, reach an impasse, take a strike, attempt to replace the strikers, and if successful, go the way of the open shop."

Events in Vermont in the 1970s illustrated a fairly typical scenario. Contractors retained the services of an attorney who had taken part in open-shop seminars sponsored by the Associated General Contractors. A Governor's fact-finding panel later concluded that the consultant and the Vermont contractors in concert had decided to bargain in bad faith with the Carpenters and Laborers unions by proposing intentionally unreasonable demands. The goal, according to the panel, was to destroy organized labor in the Vermont construction industry—an industry of which the Carpenters had been an integral part since 1890. By 1979 the union did not have a single local collective bargaining agreement in the state.

Important support for activities of this kind came from the open shop's most powerful ally, the Business Roundtable, whose members included top officers of 200 of the country's leading corporations. Just how significant the construction industry's role in the antiunion drive had been could be measured by the fact that the Roundtable grew out of a merger of two earlier antiunion organizations, the Labor Law Study Committee and the Construction Users Anti-Inflation Roundtable.

The Roundtable provides the antiunion contractors with a powerful and prestigious political lobby whose main current goal, after its recent victories in the struggle for labor law reform and common situs picketing, is the repeal of the Davis-Bacon Act. Davis-Bacon, a Depression-era law aimed at preventing the construction industry from cutting wages on federal projects, requires that wages and work rules on federally financed projects meet the standards prevailing in each area. This has come to mean union rates and work rules. A number of similar state laws establishing the prevailing wage principle of Davis-Bacon on state funded construction projects also helped the unions a great deal.

Union reactions to the onslaught were largely ineffective. Not unlike their brothers and sisters in the manufacturing sector who were forced to make concessions in order to keep plants from closing, construction workers were forced by union contractors to give back earlier collective bargaining gains because of the open-shop threat. During the 1973/1974 recession the forfeiture of pay increases became somewhat common. Numerous unions entered into "project agreements" with union contractors. The agreements were special arrangements covering large construction projects in which contractors won the right to hire supervisors independent of the unions, forbid jurisdictional strikes, slowdowns or stoppages, and to determine the number of apprentices to be hired.

The AFL-CIO sanctioned this trend at the highest level. In 1978 the Federation's Building and Construction Trades Department and the National Constructors Association (NCA) negotiated a two-year agreement designed to reduce building time and costs in heavy construction projects in order to enhance job prospects for union members. One year earlier, the NCA and the Laborers International Union reached an agreement covering the open shop states of Texas, Oklahoma and New Mexico. The pact included a no-strike pledge, limited overtime pay, and gave employers the right to determine crew sizes and dismiss employees under certain conditions.

Frustrated by the success of their adversaries, the labor movement placed a great deal of emphasis on legislative reform of existing labor law. The building trades played a key role in this effort. Their major goal was the removal of the construction unions from the prohibition against secondary boycotts embodied in the National Labor Relations Act. The law, as interpreted for the construction industry, permitted a union in a dispute with a contractor to picket only that contractor's operations. Since the construction site held a number of contractors and subcontractors, the picketing union could only disrupt a fraction of the total operation. Any refusal to work by other unions on the construction site during such a dispute constituted a secondary boycott and was therefore illegal. In their fight for common situs picketing legislation the building trades unions argued that industrial plants could be picketed without regard to the incidental effects on neutral employers and that to impose a different rule on construction sites denied construction unions and workers equal rights under the law.

But labor lost twice on common situs picketing. The first time in 1975 when, after the bill passed Congress, President Gerald Ford, under intense pressure from business and other antiunion pressure groups, reneged on a promise to sign the bill. Two years later, no such mendacity was necessary. Congress, with an even larger Democratic majority, defeated common situs picketing by a vote of 217 to 205. It was a graphic illustration of the decline of labor's political influence.

DISCUSSION QUESTIONS

1. How have dramatic changes in the nature and location of jobs since World War II created serious political and organizational problems for unions?
2. How has the struggle of blacks and women for economic justice affected organized labor?
3. Discuss the ambivalence of the AFL-CIO leadership in dealing with problems of corruption in a few of the affiliated unions.
4. What factors accounted for the tremendous rise in public-employee unionism after 1960?
5. Compare and contrast the antiunion movements of the 1920s and the 1970s. Consider both tactics and underlying philosophy.

KEY WORDS AND PHRASES

Blue-Collar Blues
Black Power
Civil Rights Act of 1964
Women's Movement
Changing Industrial Structure
George Meany
AFL-CIO

Philadelphia Plan
Equal Rights Amendment
Coalition of Labor Union Women
Public Employee Unionism
Cesar Chavez
Coalition Bargaining
Deregulation

McClellan Committee
Landrum-Griffin Act
Miners for Democracy
Occupational Safety & Health Act
Employees Retirement Income
  Security Act

Concession Bargaining
Boulwarism
Antiunion Consultants
Open Shop in Construction

BIBLIOGRAPHY

The material for this section was drawn largely from:

Aaron, Benjamin, Joseph Grodin, and James L. Sterns, eds. *Public Sector Bargaining*. Washington: Bureau of National Affairs, 1979.

AFL-CIO, *American Federationist, 1960–1980;* Industrial Relations Research Association. *Proceedings* of the Annual Meeting. Madison, Wis.: IRRA Publication Series, 1960–1980.

Barbash, Jack. "The 1980s—A New Era in Industrial Relations?" in Brochard, Michel. *Les Relations de Travail en Periode de Crise Enconomique.* Montreal, 1983.

Barnet, Richard J. and Ronald E. Muller. *Global Reach: The Power of the Multinational Corporations.* New York: Simon and Schuster, 1974.

Berman, Daniel M. *Death on the Job: Occupational Health and Safety Struggles in the United States.* New York: Monthly Review Press, 1978.

Bok, Derek C. and John T. Dunlop. *Labor and the American Community.* New York: Simon and Schuster, 1970.

Briggs, Vernon M., Walter Fogel, and Fred Schmidt. *The Chicano Worker.* Austin: University of Texas Press, 1977.

Brody, David. *Workers in Industrial America: Essays on the 20th Century Struggle.* New York: Oxford University Press, 1980.

Burck, Gilbert. "A Time of Reckoning for the Building Unions," *Fortune,* vol. 99, no. 11(June 4, 1979): 82–96.

Center to Protect Workers' Rights. *From Brass Knuckles to Briefcases: The Changing Art of Union-Busting in America.* Washington: CPWR, 1979.

Cochran, Bert. ed. *American Labor in Midpassage.* New York: Monthly Review Press, 1959.

Craypo, Charles. *Economic Bargaining Power: Case Studies in the Private Sector* (unpublished manuscript).

Edwards, Richard. *Contested Terrain: The Transformation of the Workplace in the Twentieth Century.* New York: Basic Books, 1979.

Edwards, Richard C., Michael Reich, and Thomas Weisskopf, eds. *The Capitalist System: A Radical Analysis of American Society.* Englewood Cliffs, N.J.: Prentice-Hall, 1972.

Faulkes, Fred. "Large Nonunionized Employers," in Industrial Relations Research Association, *U.S. Industrial Relations, 1950–1980.* Madison, Wis.: IRRA Publication Series, 1981.

Foner, Philip. *Organized Labor and the Black Worker, 1619–1973.* New York: Praeger, 1974.

Gordon, David M., Richard Edwards, and Michael Reich. *Segmented Work, Divided Workers: The Historical Transformation of Labor in the United States.* New York: Cambridge University Press, 1982.

Goulden, Joseph. *Meany.* New York: Atheneum, 1972.

Hall, Burton, ed. *Autocracy and Insurgency in Organized Labor.* New Brunswick, N.J.: Transaction Books, 1972.

Howe, Louise Kapp. *Pink Collar Workers: Inside the World of Women's Work.* New York: Putnam, 1977.

Josephy, Alvin M. *Red Power: The American Indians' Fight for Freedom.* New York: American Heritage, 1971.

Northrup, Herbert R. *Open Shop Construction.* Philadelphia: University of Pennsylvania Press, 1975.

Sheppard, Harold and Neal Q. Herrick. *Where Have All the Robots Gone? Worker Dissatisfaction in the 70s.* New York: The Free Press, 1972.

U.S. Bureau of Labor Statistics. *Monthly Labor Review,* 1960–1980.

U.S. Cong. House Subcommittee on Labor-Management Relations. *Oversight Hearings.* 96th Cong., 1st sess. "Pressures in Today's Workplace." 2 vols. Washington, D.C.: GPO, 1979.

U.S. Department of Commerce, *Statistical Abstract of the United States, 1955–1980.*

U.S. Department of Health, Education and Welfare. *Work in America.* Washington, D.C.: GPO, 1973.

Wilhelm, Sidney. *Who Needs the Negro?* Garden City, N.Y.: Doubleday, 1971.

Zinn, Howard. *Post-War America, 1945–1971.* Indianapolis: Bobbs-Merrill, 1973.

For additional reading see:

Conway, Mimi. *Rise Gonna Rise: A Portrait of Southern Textile Workers.* Garden City, N.Y.: Anchor Books, 1979.

Finley, Joseph. *The Corrupt Kingdom: The Rise and Fall of the United Mine Workers.* New York: Simon and Schuster, 1972.

Gould, William. *Black Workers in White Unions: Job Discrimination in the United States.* Ithaca: Cornell University Press, 1977.

Goulden, Joseph C. *Jerry Wurf: Labor's Last Angry Man.* New York: Atheneum, 1982.

Herling, John. *Right to Challenge: People and Power in the Steelworkers Union.* New York: Harper & Row, 1972.

Kazis, Richard and Richard L. Grossman. *Fear at Work.* New York: The Pilgrim Press, 1982.

Meister, Dick and Anne Loftis. *A Long Time Coming: The Struggle to Unionize America's Farm Workers.* New York: St. Martin's Press, 1973.

Sexton, Patricia and Brendon Sexton. *Blue Collars and Hard Hats*. New York: Random House, 1971.

Sexton, Patricia. *The New Nightingales: Hospital Workers, Unions, New Women's Issues*. New York: Enquiry Press, 1982.

Sheridan, Walter. *The Fall and Rise of Jimmy Hoffa*. New York: Saturday Review Press, 1973.

Spero, Stirling and John M. Capozzola. *The Urban Community and its Unionized Bureaucracies: Pressure Politics in Local Government Labor Relations*. New York: Dunellen, 1973.

Terkel, Studs. *Working*. New York: Pantheon, 1974.

Changing Times, Changing Tactics

Ironically, a prime example of the shared interests approach to industrial relations took place even as the erosion of labor's power and influence was well underway. In 1975 Secretary of Labor John Dunlop created the Labor-Management Group, called by labor journalist A.H. Raskin "the most ambitious instrument ever established in this country for the leaders of industry and labor to collaborate in the formulation of policy in areas such as trade, taxes, full-employment, energy and health care."

The Committee consisted of the chief executives of companies such as General Motors, General Electric, du Pont, United States Steel and Mobil. The counterparts from labor included George Meany and his chief aide, Lane Kirkland, from the AFL-CIO, as well as the presidents of six major American unions.

As it turned out cooperation proved to be largely a one-way street. Labor cooperated on the restriction of imports and the relaxation of environmental standards. But on labor law reform, the conduct of big business signaled that it was not willing to accept organized labor as even a junior partner in the operation of the American economy. The shock hit doubly hard because for the unions, labor law reform had little to do with companies with which they had long-standing relationships. Aimed primarily at "outlaws" like J.P. Stevens, which consistently violated their workers' rights to seek union representation, the bill, after considerable compromise, emerged as a rather mild revision of existing labor law to expedite the administration and procedures of the NLRB and strengthen penalties against violators.

It was bad enough when much of what labor considered responsible business leadership lined up with old-line union haters to defeat labor law reform. Even more menacing was the alliance between big business and groups formed in opposition to issues such as gun control, abortion, equal rights for women, and busing to achieve racial balance in the schools. This new coalition of well-organized forces demonstrated its danger to organized labor during the debate of common situs picketing when it generated some 720,000 cards and letters to President Gerald Ford urging him to veto the bill.

Business carried on the campaign against the reform bill in a tone that recalled the worst excesses of the twenties. Groups like the Business Roundtable, the National Association of Manufacturers, and the National Right to Work Committee charged that unions were about to take control of the nation and that half of the Senate had been "bought by the union bosses."

George Meany asked why business was "seeking to destroy a labor movement that has always supported and promoted free enterprise." Lane Kirkland, then secretary-treasurer and now president of the Federation, went even further in demonstrating his sense of betrayal. "Unlike employers in many other countries, American management has not been under attack by any hostile ideology promoted by labor. . . . Workers and their unions have not clamored for the nationalization of industry or for chairs and votes in the corporate board room." "We have not," he continued in obvious reference to the tactics of business in the congressional battle, "launched hate campaigns or organized fillibusters in order to thwart the legislative process and crush legitimate rights and reasonable hopes for fair play where management is concerned."

The fight for labor law reform proved to be a last hurrah for Geroge Meany, the aging leader of the Federation who over a quarter of a century had come to personify the labor movement more than anyone since Samuel Gompers. Meany died in 1980. His successor, Lane Kirkland, a member of the Masters, Mates and Pilots Union from the time of his service in the merchant marine during World War II, had spent most of his union career as a staff member of the AFL-CIO. He had long been in fundamental agreement with the vision of the labor movement held by George Meany. But most of Meany's leadership years were marked by economic prosperity and a relatively peaceful industrial relations environment. Kirkland, on the other hand, assumed the leadership of the AFL-CIO at a time of economic decline and renewed labor-management tension.

One of the major problems confronting Kirkland was the decline of union political influence. In part this could be attributed to the unions' relative success in raising the standard of living for their members. For many in the general public, workers who seemed not to fit the romantic mold of the downtrodden and oppressed were less deserving of sympathy. Frequently, the public accepted the increasingly strident antiunion propoganda from business which laid a major portion of the blame for inflation at the door of the labor movement. Even though, while the average wage nearly doubled in the 1970s, the average worker ended the decade with less purchasing power than at the beginning.

But more significant reasons for the decline in political influence included a declining union share of the workforce and the movement of industry, population and political power to the right-to-work states of the

Sun Belt. Union political strength remained greatest in the industrial states of the Northeast and Midwest, but as the economic position of these states declined, so too did their political power.

Erosion of labor's political power corresponded with a strong political offensive by business. The 1974 amendments to the Federal Election Campaign Act proved to be a bonanza for corporate political efforts. A 1975 ruling by the Federal Elections Commission established that corporations could use company funds to establish and administer political action committees (PACS). By 1980 more than 800 corporate PACS existed, as well as another 800 or more trade association and related PACS. Labor PACS remained at about 275. In the 1978 congressional elections, business and related PACS contributed a total of 22.6 million compared to 9.4 million in labor contributions.

The effectiveness of this massive power became evident in the 1980 elections when a militantly conservative Republican Party, led by Ronald Reagan, won the presidency, captured control of the Senate for the first time since 1954, and won enough seats in the House to throw that chamber under the effective control of a coalition of Republicans and conservative Democrats. Not even in 1946 and 1952 had labor suffered a defeat of such magnitude.

Even more indicative of labor's weakened political machinery was the fact that 45 percent of union households rejected their leaders' urging and voted for Reagan. Reagan's deep inroads into the labor vote obviously strengthened his decision to carry out what *The New York Times* called the "execution" of the Professional Air Traffic Controllers Organization when they carried out an illegal work stoppage in 1981. Although labor leaders gave verbal support to the air traffic controllers, by and large they stood by helplessly while the Reagan administration destroyed the union through mass dismissals, contempt citations, and decertification.

The Republican administration also brought about sweeping changes in labor law administration and policy. Although nowhere were pro-labor statutes repealed outright, much the same effect was achieved through administrative regulation and the appointment process. Davis-Bacon, minimum wage, child labor laws, the Equal Employment Opportunity Commission, and the Occupational Safety and Health law were exposed to amendment by rule. The Department of Labor, the National Labor Relations Board, and the Occupational Safety and Health Administration came under the direction of presidential appointees who made no secret of their antagonism to the laws they administered.

THE SEARCH FOR RESPONSES

In the face of the overall challenge to labor's power a merger wave took place that by 1980 had involved 119 unions in 64 mergers. One example was the formation in 1969 of the United Transportation Union (UTU). The merger of four previously independent railroad bortherhoods resulted from the shrinking of the financially troubled railroad industry. Mergers like those between the Steelworkers and the Mine, Mill and Smelter Workers; the Teamsters and the Brewery Workers; the Photoengravers, Lithographers and Bookbinders; and the Amalgamated Clothing Workers and the Textile Workers illustrated responses to labor's weakened collective bargaining and organizational situations. They demonstrated union recognition of the need to consolidate strength in a threatening economic and political climate. The return of the United Auto Workers to the AFL-CIO in 1981 also symbolized this recognition.

The AFL-CIO also committed itself to a major increase in organizational activity, most notable being a coordinated effort launched in 1980 to organize the workforce of rapidly growing, but largely nonunion, Houston, Texas. The Center to Protect Workers' Rights, the research arm of the AFL-CIO Building Trades Council, undertook extensive studies in corporate structure, the role of trade associations, and the extraordinary growth of antilabor, business-financed political action committees. The Federation also established the Public Affairs Institute to disseminate labor's point of view on important economic, social, and political issues. The Institute's mission is to counter what the AFL-CIO perceives as "the domination of the media by conservative, antiunion and big business interests with superior financial interests." And, perhaps most important of all, to counter the Reagan administration's claim that it was out of touch with its membership, the AFL-CIO leadership organized Solidarity Day, bringing close to a half million unionists and members of minority, women's, and other liberal groups to Washington on September 19, 1981 to protest the Reagan administration's policies and begin the rebuilding of labor's political influence.

Also significant were new union strategies to confront corporate power. On October 19, 1980, J.P. Stevens, the symbol of antiunionism in the South for seventeen years, recognized the Amalgamated Clothing and Textile Workers Union (ACTWU). Although the agreement covered only 10 percent of Stevens' workers, it constituted a major breakthrough, not only in terms of Southern organizing, but in terms of tactics as well. ACTWU succeeded by putting pressure on corporate partners of Stevens to resign from the Stevens board of directors because of the effect their association with the notorious labor law violator was having on the fortunes of their own companies. The final breakthrough came when the union threatened to run candidates for the board of Metropolitan Life Insurance Company, a company which held $97 million of Stevens' $226 million in long-term debt. In addition to the bad publicity, according to *The Wall Street Journal*, a contested election for the Metropolitan Board would have cost the company $5 to $7 million in mailing, legal, and other costs. Not surprisingly,

Metropolitan preferred to pressure Stevens to resolve its problems with the union.

The "corporate weapons" used against Stevens formed part of a new strategy that could inject unions into the process of financial policymaking for many large corporations and financial institutions. The potential lies primarily in the financial power of union pension funds. In 1978 these funds owned fully 20 percent of the financial securities of the country.

The irony was that in some cases these funds were being used to destroy union jobs. In 1979 the AFL-CIO convention urged that the funds be entrusted to financial institutions whose investment policies are not inimical to the welfare of working men and women. What was being suggested in rather circumspect terms was the possibility of requiring that union pension funds be invested only in unionized companies, that investments be withdrawn from companies pursuing a runaway-shop policy, and that pension fund managers buy and sell shares in companies undergoing organizing drives in order to influence management to recognize the union. But because most of these funds are either under the absolute control of management or under joint union-management committees, any change in investment policies will have to be won at the bargaining table and will have to satisfy the requirements of prudent management so that the income of retirees is protected.

Another development with potential to alter the traditional relationship between labor and management is the growing workers control movement. During the 1960s, both unions and management became concerned with the alienation of workers, the erosion of the work ethic, and the discontent of young workers. This led to a number of experiments to "humanize" the workplace through innovations in the organization of work that offered some workers more control and variety in their jobs. While these experiments gave workers the opportunity to participate in some low-level decision making, they left the power relationships between workers and managers unchanged.

The economic crisis of the 1970s extended the idea of workers control. As the economy faltered and companies closed aging plants and moved elsewhere, workers and worker-community coalitions moved to take over at least sixty threatened plants. Officials at all levels of society have endorsed employee ownership to save jobs. Ironically, the old nineteenth-century dream of producers cooperatives has been revived as a possible means to help save ailing industries. Although the goals of the new cooperative movement are purely pragmatic, the movement carries the seeds of what could become an historic democratization of American work life.

Many union leaders are wary of the new cooperative movement. Some see it as merely a "share-the-crumbs" movement, in the words of one assistant Secretary of Labor, rather than a share-the-wealth movement. To others, like Jerry Wurf, former president of AFSCME, "the concept of worker control is an exciting one, for soapbox oratory in the streets and rap sessions in the faculty lounge," but impossible under the social, political and economic system on the United States.

Yet underneath the sarcasm there is another fear, based on the meaning of worker control for the traditional role of unions. Where the workplace has been "humanized" and workers offered some modicum of participation, some unionists fear a resurgence of company unionism, and indeed, such minor reforms have become part of the open-shop movement, just as the employee representation plans played an important role in the antiunion American Plan of the 1920s. Where firms actually are transformed into producers cooperatives, unions fear the blurring of distinction between employees and employer that gives unions their reason for existence.

Still, unions were involved in some worker participation in management. The United Steelworkers, after an initial coolness to the idea, played an active role in trying to engineer what proved to be an unsuccessful community-worker takeover of a Youngstown, Ohio, steel mill shut down by a conglomerate. And the 1980 contract between the steel union and the major companies authorized the establishment of joint "participation teams" with the authority to experiment in order to spur productivity and enhance employee morale and dignity. A number of other unions such as the United Auto Workers, the Newspaper Guild, and the Bakery and Confectionery Workers are also involved in experimental "workplace democracy" programs.

Some advocates of projects such as these pointed out that the workplace committees should not replace the traditional adversary process between unions and management. Irving Bluestone, a United Auto Workers advocate of workplace democracy, explained that "while issues of economic security and continuing encroachment on what management terms its sole perogatives will remain adversary in nature, there is every reason why democratizing the workplace should be undertaken as a joint, cooperative, constructive, nonadversary effort by management and the union." And Lloyd McBride, president of the Steelworkers, rejected "the idea of people going around and condemning any move toward cooperation as being unholy and wrong." According to McBride, "the union, once it secures good wages and benefits, has a responsibility to the employer and the individual worker has a responsibility to keep the business going. . . . In many plants . . . the adversary relationship has been rigidified, (where) the two sides operate more as enemies than as employees."

Most current experiments are limited to shop floor participation in joint labor-management committees. Worker participation at the top policy making level of the corporation, long in operation to one degree or another in Germany and Sweden, has never taken hold in the United States. Part of American labor's view of the capitalist system has been that the role of unions and management are distinctly separate, that direction of the enterprise is the responsibility of management, and that union involvement in management of the firm would compromise its role as the protector of its members. That article of faith was challenged in 1980 when Douglas Fraser, Auto Workers president, became a board member of the Chrysler Corporation as a quid pro quo for the workers' sacrifices in helping the near bankrupt company qualify for federal loan guarantees.

For Lane Kirkland, the elevation of Fraser to the Chrysler Board was more of a "share-the-crumbs" program than an advance for unions. "I believe in codetermination through the collective bargaining process and I consider it fundamentally wrong to think of board membership as a substitute for collective bargaining," said Kirkland. "To put it on top of weak bargaining is a travesty."

Whether or not Kirkland dismissed the potential of codetermination and, by implication, worker control, too lightly, is impossible to say. But there is little question that whatever role labor is to play, it will only succeed if the unions remain strong. They remain the fundamental working-class institutions in a democratic society. In order to carry out their functions, unions will have to rebuild their economic and political strength through vigorous organizing and by reaching out once again to their traditional allies.

This will require rethinking some of the fundamental assumptions that have governed organized labor's role for more than half a century. Can the traditional emphasis on collective bargaining survive in an environment marked by changing corporate structures, the internationalization of business, the occupational shift from production to service and white-collar jobs, and the commensurate decline of labor's political power? Should organized labor attempt to reassert its influence in the Democratic Party, or should it once again consider the old option of independent political action? It is clear that the current union leaders face many of the same choices that vexed their predecessors over two centuries. Whatever path they choose it will have profound implications for American workers, workers for whom equality—political, economic, and social—remains a goal rather than a reality.

KEY WORDS AND PHRASES

Lane Kirkland	Air Traffic Controllers Strike
Conservative Political Action Committees	Solidarity Day
	Corporate Campaign
Union Merger Movement	Workers Control

BIBLIOGRAPHY

The material for the epilogue was drawn largely from *The Washington Post*, *The New York Times* and *The Wall Street Journal*, as well as from:

Barbash, Jack. "The 1980s—A New Era in Industrial Relations," in Brossard, Michel. *Les Relations de Travail en Periode de Crise Economique.* Montreal: University of Montreal, 1983.

Faulkes, Fred K. "Large Nonunionized Employers," in *U.S. Industrial Relations, 1950–1980.* Madison, Wis.: Industrial Relations Research Association Series, 1981.

Raskin, A.H. "A Reporter at Large (Labor)," *The New Yorker,* vol. 56 (August 25, 1980): 26–76.

Raskin, A.H. "Management Comes Out Swinging," in Industrial Relations Research Association. *Proceedings of the Annual Meeting, 1978.* Madison, Wis.: IRRA, 1979.

Rifkin, Jeremy and Randy Barber. *The North Will Rise Again: Pensions, Politics and Power.* Boston: Beacon Press, 1978.

Zwerdling, Daniel. *Workplace Democracy.* New York: Harper and Row, 1980.

Chronology

1648 Boston coopers and shoemakers form guilds.

1778 Journeymen printers in New York combine to increase their wages.

1791 Philadelphia Carpenters carry out the first strike in the building trades in an unsuccessful attempt to win the ten-hour day.

1792 Philadelphia shoemakers form the first local union organized for collective bargaining.

1794 Federal Society of Journeymen Cordwainers formed in Philadelphia.

1805 A journeymen's cordwainers' union in New York City includes a closed-shop clause in its constitutions.

1806 Philadelphia shoemakers found guilty of criminal conspiracy after striking for higher wages.

1825 The United Tailoresses of New York, a trade union organization for women only, formed in New York City.

1827 The Mechanics Union of Trade Associations, made up of skilled craftsmen in different trades, formed in Philadelphia—first city central.

1828 the Workingmen's Party formed in Philadelphia.

1829 the Workingmen's Party of New York founded.

1834 The National Trades Union, the first attempt at a national labor federation, formed in New York.

1836 The National Cooperative Association of Cordwainers, the first national union of a specific craft, formed in New York City.

1840 President Martin Van Buren establishes the ten-hour day for federal employees on public works without reduction in pay.

1842 In the case of *Commonwealth* v. *Hunt*, the Massachusetts Supreme Court holds that labor unions, as such, are not illegal conspiracies.

Massachusetts and Connecticut pass laws prohibiting children from working more than ten hours per day.

1847 New Hampshire passes first state law fixing ten hours as the legal workday.

1848 Pennsylvania's child labor law makes twelve the minimum age for workers in commercial occupations.

1852 The Typographical Union founded—first national organization of workers to endure to the present day.
Ohio passes first state law limiting working hours of women to ten hours a day.

1859 Iron Molders Union founded in Philadelphia.

1860 Successful strike of 20,000 New England Shoemakers.

1863 Abraham Lincoln issues the Emancipation Proclomation freeing the slaves.
Brotherhood of Locomotive Engineers founded.

1866 National Labor Union founded.

1867 Knights of St. Crispin, a union of factory workers in the shoe industry, founded.

1868 First federal eight-hour-day law passed—applied only to laborers, workmen, and mechanics employed by the government.

1869 Black National Labor Union founded in Washington under the leadership of Isaac Myers.

1869 First local of the Knights of Labor founded in Philadelphia.

1870 First written contract between coal miners and coal operators signed.

1873 Brotherhood of Locomotive Firemen and Enginemen founded.

1874 Cigar Makers International Union makes first use of the union label.

1875 Conviction of "Mollie Maguires" for anthracite coalfield murders—ten are eventually hanged.

1876 Workingmen's Party, later Socialist Labor Party, founded.

1877 Nationwide railroad strikes result in the calling out of state and federal troops to end the strikes.

1878 Greenback Labor Party organized by a fusion of the Greenback Party and the Workingmen's Party.

1879 Terrence Powderly is elected Grand Master Workman of the Knights of Labor.

1881 Federation of Organized Trades and Labor Unions, predecessor of the American Federation of Labor, founded in Pittsburgh.

1882 First Labor Day celebration held in New York City.

1883 Brotherhood of Railroad Trainmen founded.

1884 Federal Bureau of Labor established in the Department of the Interior.

1885 Foran Act forbids immigration of laborers on contract.

1886 Eight-hour movement leads to the Chicago Haymarket riot.
American Federation of Labor founded in Columbus, Ohio—Samuel Gompers is first president.

1887 Seven anarchists sentenced to death (five are eventually executed) for the Haymarket bombing.

1888 First federal labor relations law enacted—applied only to railroads and provided for arbitration of disputes.

1890   United Mine Workers of America founded.

1892   Homestead, Pennsylvania strike by the Amalgamated Association of Iron, Steel and Tin Workers at Carnegie Steel.

1894   Strike by the American Railway Union led by Eugene V. Debs against the Pullman Palace Car Company defeated by the use of injunctions and federal troops.

1898   Congress passes the Erdman Act, providing for mediation and voluntary arbitration on the railroads—supersedes the law of 1888.

1900   International Ladies Garment Workers Union founded.

1901   United States Steel defeats the Amalgamated Association of Iron, Steel and Tin Workers after a three-month strike.
Socialist Party of America founded.
United Textile Workers of America founded.

1902   Anthracite coal miners in Pennsylvania end a five-month strike and agree to arbitration by a presidential panel.

1903   Department of Commerce and Labor created by Congress.

1905   Industrial Workers of the World (IWW) founded in Chicago.
U.S. Supreme Court declares a New York maximum hours law for bakers unconstitutional under the due process clause of the fourteenth amendment (*Lochner* v. *New York*).

1906   Successful strike by the International Typographical Union paves the way for extension of the eight-hour day in the printing trades.

1908   Federal Court finds section of the Erdman Act banning the "Yellow Dog Contract" unconstitutional (*U.S.* v. *Adair*).
Boycott by the United Hatters of Danbury, Conn., against D.E. Loewe and Company held to be a conspiracy in restraint of trade under the Sherman Antitrust Act (Danbury Hatters Case).
U.S. Supreme Court upholds Oregon state law limiting hours for women workers (*Muller* v. *Oregon*).

1909   National Association for the Advancement of Colored People (NAACP) founded.

1911   Supreme Court upholds an injunction ordering the AFL to remove the Bucks Stove and Range Company from its unfair list and cease to promote a boycott (*Gompers* v. *Bucks Stove and Range Company*).
Triangle Waist Company fire in New York City—146 workers, mostly women, die.

1912   Massachusetts adapts the first minimum wage act for women and minors.
Textile strike led by the Industrial Workers of the World in Lawrence, Massachusetts wins wage increases.

1913   U.S. Department of Labor established.

1914 Clayton Act approved—limits the use of injunctions in labor disputes.

1915 LaFollette Seamen's Act approved—regulates conditions for seamen.

1916 Federal Child labor law enacted (later declared unconstitutional).

Adamson Act provides a basic eight-hour day for railroad workers.

1917 IWW strike in the copper mines of Bisbee, Arizona ends with deportation of 1200 strikers to the desert.

Courts uphold the "Yellow Dog Contract" and rules that union efforts to organize workers who have signed them are unconstitutional (*Hitchman Coal and Coke Co.* v. *Mitchell*).

1918 President Woodrow Wilson creates the National War Labor Board.

1919 Great steel strike under the leadership of William Z. Foster is defeated.

Boston Police Strike—first strike of public safety workers in American history.

Communist Party of America founded.

1921 Supreme Court rules that secondary boycotts are illegal and that, the Clayton Act notwithstanding, unions could be enjoined by the courts for actions considered illegal conspiracies in restraint of trade (*Duplex Printing Press* v. *Deering*).

Congress passes a law restricting immigration into the United States and establishing the national origin quota system.

1922 Coal strike in southern Illinois leads to the "Herrin Massacre" in which strikers kill twenty guards and strikebreakers.

1924 Samuel Gompers dies. William Green assumes presidency of the AFL.

1926 Railway Labor Act requires employers to bargain with employees and forbids discrimination against union members.

1931 Davis-Bacon Act provides for payment of prevailing wage rates to workers employed on public construction projects.

1932 Norris-LaGuardia Act prohibits federal injunctions in labor disputes, and outlaws "Yellow Dog Contracts."

1933 National Industrial Recovery Act (NIRA), Section 7(a), guarantees rights of employees to organize and bargain collectively.

Frances Perkins becomes Secretary of Labor and the first woman named to the Cabinet.

1935 NIRA declared unconstitutional. The National Labor Relations (Wagner) Act establishes first national labor policy of protecting rights of workers to organize.

1935 Committee for Industrial Organization (CIO) formed inside the AFL.

1936–37 Sitdown strikes aid the organization of unions in the auto and rubber industries.

1937 General Motors and United States Steel recognize the United Auto Workers and the Steelworkers Organizing Committee, respectively.

U.S. Supreme Court declares the National Labor Relations Act constitutional.

Police kill ten strikers in "Memorial Day Massacre" in Chicago during the Little Steel Strike.

AFL expels the CIO unions.

1938 Fair Labor Standards Act establishes forty-hour week, minimum wage.

CIO (Congress of Industrial Organizations) organizes as independent federation with John L. Lewis as president.

1940 John L. Lewis resigns as CIO president. Philip Murray replaces him.

1941 Ford Motor Company recognizes the United Auto Workers.

AFL and CIO give no-strike pledges for the duration of the war.

1942 President Roosevelt sets up the National War Labor Board.

National War Labor Board establishes the "Little Steel Formula" for wartime wage adjustments.

1943 President Franklin Roosevelt establishes the Fair Employment Practices Committee.

Smith-Connelly Act restricts strikes and union political activity during the war.

1946 Largest strike wave in American history occurs as miners, steelworkers, auto workers, and electrical workers strike.

United Mine Workers win health and welfare fund.

1947 Congress passes the Taft-Hartley Act restricting union practices and permitting the states to pass right-to-work laws.

1949–50 AFL, CIO, and United Mine Workers help form the International Confederation of Free Trade Unions in London.

CIO anti-Communist drive culminates in the expulsion of two unions, and nine more in the following year.

1950 United Auto Workers and General Motors sign a five-year contract with no reopening provision that provides for pensions, automatic cost-of-living wage adjustments, guaranteed annual increases and a modified union shop.

1952 President Truman seizes the steel industry when the companies reject the Wage Stabilization Board's recommendations. Supreme Court finds the action unconstitutional and an eight-week strike follows.

William Green and Philip Murray die. George Meany becomes president of the AFL and Walter Reuther of the CIO.

1953 AFL and CIO approve a "no-raiding" pact.

AFL expels the International Longshoremen's Association for corruption.

1955 Ford Motor Company accepts principle of supplementary unemployment benefits in contract with the United Auto Workers.

AFL and CIO merge with George Meany as first president.

1957 AFL-CIO expels Teamsters, Bakery Workers, and Laundry Workers for corruption.

1959 Congress passes the Labor-Management Reporting and Disclosure Act (Landrum-Griffin), which regulates the internal affairs of unions.

1962 Federal employees' unions given the right to bargain collectively with government agencies as a result of a presidential executive order.

1963 Equal Pay Act prohibits wage differentials based on sex for workers covered by the Fair Labor Standards Act.

1964 Title VII of the Civil Rights Act bars discrimination in employment on the basis of race, color, religion, sex, or national origin.

1966 Coalition bargaining occurs in negotiations between General Electric and eleven unions representing GE employees.

1968 Civil Rights leader Martin Luther King is assassinated while supporting a strike by Memphis, Tennessee, sanitation workers.

1969 A new Department of Labor drive to open construction jobs to minorities begins in Philadelphia.

1970 The first mass work stoppage in the history of the Post Office Department occurs.

Hawaii becomes the first state to allow local and state government employees the right to strike.

Congress passes the Occupational Safety and Health Act.

1973 The United Steelworkers of America and the major steel companies sign an "Experimental Negotiation Agreement" in which the union relinquishes the right to strike in exchange for binding arbitration of unresolved issues.

1974 The Coalition of Labor Union Women (CLUW) is founded in Chicago.

Congress passes the Employee Retirement Income Security Act regulating all private pension plans.

AFL-CIO creates a public employee department in recognition of the growth of public employee unionism.

1975 Eighty thousand Pennsylvania public employees, members of the American Federation of State, County and Municipal Employees (AFSCME) carry out the nation's first legal large-scale strike of state employees.

Union supported labor law reform legislation is defeated in Congress.

1977 Union-supported legislation aimed at improving the ability of building trades unions to organize and carry out effective strikes is defeated.

1980 Joyce Miller of the International Ladies Garment Workers Union becomes the first woman appointed in the AFL-CIO executive board.

1981 President Reagan fires most of the nation's air traffic controllers and orders their union, the Professional Air Traffic Controllers Association, decertified as a result of an illegal strike.

The largest labor rally in American history takes place in Washington as nearly a half million trade unionists and supporters protest President Reagan's economic policies.

INDEX